ISLAND AND EMPIRE

STANFORD **OTTOMAN WORLD** SERIES

ISLAND *and* EMPIRE

HOW CIVIL WAR IN CRETE
MOBILIZED THE OTTOMAN WORLD

Uğur Zekeriya Peçe

STANFORD UNIVERSITY PRESS
Stanford, California

Stanford University Press
Stanford, California

© 2024 by Uğur Zekeriya Peçe. All rights reserved.

No part of this book may be reproduced or transmitted in any form or by any means, electronic or mechanical, including photocopying and recording, or in any information storage or retrieval system, without the prior written permission of Stanford University Press.

Printed in the United States of America on acid-free, archival-quality paper

Library of Congress Cataloging-in-Publication Data
Names: Peçe, Uğur Zekeriya, author.
Title: Island and empire : how civil war in Crete mobilized the Ottoman world / Uğur Zekeriya Peçe.
Other titles: Stanford Ottoman world series.
Description: Stanford, California : Stanford University Press, 2024. | Series: Stanford Ottoman world series | Includes bibliographical references and index.
Identifiers: LCCN 2023057993 (print) | LCCN 2023057994 (ebook) | ISBN 9781503638723 (cloth) | ISBN 9781503639232 (paperback) | ISBN 9781503639249 (epub)
Subjects: LCSH: Civil war—Greece—Crete—History—19th century. | Muslims—Greece—Crete—History—19th century. | Refugees—Greece—Crete—History—19th century. | Protest movements—Turkey—History—19th century. | Crete (Greece)—History—Turkish rule, 1669-1898. | Turkey—History—Ottoman Empire, 1288-1918.
Classification: LCC DF901.C84 P469 2024 (print) | LCC DF901.C84 (ebook) | DDC 949.5/906—dc23/eng/20240212

LC record available at https://lccn.loc.gov/2023057993
LC ebook record available at https://lccn.loc.gov/2023057994

Cover design: Lindy Kasler
Cover photograph: Iraklio, Crete, c. 1900. Archivio Giuseppe Gerola, Istituto Veneto di Scienze, Lettere ed Arti, Venice.

To the generous people of Crete, yesterday and today

CONTENTS

Acknowledgments — ix
Note on Names and Spelling — xvii

Introduction
No Refugee Is an Island — 1

1 **Fear and Trembling in the Mediterranean** — 33
Civil War in Crete and the Birth of a Refugee Question

2 **Sheltering Mountain** — 63
The European Military Intervention and
the Exodus of Crete's Muslims

3 **Adaptability in Vulnerability** — 86
The Muslim Minority in Autonomous Crete, 1898–1908

4 **"Crete or Death"** — 108
Sounds of Protest in the Ottoman Empire

5 **Resettling the Displaced into History** — 138
Refugee Boycotters in the Ottoman Protest Movement

Conclusion
Against Violence: Worse Than Refugeehood Is Death — 164

Abbreviations Used in Notes — 183
Notes — 185
Bibliography — 225
Index — 239

ACKNOWLEDGMENTS

I would like to begin with a confession. I often judge books by their covers. Now that my book is out in the world, I think it would be only fair if I did the same for mine. But, before that, let me first thank Istituto Veneto di Scienze, Lettere ed Arti in Venice for allowing me to use the photograph you see on the cover, partially, and facing this page in full form. Much appreciation is also due to the Vikelaia Library in Iraklio for providing me with a high-resolution copy of that image. The photograph comes from the archive of Giuseppe Gerola (1877–1938), an Italian historian who traveled throughout Crete in the early years of the twentieth century to research and document traces of four-centuries-long Venetian rule on the island.

The photograph shows two boys leaning against a Venetian wall that evidently underwent some changes in the form of removals, fillings, and additions during the centuries following the Ottoman conquest of Crete in the mid-seventeenth century. The boys' identities are unknown to us, but certain details in their appearance offer clues. Both are wearing aprons, indicating that, like many of their teenage peers, they worked in a shop in this busiest city of the island. Both are in knee-high boots known as *stivania*, universally worn by Cretan men regardless of religious or regional background. The boy on the right is sporting a red fez, while the one on the left has a black scarf wrapped around his head. It is likely that the only difference in the look of these two suggests distinct religions, Islam and Greek

Orthodox Christianity respectively. Perhaps it was such indistinguishability of the two boys except through a single item that made this mise-en-scène especially interesting for Giuseppe Gerola. In the early 1900s while he was exploring Iraklio's Venetian legacy, the city's population was almost equally divided among Muslims and Christians. Having one representative from each community fit into Gerola's common practice of photographing buildings and monuments with the people living near them. By freezing both architectural and human landscapes in his still images, it was as if the historian Gerola captured distinct layers of time from the Venetians to the present. I somehow see the nature of his undertaking as akin to one of the greatest challenges of historians writing monographs: capturing glimpses of a bygone world from limited sources and organizing them in a narrative that is bounded for the sake of coherence, yet, at the same time, open-ended to imagine the unrecorded. In this book, one of my primary goals is to present a multilayered history of an island and empire by highlighting commonalities between communities. In so doing, I emphasize enduring coexistence against a history of violence.

If you walk four hundred meters from the Vikelaia Library toward the Mediterranean Sea, you will arrive on the spot where this photograph was taken 122 years ago. Iraklio's older buildings endured the test of time for centuries, but many were destroyed or badly damaged by the German air bombardment during the island's occupation in World War II. Looking closely, though, you may still recognize a small part of the high wall standing out of sight between the higher cement apartment blocks. Its concealment invites the question about what else of the complex and rich history of our lands remains hidden from our visions. When I regard the immense wall in Gerola's photograph, my mind goes to another wall. Intangible and often unscalable, this is the one erected between the common pasts of Greeks and Turks, shared histories of Greece and Turkey. Indoctrination, political crises, well-kept borders, and visa regimes have functioned to keep the wall secure. Interactions between the people of two countries, however, never stopped. And these are crucial because they reveal that the wall's foundations are weak. Over the years, during my research and travels in different parts of Greece, I lost count of the times when people had heartfelt conversations with me on our commonalities. Neither do I know the number of times I have heard that it was the powerholders, not the common folks, who thrived by stoking a hostile language. This is not a scholarly remark perhaps, but its pervasiveness makes it feel very real to me. Its authenticity is an antidote against cynicism. I would like to acknowledge this popular wisdom, of which I try not to lose sight in my book. I treat coexistence as the norm but do not intend to portray a rosy picture. I historicize, not normalize, the swerving from the typical.

This book is the fruit of many years of labor. Countless individuals have inspired and supported me during the process of research, writing, and revisions. I am pleased to acknowledge my gratitude to them. I am grateful to Aron Rodrigue for his enthusiastic support for this project. Our stimulating and lively conversations started long time ago in California, continuing over the years in multiple locations, always involving inspiring exchanges, each time helping me see my work anew and in broader terms. I thank Norman Naimark for his robust and critical reading of my prose, helping me become a better writer. I feel like the *New York Review of Books* should also recognize Norman: I became its faithful reader thanks to him. Joel Beinin opened up the world of the Arabic-speaking Middle East to me, helping me develop a fuller picture of Ottoman history. I took so much inspiration from my conversations with Shahzad Bashir on the Ottomans, Mughals, and other denizens of the past and present. With Bob Crews, the worlds of Central Asia and Iran came into view. I thank Nükhet Varlık and Ali Yaycıoğlu for supporting my scholarship, and I am thrilled to see it in print in Stanford's Ottoman World Series under their editorship.

I thank all members of the amazing team at the Stanford University Press. I appreciate Kate Wahl's guidance throughout this long process from its beginning with a book proposal to the final stages of production. I learned a lot from her sharp eye and expertise. Now I understand well that crafting a book is a phrase that better describes the author's task than writing a book. I thank Elisabeth Magnus for her superb work in copyediting. I also appreciate the assistance and support of Melissa Jauregui Chavez, Gigi Mark, and Cat Ng Pavel.

I received helpful feedback from many people when I presented parts of my research in workshops and conferences. Thanks are especially due to the organizers of the Twelfth Nordic Conference on Middle Eastern Studies in Iceland (2022); Stacy Fahrenthold and Akram Fouad Khater for the workshop "New Perspectives on Middle East Migrations" at North Carolina State

University (2022); Houssine Alloul, Enno Maessen, and Uğur Ümit Üngör for the conference "Narrating Exile in and between Europe and the Ottoman Empire/Modern Turkey" at the University of Amsterdam (2021); Aslı Zengin for the workshop "Death and Afterlives in the Middle East" at Brown University (2019); Firoozeh Kashani-Sabet at the University of Pennsylvania (2019); Cemal Kafadar for the *sohbet-i Osmani* at Harvard University (2017); Christine Philliou for the Western Ottomanists Workshop at the University of California, Berkeley (2016); the Mellon Foundation Sawyer Seminar at the Ohio State University (2014); and Dimitris Gondicas and Molly Green for the Hellenic Studies Workshop at Princeton University (2014).

I am grateful for the support provided by Stanford's Department of History, the Abbasi Program in Islamic Studies, the A. G. Leventis Foundation, the Stanford Humanities Center, the History and Middle Eastern Studies Programs at Bard College, the History and Literature Program at Harvard, and Lehigh's History Department, Center for Global Islamic Studies (CGIS), and College of Arts and Sciences.

In Crete I appreciate the warm assistance of the staff in the following archives and libraries: Historical Archives of Crete (Hania), Historical Archives of the University of Crete (Rethimno), Historical Museum of Crete (Iraklio), Municipal Library of Hania, Public Library of Rethimno, and Vikelaia Library (Iraklio). In other locations I was also fortunate to have met resourceful and helpful people. I thank the staff of Ahmet Piriştina City Archive and Museum (Izmir), Atatürk Library (Istanbul), Austrian State Archives (Vienna), Beyazıt Library (Istanbul), British Library (London), British National Archives (Kew Gardens), Ecumenical Patriarchate of Constantinople Library (Istanbul), French Foreign Ministry Archives (Nantes and Paris), Gennadion Library (Athens), Hellenic Foreign Ministry Archives (Athens), Hoover Archives (Stanford), ISAM Library (Istanbul), Istanbul University Rare Documents Library, Italian Diplomatic Archives (Rome), Izmir National Library, Library of the Parliament (Athens), National Library of Greece (Athens), Ottoman State Archives (Istanbul), and Sismanoglio Megaro (Istanbul).

I thank Panepistimiakes Ekdoseis Kritis for the permission given to use a photograph from one of their publications. I appreciate the following institutions for their permission to use material in this book: Ahmet Piriştina Kent Arşivi ve Müzesi, Bibliothèque nationale de France, British National

Archives, Centre des archives diplomatiques, Dimosia Vivliothiki Rethimnou, Dimotiki Vivliothiki Hanion, Ethniki Vivliothiki tis Ellados, Istanbul University Nadir Eserler Kütüphanesi, Istoriko Arheio Kritis, Istoriko Mouseio Kritis, Nazım Hikmet Kültür ve Sanat Vakfı, and Österreichisches Staatsarchiv. Part of chapter 2 came out in *Middle Eastern Studies* in 2018, and I thank the editors for allowing me to publish an amended and extended version here.

I had my first teaching job after PhD at Bard College, and I fondly remember the friendship of Lamis Abdelaaty, Franco Baldasso, Omar Cheta, Mar Gómez Glez, Sara Marzioli, Dina Ramadan, and Tehseen Thaver. In the next chapter at Harvard I thank Valeria Castelli, Jon Connolly, Eda Çakmakçı, Onur Günay, Lauren Kaminsky, Harry and Hripsime Parsekian, Duncan White, and Tarık Tansu Yiğit.

I found a supportive intellectual environment at Lehigh University. I thank everyone in the wonderful History Department: my mentor Bill Bulman, Bárbara Zepeda Cortés, Kwame Essien, Nitzan Lebovic, Michelle LeMaster, Ellen Zimmer Lewis, Monica Najar, Emily Pope-Obeda, John Savage, and Shellen Wu. Special thanks are due to Rob Rozehnal and the rest of my amazing CGIS community. I also thank Bob Flowers, Scott Gordon, Khurram Hussain, Rick Matthews, Allison Mickel, Annabella Pitkin, and Bruce Whitehouse.

I appreciate Yiğit Akın, Sam Dolbee, Ramazan Hakkı Öztan, Seçil Yılmaz, and Anna Zozulinsky, who read parts of the book's earlier draft and provided helpful feedback. I thank my colleagues, professors, and mentors, namely Margaret Lavinia Anderson, Cemil Aydın, Keith Baker, Halil Berktay, Lisa Blaydes, Isa Blumi, Julia Philips Cohen, Edhem Eldem, Yannis Hamilakis, Katherine Jolluck, Vangelis Kechriotis, James Sheehan, Akşin Somel, Matthew Sommers, Kabir Tambar, Thanos Veremis, Heghnar Z. Watenpaugh, and Caroline Winterer.

I thank Fırat Dernek, Ümit Kurt, Devin Naar, Nicholas Stavroulakis, and Vasso Tsiami for their friendship and many intellectual interactions over the years. The following is obviously a partial list, but I thank many souls, friends and colleagues, who have stimulated my thinking over the years: Eva Achladi, Ufuk Adak, Oscar Aguirre-Mandujano, Önder Akgül, Ayça Alemdaroğlu, Aytek Soner Alpan, Anubha Anushree, Febe Armanios, Melanie Arndt, Ebru Aykut, Zeinab Azarbadegan, Lilla Balint, John Bediz,

Stefo Benlisoy, Binyamin Blum, Fırat Bozçalı, Lale Can, Kostas Chalkias, Francesca A. and Ilhan Citak, my climbing group with André and Anna, Gwendolyn Collaço, Mehmet Çelik, Jacob Daniels, Manousos Daskalogiannis, Margia Delaki, Lukas Dovern, El Gato Dice (Dave and Bob) for the times of rhythm, melody, and poetry, Kyria Eleni in Chios for the *gouri*, Turgut Erçetin, Boğaç Ergene, Emre Erol, Basma Fahoum, Daniella Farah, Suzie Ferguson, Veronica Ferreri, Louis Fishman, Alexander Frese, Matthew Ghazarian, Dimitris Gkintidis, Ioannis Grigoriadis, David Gutman, Doğan Gürpınar, Mimi Haas, Antonis Hadjikyriacou, Vladimir Hamed-Troyansky, Natalie Jabbar, Britta Janssen, Gürer Karagedikli, Burcu Karahan, Ali Aydın Karamustafa, Katerina Katsougianni, Katy Kavanaugh, Burçak Keskin-Kozat, Varak Ketsemenian, Ohannes Kılıçdağı, Asher Kohn, Takis Kokkinakis, Yiannis Kokkinakis, Sinan Kuneralp, Selim Kuru, Harun Küçük, Efthimis Lekakis, Avital Livny, Demetrius Loufas, Georgios Michalopoulos, Owen Miller, Chula and Hubert Morel-Seytoux, Sato Moughalian, Kutay Onaylı, Danny Perez, Socrates Petmezas, Erin Pettigrew, Ramzi Salti, Margaret Sena, Phaedon Sinis, Agathangelos Siskos, Şahin Sonyıldırım, Vassilis Stavrakakis, Firuzan Melike Sümertaş, Kaya Şahin, Dario Tedesco, Tuğsan Topçuoğlu, the Tsiamis family, Arianne Urus, Mehmet Fatih Uslu, Kerem Ünüvar, Manolia Vougioukalaki, Hakan Yazıcı, Alp Yenen, Murat Yıldız, the Yılmaz family, and Christin Zurbach.

My profound appreciation goes to the entire Erotas family, and especially to my *dostaki*.

I have had the privilege of working with diverse groups of students at Sabancı University, Stanford University, Bard College, Harvard University, and Lehigh University. Teaching is the best way of learning, and I appreciate my students for making me understand and practice that.

I am grateful to Seçil for being on this *Kalos* path, from Boğaziçi in Istanbul to a ministry building in Ankara to Manayunk and the village of Hamezi. She has been my engaging reader and listener.

I thank my parents Mahinur and Ilyas for everything they have done for me in their capacity. Primary school was the only formal education they experienced. I am grateful to them for making sure that my siblings (Meryem, Şeyma, Yusuf) and I attended college. As if to make up for the absence of university degrees in past generations, I'm still hanging out on college campuses!

I began the research for this book in Hania, western Crete, and finalized the writing in Sitia, eastern Crete. The circle is now complete. I offer my heartfelt thanks to the people of the village of Hamezi, who reminded me of the warmth of my native village of Katilos in Potomya/Güneysu, Rize. I have always believed that Crete and the Eastern Black Sea are very similar in ways more than just the fact that snails are called *hohli* in both lands.

Uğur Zekeriya Peçe
Hamezi, Crete, August 2023

NOTE ON NAMES AND SPELLING

Many locales that appear in this book have multiple names and spellings with changes over time. Although it is not easy to be perfectly consistent in the use of those names, I try to strike a balance between Greek, Turkish, and English. For the places in Crete, I prefer to use the current local version. For instance, around the turn of the twentieth century, the largest city of the island was referred to in multiple ways such as Kandiye (Turkish), Candia (English), and Irakleion (Greek). The rendition of its name into English today is done in several ways: Heraklion, Herakleion, Irakleion, Irakleio, Iraklio. I opt for the last one because it is closest to the spoken language of most of the city's residents today. I follow the same logic for the other two cities of Crete: Hania and Rethimno. For the locations within the Ottoman Empire I generally use more familiar Turkish versions such as Izmir and Trabzon. For the city that is known as Thessaloniki in Greek and Selanik in Turkish, I use Salonica, which is the more common version in scholarly writing.

xvii

ISLAND AND EMPIRE

INTRODUCTION
NO REFUGEE IS *an* ISLAND

Pırağ'da Yahudi mezarlığında sessiz soluksuz ölüm.
Ah gülüm, ah gülüm,
muhacirlik ölümden beter . . .

Death in Prague's Jewish cemetery, silent and speechless.
Oh my love, oh my love,
worse than death is refugeehood . . .
 —*Nazım Hikmet, Jeseník, 20 December 1956*[1]

Under a scorching August sun in 1896, more than five thousand displaced Muslim peasants congregated outside the city of Iraklio (Candia), beside two corpses of their coreligionists. The bodies had been brought there from Larani, a village about twenty miles south. Reports conflicted as to how they had been killed. The Muslim sources claimed that the killings had occurred as the victims attempted to collect their belongings from the village now under Christian control. Rival accounts maintained that they were ambushed and shot dead by a grieving father, avenging his teenage son who had been murdered in trying to prevent the two from pillaging their farm. Before the city gates lay the two lifeless bodies to be presented to the European diplomats stationed in Iraklio as macabre evidence that death was roaming the land. It was in this heated moment that Hasan Pasha, the newly appointed governor of Iraklio, the most populous district in Ottoman

Crete, encountered the refugee villagers, a frustrated multitude denouncing the authorities and crying for passage through the gates. Anxious to keep the tense atmosphere in the city under control, he denied them permission to enter and parade the dead bodies through the streets leading to the European consulates. "If you want to continue subjecting us to the slaughter," a voice rose from the crowd as fingers pointed to the corpses, "look!" The insults from the angry group soon turned physical, with some protesters pulling Hasan Pasha down from his horse and attacking him with sticks. Thanks to several helping hands extended to the fallen pasha, he managed to move away and throw himself into a shop, finding there a side door exit into a garden. He then headed through a backstreet to the government *konak*. In this turmoil Hasan Pasha lost his fez. Lost too was the prestige that a high-ranking Ottoman administrator needed most at this time of upheaval in Crete. With the gate now under the control of the refugee demonstrators, the displaced, long made to wait in anxiety outside the city walls, poured into Iraklio.[2]

On this violent day and hundreds of others prior, most of Crete was in a state of uproar. Anchored off strategic locations along its 160-mile-long northern shore were the battleships of Britain, France, Italy, Russia, Austria-Hungary, and Germany, a collective force patrolling the Mediterranean with the avowed aim of pacifying the island and preventing the strife from spilling over into the Balkans. On the island's high mountains far from the coast were Christian insurgents in an armed struggle against the Ottoman administration as they attempted to help in the annexation of Crete to Greece. And across the island's fertile valleys, isolated villages, and coastal towns were scenes befitting a civil war: smoke rising from villages ablaze, churches and mosques demolished, Muslim and Christian cemeteries defiled, olive trees burned, vineyards destroyed, tens of thousands of civilians internally displaced, and an unknown number of islanders murdered.

The episode at the gates of Iraklio in August 1896 paints a picture of how displacement catalyzed collective action on an island. This relationship also motivates the central question that *Island and Empire* explores in a much broader context, from the late nineteenth century to World War I: How are displacement, intervention, and protest connected in the Ottoman world? The physical confrontation between the refugee villagers and Hasan Pasha sets the stage to recount a narrative of displacement and collective action, one that soon after beginning on an island became a larger story about an empire.

British author H. H. Munro, writing under the pen name Saki, quipped that "the people of Crete unfortunately make more history than they can consume locally."[3] In the spirit of this aphorism, *Island and Empire* examines the violence that enveloped Crete during the 1890s and its long-term implications at local, imperial, and transnational levels. Drawing on research in local and national archives in seven countries, I narrate a connected history of mass displacement, international intervention, and popular mobilization, three phenomena that transformed the Middle East and the Balkans around the turn of the twentieth century.

My narrative begins with a discussion of an island-wide conflict, which I treat as a civil war, during the mid-1890s between Crete's majority-Christian and minority-Muslim populations, both Greek-speaking communities. I then proceed to explore a long-lasting international imbroglio known in the diplomatic parlance of the late nineteenth and early twentieth centuries as "the Crete/Cretan question." This represented a component of the protracted Eastern question that marked the relations between the Ottoman state and European powers from the mid-nineteenth century to the end of World War I.[4] The island's governance was long stipulated as a European matter in article 23 of the Treaty of Berlin (July 1878), obliging the Sublime Porte to enact a reform program in Crete, which materialized with the signing of the Pact of Halepa near Hania (Canea/Hanya) in October 1878. The Pact launched a period of autonomy lasting more than a decade characterized by such anti-Hamidian features as a strong assembly, parliamentary elections, and political parties. As Sultan Abdülhamid suspended the Ottoman parliament in 1878, the province of Crete acquired its own.[5] At the heart of the Crete question were the conflicting visions of rule between the islanders and Istanbul as well as clashing claims of sovereignty between Greece and the Ottoman Empire over a piece of land encompassing about 3,200 square miles with a population of more than 350,000. The tremendous geostrategic value of this island came from lying equidistant from Asia Minor, Europe, and North Africa as well as from boasting the Suda Bay, host to one of the deepest natural harbors in the entire Mediterranean. What elevated an interstate dispute to a complex transnational issue was the military occupation and later supervision of Crete for about a decade by a European coalition comprising Britain, France, Italy, and Russia.[6] I argue that the displacement of around seventy thousand Muslims following the civil war and the international intervention inspired mass protests that went far beyond the scene in Iraklio with which this book began. Rather, the movement spanned the Ottoman provinces from 1908 onward, sending echoes farther afield among the Muslims living under European colonial empires in Asia and Africa as well.

My main query about how displacement and protest are intertwined generates several other questions on three levels of analysis. At the local level, I introduce the concept of civil war to analyze the conflict on the island and explain why terminology matters in how we describe collective violence. At the international level, I explore how the European intervention contributed to a civilian catastrophe and accordingly treat the dislocation of Crete's Muslim community as an early example of "unmixing of populations," which only intensified after the First World War. At the level of empire, I examine the popular mobilization around an island after 1908 and discuss how community organizers in the Ottoman world made sense of the Crete question.

I make three central contributions to the histories of violence, international intervention, and displacement. First, I examine the strife between Christians and Muslims in the 1890s as a civil war, in distinction from Greek and Turkish historiographies that have often seen it as a revolution or an uprising, respectively. I argue that these terms reproduce dominant state language about violence and reduce a complex upheaval to a primarily nationalist conflict. Defining civil war as strife between communities that are familiar with one another, I underscore the element of intimacy between the island's Christians and Muslims. In so doing, I critique sectarian interpretations of conflict that pervade both contemporary accounts and historiography. By foregrounding the human consequences of the turmoil rather than the fighting between the state and insurgents, this terminology accentuates the analytical connection between violence and displacement.

My second contribution relates to the topic of international interventions launched in regions with mixed populations. The internal displacement of Crete's Muslims that began with a civil war concluded only after the refugees' demands for repatriation to their villages fell on deaf ears. I argue that the European perceptions of the strife in terms of an incompatibility between linguistically identical but religiously distinct communities underpinned the policies that fueled the Muslim flight from Crete. Such perspectives imagined the displacement as a strategy to prevent future clashes. Historians have widely studied the aftermath of World War I as the formative period for the crafting of policies that saw the elimination of ethnoreligious diversity, through population exchanges and transfers, as a panacea against conflict. Scrutinizing the depictions of Crete's Christians and Muslims as sectarian communities harboring mutual hatreds, I offer an alternative periodization for the internationally sanctioned projects of ethnoreligious homogenization in the name of political stability. While this book, at its core, narrates a story of an empire through the prism of an island, it also intervenes in histories of imperialism with an examination of Europe's insular entanglements.

My third contribution concerns displacement, the study of which is characterized by an emphasis on resettlement and humanitarianism. Underscoring the refugees' resourcefulness rather than helplessness, I demonstrate how the Muslims, displaced from Crete and resettled in Asia Minor, Syria, and Libya, took the lead in an empire-wide grassroots action between 1908 and 1911. I argue that the islanders who had been removed from Crete became the movers of Ottoman mass politics. Composed of public rallies and economic boycotts of Greece, the popular mobilization was distinguished from earlier examples in protest-rich Ottoman history in three fundamental ways: longevity (continuous occurrence between late 1908 and 1911), scale (covering most towns and cities in every province), and novelty (use of mobilization strategies and protest practices that were unavailable during the preceding three decades of censorship and the ban on mass political assembly in the streets and other public spaces). If the Cretan refugees recast themselves after 1908 as protagonists in the mass mobilization, the routinization of protest through continuous public assemblies about Crete remade the empire. I explore how ordinary Ottomans, the islanders and others, made sense in their neighborhoods of a diplomatic question that involved multiple states.

Uprooting: A Fratricidal War

A New Testament passage in the Epistle of Paul to Titus refers to an ancient seer-cum-philosopher of Cretan origin, likely Epimenides, who profiled his own people with words far from flattering: "Cretans are always liars, evil beasts, lazy gluttons."[7] One might read this as a biblical reproach whose essentialist characterization of an insular clan would be outdated by 1895. Around this time reports on targeted killings of civilians across Crete proliferated. As bloody incidents began to foster a climate of fear and panic, multiple observers deployed an indiscriminate language to characterize the islanders or large sections of them as hyperviolent. Aristotelis Korakas, the leader of a paramilitary force supported by Athens and the son of a famous chieftain who had fought against the Ottoman administration in the past, addressed a proclamation to the Christian inhabitants of the Candia (Iraklio) province. In this document from February 1897, Korakas set out to liberate them "from bloodthirsty Turkish Cretans."[8] Several days after his communiqué, a petition sent to the Ottoman government and representatives of European states by the Muslim inhabitants of Rethimno (Resmo) accused the Christians of aiming for "the total elimination of Muslims from the island."[9]

Multiple influential figures presumed violence in Crete to be innate to its inhabitants. In early 1895, the Italian consul in Hania relayed to the embassy in Istanbul the news of various bloody crimes in western Crete, interpreting them as the rekindling of "the antagonism existing between the two opposing elements since time immemorial [*tempo immemorabile*]."[10] In 1910, when the Muslim population stood around thirty thousand with a 70 percent decrease from its pre–civil war figure, the British consul A. C. Wratislaw reported a recent rash of murders of Muslims that had punctured a period of relative peace on the island, construing them as an indication of its inhabitants' savage ways: "Crete is not a ladies' school but a mountainous country whose inhabitants, outside the towns, are in a very elementary state of civilisation," the British consul wrote. "Their manners are ungentle and their respect for private property is limited, nor can it be expected that the Christians should treat the Mussulmans any more tenderly than they treat one another."[11]

It was not only the Europeans who imagined the islanders as having fierce passions that often burst out in violence. Turhan Pasha, serving as governor of Crete during some of the bloodiest days of civil war, wrote to Sultan Abdülhamid in late 1897 that for centuries the Christians had resorted to "rebellious acts" (*hareket-i serkeşane*), revolting twenty-four times under the Venetians and seven times since 1821. The resort to sedition was in "the natural disposition" of this island's inhabitants.[12] For Mustafa Nuri (b. 1851, Iraklio), an Ottoman statesman who promoted the significance of his native land to the imperial public after 1908, ferocity characterized Crete's physical and human landscape: "Those who are familiar with the fierceness of the Mediterranean along the shores of Crete . . . could form an idea about the nature and emotions of the people inhaling the air of its raging sea and inhabiting the mountains of that rebellious [*serkeş*] island." The Cretans always lived in the extremes: "They either love, and love with passion, or they hate, and hate with passion." Suggesting that such polarity also defined the relations between the island's Christian and Muslim communities, the veteran statesman added that the Greek (*Rum*) population harbored for years a strong feeling of hatred toward the Ottomans (*Osmanlı*).[13] Nikos Kazantzakis, who was also born in Iraklio, thirty-two years after Mustafa Nuri, envisioned his home-island with a similar sentiment. For this giant of modern Greek literature, Crete was not "a picturesque, smiling place. Its form is austere, furrowed by struggles and pain." For him, the history of this island was shaped by a violent struggle between "men fighting for their freedom and oppressors raving to crush them. These Cretans have grown so familiar with death that they no longer fear it."[14]

The portrayal of Crete as a land marked by bloodshed was widely reproduced in scholarly works. The literature on its history of conflict during the nineteenth century broadly falls into two camps. While Greek historiography has traditionally treated bouts of violence as a series of revolutions that the Christians waged against an oppressive state, Turkish historiography has recounted them as revolts instigated by the agents of an irredentist Greece.[15] Both perspectives reproduce narratives that amplify the state's voice. What state-centric accounts often conceal are the social dynamics and consequences of violence. Tobie Meyer-Fong critiques such viewpoints in her discussion of the cataclysm that ravaged China during the mid-nineteenth century, a conflict bearing an incongruous mix of labels such as the Taiping Rebellion, the Taiping Revolution, and the Taiping Civil War. She posits that "an examination of the human consequences of this war has the potential to transform our understanding of this period, forcing us to rethink the priority we attach to revolution, state, and nation."[16] Meyer-Fong's point resonates with the case of Ottoman Crete as well. A binary of revolution or revolt flattens a complex conflict on the island into a neatly defined clash between insurgents and soldiers. A strife that claimed many lives, demolished countless homes, and destroyed more than one million olive trees warrants using a different descriptor to foreground the scope of ruin across the physical and human landscape of Crete.[17] I investigate the violence in Crete during the 1890s as a civil war between groups of Christians and Muslims, two native communities sharing Greek as their mother tongue and holding in common various island customs.

In studying the island-wide turbulence, the idea of revolution and revolt has proven pervasive, but this is not because it offers a cogent reflection of the experiences of historical actors swept up in a conflict. Its prevalence instead typifies histories of interreligious/ethnic violence in which the state often serves as the primary agent, against which revolts and revolutions are leveled.[18] The underutilization of the concept of civil war in Ottoman historiography is partly due to how official histories have remembered violence, a point David Armitage raises as he underlines the politicization of terminology, positing that "established governments will always view civil wars as rebellions or illegal uprisings against legitimate authority" whereas "the victors in a civil war will often commemorate their struggle as a revolution."[19] The terminology of revolt and revolution often underpins a story of morality, which partly explains why it tends to lend itself to relatively clearcut divisions.

Civil wars split societies into opposing camps. They harden existing divisions along ethnicity, religion, or ideology while simultaneously blurring the boundaries between civilians and belligerents. Part of the fighting in civil wars may occur between soldiers and insurgents, yet a clear distinction between peasants and combatants often fades into murkiness. Studying interethnic violence in Ottoman Macedonia at the turn of the twentieth century, İpek Yosmaoğlu has identified ambiguity as a defining aspect of strife. Her work features "a protracted conflict, finally a civil war, fought as an insurgency, where the lines separating fighter from civilian, perpetrator from victim, traitor from hero, were not clearly drawn."[20] Evidence of such fuzziness in the case of Crete appears in some rare photographs from local and diplomatic archives. They present motley groups of villagers in armed resistance against imperial troops. Figures 1 and 2 portray groups of Christian villagers from two nearby locations to the west of Hania. The presence of several arms-bearing young teenagers and priests demonstrates the difficulty, if not erroneousness, of pigeonholing inhabitants into two neat categories, civilians versus combatants. On their part, local Muslims formed paramilitary bands as well with a similar goal: the preservation of the lives, properties, and political power of the community they saw themselves a part of. The term *civil war*, I suggest, is better suited to capture the complexity of this internecine fighting than *revolt* or *revolution*. A lack of clear distinctions between civilians and fighters is not an attribute exclusive to civil wars. That feature, however, accentuates the process-centered character of such strife. The terms *revolt* and *revolution*, on the other hand, often simplify collective violence. They are outcome oriented and, as such, reproduce precise and teleological narratives that are favored by nationalist constructions of history. While many of the island's Christian peasants are criminal rebels in most Turkish accounts, they are revolutionaries in Greek national histories.

While the concept of civil war lends itself to a less state-centric and more inclusive narrative of violence, does it really agree with the way contemporaries perceived the conflict?[21] The example of Crete shows that multiple figures from the island and beyond regarded the conflagration as civil strife.[22] In June 1896, penning a letter from the Preveli Monastery at the foot of a mountain overlooking the azure waters of the Libyan Sea in southern Crete, the Greek-Orthodox bishop Evmenios reported the attacks

FIGURE 1. A group of partially armed peasants from the village of Platanias in western Crete, 1896. Source: Ioannis Mourellos Archive, Etairia Kritikon Istorikon Meleton/ Historical Museum of Crete.

FIGURE 2. The Ottoman Turkish caption introduces this group as "the seditious committee" (*cemiyet-i fesadiye*) in the village of Kambos in western Crete, 1896. Source: Istanbul University Rare Documents Library, Yıldız Albums.

on the Christians. He admonished the island's Ottoman administration for driving the country to a "civil war" (*emfyliōn ... sparagmōn*).[23] It was not only Christian Cretans who made sense of the conflict in this way. In March 1897, corresponding with a British navy officer to convey their appreciation for his assistance, a group of Muslim notables condemned "the murderous assaults of civil war" (*attaques meurtrières de la guerre civile*).[24]

Civil war pits neighbor against neighbor, driving a wedge between communities deeply familiar with one another. The fratricidal nature of its violence is embedded in the title of one of the greatest fictional works about the Greek civil war of the 1940s, *The Fratricides* (1955), a novel by Nikos Kazantzakis, born during the waning years of Ottoman rule on the island.[25] In the 1890s, the Paris-based newspaper *Meşveret* (Consultation) had viewed the intercommunal violence in Crete through a prism similar to Kazantzakis's. In July 1896, the leading Young Turk publication in exile summarized several letters received from Crete that related acts of brutality against civilians. Those heart-rending missives made *Meşveret* "shudder at hearing about the bloody deeds among the brothers of the country [*vatan kardeşleri*] living together for centuries."[26] Two years later, in 1898, Dionysios, the bishop of Rethimno, would write a letter to Muslim notables in each of Crete's three principal cities. Addressing the receiver of his missive as "compatriot friend," he described the bloodshed as a civil war, adding to the example of the bishop Evmenios referenced earlier. Underscoring the common island identity between Christians and Muslims, Dionysios exclaimed: "We both live in the same land, we breathe the same air, we have the same origin, the same customs, we are speaking the same language, we have the same natural vices and virtues."[27]

Dionysios's stress on the intimate familiarity between the two communities at bloody loggerheads for the past two years illustrates the pertinence of David Armitage's observation that "civil wars spring from deep and deadly divisions but they expose identities and commonalities. To call a war 'civil' is to acknowledge the familiarity of the enemies as members of the same community: not foreigners but fellow citizens."[28] In differentiating civil war from other types of mass violence, political scientist Stathis Kalyvas has already underlined the centrality of intimacy: "More than anything else, intimacy is the attribute that sets interstate war apart from civil war. . . . Violence in civil war is frequently exercised among people who share membership in a legally recognized or 'imagined' community."[29] The size and topographic variety of Crete made up an island world in which peasants living in the westernmost region of Kissamos maintained little contact with those in the region of Sitia, about two hundred miles east. By the same token, the physical and sociocultural landscape of highlanders in southwestern Crete was incomparable to that of the lowlanders to the north.[30] Nevertheless, inhabiting an island with outer boundaries clearly fixed by the sea, I argue, made an imagined community much likelier to imagine.

The dearth of civil war terminology in the examination of violence in Crete is in part related to what Ussama Makdisi calls "the impossibility of 'civil war' in the Modern Middle East," presupposing the alleged "existence of inherently primordial sectarian worldviews that persist no matter how much change and transformation occurs in the Middle East."[31] If it is reductive to frame late Ottoman history as a tale of peaceful coexistence of diverse ethnoreligious groups, it is equally misleading to recount a definitive story of fanaticism and hatred between them. Here it is worthwhile to recall Christine Philliou's point about the fallacy of binaries that "limits us to two diametrically opposed visions," situating the empire's history in juxtaposition against an idealized western European norm and constructing a past demonized as oppressive or glorified as tolerant.[32] Manifold episodes of intercommunal violence in Ottoman history do not suggest the commanding power of wholesale religious hatred in society. This plain remark could seem to be just stating the obvious, if not for the persistence of scholarship that deploys an indiscriminate vocabulary of mass hatred to study conflict.[33]

Probing the strife in Crete during the 1890s in terms of a civil war yields insights beyond an island, helping us unsettle the histories of violence that "hinge on tropes such as sectarianism, Muslim-Christian conflict, or the clash of nationalisms."[34] It calls for an explanation of collective violence rather than treating it as a historical constant. Of relevance here is the case of the Yugoslav countryside during the early 1940s, in which the tension that embroiled groups intimately familiar with one another, communities speaking mutually intelligible languages, centered on religious difference. Max Bergholz's research on a rural community in Bosnia-Herzegovina "confronts us with the notion that it is actually the violence that largely generates these concepts ['nationalism,' 'ethnic groups,' 'ethnic conflict'], enhances their salience, and makes them matter in certain moments."[35] Like Bosnia-Herzegovina, Crete had a long history as an Ottoman borderland, but in the form of an island, with a legacy of conversion to Islam and traditions shared by religiously diverse populations.[36] Similarly in Crete, the violence of civil war ruptured a society that has often known how to manage potentially inflammatory differences.

As I discuss with more detail in chapter 1, ethnically motivated murders, the spread of panic-inducing rumors, raids on villages by paramilitary groups, retaliatory attacks, and dissemination of atrocity narratives polarized Cretans along the lines of "us versus them," fault lines drawn mostly by religion. Civil war led to the breakdown of a social order sustained by shared traditions and kept intact by a perceived interest in its preservation. As Barbara Walter notes, "Most people don't realize they are on the path to civil war until the violence is a feature of everyday life."[37] In this sense the phenomenon points to an aberration from the ordinary, the explanation of which is possible only through the scrutiny of events and processes that illuminate a society's descent into violence. By utilizing the terminology of civil war I seek to eschew the trope of inherently violent communities while keeping clear of painting a rosy picture of coexistence. The term offers a corrective to such ahistorical binaries as Oriental despotism or Ottoman tolerance. As Mahmood Mamdani posits in his work on the Rwandan genocide, "Violence cannot be allowed to speak for itself, for violence is not its own meaning. To be made thinkable, it needs to be historicized."[38] The concept of civil war tosses an anchor into history.

Partition: Boundaries in Mind and Land

Amid the violence of civil war ravaging Crete, the Sublime Porte grew alarmed to find a way to safeguard its most strategic insular possession, an island with "a first-class harbour at Suda Bay."[39] In pursuit of this goal, the state entered two contests: a successful military one against Greece in April 1897 and a frustrating diplomatic one with the great powers of Europe. The war with Greece was fought in Thessaly, about two hundred miles north of Athens, although its antecedents date to a Greek military intervention, when in the winter of 1897 a detachment of around 1,500 strong under the command of Colonel Timoleon Vassos landed on western Crete.[40] The protracted, and ultimately futile, political battle that the Ottomans waged with the European coalition has mostly been studied from the viewpoint of diplomatic history. Scholars have examined how a Euro-Ottoman partnership in Crete that began with the Sublime Porte's requesting Europe's assistance in the summer of 1896 ended in the fall of 1898 when the international coalition forced all Ottoman troops to evacuate the island.[41]

The cooperation between the European coalition and the empire culminated in early 1897, when Colonel Vassos's forces closing in on Hania were halted by the combined forces of Ottoman artillery and European battleships. The Western press widely condemned this common front against Greece. The *New York Times*, for instance, evoked a famous naval battle from 1827 when the armada of Britain, France, and Russia had destroyed Ottoman and Egyptian fleets, a victory that opened the path to Greek independence. The American paper fumed that if the Western powers restrained Greece, "the glory of Navarino will be effaced. . . . When the Greeks courageously intervene to lift the yoke from their kinsmen in Crete, a cordon of warships sent by the great civilized Christian powers shuts out their succoring squadron."[42] In less than two years, however, Abdülhamid II, under

FIGURE 3. Ottoman authorities and European officers at the parade of international troops in Hania, 1898. Source: Family, Court and State Archives of the Austrian State Archives, PA XII, Liasse XXVIII, 291.

FIGURE 4. A scene from the departure of Ottoman soldiers and civil servants from Suda Bay, Crete, 1898. Source: Historical Archives of Crete, Paul Blanc Photographic Collection, 3/101.

immense pressure from the coalition, would acquiesce to his soldiers' departure from Crete. Although Crete remained an Ottoman territory on paper, the forced withdrawal of troops was a serious blow. It was this humiliation that led the Young Turks in exile and later the Committee of Union and Progress (CUP), the commanding political organization following the revolution of July 1908, to denounce the Hamidian regime.

I explore the international military intervention in Crete in terms of its impact on displacement. The uprooting of Crete's Muslims started as an internal displacement, during which a mass exodus from the countryside overpopulated the island's coastal cities. The process was completed, with no prospect of return to the home-island, when the tens of thousands of people left Crete for Asia Minor, Syria, and Libya. A census carried out in June 1900 counted the number of Muslims in Crete at 33,496, representing a 54 percent decrease from the previous one in 1881. An overlooked example of mass migration during the empire's long nineteenth-century history of displacements, the Muslim flight from Crete also tore up the bi-religious fabric of the island's populous countryside. At the end of the nineteenth century 58 percent of the Muslims lived in the countryside, as a minority among a larger Christian population. In the aftermath of the civil war and the European intervention, this ratio dropped to 21 percent.[43]

In late 1897, the Assembly of Cretans, the political wing of the armed movement for *enosis* (union) with Athens, which had by this point become a regular interlocutor with the European admirals overseeing the island's affairs, submitted a petition to the foreign ministers of the coalition powers.[44] In his report to the British foreign secretary, the general consul Alfred Biliotti picked up on the main demand of the petitioners, the complete withdrawal of Ottoman troops from the island. Emphasizing that both Christians and Muslims "are perhaps more attached to their native soil than any other race," Biliotti nevertheless noted how difficult it would be for the dislocated Muslims to return to the villages ravaged by the civil war.[45] Only the creation of a capable gendarmerie, he continued, would induce them to rebuild their lives, as it was "beyond a doubt that no native Mussulman will make up his mind to return to the country before he is quite certain that he can do so with perfect security." It appeared that the only measure for their repatriation rested on European troops to escort them and be garrisoned in the countryside until the formation of a gendarmerie, which would take a year in the most optimistic scenario. Biliotti's final sentence in his dispatch to London read like a rhetorical question: "But is such an inland occupation contemplated, or likely to be consented to by the Powers?"⁴⁶

Earlier that year, Biliotti had arrived in southwestern Crete on board a British warship to secure the release of more than a thousand Muslim villagers and scores of Ottoman soldiers. Trapped in Kandanos, a village under the blockade of the Cretan chiefs aided by volunteers and artillery from Greece, they were rescued thanks to Biliotti's intercession with the besiegers. This incident represents one of the examples whereby the goals of local actors (appropriation of Muslim property) and those of international ones (pacification of Crete) aligned. Both objectives hinged on the emigration of rural Muslims. During the negotiations Biliotti promised that he would "facilitate by all the means in my power the emigration of such of the Mussulmans of Selinos who, like those of Sitia (they asked to go to Rhodes), might be inclined to go and settle elsewhere." What he envisioned for them was more than a relocation from the island's villages to towns because "the emigration of the country Mussulmans is the best solution of the Cretan problem, and . . . their agglomeration in or round the towns in Crete would throw the emigrants into utter destitution."⁴⁷ Ten years later, with a much-diminished population in Crete, the British Foreign Office even suggested that in case of threats to their well-being the Muslim minority should be urged "to colonize a particular region of the island, where they could more easily be afforded security of life and property."⁴⁸ From the time of European military occupation in 1897 to the end of the European-sanctioned autonomous regime of Crete in 1913, on multiple occasions numerous international figures spoke of displacement as though it were the solution rather than a problem.

Laura Robson observes that "the idea that physical separation could serve as a solution to the problems of building a new world of nation-states arrived swiftly and dramatically on the global stage after the First World War."⁴⁹ Singling out the aftermath of World War I as the formative period for grand-scale projects of dislocation by Britain, France, and the League of Nations, first in the Middle East and later in South Asia, Robson also mentions several nineteenth-century harbingers of the notion of ethnic concentration through separation, which included the French settler colonialism in Algeria and early Zionist projects of transferring European Jews.⁵⁰ The treatment of displacement as a method of conflict resolution in multireligious Crete resonates with how partition during the twentieth and twenty-first centuries, "touted as a 'solution' to ethnic conflict, has invariably been associated with mass violence," as Arie Dubnov and Laura Robson argue in a synoptic and transnational account of partitions.[51] Figures 5 and 6 illustrate the division of Crete and its capital Hania into sectors between four members of the European coalition. Amounting to an administrative separation, and therefore not suggesting a partition based on ethnoreligious difference, the creation of zones, a policy that remained enforced for more than a decade, nevertheless represents an early example of colonialist license to draw lines on the Ottoman map. Crete in the aftermath of a collective European intervention offers a case that uniquely combines the method of split governance and the policy of promoting Muslim emigration.

The internationally sanctioned compulsory exchange of populations (*mübadele*) in 1923–24 between Greece and Turkey, involving the uprooting of close to two million people, had its antecedents in European responses to the Cretan refugee question. As Davide Rodogno has observed, the Cretan case of demographic engineering seems to suggest a quintessentially European approach to conflict resolution in multireligious societies.[52] I argue that this is also an Ottoman story. Indeed, one of the elements making the example of Crete stand out is that the idea of "the unmixing of populations" appealed not only to the agents of European imperialism but to some high-ranking Ottoman imperialists as well. There is much evidence indicating that the European coalition saw the mass transfer of people as a remedy against collective violence. What is less obvious is the Ottoman side of such a worldview. For instance, in August 1897, the interim governor of Crete Müşavir İsmail considered separating Christian and Muslim villages to execute an "exchange" (*istibdal*, a word related to *mübadele*) of their properties.[53] Like the two population transfer agreements that the Ottoman state reached with Bulgaria and Greece following the Balkan Wars (1912–13), the governor's exchange plan in Crete did not materialize.[54] Still, the case of Crete under European occupation and civil strife provides an earlier example that helps historicize schemes, European and Ottoman, to dislodge people in the name of peace.

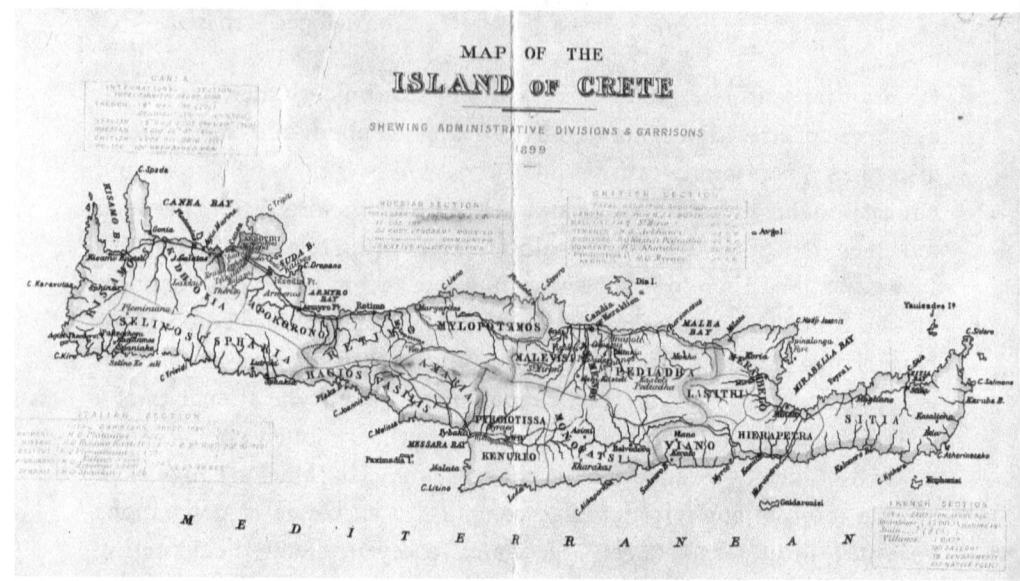

FIGURE 5. Map of the administrative divisions of the four occupying powers of Europe. Canea (Hania), Crete's capital, and its environs represent the international zone under the collective governance of the European coalition. The original map is dated February 1897 and the boxes next to each geographic section in the revised map provide information about the size of garrisons in February 1899. Source: British National Archives, FO 925/3408.

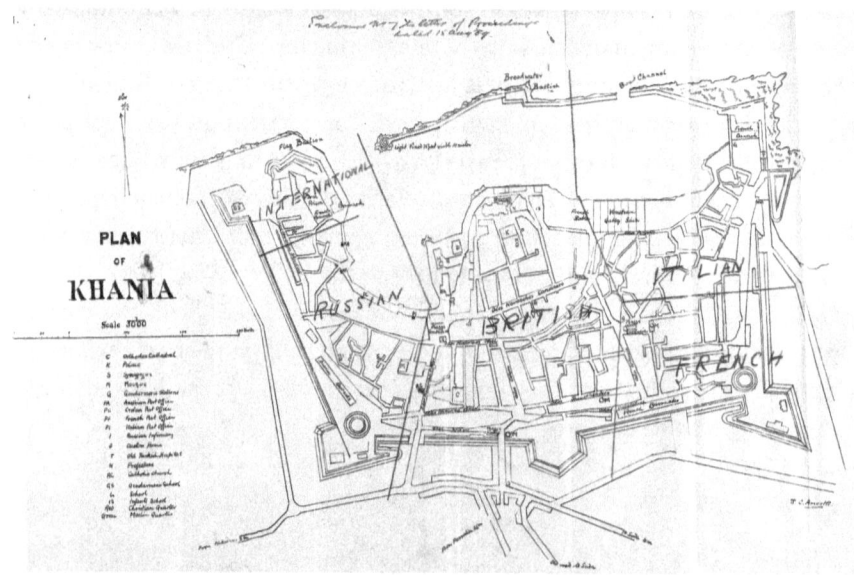

FIGURE 6. The division of Hania into four zones plus the section designated "International," a bastion where the flags of the coalition powers hoisted, 1909. Source: British National Archives, ADM 116/1078.

Against Speechlessness: The Voice of Mobilization

In June 1910, a Turkish-language newspaper *Yeni Edirne* (New Adrianople) informed its readers of a protest rally in Kavala. Reporting from that small coastal city about 150 miles southwest of Edirne, *Yeni Edirne*'s correspondent identified the steady press coverage about Crete as the main inspiration for multiple public assemblies throughout the empire since early 1909. Held on a Friday in May, a market day on which merchants and visitors from neighboring villages augmented the population of Kavala, a city famous for its tobacco industry, the rally drew a large crowd. Preferring an expansive vista, some residents stood at the windows and on the rooftops overlooking the town square. They observed with curiosity the demonstrators streaming into the square with Ottoman flags and placards that bore such inscriptions as "Crete is ours" and "Crete, or Death in Crete."[55] The latter was a variation on the ubiquitous protest chant of the period "Crete or Death" (*Ya Girit ya Ölüm*).[56] The audience responded with sustained applause to the orators, who delivered passionate speeches in Turkish, Albanian, Greek, and Judeo-Spanish, some of the languages widely spoken in the area.[57]

Unlike western Anatolia, especially the Izmir area, and northern Libya, Kavala did not receive a sizable refugee population from Crete. But like many other provincial towns from Albania to Syria, Kavala became a site for staging mass rallies during the popular mobilization that the island inspired after 1908. Setting off these empire-wide events was an announcement in October 1908 by the autonomous government of Crete to unite with Greece. Although this unilateral declaration of union received no international recognition and the island remained officially autonomous until 1913, it plunged Crete into turmoil, sending shockwaves to Greece and the Ottoman Empire.[58] The ramifications of this maneuver transcended the Mediterranean, reverberating through European capitals and as far afield as India. For instance, in June 1910, during a House of Commons debate on Crete in Britain, G. A. Lloyd articulated the possible consequences of failing to devise a solution to the satisfaction of the Sublime Porte: "The situation in the island itself would be a serious one, but it would not be confined to the narrow limits of the island itself. The effects would extend into Asiatic Turkey and beyond." Any perceived injustice toward the sultan-caliph ran the risk of further alienating many Muslims under British rule: "The breeze of dissatisfaction would spread, and have the effect of fanning the flames

ازمیرده دائرهٔ عسکریه اوکنده کرید ایچون عقد اولنان میتینغلردن بر منظره   « فوطو: حلیم لوندرات »

Grand meeting organisé à Smyrne en faveur de l'île de Crète.
(Photo: Halim.)

FIGURE 7. A protest rally for Crete staged in Izmir in 1911. One of the few visual documents related to Crete rallies, this photograph captures two features of mass politics in this period: befezzed protesters and Ottoman flags making red the dominant color in the sites of assembly and the variety of headgear indicating demonstrators' diversity. Source: *Resimli Kitap* (Illustrated Book), no. 33, October 1911.

of discontent in Egypt, and arouse the attention of many millions of our fellow-countrymen in India and elsewhere."[59] And a month later, *Tearüf-i Müslimin* (Acquainting of Muslims), an Istanbul-based magazine founded by the members of Russian Tatar diaspora, discussed the agitation that the Crete question caused among the Indian Muslims. They established committees in Bombay, Calcutta, Madras, and Singapore and rushed to the aid of the Caliphate by collecting donations for the Ottoman fleet.[60] Corroborating British fears and confirming the pan-Islamic magazine's coverage, the French diplomatic post in Calcutta would later report that Istanbul newspapers were in high demand among the Muslims of the subcontinent.[61]

When the description of the Kavala rally appeared in *Yeni Edirne* and when *Tearüf-i Müslimin* reported the distant ripples of the Crete question, the narrative constructed around it was already familiar to many in the Ottoman world. At its heart were the themes of Muslim victimhood and European imperialism readying to devour the last standing Islamic empire. In the pro-CUP press coverage of the island's affairs and of its significance for the broader Muslim world, Crete's Muslim population was featured as a beleaguered minority, severely shrunk because of mistreatment by the local government. They lived in fear under a regime that chipped away at Ottoman sovereignty and naval standing in the Mediterranean.[62] In such accounts, the island was frequently identified as "the safety lock of our [Ottoman] motherland," hinting at its importance within the interstate balance of power.[63] Writing in a special issue on Crete of the weekly *Hikmet* (Wisdom), Karabey Karabekof (b. 1874, Ganja), a doctor and the future leader of the Ittihad (Union) Party of Azerbaijan, foregrounded the island in the transimperial imagination: "For Turkey and for all Muslims, Crete is more than just a small island. It is the sentinel and guardian of our African colonies [*Afrika'daki müstemlekatımız*]." Not only the author's origins but his opinions suggested the bonds the island activated in the Ottoman world. In its potential loss Karabekof saw a domino effect: "If Crete is lost, Africa will be next. If our lands in Africa are gone, millions of African Muslims will fall under the murderous hands of enslavers, as happened in Algeria, Tunisia, and elsewhere."[64]

Hüseyin Nesimi, a key figure that I discuss in the book's conclusion, had already in the 1890s envisaged his native island as "the lock of the Aegean sea and the sentinel of Ottoman naval sovereignty in the Mediterranean."[65] Fourteen years later, in 1910, a similar vision manifested in a description by Ali Haydar Emir, a naval officer and instructor, for whom an Ottoman Mediterranean devoid of Crete resembled "an unlocked gate, thus vulnerable."[66] The same year in June a petition from a protest rally in Bozkır, a small town in central Anatolia, opened with the sentence "Crete is the safety lock of our sacred motherland."[67] As seen on the map in figure 8, the island's position in the eastern Mediterranean illustrates the aptness of this widespread metaphor.

Crete's emergence as a pressing matter in the postrevolutionary Ottoman public space cannot be explained by its key position on the map alone. Deeply symbolic factors mattered too given its history abounding with singularities. This island held a unique position in terms of generating tales

FIGURE 8. Detail from "Mediterranean Sea, Eastern [with] The Nile-Delta and the Suez-Canal," *The Times* (London, 1895). Source: David Rumsey Historical Map Collection.

of sacrifice and martyrdom, in both early modern and modern times. Its capture in the mid-seventeenth century after a twenty-one-year-long siege (1648–69) was the last major Ottoman conquest. This conquest, materializing after one of the longest sieges in recorded history, was widely recounted during the popular mobilization after 1908 in terms of "sacrificial struggles that lasted a quarter of a century."[68] And the war Crete triggered with Greece in 1897 produced a victory, not only quick but also rare in a century punctuated by Ottoman military defeats.

Perhaps no place offered a more telling test than Crete of whether the CUP, the leading political actor following the Constitutional Revolution of

July 1908, could offset the blows to the empire's sovereignty. Three consecutive days in early October are critical to contextualize this. On 5 October 1908, the autonomous principality of Bulgaria declared its independence, ending the thirty-year suzerainty of the Sublime Porte, which had been stipulated by the Treaty of Berlin (1878). On 6 October, Austria-Hungary annexed Bosnia-Herzegovina, culminating its thirty-year occupation of the erstwhile Ottoman province. In a way, these two acts merely formalized long-established de facto conditions. But they further undermined the state's prestige and soured the climate of postrevolutionary euphoria among many Ottomans. And on 7 October Crete's government proclaimed the island's union with Greece. In the dominant CUP narrative, Abdülhamid II won a war but lost Crete, a striking indication of imperial weakness during his rule. If an island exemplified previous feebleness, it could now set in motion a rejuvenation on multiple levels. This hinged on rallying the Ottomans around the question of Crete.

In his *Tanin* (Echo) editorial, Hüseyin Cahid, a leading Unionist who would soon be elected to the parliament as deputy for Istanbul, described Bulgaria and Bosnia-Herzegovina as two gangrenous provinces amputated from the empire. In the case of Crete, however, resigning to its severance would weigh heavily on people's hearts given the blood that the Ottoman heroes had shed in the plains of Thessaly in 1897.[69] In another editorial, Cahid diagnosed Abdülhamid's misgovernment and the negative public opinion that it sparked in the West as the causes of those territorial amputations. If not for the Constitutional Revolution in July 1908, the loss of Crete would be only a matter of time with "the wretched old regime keeping silent, even hiding the news from the Turks."[70]

For the CUP, Crete became a means of harnessing the power of masses toward imperial rejuvenation and consolidation. In the realm of politics, the island inspired large rallies and mobilized crowds, especially in the provinces, translating abstract rhetoric about political activism into lived experience. Protest rallies provided the CUP with an opportunity to cultivate an active political subject to be shaped in the streets. A novel choreography of protest distinguished it from earlier forms of collective action by townspeople. The formation of organizing committees, petitions sent to the capital, newspaper coverage, flags unfurled, banners inscribed, speeches scripted, and slogans repeated lodged the Ottoman protest in a modern aesthetics of performance. In the economic domain, Crete animated a boycott movement from 1909 onward, which aimed to break the strength of Greece and even of Greek Ottomans in the economy. In the military arena, it drove a grassroots donation campaign to modernize the navy before an anticipated war against a superior fleet of Greece and other external threats. In a matter of years, though, both the CUP and the empire that it commanded foundered. But all these phenomena that the island helped generate survived and left indelible marks in the post-Ottoman world.

Appreciating the uniqueness of Crete, with its fecundity of historical meanings, helps contextualize the story that I narrate in this book. But my primary interest lies more with its people than with its becoming a flashpoint between the Ottoman Empire, Greece, and Europe. In my narrative Cretan refugees hold a special place in the history of an empire marked by multiple displacements during the nineteenth century. They hail from an island with a practice of factional politics in the 1880s, thanks to the parliamentary regime instituted by the Pact of Halepa, and with a legacy of civil unrest in the 1890s. I posit that the plight and injustices of civil war only deepened their politicized sensibilities, paving the way for the Cretans' energetic activism that the CUP managed to channel into its grand project of imperial consolidation after 1908. It is illuminating to examine the Crete question as a generative crisis that afforded the CUP a means to differentiate the new regime from the Hamidian era and to redesign Ottoman politics and economy. But my main objective is to understand how survivors of the Cretan civil war emerged as a vocal force mobilizing Ottoman society.

Let us revisit the rally in Kavala in 1910, with which I opened this section. In his coverage of the event, the reporter highlighted the presence of a Cretan refugee in the crowd. The unnamed protester burst into tears as the orators delivered emotional speeches. Authentic or fictitious, the detail of a weeping refugee illustrates a publishing strategy aimed to mobilize the sentiments of the reading public. Such sentimental depiction also strikes a chord with the trope of suffering that would come to characterize much of the historiography on Ottoman refugees, a tendency that stems from the pairing of displacement with war.

In his work on mobility, Reşat Kasaba remarks that "the Ottoman Empire began and ended with migration."[71] Kasaba distinguishes between the initial and terminal migrations: the former gave birth to the empire, the latter augured its demise. Large-scale human movements during the earlier eras "helped build the empire and made mobility an integral part of it," whereas those of the nineteenth and early twentieth centuries unraveled it.[72] Kasaba's insight is emblematic of the scholarship on late Ottoman displacements. A common feature of it is the examination of mass population movements within a narrative of the waning of the Ottoman Empire. This is natural considering that it was the Ottoman military defeats that propelled a great number of civilians into the shrinking imperial territories.[73] For instance, scholars have demonstrated how a series of major conflicts during the empire's final decades, from the Russo-Ottoman War (1877–78) to the Balkan Wars (1912–13) and World War I (1914–18), led to major humanitarian catastrophes.[74] While it would be erroneous and objectionable to overlook the misery endured by the dispossessed, a lachrymose emphasis in the narrating of displacement, however, risks obscuring the examples of refugee activism.

Less obvious than the humanitarian impacts of wartime mobilization is how the displaced recast themselves in their postwar lives.[75] Shifting attention from what was done to the refugees to what they did, I foreground Cretan refugees' activism and explore how they energized Ottoman society between late 1908 and 1911. Approaching displacement as a condition that generates not only victimhood but also impetus for collective action I argue that visible segments of Cretan refugees, hailing from underprivileged classes of the island and mostly counting among the urban poor on the Ottoman mainland, drove empire-wide protests. With a focus on an understudied example of refugee activism at a time of widening public space in the Ottoman world, I join an ongoing conversation about envisioning migrants and refugees as resourceful protagonists rather than helpless multitudes.[76] Although the displaced and dispossessed were indeed people in need, the scrutiny of their involvement in the Ottoman protest movement helps "writ[e] refugees into modern history as active participants."[77] Thus *Island and Empire* offers a new perspective on refugees by featuring them not solely as the embodiment of imperial collapse but rather as leading actors in the remaking of empire.

During anti-Greece demonstrations after 1908, the Cretan refugees established a conspicuous presence in the streets. Sporadic references to them in official documents were replaced by ubiquitous commentary on their deeds, especially in the major port cities of Izmir and Salonica. They punctured the archival quiet that had enveloped them during the early aftermath of their dislocation from Crete. They morphed from the absentees of recorded history to its loud agents. They not only remade themselves but helped remake the empire by stimulating debate in print and on the street over the meanings of activism and imperial citizenship.[78] Their story provides another example of "the world refugees made," to borrow a phrase from Pamela Ballinger's study of Italian decolonization in the aftermath of World War II.[79]

In her critique of the refugee label in terms of denoting an undifferentiated multitude in misery, the anthropologist Liisa Malkki posits that the "vision of helplessness is vitally linked to the constitution of speechlessness among refugees: helpless victims need protection, need someone to speak for them."[80] Malkki's argument regarding the silencing of refugees in public coverage is also valid for the way they have been traditionally featured in history. Recent works in Ottoman studies, however, have sketched a more dynamic profile.[81] In this book, Cretan refugees are featured as protagonists of history. The exploration of their activism as protesters provides a strong antidote to the widespread representation of refugees with anonymity. If "mass displacement is taken to render refugees indistinguishable," as Peter Gatrell notes, then my goal is to highlight the centrality of Cretans in the Ottoman protest movement and narrate a story that treats displacement as a generative process.[82]

While there is an extensive historiography on the transformative impact of displaced statesmen, intellectuals, and army officers in late Ottoman history, we know much less about that of the uprooted who produced no written records about their lives and deeds.[83] In the absence of textual accounts left by refugee protesters, I seek to confront the issue of speechlessness, in the literal sense, by tracing their actions in the streets and by lending an ear to their sonorous deeds. What they lacked in self-written words, I argue, the Cretan refugees made up for in spoken words (such as the slogans chanted in the rallies) and in physical action (such as obstructive and intimidating acts during the anti-Greece boycott). Through a range of "earwitness accounts," I explore popular protest in its auditory atmosphere with the purpose of drawing our attention to the sounds of the past.[84]

In a classic study of sensory history, Alain Corbin has sketched an "auditory environment" of the nineteenth-century French countryside by tuning in to the sounds of village bells.[85] The cultivation of a sensibility for the clues of an "auditory environment" characterizes the approach of sensory history. Mark Smith regards it as "a way of becoming attuned to the wealth of sensory evidence embedded in any number of texts."[86] I draw on the methods of sensory history not only to contemplate Ottoman soundscape of protest but to amplify the sonic traces of a refugee community that has largely remained outside of historiography. As Jan Plamper observes in his work on the Russian Revolution, sensory dimensions are "key to any account that foregrounds the experience of historical actors themselves rather than, say, geopolitical rivalries, high-power politics, quantifiable social aggregates (classes, groups), or abstract socioeconomic forces."[87] Similar to the revolutionary Russian context marked by a flurry of emotion and fervor, the aftermath of the July Revolution in the Ottoman Empire offers an apt setting to examine soundscapes of protest in an era of mass politics.

In addition to underscoring the active involvement of Cretan refugees, I demonstrate how the CUP, especially through its provincial branches, commanded an empire-wide protest movement centered on Crete. The CUP leadership in mass mobilization might prompt an elusive question about the nature of protest meetings. Were they orchestrated or spontaneous? Did they indicate forced gatherings or express popular will? European diplomats often explained away the Crete rallies as artificial events manufactured by the CUP.[88] In such accounts they heard the sounds of protesters, Cretan refugees in particular, as signs of unruliness and fanaticism. In Turkish sources, on the other hand, demonstrators became the mouthpiece of an Ottoman nation, a multiethnic collective predominated by Turks and Muslims. Their sounds announced readiness to die for an island and empire. By foregrounding the soundscape of protest, I ask questions different from those related to the autonomy and function of crowds.[89] Primarily, I seek to identify the sounds that emblematized mass gatherings in the late Ottoman Empire. I ask not only what the protesters shouted but also what the uninvolved may have heard. During the several years following the Young Turk Revolution, recurring Crete rallies with their formulaic script and form introduced townspeople to a novel phenomenon. Thus I am especially interested in understanding how mass politics was experienced as a process, rather than examining it from a normative or functionalist viewpoint.

Scholars have deftly investigated the increasingly visible crowd as a daunting force and as the physical manifestation of public opinion in the streets during an era of parliamentary politics.[90] Within that genre, some informative research has covered public meetings and demonstrations set off by Crete, treating them as "one of the main elements of the collective action repertoire of Turkish nationalism."[91] Rather than employ Crete as yet another example to articulate the heightened visibility of crowds wielding a nascent force of nationalism, I seek to probe the sensory aspects of their involvement in Ottoman mass politics. Doing this, I argue, helps us grasp the basic audible mechanisms through which collective political action came to life through protest.[92]

Sources and Chapter Plan

Methodology and sources are tightly interwoven in historical scholarship, and this book is no exception. In other words, writing a transregional history with one place at the core requires a utilization of diverse sources that illuminate the multiplicity of perspectives about that locale and its broader world. *Island and Empire* weaves a narrative of connectivity by drawing on a variety of documents in multiple languages to transcend the insularity of chronicles centered in a single national context. The sheer extent of multilingual documents related to Crete is a corollary of the rival claims over the island. The volume of documents generated on and about this island grew during the late nineteenth century when a military intervention, and later occupation, by the European quartet turned the international spotlight on it. During the civil war of the 1890s, not only blood but also much ink was spilled in Crete. Western diplomats sent daily dispatches to their superiors. European admirals compiled detailed reports. Ottoman administrators penned alarming accounts to the Sublime Porte and Yıldız Palace. Christian insurgents exchanged letters with various committees in Athens striving for Crete's unification with Greece. Documents housed in Athens, Istanbul, Kew Gardens, Nantes, Paris, Rome, and Vienna allow me to present the gamut of official observations relating to the Crete question. Insights drawn from those archives, however, transcend state perspectives. Petitions and letters that the islanders submitted to the coalition forces stationed in Crete amount to hundreds of pages, making the state archives in Europe and Turkey a treasure trove of local history. Such materials offer a portal into a lost world, documenting how Christian and Muslim civilians perceived the strife that tore apart their home-island. Still, the plethora of perspectives from afar, whether from the seat of the sultanate in Istanbul or from the Quai d'Orsay in Paris, entail the temptation to carry the historian away from the internal dynamics of a large island like Crete. It is at this point that local collections such as those in the Historical Archives of Crete in Hania and in multiple municipal libraries across the island come to the rescue. The rich holdings of these institutions helped me remain attentive to "the internal differentiations and relations of power within the island itself," taking to heart Antonis Hadjikyriacou's suggestion that "to focus exclusively on external impositions is to forget the internal ones."[93]

Island and Empire is organized into five chapters that proceed chronologically and thematically. Chapter 1 zeroes in on the island to examine the conflict that I conceptualize as a civil war. The chapter's primary question is how an atmosphere of insecurity fostered by a series of targeted murders in 1895 morphed into a civil war that enveloped the island in less than a year. When the strife died down in late 1898, it would leave in its wake a radically transformed human and physical landscape with the displacement of more than a hundred thousand civilians across religious lines and the destruction of around one million olive trees. Those uprooted during the civil war came from an overwhelmingly rural Muslim background, a fact born out of the Island's demography, with Muslims constituting a majority in the coastal towns and a minority in the interior country. After a period of internal displacement in the towns, the majority of Muslim refugees left the island altogether, from causes that I explore in chapter 2. The main question here is how international military intervention paved the way for their massive exodus to Asia Minor, Syria, and Libya. This chapter treats the island's topography as a key factor shaping the European coalition's operations and objectives in Crete. One answer to the conundrum of how an Ottoman military victory against Greece in 1897 failed to translate into a favorable scenario in Crete is its mountains. Shielded by cliffs and gorges, both in generous supply on the island, the peasant fighters, a social group sharing much in common with Hobsbawm's bandits-cum-revolutionaries, knew how to harness geography in negotiations with the European admirals and consuls.[94] Chapter 3 presents the story of the Muslims who remained on the island, numbering around thirty thousand—a community much diminished from its pre–civil war figure of about one hundred thousand. The fundamental question in the third chapter is how this minority reckoned with displacement as a broadly defined phenomenon, not merely a physical experience but a condition associated with losing the privilege and security of being governed by an Islamic empire. I focus on the strategies of the minority to carve out a vibrant space for themselves in a new polity that retained few traces of the former regime. This is a story of Muslim Cretans' adaptability and resourcefulness amid an awareness of fragility and, at times, a premonition of peril. While various examples of publicly voicing allegiance to the new regime speak to a process of adjustment, the examination of the mass eviction of Muslims from Spinalonga, an islet off the coast of Crete, under the pretext of turning it into a leper colony illustrates the community's vulnerability during the 1900s.

The first three chapters of the book discuss how civil war and its aftermath created a displaced population of around seventy thousand Muslims. These refugees left their marks in history as they strove against the injustices of displacement. Sometimes they physically confronted high-ranking Ottoman administrators, and many other times they petitioned European officials to make their voices heard. The marks they left in history were mostly kept in bureaucratic folders away from public gaze. The final two chapters are the story of refugee protesters in full view. They explore how Crete and its refugees electrified the Ottoman Empire in the wake of the Constitutional Revolution in 1908. Chapters 4 and 5 cover the emergence of mass rallies and a fierce boycott against Greece, widely dubbed economic warfare that at times targeted Greek Ottomans and others that did business with the boycotted. I first discuss a network of activists composed of writers, intellectuals, journalists, and politicians. Hailing from relatively privileged backgrounds with Cretan roots, they were all based in Istanbul. They performed formative roles in terms of raising awareness about their native island. I credit this circle of public figures with crafting what I term Cretespeak, an emotive language comprising various elements that rendered the island legible to a transregional public. Shifting the focus from middle-class figures to masses, the remainder of the fourth chapter scrutinizes the soundscape of protest. I turn to the streets and the squares where mobilizing crowds, among them vocal and highly visible Cretan refugees, cried out the grim refrain of late Ottoman protests, "Crete or Death." Perhaps Crete was no longer an indisputable part of the empire, but the Cretans absolutely were, and they made their presence felt. Continuing the topic of collective action in the streets, chapter 5 examines the boycott movement that spanned the empire, affecting especially the towns and port cities that had become new homes to those displaced from the island a decade earlier. The refugee boycotters were mostly anonymous, unlike their co-islanders who formulated Crete-speak through solemn speeches and articles. Not in refined words but in much-talked-about and sometimes aggressive street acts lies their legacy in late Ottoman history. The overarching question in the final two chapters is how to make sense of a sweeping protest movement against the backdrop of a history of civil war and displacement.

Nazım Hikmet (b. 1902, Salonica) has opened this introduction by musing, "Worse than death is refugeehood." *Island and Empire* closes with a titular twist to his mournful line. The book's conclusion, "Against Violence: Worse Than Refugeehood Is Death," discusses the sorrowful and illuminating case of Hüseyin Nesimi, an intellectual and civil servant native to Crete with a heavy experience of displacement. Nesimi's life was cut short while he sought to rescue Armenian Ottomans from certain death in 1915. The book's final section shows how the legacy of violence and displacement in Crete persisted beyond it after 1914.

A final note is in order before I dive into my historical narrative starting in the 1890s. One of my goals in this book is to call into question the widespread distinction between terms used to denote notable public figures experiencing displacement versus anonymous individuals. While the word *émigré*, mostly used for those leaving their homeland for political reasons, is usually reserved for people of relatively privileged backgrounds, the word *refugee* mostly covers members of an anonymous and undifferentiated mass. This variation pervades scholarly and popular writing alike. Such differentiation, I argue, reflects an artificial separation of displaced individuals into two groups on the basis of privilege and cultural capital. Rather than illustrating historical actors' own self-definition, it often implies hierarchical categorizations of historians. In this book, I use the descriptor *refugee* to refer not only to illiterate Cretan protesters in Ottoman streets but also to intellectuals and other notable public figures uprooted from their native island (*muhacir*, whose historical usage was not necessarily class specific, is the best approximation in Turkish). This is not just a matter of nomenclature but an analytical preference that is inseparable from one of my central arguments: the emergence of a new Ottoman mass politics, both as a discourse and as lived experience, was a process driven by a multiclass community of displaced islanders. Further encouraging me to jettison elitist distinctions among the displaced are Nazım Hikmet's lines opening *Island and Empire*. Whatever class-related privileges this prominent poet possessed, he imagined his exilic condition in eastern Europe in terms of being a *muhacir* or refugee. With this word he made sense of his own uprootedness, situating his exile within the long genealogy of Ottoman and post-Ottoman displacements.

ONE

FEAR *and* TREMBLING
in the MEDITERRANEAN

Civil War in Crete and the Birth of a Refugee Question

If a high-ranking Ottoman official hoped for an appointment to enjoy some peace of mind with manageable administrative challenges, Crete during the 1890s would be an unlikely province to grant that. In the middle of that decade, revenge killings involving Muslims and Christians fostered an atmosphere of fear and insecurity that soon spiraled into an island-wide civil war.[1] The tension was exacerbated by Crete's financial woes that delayed salary payments to the gendarmerie, rendering the security forces disgruntled and potentially unruly, just when they were needed most urgently.[2]

Crete in the mid-1890s changed governors like gloves. The release of the renowned governor Alexandros Karatheodoris Pasha from the Cretan imbroglio came with the sultan's recalling him in March 1896, a decision that seemed to have disconcerted local Christian and Muslim notables alike.[3] Karatheodoris Pasha had replaced Turhan Pasha a year earlier. And now it was the turn of Turhan to replace Karatheodoris. Known as Turhan Pashë Përmeti in his native Albanian, who years later in 1914 would serve as prime minister of Albania, he spoke perfect Greek, one reason for his appointment to Crete. Reporting at the time of Turhan Pasha's recall from the island in March 1895, the veteran British consul Alfred Biliotti remarked that Turhan Pasha "was not the man for Crete."[4] A book published in 1897 in

Paris by the Muslim Philanthropic Alliance of Crete seconded this assessment, identifying Turhan Pasha's biggest weakness as his inability to comprehend the gravity of the situation on the island.[5] Corci Berović Pasha's exit from Crete, on the other hand, involved high drama. Before arriving in Crete to assume the heavy mantle of governor, Berović had succeeded Karatheodoris as the top administrator of the autonomous island province of Samos. In February 1897, having filled the office of governor of Crete for about half a year only, Berović sought refuge on a Russian warship, from which he embarked onto an Austrian Lloyd steamer to flee for Scutari near the Adriatic.[6]

While Berović Pasha was anxious to flee the turbulent island for his native Scutari, Greek ironclad *Hydra* and the gunboat *Sfaktiria* had arrived off the coast of Hania. In the meantime, Ottoman infantry had been clashing with the insurgents in the hills overlooking the city whose Christian neighborhood lay in rubble after a fire caused by internecine fighting among its residents.[7] When the squadrons commanded by the European admirals anchored in Cretan waters on 11 February, the island was in dire straits. The heightened climate of tension during the winter of 1897 proved Karatheodoris Pasha right for saying, a year earlier, that he had "no hope for the future in Crete and thought that things must go on from bad to worse."[8] In the words of Victor Bérard, French diplomat and author of multiple books on politics and history, while "the Muslim populace, as the masters of the cities, had just set Canea [Hania] ablaze and besieged the Christian quarters of Rethimno and Candia [Iraklio] . . . the insurgents, as the masters of the rest of the island, proceeded to ransack the Muslim villages."[9]

Among the multiple upheavals that Crete witnessed during its turbulent history, the civil war of the 1890s marked the most catastrophic. It was also more sweeping than earlier ones that had already caused immense devastation. The British geologist and hydrographer T. A. B. Spratt, for instance, had observed during his travels in the 1850s and '60s that "ruin meets the traveller in every village, the result of a devastating war lies impressed upon the face of the land and upon many a countenance still, and a sorrowful tale is ever ready for his ear."[10] Bringing havoc to all parts of the island, the final strife of the nineteenth century produced a massive uprooting of both olive trees and humans. Its destructiveness marked a reversal of a relatively peaceful period starting in 1878 when the island had obtained a special parliamentary regime along with a great degree of autonomy. The

FIGURE 9. Devastation in Hania in the wake of the flames, 1897. Source: Family, Court and State Archives of the Austrian State Archives, PA XII, Liasse XVIII, 282.

FIGURE 10. Julius von Pinter, the Austro-Hungarian consul in Hania, reported that the fire had destroyed seventy-three Christian and eleven Muslim homes in addition to eighty-three Muslim and fifty-one Christian stores. Source: Family, Court and State Archives of the Austrian State Archives, PA XII, Liasse XXVIII, 282, 1897.

FIGURE 11. The flags of six European powers together with the Ottoman flag in Hania, 1897. Source: Pantelis Sygkellakis Collection, Municipal Library of Hania.

year 1878 represented a watershed. It suggested that there was a remedy to cycles of violence and it lay in serious reform. It proved that conflict was not a constant. Known as the Pact of Halepa, the liberal reform document of 1878 set Crete on a political trajectory distinct from most of the empire. At the time of its signing, Abdülhamid II had just dissolved the Ottoman parliament, initiating a period of autocratic rule. But not in Crete.

With the Pact of Halepa, the Christians who made up about two-thirds of the island's population turned their demographic advantage into political power. The number of deputies in the influential general assembly was specified as forty-nine for Christians and thirty-one for Muslims. If the Halepa regime reversed the long-held Muslim dominance in local administration, an imperial edict of 1889 curbed the growing authority of the Christians and the island's autonomy together with it. They responded to Istanbul's heavy intervention by boycotting the elections. This prevented the general assembly from convening until the appointment of Karatheodoris Pasha as governor in 1895, which happened after a five-year era of Muslim military governors.[11]

The restriction of government privileges was a blow mainly to privileged Christians and had only a limited effect on peasants, whose labors kept the island's rural economy running. But when the political disgruntlement combined with a severe economic crisis, a recipe for more general strife was concocted. As Manos Perakis explains, failed harvests, a global drop in produce prices, and indebtedness further worsened by dependence on private lenders due to the absence of a credit bank created a burdensome situation for small producers. With little to lose under such tough circumstances, the rural poor did not really see the prospect of uprising as an extremely risky undertaking.[12]

My narrative in this chapter begins against such a backdrop of dire straits on the island. The short span of time in Crete's history from late 1895 through 1898 could easily lend itself to a monograph-length exploration of the intricate web of relations that involved multifarious actors with distinct interests.[13] There is ample archival material for a thorough investigation of the divergent visions of high-ranking Ottoman commanders, the sultan's top civil servants, European admirals and consuls, native notables, and Cretan chiefs and Hellenic officers intent on annexing the island to Greece. In this chapter I pursue a more focused goal. I examine the catastrophic consequences of the violent conflict in Crete for its ordinary inhabitants. I am especially interested in probing the turmoil as a civil war and charting its impact in terms of the mass internal displacement of rural islanders. The main reason for their dislocation lay in the complete breakdown of public security across the countryside in the island's interior, unlike in the coastal cities, where from February 1897 onward European and Ottoman troops were stationed.[14] The lens of civil war lays the emphasis on the broader island society, shifting away from the traditional focus of historians on the fighting between the state and insurgents aided by Athens.

The first section of this chapter narrates how sporadic violence and collective insecurity in parts of Crete escalated to island-wide strife and civil war. After presenting a picture of disorder in the countryside and cities, I examine intimacy as one of the defining features of civil war. I then substantiate my usage of *civil war* as the terminology that best captures the experiences of islanders by locating the concept, in its verbatim form or connotations, in the remarks of contemporary figures who witnessed and, in the case of several, bore the brunt of violence. Having identified this usage in the lexicon of multiple actors in 1890s Crete, I explore the dispossession and displacement of tens of thousands of rural Muslims as one of the primary dimensions of civil war. My analysis also acknowledges the displacement of Christian islanders, an uprooting as unjust and painful as that of the Muslims, yet much smaller in scale.

Dread in the Hills

During the waning months of 1895, the steady deterioration of public security in Crete generated a fertile environment that would carry a small insurgent band named Epitropi (Committee) from relative obscurity to popularity with a large section of the Christian population. Epitropi had entered the stage in late 1895 with a whimper, drawing only limited participation from the rural inhabitants. Formed in the mountainous western Crete under the full title of the Central Revolutionary Reform Committee of Crete (Kentriki Epitropi tis Metapolitevsis Kritis), it soon began to be known simply as Epitropi. As the public unrest in Crete progressively worsened with no visible sign of improvement, the guerrilla band proved capable of exploiting the atmosphere of insecurity and instability to boost its appeal among the broader Christian population. Around this time, the forces tasked with safeguarding the inhabitants of a large island were in urgent need of reform that required considerable funds from Istanbul, slow to trickle out if they did at all. In September 1895, governor Karatheodoris Pasha dispatched a cipher telegram to the Sublime Porte, informing the grand vizier of a gathering organized by *cemiyet*, that is, Epitropi, with the goal of signing a collective petition to demand administrative reforms. At this early stage of limited peasant mobilization, the island was still imagined within the framework of the empire. Their main demands revolved around restoring the administrative privileges that the Sublime Porte had rescinded in 1889 and bolstering the island's autonomy. Given the small number of participants from the districts of Apokoronas and Rethimno, Epitropi decided to put off petitioning the authorities until a more suitable occasion, awaiting the involvement of more villagers from other districts in western Crete.[15]

On the penultimate Sunday of September 1895, a larger gathering of around five hundred people, almost all armed, took place in Krapi, on the slopes of the Lefka Ori (White Mountains). At this assembly, the participants discussed a detailed reform proposal. The approved document contained the following demands: the sultan's appointment, for a five-year term, of a Greek Orthodox governor who would be vested with the authority of sanctioning the laws passed by a popularly elected general assembly; the formation of a ten-member council to assist the governor, which would be composed, in proportion to population, of five Christians, three Muslims, and two delegates from the European consular corps; the limiting of Ottoman troops to four thousand soldiers garrisoned only inside the fortresses rather than possessing freedom of movement across the island; and the exemption of Crete from commercial treaties between the Sublime Porte and the European states unless they were also ratified by the island's parliament. An Italian consular report noted the reverberations that this gathering in the mountains produced in Hania, the administrative capital of Crete. Wary of an island-wide spiral into chaos as witnessed several times in the preceding thirty years, "the most intelligent and wisest leaders" of the urban Christian population initially harbored a strong opposition to armed assemblies in the countryside. Recently, even they had begun to acknowledge, however, the need for major reforms to ensure the safety of their coreligionists.[16]

The concerns over the safety of civilians that the Christian notables expressed in September 1895 were not unknown to Karatheodoris Pasha. He had informed the grand vizier six months earlier, days after his appointment as governor of Crete, about the emergence of a perilous social atmosphere. It was fostered by a kind of a rumorscape. Collective misinformation and commonplace incidents blown out of proportion collapsed the distinction between fact and hearsay. Referring to the situation in western Crete, the governor's report noted that recent murders had set off rumors that convinced the inhabitants of the presence of cabals committing targeted ethnopolitical killings. Such rumor-fed convictions generated feelings of "aversion and hostility" (*bürudet ve zıddiyet*) in intercommunal relations to such a degree that people on both sides ceased to exchange greetings.[17] In his report on the series of homicides that started to multiply in the summer of 1895, especially in the southwestern district of Selinos, the British consul Alfred Biliotti mentioned a presumption held by certain Christians. They believed that a native gendarme had brought to Selinos a hit list issued by a secret committee of Hania Muslims, the killing orders to be carried out by his sons.[18] Zahid Chaudhary's remarks concerning the inflammatory capacity of collective misinformation during the Sepoy Mutiny of 1857 shed light on social tension in Crete as well. Especially in an agitated environment, rumors "derive their force from collective and repeated circulation. The standard of truth, in fact, is irrelevant to the rumor's effects."[19]

Plentiful were such examples showcasing how threads of violence bound the countryside and the cities. For instance, in early September of 1895, to avenge one of his relatives shot dead in Hania, a man murdered a random Muslim customhouse officer in a coffeehouse several hours from the city. In the district of Kissamos, some twenty miles west of Hania, roused by the killing of a Christian, his coreligionists surrounded the village where the crime was perpetrated. The exchange of shots left one Muslim dead. Biliotti noted that such incidents plunged the peasants into terror. They felt compelled to form groups of seven or eight people to carry the grape harvest to urban markets more safely. The approaching olive season amid deepening insecurity invited more woes. Biliotti, whose informed dispatches from around the time of Karatheodoris's appointment to Crete in the spring of 1895 had struck a tone of optimism about interfaith relations, now expressed gloom. He observed that the Christian majority now believed that "the amelioration which they long for cannot be obtained by a change from a Mussulman to a Christian Vali, or vice versa, but that there must be a radical change in the present mode of governing the island."[20]

In a country rife with insecurity, the emergence of an armed group, Epitropi, albeit small initially, conveyed the promise of refuge to many villagers. The experience accumulated from multiple incidents over the years had taught the peasants of Crete to distrust and fear the state, including its local appendages. In this atmosphere of chaos, Dorotheos, the bishop of Kissamos and Selinos, expressed indignation at the irregular bands of Muslims, which, he claimed, received assistance from Ottoman troops: "Jealous of Kurdish exploits against Armenians and benefiting from the weakness and malevolence of the government, [Muslim Cretans] launched a war of extermination [*polemon eksontōseōs*] against the Christian element."[21]

Earlier episodes of unrest in nineteenth-century Crete had familiarized the islanders with such crimes as the profanation of sacred sites, the destruction of fields and olive oil workshops, and the theft of livestock. Against this historical backdrop of strife, novel outbreaks of violence in the mid-1890s generated consternation rather than surprise. And on this wave of fear and trembling Epitropi rose to a position of influence and command beyond its initially narrow radius. In early November 1895, its members advanced from the western district of Apokoronas to Argyroupoli, a village about a seven-hour march southeast in the Rethimno district. Their goal was to ascertain if there was any truth to the allegations of profanation of a chapel by the soldiers. Other similar instances of active involvement in local affairs indicated that Epitropi had begun to take on the mission of shielding the Christians from mistreatment and abuse.[22]

In the initial stages of its existence, Epitropi refrained from skirmishes with the Ottoman soldiers. During this time its primary goal was still to seek the implementation of wide-ranging reforms in the local administration. Another reason for its policy of avoidance was its modest size. Before long, however, the band began to see its ranks expand. In late November 1895, the Ottoman authorities received the intelligence that Epitropi was preparing to move from Apokoronas to Kampoi, a natural stronghold in high altitudes a five-hour march northwest. The government dispatched troops with the goal of putting an end to the band's operations once and for all. As soon as the first detachment sighted Kampoi, three village elders ventured to meet the commander. They tried to reason with him, asking for permission to persuade Epitropi to leave the village to prevent bloodshed. Unmoved by the supplications, the commander proceeded toward Kampoi. A hail of bullets welcomed his unit. Another detachment of five hundred soldiers headed to the village by another route engaged Epitropi. Although the band numbered only around fifty men, the assault by Ottoman troops quickly attracted about five hundred armed peasants from neighboring villages rushing to aid Epitropi. In the skirmish, somewhere between six and twenty soldiers perished. Also gone was a rather passive stance of the peasants toward Epitropi. A third detachment of about two hundred soldiers made no engagement and returned to Vamos, a four-hour march east of Kampoi, when they heard the tolling of church bells all around them, an auditory cue for villagers to arm themselves. Rural inhabitants of western Crete, who had previously entertained mixed feelings about the armed band, might have strongly preferred to stay out of a fight with the soldiers. But when they were confronted to choose between the troops and the insurgents, picking a side must have come as easily as harvesting olives or grazing goats. The peasants of Crete increasingly came to regard Epitropi as their guardian. For some of them, going down to Hania on market days entailed humiliation at being treated rudely during the confiscation of their arms at the city gates. Particularly for people with such experiences, Epitropi held the promise of restoring dignity. They justified being armed, mostly with knives, which were universally carried on the island, by claiming that they did so "to defend themselves as the government fails to protect them on the roads."²³

The disintegration of state authority and a deepening sense of insecurity among the population go a long way toward explaining Epitropi's growing prominence. It is also important to recognize the broader international setting to contextualize the emergence of this armed band. In a proclamation issued in November 1895, Epitropi defined its self-assigned role as fighting against "the miserable situation that has been reigning in our unfortunate country on account of the abolition of our privileges in 1889."²⁴ Its statement dated the main reason for the turmoil in Crete to 1889, but not until late 1895 did the instability come to a head. Epitropi alluded to a long string of struggles throughout the nineteenth century against Ottoman rule. Earlier attempts to annex Crete to Greece had failed because of the relative vigor of the empire and the European policy of maintaining the status quo on the Eastern question. Now, however, the international conjuncture presented an opportune moment for the age-old struggle. Objectors to Ottoman rule in Crete found a sympathetic European audience already aroused by the coverage of Armenian massacres in Anatolia.²⁵ "Now that Turkey is in domestic paralysis and the civilized world's attitude toward it is unfavorable, the Cretan people deem the present moment ripe to demand . . . the restoration of those rights of which we were stripped unilaterally and unlawfully," Epitropi proclaimed. The armed band saw the restoration of the extensive autonomy Crete had enjoyed until 1889 as the first step toward ameliorating the general situation. The definitive solution to periodic crises on the island, however, lay in union with Greece.²⁶

The combination of internal volatility and a favorable international context helped Epitropi quickly expand its operations. Partly inspired by a highbrow irredentist agenda formulated in Athens, the organization's literate cadre was composed of a small group of middle-class professionals.²⁷ Mostly educated in that city, they embodied the romantic spirit of nineteenth-century nationalism and spelled out resistance against the Ottoman state by invoking the modern history of Crete. In a March 1896 proclamation addressed to "the liberated and enslaved Greeks and the freedom-loving children of the civilized world," Epitropi listed a litany of uprisings from the previous decades. "When Hellenism waged a battle in 1821 against Turkish despotism, fighting the forces of the sultan and of

Egypt," its statement opened, and it went on to decry Ottoman dominion over the island after the founding of an independent Greece. Unlike the inhabitants of the regions liberated after 1821, Epitropi continued, the Cretan revolutionaries had failed to persuade the Europeans to make the sultan bestow a tolerable regime on the island. "Only after the Revolution of 1878 our country acquired with the Pact of Halepa a set of privileges, which were eventually abolished in 1889."[28] According to this narrative of disappointments, it was the unlawful abolition in 1889 of the privileges granted in 1878 that had caused the conflict that laid waste to Crete. "Murders committed against Christians across the countryside and before the city gates by the hordes of Turkish killers with the knowledge of the Turkish administration" prompted Epitropi to take on the task of avenging the persecuted.[29] Before long, the disturbances spread and entered through the city gates.

Panic in the Cities

If truth is the first casualty in times of war, in Crete it had already died when the strife descended from the mountains into the coastal cities. Abundant stories and reports caused panic before they turned out to be fabricated. On an early summer morning in 1896, the staff of the British consulate in Hania were startled by a sudden rush of urban residents into their premises. With the consular guards shutting the building's door to prevent overcrowding, those who were slow to take shelter there ran along the quay in great panic. Some forced their way into the customs building. Others hid behind casks on the docks. The remaining few jumped into the sea and swam toward the boats. It was the circulation of an unfounded rumor by a police officer, Vassilis Georgiadis, that had startled the people of Hania. Early in the morning a barber had shared with him the fake news that Ottoman military authorities had distributed cartridges to Muslim civilians. Further disconcerting Georgiadis was another piece of uncertified information that two Muslims wounded by Christians in a nearby village would be brought to Hania. He knew well that the sight of their bruised bodies would exacerbate the restlessness in the city. The alarmed police officer rushed to the Christian stores and warned their owners of a looming massacre, leading many to arm themselves and wait at the windows ready to fight. Fortunately, Ottoman civil and military authorities managed to de-escalate the tension. Praising their effective action in an atmosphere charged with explosive rumors, the British consul Alfred Biliotti noted that he deemed "panics for which no exact reason can be assigned far more perilous than real known danger."[30]

In a city where every house was home to revolvers and knives, the maintenance of public order proved an arduous task with the whole population becoming "so terror stricken as to take fright at every noise that is made." Any sound resembling a gunshot would prompt a flight, as in the case when a man driving nails in a door scared his neighbors, causing people to launch a frantic rush for shelter.[31] When Biliotti described in July 1896 the frequent outbreaks of mass panic in Hania, he sounded like a social psychologist with an interest in crowd behavior. "The more futile the cause, the more the impending danger is serious," Biliotti observed, "for it rests not on an incident which can be controlled or explained the moment it takes place, but in the imagination of the whole population, which has gradually grown to that state of nervousness and excitability that the general feeling seems to be 'kill not to be killed.'" He added that "no immediate remedy but time is capable to cure this deep-rooted disorder of the imagination."[32] The clock was ticking, however, not to alleviate but to aggravate the excitement. With every delay in reforming the island's embattled institutions to the satisfaction of its inhabitants, the Christians' faith in peaceful transformation dimmed. With every new village pillaged and devastated by Christian or Muslim bands, the desire for coexistence waned. With every new perpetration of atrocities, the atmosphere of fear and trembling became too thick to dispel, soon turning into island-wide strife.[33]

In April 1896, a confidential letter by Aristidis Kriaris, a prominent pro-Athens Cretan politician, portrayed the general situation on the island in a language evoking civil war.[34] "Our country remains in a very critical situation," his alarming note to Alexandros Skouzes, foreign minister of Greece, warned. "Frightful anarchy, rupture of communications, stagnation of business, and ravaging poverty" put Crete in dire straits. The civilian administration deserved the blame for the inertia of its officials amid the imprisonment of the innocent, unlawful arrests and ill-treatment of Christians. The military authorities disdained anything beneficial for the country's development. Afflicted by serious financial troubles, the government fell behind on salary payments, one consequence of which was rampant discontent and periodic mutiny and desertion in the ranks of the gendarmerie. For Kriaris the crisis was systemic above all else. And its social impact was catastrophic with the steady radicalization of certain sections of the population. Society was ravaged by "racial murders [*dolofoniai fyletikai*], ferocious fanaticism of both elements [Christians and Muslims], hostility of native Turks, coteries of beys,[35] committees and assemblies of Christians, assaults by the army that in turn provoke counterattacks and bloody clashes."[36]

Kriaris's gloomy report was penned not long after the end of Karatheodoris Pasha's governorship in Crete. Although his post had lasted only about a year, it proved long enough to disillusion the experienced bureaucrat with the state machinery. Resolute and well versed in the island's character, he commanded respect of Christians and Muslims alike but faced hurdles on his path. For instance, it was reported that Karatheodoris Pasha had asked for military reinforcements to better deal with the worsening situation. His request was turned down by Hasan Tahsin Pasha, the military commander of the island. Some Muslim Cretan sources, likely supportive of Young Turk views, claimed that Hasan Tahsin had purposely caused difficulties for the governor since he aspired to replace him.[37] In the end, the overall turn of events distressed Karatheodoris Pasha about the island's future, a dismay that Kriaris, and other native notables, shared for different reasons.

When the Sublime Porte announced the reintroduction of the provisions of the Pact of Halepa in June 1896, neither the Christian nor Muslim deputies of the Cretan Assembly expressed satisfaction. As winter melted into spring, the situation in Crete had deteriorated to such a degree that the restoration of a reform pact that had kept the island in relative peace and prosperity for a decade fell short of promising a return to better times. Remedies that less than a year ago had promised peace were now obsolete. The deputies remained doubtful whether the Pact of Halepa could pacify Crete under the present circumstances. This illustrated the quick turn of events given that only less than a year earlier the deputies had worked harmoniously under the presidency of Karatheodoris Pasha. Once the civil war was in full swing, strategies that would be effective in ordinary times became futile. Causing island-wide destruction and displacement, civil war resisted normalization.

The Muslim deputies dreaded any reforms that would favor the majoritarian demands.[38] One day before the opening of the assembly, they presented to the European consuls a petition bearing twenty-one signatures in which they argued that the Pact of Halepa undermined the minority interests. The document spelled out the reasons why it failed to "protect the established moral and material rights of the Muslims." Fully aware of the decisive power that the European governments held over the political future of Crete, the deputies exhorted the consuls to "take interest in the rights and fate of the minority [kısm-ı ekalliyet] and not to sacrifice them to the excessive and radical demands of the majority."[39]

Two days after the opening of the assembly, it was now the turn of thirty-nine Christian members of this body to lodge a petition of complaints and demands. The document submitted to the governor in mid-July 1896 consisted of requests for several critical amendments to the Pact of Halepa. The petitioners presented an identical copy to the European consuls. An appendix added to that version illustrates how they narrated the island's recent history. A turning point in that historical framing was 1830. It was an auspicious year for the founding of independent Greece. But it also marked disillusionment with the great powers of Europe for not making Crete and Samos, two islands that had witnessed pro-Greece movements during the 1820s, part of the newborn kingdom: "Having acquired a just system of government by the imperial edict of 1832, Samos has been thriving and prospering from that date, but beyond certain alleviations in taxation . . . nothing was done for Crete."[40] The dislike of the local administration and the favorable international context during the Russo-Ottoman War of 1877–78 combined to incite some Christians to launch an uprising, which culminated in the Pact of Halepa. The deputies considered the Halepa regime as the herald of prosperity on the island. Governors now enjoyed prerogatives shielding them against both the centripetal influence of Istanbul and meddlesome military commanders in Crete. In this period of enhanced autonomy the islanders finally began to reap the benefits of self-rule.[41]

The era of prosperity, however, proved short-lived. In 1889 the central administration abolished most of the privileges that it had granted to the island a decade earlier, setting off, in the words of the Christian deputies, "a state of chronic disorder such as we had never seen before." In describing the ensuing ill effects, the deputies minced no words: "The courts' constant acquittals of criminals by government orders, the excessive granting of amnesty and often to repeat offenders, the squandering of public funds, and corruption became commonplace in the administration of the island." In this environment of injustice, well-intentioned and law-abiding segments of society grew despondent and indignant. Homicides surged and armed bands multiplied. Low in support and resources but high in obstacles set by the military authorities, the illustrious governor general Karatheodoris Pasha, who had enjoyed especially high popularity with the Christians, lost the prestige he had commanded earlier. In despair, he left the island.[42]

The chaotic situation weakened any remaining interest to return to status quo ante through the reinstitution of the Pact of Halepa: "Even the most moderate inhabitants became convinced that efforts in that direction would not be justified, either morally or practically." And more than that, many came to advocate "the necessity of obtaining by arms and at all sacrifices a definite deliverance from their misery, by the annexation of the island to Greece."[43] Why rebuild the destroyed villages, the Christian deputies asked, so that they would become fodder for wrongdoers and would be set ablaze again at the emergence of the next conflict?[44] It should be noted that both the historical narrative and the reform proposal bear a striking similarity to the language and content of the resolutions, referenced earlier in the chapter, that Epitropi passed in the mountains of western Crete in September 1895.[45]

At the heart of the Christian deputies' demands lay a radical reformulation of representation in the general assembly and the administrative council. Although the legislative mechanism introduced by the Pact of Halepa required a two-thirds majority for the passing of laws, the Christian deputies now advocated for its replacement with the principle of absolute majority. The Muslim deputies deemed this unacceptable for two reasons. First, they argued that they deserved stronger political representation because they held more land. Even though the Muslims were a minority, they controlled "possessions of more considerable value, and thus are more attached to the country." The second reason for their opposition pertained to their distrust toward the island's inhabitants who, in their privileged eyes, were lacking in education and manners. They had already proven that "in the case of one of their two elements [Christians and Muslims] enjoying an absolute majority in the general assembly and administrative council, they would be incited by fanaticism to trample the rights and interests of the minority."[46]

Another point, with which the Muslim deputies took issue, concerned the state language. Instead of a bilingual governance introduced by the Pact of Halepa, the Christian deputies proposed the exclusive use of Greek in the proceedings of tribunals, state councils, and other administrative offices. Both communities spoke Greek as native tongue, but the Muslim deputies remained steadfast to preserve Turkish as one of the two official languages of the land. They regarded it as one of the few threads binding them to the imperial state. "While speaking Greek patois in daily life," the deputies pointed out, "Muslim Cretans preserve their particular and national language [*leur langue propre et nationale*], Turkish, which they make use of in writing."[47] The tongue they used in quotidian life made them Cretan and the one they employed in lawmaking, Ottoman. They desired to retain both.[48]

What's in a Name? An Intimate War

A violent intercommunal discord was born out of Crete's socioeconomic dynamics, the collapse of state authority, and the pervasive atmosphere of fear in society. Drawing on Stathis Kalyvas's remark that "intimacy is essential rather than incidental to civil war," I treat the conflict in Crete as an internecine strife between Christians and Muslims holding in common a set of cultural characteristics.[49] The conceptualization of this bloody antagonism as a civil war rather than a revolt sharpens the fact that these two communities were bound to one another through intimate ties despite the sporadic outbursts of hostility pitting them against one another. A common language constituted one of the principal factors establishing intimacy.

Whereas the Muslim deputies distinguished between the written and spoken language, their remarks were mostly valid for those from an upper social class like themselves. But the large number of Muslims who were illiterate members of agricultural classes spoke the Cretan dialect of Greek exclusively, with little or no knowledge of Turkish. An example from a festive occasion of the Annunciation on 25 March 1892, coinciding with the anniversary of the Greek Revolution of 1821, illustrates the potentially irritable intimacy formed by language and music. Antonis Trakakis, a native narrator reminiscing about his youth in the countryside of southwestern Crete, remembers that day mostly for the lasting impression that Turkish dancers left in his adolescent mind. Trakakis writes how a group of Turkocretans, whom he plainly calls "Turks" (*oi Tourkoi*), masterfully performed the most demanding of local dances while the inhabitants of the small town Palaiochora in the district of Selinos socialized in the village coffeehouse. Following the dances, the Cretan lyra began to play *rizitika*, songs of old

Crete endemic to its western mountains. The dancers, however, refrained from singing because the song lyrics were rife with allegories offensive to Turks.⁵⁰

Scholarship has traditionally treated the island's eventful history as an appendage to the grander narrative of the Ottoman Empire or the Greek Kingdom. In such accounts, while Turkish historians have studied the turbulent 1890s as a series of revolts in an unobtrusively governed province, Greek scholars have viewed the same interval as a chain of revolutions against an oppressive regime.⁵¹ More recent examples that, in one way or another, fall within such historiographical approaches demonstrate the commanding presence of the terms *revolt* and *revolution*, instead of *civil war*, in making sense of the past.⁵²

What eluded the scholarly gaze of historians was obvious to multiple contemporary observers in Crete. In a long petition to the Ottoman governor of Crete, Evmenios, who taught at the Theological School of Halki in Istanbul before his appointment to Crete as bishop of Lampi and Sphakia in southwestern Crete, reported the looting and murders perpetrated by Turkocretan bands in the district of Agios Vasileios. They committed their misdeeds, Evmenios wrote in June 1896, before the eyes, and sometimes even with the assistance of, imperial troops nearby. He maintained that his flock had so far acted responsibly, bearing in mind duties toward the administration and humane feelings toward the fellow islanders. But the bishop declared that community leaders like him were beginning to find it hard to restrain the indignation of the offended and injured Christians. Evmenios concluded that the Ottoman administration, for its failure to impose discipline on the troops, would be blamed for the outbreak of a "civil war" (*emfylion*).⁵³

In March 1897, a group of Muslim notables from Hania addressed a letter to R. N. Custance, the captain of the British battleship HMS *Barfleur*, to express their gratitude for the protection he offered to the Muslim population. Written in French and bearing six signatures, the text featured the phrase *attaques meurtrières de la guerre civile*, rendered in the English translation of the document as "the murderous attacks of civil war."⁵⁴ Earlier in February 1897, F. C. M. Noel, the commander of the torpedo cruiser HMS *Scout* operating in Suda Bay, had written to Captain Custance that the district around the strategic harbor "has been, in common with the surrounding country, in a dreadful state of disorder and anarchy. Acute civil war has been raging between the Christian and Mussulman population, accompanied by wholesale destruction of property."[55]

Even representatives of the Ottoman state invoked an imagery of civil war in making sense of the conflagration in Crete. Given the absence of the term in late nineteenth-century Turkish, I propose that the phrase that most closely approximates the concept is *mukatelat* (mutual killings). *Mukatelat* summons the image of a society disintegrating because of reciprocal clashes among its constituent elements, united by a shared culture yet divided by clashing visions.[56] About a month after Evmenios warned of an imminent civil war, a cipher telegram that Corci Berović and Abdullah Pashas, the governor and the general commander of Crete respectively, sent to the Yıldız Palace informed the sultan of the continuation of *mukatelat* on the island.[57] In another example, this time from the higher echelons of the state, the resolutions of a council of ministers meeting in April 1897 mentioned "mutual killings and bloody incidents [*mukatelat ve vukuat-ı hunrizane*] witnessed between the segments of imperial subjects who are equal in the eyes of the exalted sultanate."[58] The word *mukatele*, in singular form, usually corresponded to a clash or single episodes of violence, as when it was used to describe the street clashes between Christians and Muslims in Hania in May 1896.[59] I argue that the suggestion of regular and continuous collective violence in the two examples above makes the plural form *mukatelat* a fitting word to connote "civil war" in Ottoman Turkish. Only through the plural form does the sense of the collective in the concept of civil war come into plain view.

The easterly spread of the strife that had remained mostly restricted to western Crete until mid-1896 also evinces the aspect of plurality and collectivity in civil wars. The violence truly morphed into civil war only after it began to spiral into an island-wide phenomenon. In a detailed report to the Austro-Hungarian foreign minister, consul Julius von Pinter described the breakdown of coordination and cooperation between the governor and military authorities. This led, especially in the Iraklio area in the east, to catastrophic consequences whereby "the richest province of Crete now resembles a wasteland."[60] The conditions in that province, Pinter observed, "have developed into a kind of a civil and racial war [*Bürger und Rassenkrieg*]."[61] Drawing on reports from Muslim and Christian notables, in addition to a document compiled by the Italian vice-consul in Iraklio, the Habsburg consul submitted to Vienna an appalling figure of devastation in eastern Crete. He calculated that a total of 235 Christian and Muslim villages had been partly or completely destroyed. All the churches in the ravaged Christian villages and ten mosques in various districts had been razed. With the violence perpetrated on the natural environment, including the destruction of carob and olive trees and the grape harvest, he anticipated that the financial damage would amount to many millions of franks.[62]

The spread of the conflict to the relatively tranquil eastern parts of the island occurred in tandem with mounting social and political pressure in Greece for a direct involvement in Crete. Thousands of Cretan refugees in Athens were especially vocal with demands for intervention, both to safeguard their Christian co-islanders and to execute the long-cherished ambition of separating the island from the Ottoman state.[63] Stirred into action by irredentist patriotism, those who aspired to a common future with their

FIGURE 12. A group of Cretan fighters in the western village of Tzitzifes. Kostaros (b. 1806), the one singled out in the picture, was a famous chief during the fierce struggle against the Ottomans between 1866 and 1869. He was ninety years old at the time of the taking of this photograph. Standing near him is a boy posing with a rifle and ammunition, indicating the cross-generational and civilian nature of armed resistance. Source: Family, Court and State Archives of the Austrian State Archives, PA XII, Liasse XXVIII, 280, 1896.

Cretan brethren under the wings of an enlarged Mother Greece contributed to the cause of liberation from the Ottoman Empire.[64] If the strongest insistence to take a bolder stance in Crete came from the vocal island diaspora in Greece, multiple Pan-Hellenic committees and parliamentary deputies too clamored for an intervention. Roused by "the latest sufferings of the barbarian-slayer Great Island," a group of university students based in Athens formed a committee aiming to aid the Cretan struggle from afar. Maintaining regular correspondence with Epitropi, they managed to ship fifty thousand bullets and fifty rifles to Crete.[65] Accompanying the intensified public agitation were increasingly larger donations, more ammunition, and growing numbers of recruits destined for the island. Finally, in early 1897, Hellenic officers, torpedo boats, and even a warship followed suit.[66]

An illustrative figure for the Crete connection in Greek irredentism is Aristotelis Korakas, the son of Michail Korakas (1797–1884), one of the most prominent chieftains in nineteenth-century armed struggles against the Ottoman regime on the island.[67] The young Korakas, born in 1858 in Pombia, a village thirty miles south of Iraklio, served as a captain in the Greek military detachment, leading a volunteer corps operating in the countryside of eastern Crete.[68] If part of his mission was performed with a rifle in hand, another of his crucial roles pertained to the dissemination to islanders of the purpose of the Greek military presence in Crete. In February 1897, through one of his circulars shared with small irregular bands in eastern Crete, Korakas declared that the king of Greece had sent his son, Prince George, along with his troops "in order to liberate us from the hordes of bloodthirsty Turkocretans and euphemistically named the regular imperial Turkish army." Emphasizing the urgency of putting aside past frictions among themselves, he urged Christians to rally around the banner of Mother Greece, for the fighting in Crete was done in the name of "the nation, king, and freedom."[69]

In a proclamation issued the same day, Korakas addressed the Turkocretans, whom he had called "bloodthirsty" in his circular to the Christian bands. He declared Greece's military presence on the island to be a mission of peace to safeguard the lives, property, and honor of the population "because the ailing and paralyzed administration of the sultan's government is unable to fulfill that." He assured the Turkocretans that the king of Greece bore no ill will toward those who committed disgraceful acts against Christians, with whom they shared a "common race [*omofylos*]," a word that recalls my earlier mention of the Greek terminology concerning civil war. Once we recognize that both *emfylion* and *omofylos* are terms related to race, with the former denoting internalness (within race) and the latter sameness (same/common race), it becomes obvious that Korakas, too, viewed the collective violence in Crete through the lens of a civil war between two indigenous island communities. For him, only one of them was in the right.[70] The same month, Korakas informed Papadiamantopoulos, aide-de-camp to the king, about the details of a battle before the gates of Ierapetra, a small town in southeastern Crete. He mentioned how "the freedom-defending cannons blew up the barbarian hordes of the Crescent, destroying the walls of the town, houses and mosques under which infidels remained buried." Amid joyful cries of *Enosis!* (annexation to the motherland), a cannonball tore to pieces the roof of a minaret and the crescent upon it, "the symbol of ruthless oppression that many millions of our Christian brethren endured for centuries, to the disgrace of the civilized world."[71]

Burning the Olive Branch: A Civil War of Displacement and Dispossession

Civil wars are humanitarian catastrophes with the extremes of violence they unleash and with the enormity of displacement and dispossession they generate. The one in Crete was no exception in either regard. There, tens of thousands of internally displaced Muslims fell into a life of destitution in the cities while thousands of urban Christians sought refuge in the interior villages and in Greece. Fifty years after the conflict, poet Lefteris Alexiou (b. 1890, Iraklio) thought back to his flight from Crete to Greece: "jammed like sheep" onboard the Austrian Lloyd steamer, he had departed with his family without knowing where they were headed. "But in our wounded heart of a child we sensed that we were now a homeless bunch of outcasts. We had neither a country nor a hearth. We felt the torment awaiting us in the foreign land we were destined to."[72] Around the time of the Alexiou family's exile, in Rethimno, to the west of the poet's native city, the Christians sent an anguished note to the French vice-consul in late August 1896. They described the columns of smoke rising from the nearby villages as the visual sign of destruction perpetrated by native Turkocretan bands.[73] "We are also the subjects of the sultan and . . . demand the execution of strong measures against the acts of robbery by the Ottoman hordes," the petitioners declared.[74] This petition resembled another striking document in terms of content, a complaint made at the end of May 1896, which bore the signatures of around three hundred individuals hailing from thirteen villages near Rethimno. In it, the Christian villagers asserted that they were "peaceful and loyal subjects of the sultan." They accused the district's Ottoman administrator of not taking necessary measures to prevent the pillage and destruction of their fields and properties.[75]

In his dispatch to the embassy, the Italian consul Augusto Medana reported that during the waning days of July 1896, the fertile plains to the south of Iraklio began to witness a massive flight of Muslims. He associated their exodus primarily with misgovernance in that province. The administration's security-related decisions, such as the withdrawal of the blockhouse garrison from several locations, left the peasants fearful of their lives in those southern districts about thirty miles from the nearest city. They were now exposed to deadly attacks by irregular bands of Christians. On 29 July, around five hundred Muslim families left the southern villages of Moires and Moroni at the fall of dusk. In the village of Agioi Deka, a skirmish resulted in the deaths of an entire Muslim family, including two children, in addition to two Christians. Further inspiring mass flight from obvious insecurity and probable death, this atrocious incident served to fill the periphery of Iraklio with "a very sorrowful horde of emigrants, agitated by fear, resentment, pain of having had to abandon their own hearths and furnishings and the rich harvest of the fields."[76]

Estimating that around ten thousand Muslim refugees were found in Iraklio, the island's most populous city, the Italian consul expected this figure only to rise with the continuing waves of the displaced from the interior districts.[77] When he updated the ambassador nine days later, the number of refugees in Iraklio had already doubled and stood at more than twenty thousand, large enough to form a town of its own. The Italian consul added that over half of the city's Christian population had fled by sea to seek refuge in Greece, leaving behind vacancies to be filled by some of the displaced Muslims.[78] It should be emphasized that for most of these refugees, the condition of dislocation lasted many months. When the British consul Alfred Biliotti reported two years later on the situation in Iraklio, the city was home to around thirty-four thousand Muslim refugees while about eight thousand Christians had already departed it. In this overcrowded city, shops belonging to Christians were looted and then converted into dwellings. These windowless narrow spaces sheltered families with as many members as ten, who grieved the loss of relatives and friends and resented being deprived of all their worldly possessions in the ravaged villages out in the open fields of the countryside.[79]

As 1896 wore on, accounts of displacement from across the island multiplied. Muslims and Christians sought to appeal to the humanitarian sentiments of Ottoman and European authorities through petitions that conveyed their plight. Obviously, the loss of one's properties and fields came as a heavy blow, given that in most cases they constituted everything that a refugee family had previously possessed. Staying alive, however, must have offered some consolation to those who lost everything. After all, death was not a distant possibility but a common feature of the civil war in Crete in addition to the destruction of houses and olive orchards. And as eye- or earwitnesses, the displaced were certainly aware of atrocities around them. One such atrocious incident occurred in the night between 26 and 27 August 1896 in the village of Anopolis, only about ten miles from Iraklio. It became the scene of a slaughter of no fewer than thirty-two Christians.[80] When the horrendous news reached Iraklio, the city's Christian residents tasked Mathaios Zahariadis, a constable at the tribunal, with the investigation of the incident. Zahariadis set out to a neighboring village of Hersonissos, where he located the inhabitants of Anopolis. Drawing on survivor testimonies, Zahariadis reported that upon the arrival of an armed band of native Muslims, some villagers had managed to take refuge in a cave nearby. From there they saw a monk named Hadji Jeremiah, aged sixty, exchanging fire with the attacking party. The monk shot dead one member of the assaulting group. Outnumbered and wounded in the chest, he soon fell. Having cut off the monk's ears and nose, the attackers set his body ablaze by lighting the icons they had seized from the nearby church. Three days after the atrocity, Zahariadis proceeded to the site of the carnage, where he saw corpses partially eaten by dogs. He saw the burned body of Hadji Jeremiah and the corpse of another monk, Ignatius, aged seventy, with his head severed and with his nose and the fingers of his right hand cut off.[81]

Only a few months after the Anopolis atrocity, the easternmost region of the island witnessed new mass killings, as horrifying, yet of much larger proportions. During the early days of the month of Ramadan, a group of armed bands slaughtered more than eight hundred Muslim peasants from multiple villages in the area of Sitia about eighty miles east of Iraklio.[82] In

February 1897, the local administration in Iraklio cabled to Istanbul the horrid news of "annihilation, the description of which would tear hearts apart." The massacre carried out by local bands and volunteers from Greece, the telegram continued, was "a bloody act of savagery, the likes of which even the ancient times did not record."[83] In a telegram sent to the Russian vice-consul in Iraklio, a group of Muslim notables from that city reported this "truly bloody massacre" and requested the formation of a European commission to investigate it.[84] The insurgents managed to hide for a while the traces of mass violence in faraway locations at a time when land communications were cut off because of clashes. An inquiry launched by the officers of the British HMS *Nymph* produced no results. The cruiser's commander, according to the Austro-Hungarian consul, even referred to it as a fabricated massacre. The investigation carried out by the officers of the French ironclad *Chanzy*, however, yielded evidence of charred corpses of Muslims buried under the ruins of the demolished houses in multiple villages. In his detailed report, complete with figures and photographs, the Austro-Hungarian consul Julius von Pinter informed the foreign minister of the audience he had had with Franz Joseph on his visit to Vienna. At the meeting the emperor appeared interested in obtaining more details from the consul regarding the Sitia massacre. On the basis of the details that the consul received from Axelos Efendi, the district administrator of Sitia, a total of 884 Muslims had been killed in twenty-one villages across the district, among them 201 boys and 168 girls.[85] In a three-volume book dedicated to recording atrocities against Muslim Cretans, Hüseyin Nesimi described the Sitia massacre as the peak of brutality that would "elicit even the pity of demons, creatures of fire."[86]

Embodied evidence of the atrocities surfaced in early March 1897 when a number of survivors arrived in Iraklio, among a group of about four hundred refugees on board the imperial steamer *Inayet*. The writer, apparently a doctor, of a letter shared with the British consul mentioned that he had examined nine wounded women and children, among whom a boy, aged four, bearing a twelve-centimeter-long cut on his neck and a firearm wound on the back of his feet.[87] Soon after, the little boy succumbed to his injuries. The photograph of this unfortunate boy was published with all its graphic details in a small Turkish book eight months after the massacre. The book also visually documented several other child survivors with injuries and mutilations on their bodies. Deemed harmful by the Ottoman administration, it was banned.[88] As anthropologist Jason De León points out in his ethnography on deadly border crossings in the Sonoran desert of Arizona "There is no easy way to represent violence" and "Words alone could never capture the complexity, emotion, or realities of the violence."[89] In 1897, Hüseyin Nesimi and Mehmet Behçet, the authors of the banned Turkish book, had thought similarly about the indescribable aspect of violence on their native islands. They remarked that "neither pen nor picture could characterize and describe" the tragedy of Crete's Muslims.[90] When Biliotti visited Iraklio in late March, he saw, in the hospital and in a Muslim house, a total of nineteen injured survivors, most of them women and children. He noticed in the bodies of the victims many scars from the atrocities, mostly inflicted with bayonets and daggers. The consul found it hard to explain why a massacre of such proportions had occurred in a region that had historically been known as the most peaceful in Crete. He wrote that the only reasonable interpretation was that the perpetrators of the massacre "seem to have been taken with a sort of frenzy, which can only be explained by the terror of being killed if they did not kill their enemies."[91]

The Austro-Hungarian consul also underlined the anomaly of such a massacre in a historically tranquil region of the island. His explanation hinged not on psychology but on the politics of civil war, claiming that the scale of atrocities across twenty-one villages suggested a premeditated act. Although lacking the smoking gun, his sources blamed Amvrosios Sfakianakis, the bishop of Sitia, who reportedly had encouraged the insurgent chiefs to eliminate the Muslim population. This policy, the consul maintained, fit the overall purpose of many resisters to the Ottoman regime, whose hold they sought to break by steadily weakening Crete's native Muslim population.[92] The consul's observations on the motives for killing in the hinterland villages of Sitia resonate with other cases of mass violence under conditions of state collapse. For instance, in an inquiry into the unfolding of carnage in small towns across eastern Europe during the earlier phase of World War II, Jeffrey Kopstein and Jason Wittenberg view pogroms as "a strategy whereby non-Jews attempted to rid themselves of those whom they thought would be future political rivals." They further add how priests, as figures of authority in smaller communities, retained the power to either avert or incite violence.[93]

With an estimated death toll of 884, the killings in February 1897 across multiple villages in the island's easternmost region became the bloodiest massacre of the Cretan civil war. It occurred several weeks after another case of mass violence with a death toll somewhere between 115 and 153 Muslim villagers, this time perpetrated in Crete's westernmost region. The inhabitants of the village of Sarakina, situated in the mountains ten miles north of the Libyan Sea, decided to emigrate en masse as they began to feel more fearful in an atmosphere of escalating insecurity. Christian chiefs from the neighboring villages offered to convey them to the nearest coastal town. Only half an hour after they left Sarakina, a shot was heard from the back rows of the procession, which was followed by a hail of bullets on the marching villagers. According to Biliotti's account, based on the testimony of one Muslim that was also confirmed by Christians, a villager's resistance to being disarmed had caused a commotion that quickly led to a bloody rampage. Biliotti noted that the chiefs and others deplored the massacre deeply. But he also added that his sources had informed him that after the confusion ended, all the wounded men and some children were killed. Between twenty-eight and forty-four villagers made it alive to the coastal town of Palaiochora, from where they were brought by ship to Hania and taken to the hospital for treatment.[94]

Occurring around the same time in early 1897 on two opposite ends of a large island, the Sitia and Sarakina massacres illustrate how violence enveloped the whole of Crete. They represent the bloodiest episodes of the civil war. As such, they feature a dark side of interreligious coexistence in the late Ottoman Empire. But such occasions of carnage also involved many attempts to prevent bloodshed and rescue the victims. Although only some of them are documented, they stand as powerful testaments to the strength of intercommunal bonds. This brings us back to the intimacy of civil war and specifically suggests that there are always stories, powerful yet lesser-known, to upset enduring narratives of sectarianism in history. For instance, from the testimony of survivors from the Sitia region, Biliotti reported that Captain Mihalis Alexakis and his brother Nicolas, with the support of more than two hundred followers, rescued forty-five Muslims, mostly women and children, from the cave in which they had taken refuge. In another example, four Christians from the village of Sfaka, named Rousselakis, Captain Manolis Boyatzis Roussos, and Nicolas and Giorgios Frangoulis, conveyed twenty-five of their neighbors to the safety of the coast. Outside of the village they were stopped by a band of seventy intent on killing the Muslims. The four men stood in front of the Muslims and "declared

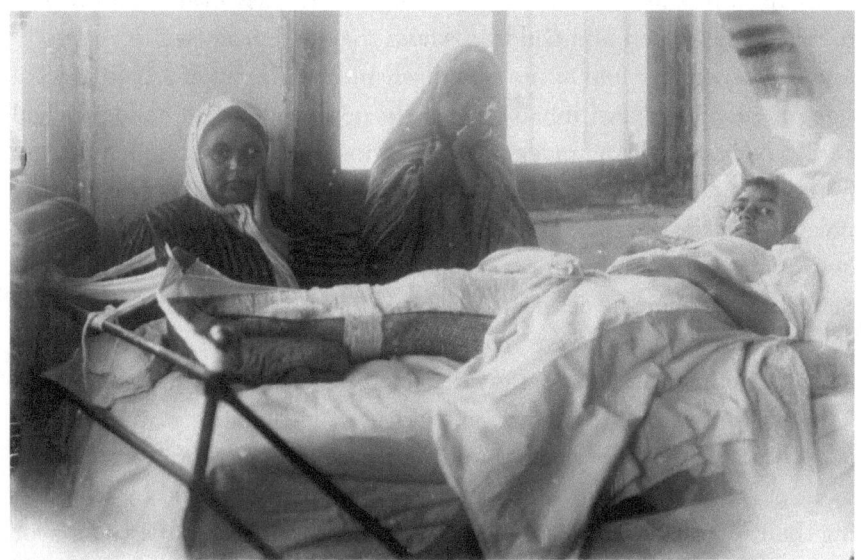

FIGURE 13. Survivors from the Sarakina massacre being treated in the Hania hospital, 1897. Source: Family, Court and State Archives of the Austrian State Archives, PA XII, Liasse XXVIII, 286

FIGURE 14. More survivors from the Sarakina massacre in the Hania hospital, 1897. Source: Istanbul University Rare Documents Library, Yıldız Albums.

to their co-religionists that they would have to pass over their corpses to reach the women and children whom they had promised to rescue."[95] And on the western end of the island, when the villagers of Sarakina were slaughtered in a ravine, inhabitants of the nearby village of Kandanos had been anxiously waiting under the siege of insurgents, an episode I discuss in the next chapter. One of the Cretan chiefs told Biliotti that he saw the prospects of the Kandanos residents as far from promising but added that he would do everything in his power to save the village's Muslim mayor Yanitsarakis, whom he described as "his intimate friend."[96]

Survivors of these massacres followed in the footsteps of thousands of Muslim Cretans who had already departed the island. As they sought the help of European and Ottoman authorities, the remaining Muslims frequently stated that they had become the target of orchestrated attacks, the main purpose of which was to remove them from the island by stimulating their migration. For instance, in September 1897, the mufti and mayor of Hania petitioned the European ambassadors to denounce "the bandits" (*eşkıya*) who continued burning the trees owned by Muslims across the island. They would cross over the cordons, security lines drawn by the international troops extending several miles inland from coastal towns, to carry away cattle, sheep, and goats. Such acts by "the bandits," the petitioners declared, "aimed to trigger the emigration of the Muslims."[97] Some substance to those claims can be located in the call of a notable Christian leader to his coreligionists. Hatzimihalis Giannaris (b. 1833), one of the most eminent chieftains and commander in chief of the Kydonia region in the foothills of the White Mountains in western Crete, underscored the centrality of the land question in the civil war. In May 1897, when a large amount of fertile land was coming under Christian control after the mass exodus of rural Muslims, he addressed the population of his native Kydonia. He began with a reminder that "the first and foremost indicator of civilization is the respect for life, honor, and property, regardless of ethnicity or religion."[98] Deploring the immense loss of Muslim and Christian properties throughout the island, the renowned chieftain saw the reason for the destruction of Muslim properties in the Kydonia region as the burning of Hania's Christian neighborhood earlier in 1897. Nevertheless, he disapproved devastating deeds of vengeance, for "The houses and trees are more than ephemeral possessions belonging to our generation alone. They belong to the motherland and our children. The properties owned by the Muslims today could belong to Christians tomorrow, and vice versa."[99]

Several reports from September 1897 yielded the findings of an inquiry in the Kydonia region that was carried out by an international commission charged with assessing the damage against Muslim properties. The investigation, covering forty-one villages, revealed the scale of destruction that had induced the Muslim petitioners to ask for help and Hatzimihalis Giannaris to appeal for restraint. In presenting the commission's findings to the embassy, the Italian consul Augusto Medana noted that in certain villages of Kydonia, the proportion of trees destroyed reached a staggering 90 percent, well above the regional average of 55 percent. In the village of Sempronas, for instance, of around a total of 1,600 olive trees, 1,200 were burned. About 500 chestnut trees as well as all the fruit-bearing trees were cut down. A likely reason for the enormity of the devastation lay in an earlier incident, illustrating the circular pattern of civil wars. In 1896 the Ottoman troops had rescued eleven Muslim families trapped in Sempronas and set the Christian quarter on fire before marching back to Hania. In the village of Mouriziana, on the other hand, only 50 olive trees out of around 500 were destroyed, suggesting the pattern of geographic variation in the violence of civil wars. It was the stronger interreligious bonds that likely saved most of the trees in Mouriziana. Thanks to the cordial ties maintained with the villagers, the Muslim Hasapis family lost only 6 olive trees. For the Italian consul, the explanation for the widespread destruction of Muslim properties was clear "when one considers that the aim of Christians was to make it impossible for Muslims to return to the interior and to force them to get rid of their possessions at a cheaper price."[100]

In parts of the island, the civil war left in its wake scenes of ruin that would remain desolate for many years. Writing about his travels in an isolated district of eastern Crete in 1912, Arnold Toynbee would later recall that "the landscape was the bare limestone mountain-side characteristic of the Aegean. Villages were rare, and some of them had been sacked during the civil war of 1897 and not reoccupied."[101] Would he have also noticed some dead tree stumps? It is untold, but one thing is certain: the magnitude of environmental devastation wrought by the civil war was immense. The real scale of the destruction of olive trees, which struck a heavy blow to their planters and caretakers, to the island's political economy, and to its flora and fauna, would surface only after the country began to heal from the scars of violence.[102] In a 1906 study published by Antonios Giannaris (b. 1852), a philologist by training and nephew of the chieftain Hatzimihalis Giannaris from the Kydonia region, it was estimated that 1,062,770 olive trees had been destroyed between 1896 and 1898. Given that the total number of olive trees were calculated to be 6,943,320 in all of Crete, the civil war suggested a socioeconomic and environmental disaster.[103]

TWO

SHELTERING MOUNTAIN

The European Military Intervention and
the Exodus of Crete's Muslims

A letter published in the 7 March 1902 issue of *Nea Erevna* (New Inquiry), a major newspaper from Crete, provided a poignant account of Muslim refugees whom a traveling reporter encountered in Istanbul. Two words uttered in the island dialect of Greek interrupted the reporter's pondering of the Byzantine monuments in a poor and ancient quarter of the city: "Sir, please." Turning back he saw a baby held by his parents and a five-year-old toddling behind them.

> From the way they were dressed I realized that they were from Crete.[1] I stopped and asked them what they wanted. "Could you show us, sir, where they're distributing money for the *muhacirs*? We tried to find out from those living in this neighborhood, but we didn't understand what they told us." ... In order to have a better idea about their situation, a family hailing from a village near Rethimno, I decided to accompany them to their dwellings. "Daddy," complained the weeping five-year-old, "I will sit here. I cannot walk any longer." My eyes caught the sorry sight of the unfortunate father, who raised his gaze to the sky and exclaimed with a voice that trembled my heart: "May the curse be on those who brought us here ... those who lied to us that all our needs would be taken care of."[2]

The story of these destitute Muslims, unable to comprehend Turkish and outwardly indistinguishable from the rural Christians in Crete who donned similar clothing, conveyed the condition of being a stranger in a faraway land.[3] This was a foreign place, stressed the reporter, where the unusual cultural traits of Cretans—such as eating snails—prompted some Anatolian Muslims to call them "Muslim infidels" (*mousoulmangavourides*).[4]

This family, like thousands of others scattered across the Balkans, Asia Minor, Syria, and Libya, ended up on the coasts of the Ottoman Empire because of the civil war that engulfed Crete at the close of the nineteenth century. In the space of three years from late 1895 through 1898, the largest Ottoman island turned into a battlefield spanning 160 miles from east to west. During this fateful period, hundreds of islanders perished while many tens of thousands lost their homes and properties, ending up as refugees, first internally and then on faraway shores. After the occupation of Crete by a European coalition, a council of admirals representing Britain, France, Italy, and Russia instituted a military cordon extending several miles inland from the coastal towns. Operating at a safe distance from the reach of the Ottoman troops, which the European powers kept from performing military operations, the insurgents reigned beyond the cordons in the island's interior. In those parts lay an expanse of mountains and valleys that from 1896 onward became bereft of rural Muslims as they began to seek refuge in Hania, Iraklio, and Rethimno. The administrative machinery run by the insurgents amounted to a provisional government, complete with assemblies to deliberate local affairs and village guards to provide security. Shy of launching a risky military campaign against the Cretan fighters in their native rugged terrain, the European powers remained cognizant of how the island's geography strengthened their hand as Crete's future was negotiated.

Commenting on the strife in Crete around this time, the Paris-based *Meşveret*, a prominent Young Turk publication in exile, offered a diagnosis for the roots of bloodshed, not only in Crete but throughout the empire under Abdülhamid II: "This senseless deluge of blood results from the absence of a justice-driven government that would instruct and guide the populace according to the principles of fraternity."[5] At the time of *Meşveret*'s publication of this indictment of the Hamidian regime, the imperial authorities were desperately trying to safeguard Istanbul's hold on Crete, an immensely strategic island. As the Crete conflict became internationalized with the involvement of the European great powers, the British foreign secretary remarked that "so many interests were bound up in Crete, and so much jealousy existed, or had existed in the past, with respect to any exclusive influence over it, that I did not imagine that any of the Powers of Europe would desire to take isolated action with respect to it."[6]

Such views of the Marquess of Salisbury hinted at potential frictions between the partners of the European coalition. Nevertheless, the European states put up a united front at least in one crucial matter related to the Crete question during the 1890s: the withdrawal of all Ottoman soldiers from the island. A decisive incident that broke the Sublime Porte's resistance to the evacuation of Crete came in the form of a riot in Iraklio in early September 1898 with the leading involvement of a group of tormented Muslim refugees from the interior.[7] Fourteen British soldiers, the British vice-consul Lysimachus Kalokairinos, and scores of civilians from the local Christian population perished in this act of mass violence. Gone were also any hopes of the Ottoman state to maintain troops in Crete.[8] Reputed to be a sovereign capable of manipulating the rivalries between foreign states, Abdülhamid II was also a realist who knew when it was time to yield to the pressures from a united Europe. The sultan acquiesced to the military and administrative evacuation of Crete in late 1898. The island's constitution drawn up in 1899 proclaimed Crete as an autonomous polity under the administration of a high commissioner selected by the European coalition. Prince George, the second son of George I, the king of Greece, became the first appointee occupying that post. The new regime was designed to operate under the suzerainty of the sultan, an arrangement that proved mostly symbolic, a physical manifestation of which appeared in the form of an Ottoman flag flying on an islet in Suda Bay of western Crete.[9]

One of my aims in this chapter is to explain the conundrum of how a clear military victory against Greece in 1897, a deviation from the defeat-laden nineteenth-century history of the empire, failed to produce for Istanbul the anticipated result of consolidating its grip on the island. Perhaps the most straightforward and traditional manner of interrogating this paradox of radical shrinkage of imperial command over Crete despite a military success would be through the prism of diplomatic history by analyzing various calculations and deliberations of the European powers within the framework of the Eastern Question. I do not disregard the merits of such an analysis. I offer, however, an alternative approach that locates the core of the matter on the island. I posit that the Cretan fighters masterfully harnessed the rugged terrain to their advantage in negotiations with the European officers. Mostly peasants or shepherds, they were the children of the countryside, naturally at home among a welcoming rural population. The risk-averse European coalition eschewed dispatching troops inland beyond the protection of the guns of its battleships, thus keeping its forces concentrated along several coastal points. Sheltered by a jagged landscape whose precipices and gorges offered natural bulwarks against conventional armies, the Cretan fighters found another source of aid in Western capitals in the form of powerful anti-Ottoman public opinion. This was yet another factor reinforcing the European reluctance for military engagement in Crete.

Following a discussion of these two factors, geographic and political, the chapter examines the opposition to the presence of imperial troops on the island. Their removal constituted the main demand of the Cretan fighters, which the European coalition viewed positively. The chapter then turns to the question of internal displacement through the example of tens of thousands of Muslim refugees waiting in limbo in Crete's coastal cities. On multiple occasions, the displaced and the dispossessed hailing from the fertile interior implored the European coalition to be resettled in their villages. The repatriation rested on the implementation of two interrelated measures: first, the creation of a generous European fund for the reconstruction of the villages devastated in the clashes; second, robust protection by the European troops until the restoration of peaceful interactions between civil war–struck native Muslim and Christian populations. To their chagrin, however, the uprooted villagers encountered an international coalition unwilling to execute those onerous undertakings. Finally, this chapter also explores sectarian stereotypes held by multiple European decision-makers as one of the factors contributing to the policy of inaction regarding the repatriation of internally displaced Muslims.

Mountain Fastness, European Hardness

"The Mediterranean is not so much the sea between the lands," J. R. McNeill asserts, "but the sea among the mountains."[10] In examining the Crete question, scholars have mostly overlooked the island's topography as a primary factor shaping the conflict around the turn of the nineteenth century. Geography's absence is all the more glaring given how large the mountains loom before the eyes of researchers visiting the archives and libraries in Crete today, especially those located in Hania. It was no coincidence that western Crete's rugged landscape begot all the major uprisings, as far back as during the medieval Venetian dominance, and as recently as in the resistance against the Nazi occupation of the island during World War II.[11] Living among supportive villagers in a terrain prohibitive to conventional armies, native fighters on multiple occasions during the nineteenth century enjoyed a literal upper hand over the Ottoman troops trying to ascend into the mountains.[12] When the European coalition landed troops on the island in 1897, it did so with the awareness of military challenges in a geography like Crete. The knowledge of the perils lurking in the mountain passes and gorges of the interior led the coalition to operate on the coast and along a narrow military cordon in the vicinity of coastal cities. In his autobiography the British admiral Reginald Bacon offers a clue to this military policy. In explaining Britain's occupation of Cyprus following the Congress of Berlin in 1878, Bacon claims that the British cabinet in fact entertained the possibility of occupying Crete instead. Even though Crete was an "incomparably better naval base, having a first-class harbour at Suda Bay," it presented a significant disadvantage: "It was very mountainous, so much so, that the War Office estimated that it would take an Army Corps to subdue any rising that might take place among the natives."[13]

In October 1897, Paul Blanc, the veteran French consul in Crete, considered a hypothetical scenario in his detailed report to the Quai d'Orsay. At this point, the Sublime Porte, with boosted confidence thanks to the military victory against Greece in April 1897, had grown frustrated with the coalition's intransigence toward its requests for stronger involvement on the island. Blanc hypothesized an eventuality in which the Europeans evacuated Crete and allowed the Ottoman state to dispatch around fifty thousand troops for the island's pacification. If he had believed that this measure could indeed end the disorder in Crete, the French consul continued, he would have assented to it, but only with a heavy heart since it would signify "the moral bankruptcy of Europe in the Orient." Attempts to subjugate the insurgents by using regular troops would be reckless considering "the mountains of Crete, inaccessible refuges sheltering fifty thousand rebels well equipped with arms and munitions." Still seething from the defeat of April 1897, Greece would be incapacitated to aid them, but the resourceful

Hellenic committees would continue smuggling arms and ammunition on small fishing boats into the island, its long coastline defying an effective naval blockade. For Blanc, all these factors suggested that a militaristic approach to the issue would prolong the insurrection indefinitely. He added that during a fierce conflict in Crete between 1866 and 1869, the Ottomans had never managed to become the masters of the situation, despite amassing more than one hundred thousand troops on the island and running a strong naval squadron to blockade it.[14]

A report that Turhan Pasha sent to Sultan Abdülhamid in November 1897 echoed some of Paul Blanc's observations. The former governor of Crete pointed out that the rebels basked in the comfort of knowing that the European coalition made no plans to confront them on the inhospitable terrain. They saw no reason to break "the carefree spell of waiting in the mountains" with ample provisions.[15] Turhan Pasha anticipated that they would bide their time until the acquiescence of the European powers to their demands, the foremost among them the complete withdrawal of

FIGURE 15. Waterfront of Hania crowded with locals and European soldiers, 1897. Source: Family, Court and State Archives of the Austrian State Archives, PA XII, Liasse XXVIII, 288.

imperial troops from Crete. He was loath to accept such a request given the military victory against Greece seven months earlier.[16]

The natural advantage that Crete's mountains provided to the belligerents had also been recognized by the British consul Alfred Biliotti in late 1895. In a meeting with governor Alexandros Karatheodoris Pasha, Biliotti talked about some of the features of guerrilla warfare on an island like Crete. The consul observed that "owing to the mountainous nature of the country and to the facility it afforded to the natives to lay in ambush, the casualties were always heavier amongst the soldiers" and that "such a result was considered by the Cretans as a victory and as such encouraged the Christians in Crete to join the armed bands."[17] In his report to the Marquess of Salisbury, the consul claimed that Karatheodoris Pasha concurred with his point that "it was impossible for a military force to come up in the mountain fastness of this island with so small an armed band as the Epitropi, whose real strength consists in the facility of dispersing."[18] At a time when the image of the Sublime Porte across Europe was at its nadir because of the Armenian massacres in Anatolia, a large-scale military operation against the Cretan fighters would cause a strong outcry. Thus, Biliotti continued, "There would be an endless series of reports of atrocities, which, whether true or false, would not fail *at this moment* to excite public opinion in Europe against the Imperial Government *more than at any other time*."[19]

Biliotti's remark about the excitability of European public opinion, at this juncture in particular, should be understood in the context of widely publicized horror stories about the Armenian massacres in Anatolia.[20] At such a time, the Western public would also decry any large-scale military operation to be launched by the European coalition, interpreting it as siding with "Turkish tyranny."[21] Indeed, as the violence enveloped Crete, Ottoman diplomatic missions in European cities kept track of the associations that aimed to rally the public in favor of the Cretan fighters.[22] In September 1896, the ambassador in Rome informed the foreign ministry of anti-Ottoman reactions to the violence in Anatolia and Crete. Detailing various deeds of the Italian activists "who were following in the footsteps of Gladstone, a sworn enemy of the state and religion," the ambassador mentioned the societies founded in cities like Venice and Milan by "ruffians blind with ignorance and bigotry." Describing those associations as being "reminiscent of Crusader assemblies," the ambassador expressed concern about such pamphlets and publications assaulting the Sublime Porte and Islam.[23] Several months later, the consulate in Naples sent a similar dispatch to the foreign minister Tevfik Pasha, informing him of an appeal issued by the Neapolitan committee Pro Candia (For Crete), a document that used scathing language against the state. The Greek Ottoman consul Loghadis wrote of his dismay at what he had for a while considered "the systematic and entirely unjustified Turkophobia displayed by the Neapolitan press, one of the most influential in all Italy." Adding that the committee's appeal was also placarded in various locations throughout Naples, Loghadis informed Tevfik Pasha that he had lodged a protest with the local authorities for the removal of notices offensive to the Ottoman state.[24] A telegram sent by the embassy in London seemed no different from many other examples until the ambassador underlined one critical point. In a report attached to his telegram, he presented the details of a well-attended soiree held at St. James's Hall in London under the auspices of the Byron Society. What made the event worthy of description was the participation of the Greek chargé d'affaires and about twenty Armenian revolutionaries. The Armenians, to whom the ambassador paid special attention, greeted with an enthusiastic ovation insulting remarks against Abdülhamid II. Before the crowd dispersed, women carrying trays collected donations for Crete.[25]

"Rome Was Not Built in a Day": The Question of Ottoman Troops in Crete

Outside a *cordon militaire* of a few miles' radius instituted by the European coalition around the island's overcrowded coastal cities, Crete's fertile lands came into the exclusive possession of the Christian population following the mass exodus of Muslim peasants into the cities. The overcrowding of urban spaces generated new challenges and deepened the frustration of the Muslims. They resented the Christians who were trespassing on their properties that lay outside the narrow cordons and were reaping the crops there. A report prepared by the Italian consul in August 1898 conveyed alarm about the dangers of collective indignation on the island. The document's prescience would manifest itself in less than a month when a group of Muslims rioted in Iraklio, claiming the lives of fourteen British soldiers, the British vice-consul, and scores of civilians from the Christian population. In his report, the Italian consul Augusto Medana informed the embassy that in late June 1898 a commission of Muslim notables had visited Fyodor Schostak, the Russian superior commander in charge of the

Rethimno sector, the zone under Russian control according to the power-sharing arrangement among the four-member European coalition. They asked for permission to cross the military cordon with the protection of European troops so that they could gather the valonia harvest of their fields. Describing the pleading population as "dispossessed and displaced, in vain invoking to be able to collect the crumbs of their properties," Augusto Medana thought that it would be no surprise "if the Muslim element, faced with the impotence of its own central authority to defend it and the abandonment of the Powers, draws advice from its nefarious instincts and rebels against the provocations of Christians, who exploit the present situation to their exclusive advantage." Adding that the council of admirals shared his fears about the present situation, the Italian consul expected them to devise necessary measures to avert the brewing storm.[26]

Hearing about this plea, a group of Christians from the several villages in the Rethimno area wrote to Fyodor Schostak. They could not guarantee the Muslims' security if they were allowed to pass the cordon to harvest what belonged to them. In perfect tit-for-tat logic, they mentioned how many Christian inhabitants of Rethimno had had to abandon their houses with all the immovables inside, only to have them looted soon afterward under the eyes of the Ottoman authorities. The petitioners added that their Muslim compatriots also benefited from the trading of Christian property that they came upon in the vicinity of Rethimno, in addition to profiting off many trees they cut down and sold as firewood.[27] Claiming that in the current situation the Christians were not less miserable than the Muslims, the villagers advised against permission to cross the military cordon. They warned of a disaster to ensue in the event of consenting to their request because then "no force can stop the famished population of the countryside from destroying out of spite the Muslim trees, which they have hitherto preserved." The petitioners demanded that the status quo continue "until the departure of the Turkish troops" from the entire island.[28]

Such an attitude suggested how an old aversion to the presence of imperial troops in Crete had only deepened in recent months. When the Christian deputies had prepared a set of reform proposals in July 1896, an article relating to the maintenance of soldiers in Crete had caused a rift with their Muslim counterparts. The Christian deputies insisted that the governor general's ability to dispatch troops in case of disturbances be subject to authorization from the administrative council, a body to be elected in proportion to the size of Christian and Muslim populations. Deeply distrusting their rivals, the Muslim deputies deemed it unlikely that the Christian councilors would "consent to the dispatching of a military force against their coreligionists, armed with the intention of injuring Muslims."[29] Soon after, however, the Christians would shift away from proposing reforms and, instead, insist on the necessity of total withdrawal of Ottoman troops from the island.

An incident in late 1896 provides an example of the distrust felt by certain vocal Christian notables toward Ottoman troops. In the corridors of the courthouse in Hania, Badirakizade Hüseyin Bey, a leading Muslim Haniotis, got into an altercation with the Christian vice-prosecutor general. Having found out that Badirakizade had been taken into custody for his aggressive conduct, a Muslim crowd gathered in front of the governor's office to demand his release. In his report to Istanbul, Governor Corci Berović Pasha justified his yielding to the crowd's pressure as the only measure to deescalate the tension.[30] The Christian administrative councilors, however, claimed that Berović felt compelled to release Badirakizade because his plea for military assistance was disregarded. They saw this incident as another indication that "urban Christians lack the army's protection when needed."[31]

In October 1897, a revolutionary assembly of Cretans convened in Melidoni, an inland village twenty miles east of Rethimno. Following the meeting, members of the group sent a memorandum to the Italian admiral Felice Napoleone Canevaro, the commander of the international squadron overseeing the military situation in Crete.[32] Chaired by Ioannis Sfakianakis and counting among its members Eleftherios Venizelos, the future prime minister of Greece, the assembly provided an in-depth explanation of why they opposed Ottoman troops in Crete.[33] Their reasoning rested on numbers. The census of 1881, which the assembly considered the only reliable count, had recorded the total number of inhabitants as 276,208, among them 202,934 Christians and 72,353 Muslims.[34] Using these figures, deemed unreliable by the Sublime Porte, the assembly broke down the island's Muslims into three distinct categories.[35] The first segment was the largest, composed of those living in urban areas. Given the greater Muslim presence in such locations, "it is the Christians of the cities rather than Muslims," the memorandum maintained, "who have grounds for not feeling safe and who would have to be protected if Turkish troops continued to be stationed there."³⁶ The second group lived in the vicinity of cities, in which they could always take refuge if needed. The final portion involved about fifteen thousand people scattered across the countryside. They constituted the most vulnerable section of the native Muslim population, for they lived far from the administrative centers among a much larger Christian majority. But even in the times when the soldiers used to move about without obstruction, "they were of little use to the Ottomans [*Othōmanoi*, used interchangeably in the text with *Mōamethanoi* and *Mousoulmanoi*, "Mohammedans" and "Muslims," respectively]." The revolutionary assembly argued that the presence of troops not only failed to safeguard the minority but actually imperiled them: "They only egged them on against the Christians, exposing them to animosity and reprisals."³⁷

Having reminded the admirals of the multiple assurances by the European coalition for the demilitarization of the island, the memorandum stated that the recent history of clashes with the Christian groups made the future of Ottoman troops in Crete untenable. Reflecting the training of its president Ioannis Sfakianakis, a physician by profession, the revolutionary assembly made use of medical metaphors to argue its case: "Their presence will have the effect of a foreign organism in the body politic, incessantly stirring up inflammation." So long as the Ottoman garrisons remained, the Muslims would never be disabused of the belief that they could help further militarize the country by fomenting disturbances and attain once again their former preponderance. "And the Christians will continue suspecting the worst of both the soldiers and their Ottoman fellow-citizens. The antagonism to be kept up between the two communities will, sooner or later, result in fresh clashes."³⁸ The members of the revolutionary assembly believed that an island freed from Istanbul's backfiring meddling would finally obtain a sustainable regime, under which its inhabitants, regardless of religious difference, could finally reap the benefits of coexistence.

According to the French consul Paul Blanc, such stiff opposition to Ottoman soldiers was rooted in Crete's recent past. In early 1898, his confidential note to the French embassy in Istanbul underlined that the pacification of Crete would be impossible "without the departure of the Turkish army."³⁹ Blanc's long probe into the deeper causes of the matter began with the argument that "there is no doubt that Crete is the place where the Turkish soldier is least savage." It was true that the Christians fought him fiercely during extraordinary times of insurrection, but they also knew to respect him when things got back to normal. Seeking the intervention of soldiers to prevent periodic outbreaks of infighting between factions from escalating was a common feature in Cretan politics. And when the countryside descended into violence, the Christians who had no desire to seek refuge in the mountains to fight for independence could instead find shelter in the well-protected cities.

Then why was it, Paul Blanc seemed to wonder, that "now the Cretans feel the strongest hatred toward the Turkish soldier?" His answer suggested a connection between two landscapes of synchronous violence: "It is because, desiring to march in the footsteps of his comrades in Armenia . . . he has become, in recent years, the principal disrupter of order and an avowed enemy of everything Christian." Far from acting as a barricade between warring groups, "the Turkish soldier has now become a blind instrument . . . respecting neither innocent individuals nor Christian properties but plundering, burning, vandalizing, and engaging in all kinds of savageries with euphoria."[40]

In the face of strong opposition to Ottoman soldiers from all quarters, Abdülhamid II regarded the stationing of troops in Crete as a critical prerogative that he did everything in his capacity to preserve. Judgments of his most notable servants reassured him of such position. In a November 1897 memorandum to the sultan, Turhan Pasha drew on his recent experience as governor of the island to convey an assessment on this question. He penned his report as the European coalition was busy weighing the merits of alternative models of autonomy. Regardless of particularities of the future regime, any weakening of Istanbul's hold would suggest a deterioration in the status of the Muslims for being a minority (*ekalliyet*). The heart of the matter was military: "Should imperial troops depart from the island, the Muslim population will be left unprotected against the arbitrary treatment of their enemies, who have committed endless crimes during the recent disturbances."[41] Turhan Pasha correctly anticipated that the European powers would bring up as a precedent the case of Samos, an autonomous Aegean island hosting only a negligible number of imperial soldiers. As if to imply that the only commonality between the two islands was the Mediterranean surrounding them, Turhan Pasha underlined that Samos was "two steps away" from Asia Minor and ten times smaller than Crete. While Samos's population stood at about forty thousand with an inconspicuous Muslim community, three hundred thousand people, a third of whom professed Islam, called Crete home. He emphasized that the significance of Crete's Muslim community was not to be gauged by size alone, for they possessed far more land and other real estate than Christians.[42]

As early as late 1897, the European coalition began to express open opposition to the presence of Ottoman troops in Crete. This is unsurprising given the adamance of the insurgents in this matter and in light of the earlier discussion about European reluctance to mount military campaigns in the mountainous interior. Should the European powers concur with the Sublime Porte's demands to maintain garrisons on the island, the British foreign secretary observed, "they would greatly disappoint the expectations which the majority of the Cretan people have been led to entertain."[43] The expectations that the Marquess of Salisbury referred to had been raised by numerous interactions of the European officers with the Cretan chiefs. To give but one representative example, Colonel Mainwaring, a British military commander in Crete, assured the notables of Archanes, one of the richest eastern villages near Iraklio, that the Christians would soon take over the island's administration. He responded to the villagers' complaint about the Muslims' boycotting by urging them to return the lands that they had unlawfully acquired. Once this was done, he promised, "the administration of the towns can be handed over to you and thus the government of the island assured to you." He asked for their cooperation and patience for it was unrealistic to expect to obtain the reins of government at one stroke. After all, "Rome was not built in a day."[44]

An Island Unmixed

Another critical example emblematic of "the expectations which the majority of the Cretan people have been led to entertain" surfaces in an episode from March 1897 centered on the inland village of Kandanos in southwestern Crete. The Kandanos case involves an extraordinary situation of the European coalition embarking on a military excursion to liberate besieged Muslim villagers. As exceptional as it seems, even this episode, in which the Muslim peasants were transported to the relative safety of Hania, rhymes with the general European policy of avoiding armed encounters with the insurgents. In attempting to persuade the Christian chiefs to lift the siege of Kandanos, the European officers relied on words and promises rather than force. In his negotiations with the insurgent leaders around Kandanos, British consul Alfred Biliotti assured them that the lifting of the siege would pave the way for the emigration of the Muslims. Before long, the departees' properties "would fall into their hands without any bloodshed." Biliotti assured the chiefs that their cooperative attitude would predispose the European coalition to establishing an autonomous regime in the near future.[45] Such promises achieved short-term goals by keeping European troops clear of skirmishes with the native belligerents. But they helped tear up, and in certain areas destroyed altogether, the bi-religious fabric of the countryside.

The Kandanos episode suggests that the European coalition viewed the Muslims' emigration from Crete as the best solution to the conflict. When Biliotti met with the insurgent chiefs around Kandanos, the most powerful weapon in his arsenal of promises was to assure them that he would use all his power to facilitate Muslim emigration from the Selinos district, an area that included the besieged village. In his dispatch to the Marquess of Salisbury, Biliotti acknowledged that "the emigration of the country Mussulmans is the best solution of the Cretan problem."[46] Having convinced the insurgent leaders to lift the siege, Biliotti, accompanied by a group of European military officers, began preparations for the Muslims' departure. During the march to the shore about ten miles away, the insurgent chiefs' efforts fell short of preventing the marauding bands from plundering the convoy, leaving the expelled only with the clothes on their backs. "The whole thing was a wild, confused, and distressing scene," Biliotti remarked, "which certainly cannot be forgotten by those who witnessed it."[47]

The book *Cretan Sketches*, which R. A. H. Bickford-Smith published in 1898, drawing on his experiences during the time he served as a commissioner of the Cretan Relief Committee, provides a rather different description of the same scene.[48] Instead of Biliotti's depiction of a miserable exodus, the reader is offered, in a section titled "Houristan," some flippant musings about women.[49] According to Bickford-Smith's account of the Kandanos campaign, what the European soldiers found hard to forget was the sexual charm of the Muslim women, not the "wild, confused, and distressing scene" of the marching villagers as recounted by Biliotti. During the long march of the relieved villagers to the port of the Selinos district, the beauty of the Muslim women made for a topic of "absorbing interest" as the military convoy trekked down from Kandanos. "Having left home early and in confusion, [this beauty] was much more shown than Mussulman beauty usually is. They had not half a dozen veils between them."⁵⁰ The Kandanos episode, thus described by the British commissioner of the Cretan Relief Committee, signaled a somber future for religious coexistence in Crete. The European coalition deemed the operation of evacuating the besieged villagers a success. This ostensible accomplishment, however, came only after promises to the Christian chiefs that the area would be stripped of its Muslim population, hence enabling Christians to acquire the abandoned lands of their erstwhile neighbors.

In August 1898, the senior British naval officer Captain Hallett acknowledged that the repatriation of Muslim refugees to their villages could be achieved only through contributions from each European power of occupation, or by the raising of a loan. In view of the large number of refugees, which would render such an action prohibitive, he mentioned this not as a realistic option but rather as an ideal arrangement. Even in the unlikely case of funneling generous sums for the relief of the refugees, Hallett doubted that they would return to their villages. Especially at a time of profound mistrust toward their Christian co-islanders, they would feel prone to attacks from armed bands in the absence of Ottoman troops in the interior.⁵¹ Earlier during the conflict Biliotti had already noted that the only measure that could induce the Muslim refugees to return seemed to be "for international troops to convoy them back, and be stationed in each important center of Moslem population until such time as the reformed gendarmerie is in quite efficient working order."⁵² Well aware of the priorities of the European coalition, which did not include the implementation of costly and perilous measures to ensure the refugees' repatriation, Biliotti had posed a rhetorical question to the Marquess of Salisbury: "But is such an inland occupation contemplated, or likely to be consented to by the Powers?"⁵³

When Ottoman troops evacuated Crete in the fall of 1898, tens of thousands of Muslim villagers remained in overcrowded cities. Those homeless peasants eagerly awaited assistance to help them move on with their lives free from harm. The likelihood of attacks by armed bands and by those bent on reprisals against violence perpetrated by the Muslims during the civil war was so high that the Christian chiefs' pledges of safeguarding their well-being failed to reassure them. Under such circumstances, a petition that bore about ten thousand signatures communicated the depth of anxiety. In this massive document addressed to Queen Victoria, the Muslim population of the Iraklio/Candia district asked for concrete guarantees, such as military protection by British soldiers. It called on the queen's government as "the greatest Islamic state in the world" and demanded that the British crown "take under its aegis and direct protection the Mussulmans of Candia, as the Catholics of the Levant are under the protection of France."[54] The petitioners found it hard to find comfort in the promises of safety when they saw all around ravaged olive trees and fruit orchards that until recently had been the mainstay of their subsistence. Disbelief was embodied in the stones looted from the partly demolished houses. Despair was substantiated by the mosques destroyed or converted into churches and by the land grabbed. "Now even we see them feeding their flocks on our land so as to destroy the shoots of the olive trees already cut down and irreparably ruin these trees, our only hope in the future."[55]

The British authorities in Iraklio refused to accept the petition.[56] It remains uncertain whether this plea was ultimately brought to the attention of the British sovereign, given that the petitioners intended to mail their appeal directly to Queen Victoria as well. What is certain is that they received no satisfactory response to the request for military protection.[57]

In a detailed missive sent to the foreign minister Théophile Delcassé in 1899, the French consul Paul Blanc mentioned that he had repeatedly reported on the massive emigration from Crete as a phenomenon of "necessity and inevitability" (*nécessité et fatalité*).[58] Blanc exonerated the European coalition and the island's new government of responsibility for this exodus. Hadn't they repeatedly assured the Muslims that they would keep them safe? He linked the primary impetus for the mass flight, a hard choice given "the profound sense of attachment to native soil, particularly among islanders whose homeland has visible limits," to a unique Muslim psychology. Blanc emphasized that the great majority of the Muslims descended from Christian converts around the time of the Ottoman conquest in the seventeenth century, "preferring to dominate rather than be dominated." On this history of being renegades hinged their fanaticism: "Having sucked the spirit of hatred with their mother's milk, can anyone expect them to give up [their old habits] and recognize the current state of things and the supremacy of the Christian element?"[59]

What transpired in Crete during the late 1890s, Blanc added, had already occurred during the Muslim emigration from Bulgaria and Eastern Rumelia to the Ottoman Empire in the 1880s. Drawing on his observations in the Balkan city of Edirne, while he had served in the French Consulate there,

Blanc mentioned a visit that he had paid to a "mohadjir" camp in the area. In conversations with the refugees, he claimed, they had all given the following answer as the reason for abandoning their homes: "We left our homeland because the Bulgarians wanted to forcibly unveil our wives and compel us to attend church." Similar statements that Blanc claimed he heard from the Muslim Cretans resonated with his observations in the Balkans. The French consul concluded with overconfidence that the emigration from Crete was an inevitable phenomenon that "should be seen as favorable for the pacification of the country and for the maintenance of order."[60]

The influential consul viewed mass emigration through the prism of two distinct historical phenomena, one distant in time and the other distant in space. The conversion of Crete's native Christians to Islam in the seventeenth century and the exodus of Bulgarian Muslims during the 1880s held up a mirror to present conditions on the island. In such a culturalist framing, the mass of refugee islanders, most of them peasants from the interior, were perceived to be captives to an imagined culture, not unlike Indian migrant workers across the Bay of Bengal in the late nineteenth century. Colonial accounts of migration, whether in the Mediterranean or the Indian Ocean, are often commentaries on freedom of choice or lack thereof. This is what Sunil Amrith reminds us too with the example of a British official in Madras who ruled out as erroneous any correspondence between Indian migration to the Bay of Bengal and "the spontaneous emigration of a free and intelligent people in England and elsewhere."[61] In the case of Crete, essentialist interpretations of migration obfuscated a naked reality: the Muslim displacement was largely rooted in tangible security concerns, which the European coalition did little to assuage.

In reporting on the question of mass emigration from Crete, Biliotti, a relative of Blanc's through his wife Marguerite, differed, both in tone and content, from Blanc.[62] Rather than making grand statements about Muslims' allegedly unchanging and universal behavior, Biliotti cited concrete factors such as robust military and financial assistance as the prerequisites to halt their flight. Not only was he perceptive enough to predict that the lack of support would lead to a mass exodus, but he was too well versed in the ways of European diplomacy to entertain any scenario where such assistance would materialize. Half a year after the Muslims' petition to Queen Victoria and two months after Blanc's report regarding the mass emigration, Biliotti wrote to London in May 1899. He noted that whenever he encouraged the refugees languishing in the cities to return to the countryside they wondered if they could count on a continuous occupation of the island by British troops. His negative answer convinced many that emigration was preferable to staying with a sense of unease about an uncertain future.[63]

If the almost complete disappearance of the rural Muslim population proved a boon to some islanders by allowing them to come into possession of the abandoned properties, the sudden decline in Crete's agricultural class meant hardship for the island's economy. In early 1900 when Prince George, the high commissioner of Crete, entertained the possibility of the return of some Muslims to their villages, Blanc objected by pointing out that "the Muslims of Crete left their homeland as the Muslims of Bulgaria, Eastern Rumelia, and Thessaly did before."[64] Blanc claimed that "the Muslims would never agree to living under a regime, however liberal, in which the reins of government are held by the Christians." As he had remarked on previous occasions, Blanc argued that these emigrants followed "an impervious law of fatality against which no force could react." Those hesitant to depart from Crete, the French consul maintained, were persuaded by the sultan's agents to leave a country "in which the Muslims would no longer be the masters." Blanc scoffed at what he saw as Prince George's naïveté and "benevolent inexperience that led him to dream such a dream." The extent of the ruin caused by the latest unrest in Crete was so enormous that it would invalidate any project aimed to repatriate them. "Christians and Muslims were engaged in a war of Apaches and Vandals," Blanc remarked. "It is, hence, a utopia to suppose that the stroke of a magic wand will suffice to reinstall them in their villages and ensure the well-being of eighty thousand people lacking in all the resources."[65]

The first census carried out by the autonomous government of Crete around the time of Blanc's report in 1900 makes evident the near-complete disappearance of religious diversity in the countryside. The mass displacement caused by civil war and European intervention rendered the Muslim minority of Crete largely an urban community, reversing a centuries-long pattern. Within a total population of 303,543, Muslims stood at 33,496, a figure 54 percent lower than the one recorded in 1881. A more telling consequence of the cataclysm of the civil war is provided by a comparison of the population data from 1881 and 1900. While 58 percent of Muslims lived outside of the three major cities in 1881, by 1900 the rural ratio within the overall Muslim population had dropped to 21 percent.[66] Living in villages and small towns scattered across the interior, rural Muslims lacked the relative security that their urban coreligionists enjoyed thanks to having larger numbers in proximity to European consulates, whose protection they invoked frequently. Smaller communities in the countryside produced greater security concerns, as indicated by the appeals of Muslim peasants in early twentieth-century Crete.

A petition that the inhabitants of Arkalohori, a small town about twenty miles south of Iraklio, addressed to the commandant of the gendarmerie in May 1908 offers a glimpse into security concerns of ordinary people. Signed by a religiously mixed group of petitioners from that town, which had a population of 973 Christians and 329 Muslims according to the census data from 1900, the document conveyed people's anxiety about the authorities' decision to relocate the Arkalohori gendarmerie station. Emphasizing the necessity of functioning law enforcement in their district, the townspeople stated that throughout the period of "Turkish rule," multiple locales across Crete had functioned as meeting points where people from neighboring areas gathered every Friday for commercial purposes. Villagers sought buyers for their cattle and crops, merchants pursued profitable business connections. On these occasions of vibrant economic activity, the bustling market towns saw their small population increase exponentially. Arkalohori, among such commercial posts, would attract crowds of visitors at times numbering more than four thousand. Multitudes of strangers would sometimes include wayward characters. Inebriated with wine and prone to crime, they would harass and even harm peaceful villagers returning home after sunset. For fear of robbery, merchants would feel compelled to take their unsold merchandise with them, rather than leaving it stored in the shops until the next market gathering. And for exactly these reasons the Ottoman administration of Crete had established a strategic gendarmerie station in Arkalohori.[67] The petition also communicated the sense of vulnerability expressed by the minority. "We have been coming here because the gendarmerie has so far protected us," the Muslims were heard saying. They wondered, "If they move it away, who is going to safeguard us? Who is going to stop an intoxicated man intent on causing me harm? Who is going to prevent a criminal from robbing me outside of my village?"[68]

Reporting to London regarding the Muslims' security complaints, the acting consul general Ronald Graham had noted in August 1906 that "the Mussulman has come to enjoy here the unenviable position of the Jew in

Russia—that of being regarded as a providentially provided safety-valve for popular over-excitement, and if there is violence in the air he or his property is likely to suffer."[69] Two years later, the Muslim deputies of the Cretan Assembly paid a visit to the British consul Arthur Peel, describing the condition of the population in similar terms. Concerned about the scheduled withdrawal of European troops of occupation from the island, Peel's visitors pointed out that the departure of the international forces could reignite the embers of the old animosity between the communities. Perhaps the local government would strive to safeguard the minority, the deputies hypothesized, but even that would fail to curb "the popular excitement," jeopardizing a small community against a three-hundred-thousand-strong majority.[70]

The small peasant proprietors outside the cities often bore the brunt of insecurity. An emblematic example is provided by an incident from the mixed village of Larani, about twenty-five miles south of Iraklio.[71] One day in September 1907, Mehmet Nazifakis and Arab Bekrakis, two shepherd boys aged fifteen and seventeen, were murdered on their way to the village, one having his throat slit, the other being beaten to death with a stick. A petition by the Muslims of Larani to the French vice-consul mentioned that a day after the murder, while the corpses still lay at the crime scene awaiting the legal proceedings to be finalized, hundreds of armed men from neighboring villages dashed to Larani. Agitated by the rumor that a Christian had fallen victim to a revenge killing, the armed crowd questioned the Muslim inhabitants of Larani to ascertain the facts.[72] The official report of the gendarmerie confirmed the falsity of the hearsay. It further noted that a twelve-year-old Christian boy, now under arrest, had spread the rumor that the Muslims of Larani killed his brother to avenge the shepherd boys. The gendarmerie report, however, pointed out that the men rushing to Larani comprised forty-seven people, only three of them armed. They left the village peacefully after assurances that the rumor was false.[73] Shaken by the events, the Muslims of Larani likened the small number of rural Muslims to "a drop in the ocean" and implored the protection of the French authorities.[74]

While the question of insecurity in the countryside concerned every inhabitant, Muslim and Christian alike, the examples of Arkalohori and Larani underscore how those anxieties intensified in the case of a small minority. Throughout the period of autonomy Muslims frequently described themselves as a beleaguered community with a desperate need for safety. Because the European coalition took on the official task of ensuring the minority's security, the impending departure of its troops from Crete added a sense of urgency to Muslims' pleas for protection. The withdrawal of international garrisons constituted one of the major decisions that the European powers took in the wake of the Theriso uprising (1905-6), a major upheaval named after the inland village that served as the epicenter of the movement. This was a large-scale insurgency that Eleftherios Venizelos, future prime minister of Greece, orchestrated against the high commissioner Prince George. Like the civil war of the 1890s, the turmoil, initially confined to an isolated area in the mountainous countryside of western Crete, spread to other parts of the island, reducing the government to a nominal existence everywhere but in few districts occupied by European troops. As the Theriso insurgents established a revolutionary government in the interior, the European coalition saw two possible courses of action: concentrate its military presence in the cities to prevent them from gaining control of government buildings and the customs there; or crush the insurgency by dispatching many soldiers into the mountains of western Crete. If the former would plunge most of the island into chaos, the latter would cause the coalition serious casualties and exorbitant financial costs. The Europeans followed a path they had already trodden during the 1890s, resorting to the negotiation skills of their officers with the fighters rather than mobilizing troops against them.[75]

The general situation around the time of the Theriso uprising bore a striking resemblance to the tumultuous 1890s in terms of the impact of violence on the rural Muslim population. In discussions with his counterparts regarding the future of Crete, Italian foreign minister Tommaso Tittoni acknowledged that the withdrawal of international troops would produce negative effects for the minority. He argued that the best remedy against such security concerns was probably the immigration of Muslims to Asia Minor.[76] The British officers responded to this question with their own imaginative solutions. In October 1906, the British Foreign Office declared its confidence regarding fair treatment of the minority under the post-Theriso regime that replaced the administration of Prince George. It nevertheless added that, in case the necessity for special protection arose, Muslims should be induced "to colonize a particular region of the island, where they could more easily be afforded security of life and property."[77] British consul Esme Howard anticipated a massive Muslim flight after the withdrawal of European troops. He pointed out that "they would also sell or let their properties for a song, and, if possible, leave the island under the influence of panic." Howard, therefore, proposed a scheme to compensate those wishing to emigrate for the value of their immovables.[78]

Typical perceptions of the European coalition regarding the place of the Muslim minority in Crete stitch together two transformative periods in the island's history. I argue that during both the mid-1890s and mid-1900s the European powers imagined the island's communities in terms that evoked "the unmixing of populations" *avant la parole*.[79] The coalition launched no concrete policies to remove the Muslims from Crete. Its reluctance to reconstruct the destroyed villages and provide military protection, however, more than facilitated their emigration. Especially during the 1890s, the European coalition predicated its actions, or lack thereof, on the assumption that religious coexistence was a chimera and policies in its pursuit would invite nothing but more bloodshed. Such beliefs harbored by foreign decision-makers wielding the power to shape the island's future played a crucial role in the mass flight. By the waning months of the nineteenth century the great majority of the internally displaced Muslims would leave Crete.

Such approaches to violent conflict in a multireligious setting like Crete were by no means the exclusive purview of European decision-makers. The notion of "the unmixing of populations" obviously informed European colonial policies in Crete. What is less clear is that it also appealed to certain Ottomans, civil servants and local notables alike. In August 1897, when the Sublime Porte still held a degree of authority, albeit much weakened, in Crete's affairs, the island's interim governor *Müşavir* İsmail sent a confidential note to the Yıldız Palace. In it he revisited a proposal that he had broached to the sultan's secretary in a cipher telegram in April 1897.[80] At that time more than forty thousand rural Muslims had been internally displaced to the coastal cities.[81] The governor mentioned how the discord and animosity embittered people. He underscored that the devastating situation victimized the minority especially, with atrocities and destruction of olive trees, jeopardizing the bi-religious life in Crete's mixed villages. For the sultan and the Sublime Porte, the pressing urgency concerned the matter of safeguarding the Muslim population. The interim governor suggested a separation of Christian and Muslim villages to undertake an "exchange" (*istibdal*, related to the better-known word *mübadele*) of their properties. He also underlined that some of the Muslim notables lent support to this idea.

He acknowledged the economic harm to be brought to the Muslims, a minority in possession of more land than the majority. The interim governor maintained, however, that the benefits would outweigh the costs, as gathering into clusters would strengthen them against the Christians who had long cherished the ambition of evicting the Muslims from Crete.[82]

When *Nea Erevna* published in March 1902 the sorrowful tale of the destitute Cretan refugee family in Istanbul, Ottoman newspapers, under the heavy hand of Hamidian censorship, had been keeping silent about Crete and its refugees. Such silence continued until the Constitutional Revolution of July 1908. Following the Cretan government's declaration of union with Greece in October 1908, the coverage of island affairs suddenly became front-page news in the press. If the story of the unfortunate refugee family evoked sympathy in *Nea Erevna*'s readership in 1902, six years later, continuous reports about the plight of many more Muslim Cretans began to electrify the imperial public.

The preceding pages have shown that the Cretan fighters harnessed geography to make the European coalition, albeit already sympathetic to them, accept their main demand, the departure of Ottoman soldiers. This was a significant accomplishment given the clear Ottoman victory against Greece in 1897. The insurgents' struggle also resulted in the displacement of Muslim islanders, who emerged a decade later as the drivers of a protest movement, a story that I narrate in chapters 4 and 5. There is a parallel between these antagonists from common class roots. Christian fighters and Muslim refugees are joined by a rural island background. I envision both groups as mostly anonymous but influential protagonists of history, performing fateful roles in shaping an island and empire. The former conducted an effective armed struggle in the mountains of Crete, while the latter waged economic warfare in the streets of the Ottoman Empire.

But before I turn to the examination of post-1908 protests, a phenomenon marked by the strong influence of Cretan refugees, I explore in the next chapter the condition of being a diminished Muslim minority in Crete. The sorrowful account of civil war and displacement in chapters 1 and 2 should not obscure the stories of those who chose to stay on the island. Their life stories illustrate the Muslim minority's adaptability amid disruptive transformations, which followed on the heels of the disappearance of the Ottoman state from Crete in all but name.

THREE

ADAPTABILITY *in* VULNERABILITY

The Muslim Minority in Autonomous Crete, 1898–1908

Mustafa Deliahmetakis sought to stay out of the limelight throughout his mayoral tenure in Iraklio, the largest city in Crete. His mayoralty overlapped with the first decade of the autonomous regime installed in Crete at the end of 1898, following the departure of Ottoman soldiers and the appointment of Prince George as high commissioner. Deliahmetakis managed to maintain a low political profile until his name came up as part of the allegations that the Muslim population of Iraklio were plotting disturbances to prevent the withdrawal of European troops from Crete scheduled for 1909.[1] In an attempt to disassociate himself from the accusations that would certainly cast doubt on his loyalties to the autonomous administration of Crete, he sent a letter to *Kiryks* (Herald). This was an influential newspaper serving as the mouthpiece of Eleftherios Venizelos's political party. The Venizelist daily published his note on 1 July 1908. In a concise statement, the mayor vehemently denied the rumors, condemning their circulation as a scheme to sow discord between Christians and Muslims. Mustafa Deliahmetakis underscored his obedience to "the laws of my fatherland" (*Nomous tēs patridos mou*).[2]

I posit that the words *laws* and *fatherland* combine to offer a glimpse into how a principal figure of Turkocretan minority defined himself as a citizen and islander during the early twentieth century. If through the word *laws* Deliahmetakis expressed his loyalty to an autonomous regime run largely by his Christian compatriots, the notion of "fatherland" anchored him firmly on Cretan soil, independent of the character of its governance. This plain declaration by the mayor of Iraklio countervails blanket statements by the Europeans who wielded influence in shaping the island's political future. For instance, during an early phase of the autonomous regime in Crete, the French consul Paul Blanc had claimed that it was impossible that the Muslims would accept "living under a regime, however liberal, in which the reins of government are held by the Christians."[3] Obviously, Blanc did not suggest that all Muslim Cretans without exception would express a sweeping dislike of a Christian-controlled regime. Such a view expressed by the doyen of European consular corps in Crete, however, helped normalize the mass flight from Crete. It obscured the reality that the emigration was greatly facilitated by the European coalition's unwillingness to assuage the minority's security concerns. For the French consul, the Muslims' departure entailed both "necessity and inevitability" (*nécessité et fatalité*).[4] It was imagined to be necessary for the prevention of future conflict. It was thought to be inevitable because of an alleged Muslim fanaticism, making the acceptance of Christian rule next to impossible. The connotation of predestination surrounding the word *fatalité* fit well into the long-held trope of Islamic fatalism in the Western imagining of Turkish Muslim communities.[5]

Such a bleak view of an influential European consul suggested that the Muslim flight from the island was voluntary. What is more, it implied a lack of faith in their prospects under an autonomous regime. The perceived incompatibility of Muslims with Christian rule resonates with the way historians have traditionally studied this island community. In the scant historical literature on Muslim experiences during the period of autonomy, mundane dimensions of being Muslim in autonomous Crete have been often overlooked. This has produced a dismal conception of history that has viewed the condition of remaining Muslims in the territories lost by the Ottoman state through the lens of tragedy, omitting examples of coexistence and intercommunal cooperation although these were standard features of everyday life.[6] Such accounts bring to mind not only European sectarian viewpoints from the turn of the twentieth century but also perspectives that would abound in the pro-CUP Ottoman press after 1908. Both of them saw the vision of a functioning multireligious society during the period of autonomy as a chimera. Underscoring the adaptability and resilience of the Muslim minority, this chapter discusses various cases of cross-religious interactions, examples made all the more striking considering the enormity of the havoc and the brutality of the violence wrought by the recent civil war.

In her work on this minority in autonomous Crete, Elektra Kostopoulou upsets the narrative of victimhood, citing that "from the point of view of some of its members, the Muslim community was growing." Arguing that the rate of decline in the number of Muslims exceeded that of the amount of their properties, Kostopoulou maintains that the remaining minority saw its potential income increase, concluding that "becoming a minority in numbers is not necessarily a negative."[7] This observation may encapsulate the condition of some urban dwellers who managed to collect revenues from estates in the country. For a more rounded picture of the Muslim minority in autonomous Crete, however, it is helpful to consider the case of smaller groups living farther from the cities. A minority within a minority, rural Muslims lacked the comparative advantage that their urban counterparts enjoyed thanks to greater numbers as well as recourse to the local government and European consulates.

In the following pages I explore a little-told story of a Muslim minority in the wake of the passing of an Islamic empire from the island. Being Muslim in autonomous Crete involved the periodic risk of facing intimidation or assaults on one's body and property, a chief cause of emigration. Being a member of the minority during the 1900s also provided the chance to drive a process of self-fashioning and of seeking novel modes of coexistence with the Christian majority. After all, these two communities held much in common, such as the Cretan dialect of the Greek language, a proud fascination with the seventeenth-century epic poem *Erotokritos*, and a culinary affection for the island's snails.[8] In this regard, my framing of Muslim experiences during the period of autonomy entails both vulnerability and adaptability.

This chapter builds on the narrative of the preceding sections in which I have discussed the concrete factors, both internal and external to the island, that set off the mass Muslim emigration from Crete. I draw on the case of the diminished minority of 33,496, a large fraction of whom, according to the 1900 census, resided in the island's three main cities. I argue that in their decision (and ability) to stay lies a story of resilience in the face of deeply changed political and demographic circumstances after the passing of the Ottoman state in all but name.[9] By merely staying on the island, thousands of families became a living refutation of indiscriminate statements such as those made by Blanc about an alleged Muslim mentality. More importantly, the active presence of a Muslim minority in Crete, until it was terminated by an international treaty signed at Lausanne in 1923, showcases a community's adaptability to a radically transformed sociopolitical setting.

Unlike Mustafa Deliahmetakis and several other figures that I discuss in the next pages, most Muslim Cretans left no documentary traces that would offer clues to how they operated in a post-Ottoman setting as members of a minority. We are fortunate, however, to have archival sources that illuminate a curious case in which the administration evicted scores of Muslims from the nearby islet of Spinalonga to turn it into a leper asylum. I close the chapter with an examination of this episode to disinter nonelite voices. I demonstrate how a group of illiterate poor islanders tried to navigate a labyrinth of legal obstacles in search of justice and fairness. They waged an uphill bureaucratic battle, lodging many petitions of protest with local and international authorities in the hope of forestalling exile and, when this failed, of at least obtaining a fair indemnity for their properties. Defeated perhaps, their efforts nevertheless shed light on the activism of the displaced, suggesting a rebuke to perceptions of refugee passivity or Muslim fatalism.

The exploration of minority viewpoints from autonomous Crete helps us understand the empire's violent demise and its concomitant possibilities. In this regard, the story in this chapter connects to the vibrant scholarship on imperial legacies and postimperial subjectivities in the broader Ottoman world. This is an account of Muslims in autonomous Crete seeking to carve out a space for themselves during "an era of rupture and transition," in Devin Naar's characterization of the post-Ottoman period for Salonican Jews as Greek subjects.[10]

"Long Live Our Prince George!": Muslim Cretans as Autonomous Subjects

On 21 December 1898, Prince George of Greece arrived in Crete as high commissioner, a post created by the European coalition composed of Britain, France, Italy, and Russia despite the objections of the Sublime Porte.[11] The British consul Alfred Biliotti reported that days before the prince's arrival, the Christian population had begun preparations to give him a warm welcome.¹² Portraits of the prince and flags of the European coalition and of the newborn Cretan state decorated house and store fronts along the route from Suda Bay, where Prince George disembarked, to the government *konak* in Hania. From the balcony of the *konak*, which had until recently served as the seat of the Ottoman administration, the prince addressed the jubilant crowd.¹³ Throughout the joyous celebrations day and night, the Muslims of Hania mostly remained in their homes. The following day, however, they responded warmly to Prince George's gesture for dialogue with the community. As a token of appreciation for the interest shown by the prince, who visited the director of the *evkaf*, the institution running various communal affairs, many illuminated their residences and stores after the fall of dusk.¹⁴

Prince George's initial interactions with the Muslim community soon gave way to a more substantive engagement. In early January 1899, the prince entered the Hünkar Camii (Sovereign's Mosque), Hania's principal mosque, named for Sultan Ibrahim, who had sat on the throne during the island's conquest in the mid-seventeenth century. The new ruler joined a devout congregation performing a special service for him.¹⁵ Figure 16 illustrates this historic moment. It provides a visual documentation of the faces in the crowd and the stares that sized up the new ruler as he was getting ready to leave Splantzia Square, the central venue of Muslim public life in the city. The Hania correspondent of *Anagennisis* (Rebirth), a newspaper based in Rethimno, reported that many Christians joined their Muslim co-islanders during the religious ceremony inside the mosque. At the conclusion of the service, Prince George proceeded to the courthouse in the company of several imams and Muslim notables. Among the latter was Hüseyin Naimbeyzade, a notable personality in the Hania community, who exclaimed in Turkish, *Prensimiz Yorgo çok yaşa!* (Long live our Prince George!)—words that the newspaper rendered in Turkish with Greek characters.¹⁶

This four-word exclamation, *Prensimiz Yorgo çok yaşa!*, paralleled a widespread public expression of political loyalty during the reign of Sultan Abdülhamid. Offering a celebratory veneration for the sultan's authority, *Padişahım çok yaşa!* (Long live the sultan!) was the most conspicuous phrase inscribed on banners and voiced by participants on various occasions such as the launching of public works and the taking of group photos for commemorative or propaganda purposes. In late nineteenth-century Hania, the longtime capital of the island where the sultan's sway prior to the proclamation of autonomy proved more robust than in the periodically re-

FIGURE 16. The Hünkar Camii can be partially seen on the right-hand side of the photograph. The crowd formed around the prince's carriage is religiously mixed. The multitude of fezzes and turbans point to the larger Muslim presence on this occasion, 1899. Source: *Kriti, 1898–1899: Fotografikes Martyries apo to Prosopiko Lefkoma tou Prigkipa Georgiou* (Iraklio: Panepistimiakes Ekdoeseis Kritis, 2009).

calcitrant countryside, these words embodied the sunset of sultans over Crete. This plain formula uttered by a prominent figure casts light on how quickly certain segments of the urban Muslim population adjusted to the transformed political context. Only about two years earlier in 1896, Hüseyin Naimbeyzade, as a deputy in the Cretan Assembly, had signed a petition addressed to the European consuls. In it, Naimbeyzade, along with his colleagues, had pointed out that "while speaking the Greek patois in daily life, Muslim Cretans preserve their particular and national language [*leur langue propre et nationale*], Turkish, which they make use of in writing."[17] In light of this, it is hard to miss the significance of Naimbeyzade's using a perceived national language for expressing his recognition of Prince George as a legitimate sovereign under a novel regime of autonomy.

The Muslim population of eastern Crete too welcomed the high commissioner with sober enthusiasm during his tour of the area in May 1899. Alfred Biliotti reported that Christian and Muslim inhabitants of Iraklio gathered in huge numbers for the occasion, "most of whom had not met each other since the struggles of the last three years," and that they "so behaved that there has not been a single case requiring the intervention of the police."[18] One of the highlights of Prince George's visit took place in the office of the *evkaf*. Fazıl Bey, a young man attending the University of Athens, delivered a welcome address in Greek, a performance that deeply impressed the prince.[19] In the spacious mansion of Mustafa Deliahmetakis, the mayor of Iraklio, Prince George met with several Muslim and Christian functionaries of the city.[20] As in Hania five months earlier, the high commissioner paid a visit to the city's principal mosque, in which the imam recited prayers for the ruler's well-being and success. On the same day, the prince also proceeded to Gazi, a majority-Muslim village outside of Iraklio to the west, where he was given a warm reception inside some of the dwellings.[21]

These examples from the earlier phase of the autonomous regime in Crete indicate the openness of multiple Muslims to the new regime. On some occasions, this attitude was made evident extemporaneously, as in the case of Hüseyin Naimbeyzade's public pronouncement of loyalty to the sovereign. On some others, it was recorded ceremoniously, as in the example of the mufti of Ierapetra, a coastal town in southeastern Crete.[22] In December 1901, the mufti took an oath of allegiance to the new regime in the presence of Prince George and the minister of education, Antonios Voreadis. In the formal ceremony that took place in the princely residence in Halepa, a wealthier suburb of Hania, the Muslim cleric declared his loyalty to "the fatherland and the sovereign" and his "obedience to the constitution."[23]

While various notable Muslims took on official roles in the government, some middle-class urban Muslims joined their Christian compatriots in grassroots initiatives that proliferated around the turn of the twentieth century. If the Muslim functionaries declared allegiance to the autonomous regime by taking an oath before the higher authorities, the participation of urban Muslims in civil society associations expressed another form of loyalty to the new regime. After all, such organizations operated under the mandate and supervision of the Cretan state, the architects of which were deeply conscious of the new regime's divergence from the Ottoman system. With areas of specialization ranging from athletics to philanthropy to arts and letters, manifold voluntary associations boasting multireligious membership began to bolster civic life on an island with a recent history of violent destruction. These organizations became operational once the government approved their charters. *Episimos Efimeris tis Kritikis Politeias*, the official gazette of the Cretan state, publicized the activation of these civic initiatives.

In late December 1899, the official gazette announced the birth of the Gymnastic Society of Halepa. The first article in the charter of the association laid out its main goal as the promotion and dissemination of interest in athletic activities among citizens "regardless of religion." Article 2 specified the establishment of a gymnasium in Halepa and mentioned the training of the association's members through a program of exercise, field trips, and preparation for athletic contests. Article 52 set 25 March and 3 November as special occasions to hold competitive events in which the winners would be honored publicly. These two deeply symbolic dates make evident the link between sports, politics, and civic identity. While 25 March marks the independence of Greece from the Ottoman state, a process starting in 1821, 3 November commemorates the autonomy of Crete, celebrating the date when the last imperial troops departed it in 1898. Chaired by Konstantinos Manos, with Ali Talat Mollazade serving as vice president, the association had thirty-two members, two of them Muslim.[24] Around the same time, an association with a similar character and mission began to operate in the majority-Muslim city of Rethimno.[25] Entering the civic life of the city under the name the Gymnastic Society of Rethimno, the organization was headed by Emmanouil Generalis.[26] Three Muslim names appear among the forty-six members listed in the official gazette. The first article of the association's charter specified that it would maintain communication with organizations pursuing similar goals "in Crete and *in the rest of Greece*," a choice of words that rendered the island part of Greece in aspiration if not in reality.[27]

The earliest gymnastic clubs founded during the period of autonomy cultivated a notion of virile masculinity, paralleling the self-image of the young state, which saw itself as the antithesis of a decrepit Ottoman regime.[28] Quite a few civil society initiatives channeled their energies toward urban women with programs designed to promote involvement in domesticated economic life. The Association of Christian and Ottoman Women (Syndesmos tōn Hristianōn kai Othomanidōn Krissōn) stands out among such organizations, drawing the attention and interest of the public when it became operational in 1901.[29] Seeking to develop weaving and various handicrafts deemed suitable to conventional female gender roles, it aimed to support financially disadvantaged women by creating steady employment. The association's charter set forth the objective of expanding the organization from its base in Hania into other cities and towns of Crete by establishing local branches.[30] Headed by Anna Gerasimidou, it was served by two vice presidents, Errieta K. Manou and Zeynep Mehmet Hamitbeyzade.[31] Its fourteen founding members were evenly divided between Christians and Muslims.[32] In a November 1901 issue, the Hania daily *Nea Erevna* introduced the Association of Christian and Ottoman Women to its readership. A weaving workshop running in a little corner of Halepa, which the newspaper claimed had remained underadvertised, became the association's main operation. Women learned not only to make dresses but to mend relations, "leaving behind the hatred of old times and working with zeal for the progress of women in the common fatherland."[33] Six months later in April 1902, *Nea Erevna* updated its readers about a new training program to furnish women with vocational skills such as cutting and sewing dresses, and drawing.[34] A month later the same newspaper announced the opening of an exhibition in the public gardens of Hania to showcase the artifacts produced by women who were trained by the association. The event aimed both to recompense indigent women with the revenue from the sale of lottery tickets and to raise the organization's visibility.[35]

In addition to supporting various civil society initiatives, lottery tickets sold in Crete functioned to raise funds for the Greek fleet. Throughout the period of autonomy, newspapers urged the public to make donations to the navy fund. For instance, multiple issues of *Nea Erevna* in 1906 came out with front-page announcements in large fonts that encouraged readers to buy lottery tickets for the benefit of the Greek fleet. That these tickets were available for sale at post offices across the island indicated that the autonomous administration was actively involved in a campaign to consolidate Greece's naval standing in the eastern Mediterranean.[36] Figure 17 provides a visual documentation of this press campaign. It shows an eye-catching text from the front page of the Rethimno daily *Anagennisis* proclaiming to its readers that "as much as you desire the grandeur of the nation, buy the lottery for the national fleet."[37]

The Cretan state lacked the right to establish its own naval fleet. The authorities instead endeavored to strengthen the navy of the nation that they aspired to make the island an official part of. The administration's active

FIGURE 17. Upper part of the front page of *Anagennisis*. The image is from the photograph of a microfilm, thus the black background. Source: *Anagennisis*, 15 July 1907, Public Library of Rethimno.

participation in a Greek national project illuminates Crete's trajectory years before its declaration of union with Athens in 1908 and that union's realization in 1913. For instance, in 1904, the Cretan Ministry of Education and Religious Affairs prepared a directive for school teachers and Greek Orthodox church councils throughout the island. Describing the main purpose of education as imparting the love of motherland to students from an early age, the circular called for donations to the navy fund. The ministry requested every school to form a committee to oversee the collection of contributions for the Greek fleet. These committees were also tasked with the transmission of donations to the ministry in Hania at the end of each month. The formulators of this initiative knew that the contributions from children would amount to little pecuniary value. The standard to evaluate the merit of this program, however, was not a monetary one. Envisioning schoolchildren in Crete as "the future citizens of the Hellenic homeland," the educational authorities identified the value of this motion in terms of warming impressionable youth to mainland nationalism in a performative fashion.[38]

The section of the directive addressed to the metropolitan of Crete urged active participation of the clergy in the fundraising campaign. It asserted that being a true Christian rested on being a patriotic citizen. The ministry's text invoked the example of Germanos, the metropolitan of Patras on mainland Greece, who was believed to have raised in 1821 the banner of revolution against the Ottomans, with the outcry "For faith and fatherland" (*yper Pisteos kai Patridos*).³⁹ The minister of education demanded the solicitation of donations from churchgoers every Sunday.⁴⁰ Two months after the ministry appealed to the island's metropolitan, the bishop of Kydonia and Apokoronas in western Crete issued a call for contributions to the navy. Characterizing the mission of strengthening the Greek fleet as a religious and national duty against "savage and barbarian foes of Hellenism," he implored the parish committees to educate the population about the significance of working for this objective.⁴¹ In February 1905, the villagers of Spilia, near the western town of Kissamos, mailed their donations to the Hellenic ministry of economy in Athens. An attached note described the purpose of contributions as a gesture of obedient devotion to "our homeland, free Greece."⁴² A committee made up of a priest and a primary school teacher oversaw the collection of the funds. It is in such details that we can locate the importance of two institutions, church and school, for disseminating an Athens-centered outlook and laying the groundwork for an anticipated union with Mother Greece.⁴³

Although the official promotion of the navy fund campaign remained mainly within the purview of the Ministry of Education and Religious Affairs, calls for participation in this national effort circulated through other state departments as well. In March 1906, an Interior Ministry directive addressed to functionaries throughout Crete opened with an account of Greek naval victories, among them the Battle of Salamis against the Persian Empire in 480 BCE under the command of Themistocles.⁴⁴ The ministry counted on everyone "to give up half of their daily bread in order to buy the lottery." Its circular advanced the goal of making Greece glorious again, enabling it to safeguard the rights of the Cretans' "unredeemed brothers groaning under the yoke."⁴⁵

The island press kept the public abreast of the donations accumulating in the navy fund. Lists of contributors that appeared in newspapers mostly recorded the modest quantities collected in Christian schools.⁴⁶ Frequent donors also came from the ranks of other public institutions. For example, the names of Hania-based civil servants who donated 2 percent of their monthly salary were published in an August 1904 issue of *Nea Erevna*. In a brief statement addressed to the mayor of Hania, twenty-six functionaries committed a monthly pledge. Five Muslim names stand out among this group.[47] Similarly, one of the contributors from among the fourteen employees of the Hania public hospital was a Muslim.[48]

We have no documents that intimate, let alone explain, the true motivations of Muslims in donating to the navy fund, a public subscription campaign animated by expansionist Greek nationalism. Furthermore, in the absence of sources to record the monetary contributions of Muslim islanders at the grassroots level, it would be problematic to take the above examples at face value and interpret them as indications of genuine enthusiasm. Writing them off as gestures motivated solely by a desire to preserve one's employment or as indications of succumbing to peer pressure, however, would be erroneous too. Such shortcuts to analysis come at the expense of depriving the Muslim contributors of autonomy in their decisions and actions. Their example twists the neat conclusions of nationalist readings of the Ottoman past in which certain actions of Turks/Muslims are deemed anomalous, to be either ignored or explained away as artificial. It also upsets common Western stereotypes of the early twentieth century, attributing predetermined characteristics to Muslims, such as intransigence toward a Christian-controlled polity.

In the Service of the Fatherland: Keeping Muslims Safe

In late November 1898, three weeks after Ottoman troops fully evacuated Crete, Emmanouil Angelakis (b. 1856) delivered a public address in Ierapetra, a town on the southeastern coast.[49] Angelakis was a notable figure in local politics during the late nineteenth and early twentieth centuries. He served as the deputy of Sitia in the Cretan Assembly in the 1880s and as the prefect of the Ierapetra district following the establishment of the autonomous regime.[50] Angelakis began his speech by remarking how the recent civil war had wreaked immense devastation throughout the island. Of all the multiple periods of foreign rule in Crete, he asserted, the last two centuries marked the darkest times. During that era foreign despots trampled over the lives, honor, and property of the islanders. Istanbul's heavy hand drove a wedge between Christians and Muslims. The rest of his discourse emphasized commonalities between them: "Until today what has separated us from the Ottomans [i.e., Muslim Cretans] was the tyrannical government, the alien conqueror." The auspicious intervention of the European great powers, however, removed this barrier. And this division no longer needed to continue, especially because "we Christians and Muslims are the children of this common motherland. We speak an identical language, maintain the same habits and traditions." Angelakis spelled out an island identity shared by both communities. At the same time, he subsumed it under a loftier belonging to Greekness and denied agency to previous generations of Muslim Cretans by adding that "the blood in our veins is Greek. I believe that everyone knows that if they believe in Mohammed it is because tyranny forced them to do so. Their ancestors believed in Jesus as we do."[51]

Having established a common cultural ground, the veteran local politician addressed the pressing matter of security. For some time, this had been the main preoccupation of the diminished minority. He argued that Christians were duty bound to prove "to our protectors [guarantor powers of Europe] that it was not any savage instinct that led us to rise up but an ardent desire to liberate ourselves from a savage subjugation." Not only humanitarian principles but "the political interests of our country," according to Angelakis, dictated the fair treatment of the minority.[52]

The withdrawal of Ottoman troops in late 1898 made many members of the Muslim community feel that they lost an old guardian. In the aftermath of the departure of the sultan's soldiers, the European powers exhorted the Cretan government to ensure the safety of the minority. It is in this setting that the meaning of Angelakis's phrase "the political interests of our country" should be understood. As early as December 1898, a joint proclamation by the admirals representing Britain, France, Italy, and Russia specified that the foremost task of the new autonomous regime was to institute a government capable of safeguarding everyone's life and property regardless of religious differences.[53] Although the massive emigration following the civil war dramatically lowered the Muslim population in Crete, they still constituted approximately one-tenth of the population. The 1900 census yielded a count of 303,543 residents in Crete, 11 percent of whom were Muslims. With 93 percent of the Christians residing in the countryside, the Muslim population in the cities of Iraklio, Hania, and Rethimno stood at 49, 44, and 62 percent, respectively.[54] Despite constituting only 4 percent of Crete's total inhabitants, rural Muslims boasted an importance disproportionate to their negligible size. At stake for the higher authorities of the Cretan state was the standing of the new regime in the eyes of the European powers. Any incident of racially provoked violence against the

Muslims would be a blow to the credibility of the nascent regime, signaling that the government had failed in its promise to safeguard a minority.

In June 1902, four Muslim boatmen were murdered in the isolated southwestern region of Sphakia, an atrocity that deeply disturbed the Muslim minority and disconcerted many of their Christian co-islanders. The crime represented the most serious instance of violence targeting the Muslims after the establishment of an autonomous regime, a period that public figures such as Emmanouil Angelakis had saluted as the harbinger of peace. Fully alert to the international repercussions of brutalities against Muslims, high commissioner Prince George issued a proclamation to the inhabitants of the Sphakia province. He exhorted everyone to help the authorities locate the criminals. The deleterious impact of such crimes, he warned, would transcend the western province and implicate the entire population.[55]

Mentioning the moral hazard that this incident would pose to the autonomous regime, the Hania daily *Patris* (Homeland) wrote soon after the murders that "if the proud people of the Sphakia mountains desire to deliver themselves from this opprobrium," they were obliged to surrender the perpetrators to the authorities. The Ministry of Interior announced that it would reward anyone assisting law enforcement to apprehend the murderers.[56] Three days later, *Patris* published a front-page editorial penned by Charalambos Pologeorgis, a notable political figure during the period of autonomy who at the time served as deputy in the Cretan Assembly. This deplorable incident offered Pologeorgis an occasion both to indict the former Ottoman regime and to affirm the fundamental difference of the present autonomous government. While the previous rulers had protected certain groups of criminals, the Cretan state promised to lead the country toward progress and civilization by curing the ills of history. For that very reason, the government was obliged to locate and punish the perpetrators of this heinous crime. He linked the motive for the murders to the ancient custom of vendetta, particularly rampant in the mountainous region of Sphakia. Four unfortunate boatmen, Pologeorgis noted, were the innocent victims killed in retaliation for the murder of a Sphakiot man, Georgios Polakis, by three Muslims in Hania several years prior.[57]

Frightened and outraged by these murders, a group of Muslims gathered in Hania's Hünkar Mosque, where they had welcomed Prince George only three and a half years earlier. Now they were trying to brace themselves against the aftershocks of this crime. In the petitions they sent to the Sublime Porte and to Giulio Prinetti, the Italian foreign minister, who headed the international commission in Rome for the affairs of Crete, they decried the hostility that certain segments of the Christian population harbored toward them. Bearing the brunt of such antagonism were the smaller numbers of Muslims scattered in the countryside. The petitioners underscored the guarantees of protection that the European coalition had made to the community when its troops replaced the Ottoman soldiers. The petition bearing 104 signatures identified the underlying motive behind anti-Muslim crimes as that of panicking the minority into selling their properties, compelling them to "abandon the country where we were born and raised by our fathers."[58]

The multiple pockets of the Muslim population that were scattered across the countryside lacked the relative security enjoyed by their more numerous coreligionists in the cities. Living in the countryside deprived them of the chance to invoke the protection of European consulates, which urban Muslims often did. If the lack of effective safeguarding by the local administration infused many rural inhabitants, Christian and Muslim alike, with a feeling of insecurity, this anxiety grew more profound in the case of rural Muslims. As suggested earlier by Charalambos Pologeorgis, unresolved conflicts dating to the recent civil war made likelier targets out of Muslims, whose modest population turned them into vulnerable victims. The prospect of taking over or even plundering their property incentivized the offenders. Reporting in June 1906 about the growing assaults on Muslims with the breakdown of public order during the Theriso uprising, the British consul Esme Howard captured the condition of the Muslim peasants well. According to the consul, they constituted "the class whose voices are least heard." They endured intolerable hardships, "sometimes by serious attacks on their lives and property, and sometimes by a systematic policy of pinpricks. The object apparently is always the same: to induce them to sell out at any price and leave the country."[59]

An inventory drawn up by the Italian commander of the Cretan gendarmerie in 1906 sheds further light on the political economy of insecurity, especially in the countryside. The gendarmerie's list estimated the approximate total value of the Muslim property in Crete as 35,138,660 pounds, of which properties valued at 6,150,387 pounds were rented to the Christians and the remaining amount were held by the Muslims. It is important to note that only 32 percent of Muslim properties were located in the three major cities of Iraklio, Hania, and Rethimno. Sixty-eight percent of the total Muslim wealth lay outside of these cities, in an area inhabited by 11,599 people, a figure representing only 35 percent of the overall Muslim population.[60]

With the vast and fertile countryside containing a large amount of Muslim wealth yet hosting a modestly sized Muslim population, the fields of agriculture frequently became crime sites. One April day in 1907, Ali Baroutakis, accompanied by his companion Muharrem Gamalakis, proceeded to a field over whose ownership he had been in conflict with Stilianos Arkhontoulakis. When the two arrived at the field that Ali Baroutakis claimed to be his own, they found Stilianos Arkhontoulakis working the land together with his twenty-year-old son Georgios. At once, the old dispute between them flamed up. Ali asked his companion Muharrem to fetch the village headman, a trusted figure on the matter of land boundaries, to help settle the issue. As Muharrem headed for the village, the father and son attacked Ali, hitting him lethally with spades. When Muharrem returned to the field with the village headman, he immediately reported the crime to the gendarmerie, which apprehended the spade murderers based on the testimonies given by three individuals. At the military tribunal in Iraklio, where the father and son were found guilty of murder, the prosecutor pronounced in his opening address that "in order to understand the motive of the crime it is necessary to know the Cretan character." Desire to control and own land was often unquenchable: "To a Cretan, so great is his love of the soil that, if he sets his heart upon obtaining a plot of land, so deep-rooted is this feeling that nothing will prevent him from committing any crime to accomplish his object."[61]

The strategic significance of safeguarding the minority was also underscored by Eleftherios Venizelos, a key figure in Cretan politics and the future prime minister of Greece. When Venizelos visited Iraklio in 1907 as part of an electoral campaign for the Cretan parliament, he commented on the matter of security, emphasizing its relevance for Crete and beyond. He underscored the importance of making Muslims feel safe "as a patriotic duty not merely because of the assurances given to the Powers with a view to effecting the withdrawal of the international troops." For Venizelos, Crete functioned like a laboratory in terms of ruling over a sizable non-Christian minority. He argued that the governance of this multireligious island would serve as a useful model that an enlarged Greece could imitate in the future.⁶² In a remark that would soon prove prescient when Greece significantly expanded its territory under Venizelos's leadership in the Balkan Wars (1912–13), he stated that Greece would absorb new Muslim communities after a likely extension of its northern borders. If the Cretan government could now inspire safety and confidence among its own Muslim subjects, it would reflect favorably on their coreligionists in the Balkans.⁶³

A year later, in May 1908, a similar argument was echoed in an anonymous article in the Hania daily *Kiryks*, the mouthpiece of the Venizelist party, which frequently published unsigned opinion pieces. The column, likely written by Venizelos himself, acknowledged the apprehension that many Muslims felt about the scheduled withdrawal of European troops from Crete, a move widely perceived to bring it one more step closer to a union with Greece. Venizelos sought to assuage the fears of his Muslim co-islanders. He argued that the reason for "the savage antagonism" that pitted the two communities against one another lay not in religious but in political differences between them. He sought to assure the minority of the good intentions of both Cretan and Greek governments. Venizelos emphasized that "the supreme national interest" (*yperteron ethnikon symferon*) of the Christians was to prove that, in Crete under Greek administration, Muslims would enjoy security and full equality with the majority.⁶⁴

Evicting Muslims, Enclosing Lepers

Throughout the period of autonomy, various notable public figures perceived a link between fair treatment of the Muslim minority and the general interests of the country. Given the multiple declarations about such a connection, a mass expropriation and eviction from the early 1900s presents a confounding case. The heart of the controversial matter lay on the islet of Spinalonga, situated a stone's throw from the northeastern coast of Crete. Before the civil war, this tiny piece of insular land had boasted an exclusively Muslim population of around 1,800, all residing within the confines of a Venetian fortress.⁶⁵ In 1903, the government initiated the expropriation of the properties of the Spinalongans, setting off the process of evacuating the remaining 330 of them. It proceeded to relocate all the lepers of Crete to Spinalonga.⁶⁶ Around the time of repurposing the islet into a leper colony, 378 people were estimated to be carrying the infection throughout Crete.[67]

Engaged in fishing, small-scale trade, and agriculture along the opposite coastline, the inhabitants of Spinalonga petitioned the Cretan government in 1903, pleading the authorities to rescind the decision of expropriation. The petitioners referred to the islet's remaining seventy-five families as the still-standing members of a centuries-old population, a great part of which had emigrated to the towns in Crete and Asia Minor in the aftermath of the civil war. They pointed out that the policy of expropriation and ensuing expulsion from their native land would lead to the inevitable dissolution of a modest yet long-established community.[68] The administration, however, appeared determined to finalize its policy. Obliged to compensate for the expropriated possessions, the government charged the prefect of the Lasithi province and a magistrate with the assessment of the value of property owned by the Spinalongans. The commission determined the amount of compensation as 13,005 francs, based on the estimated value of the total property of Spinalonga Muslims. This figure, however, made up only about 10 percent of the total claims, amounting to 127,750 francs.[69]

Taken aback by the low indemnity figure, the Spinalongans began the laborious process of seeking a fair sum for the islet village turned into a leper asylum. Five representatives of the community approached the French authorities first. The easternmost provinces of Crete, of which Lasithi was part, had fallen under the supervision of France according to the arrangement among the four-state European coalition. They paid a visit to the French vice-consul in Iraklio in October 1904, informing him of the notice they had received from the prefect of Lasithi, which had ordered them to evacuate Spinalonga in fifteen days. The directive from the prefect had arrived with a menacing warning that those failing to depart from the islet within the prescribed timeline would be considered part of the leper colony. They would be completely walled off from the outside world. Accusing the administration of what they believed to be a glaring underestimation of the value of their holdings, the claimants told the French vice-consul that they would take the first boat to Hania to lodge a complaint with the consular body.[70]

In response to the petition that the Spinalongans submitted to the consular body, the European consuls sent a collective note to Cretan authorities. In its reply the Ministry of Interior defended the legality of the expropriation, adding that the petitioners retained the right to sue the government if they were dissatisfied with the amount of indemnity. In his report to the British foreign secretary, the consul Esme Howard stressed the difficulty, if not impossibility, for the exiled Spinalongans, most of them poor fishermen, to pursue a legal action against the state. He wrote that the villagers had never accepted the sum of 13,005 francs placed at an Iraklio bank for their disposal and that the matter had lain dormant until recently when the Spinalongans had once again approached the consuls. While the Cretan government argued that the case fell within its purview alone, the British consul thought otherwise. For Esme Howard, the matter also concerned the consuls because the European powers had undertaken the task of protecting the interests of Crete's Muslim minority.[71]

As the consuls began discussions with the Cretan government to put together a commission of inquiry for reappraising the value of Spinalongans' properties, the displaced Muslims brought their case before the court of first instance in Lasithi. A commission of experts appointed by the court carried out an examination in Spinalonga. The resulting court verdict delivered in July 1906 awarded the claimants an indemnity of 35,136 francs, which represented only about 27 percent of what they had demanded. In the same month, the government lodged its own appeal, which the court of appeal in Hania accepted in December 1906, reducing the amount of indemnity to 11,509 francs.[72]

During this complicated legal process, the exiled Spinalongans submitted scores of petitions to French diplomatic authorities. For instance, Hasan Seyidakis, a Spinalongan residing in Iraklio, appealed to the commander of French troops of occupation in eastern Crete. In his petition from July 1906, Seyidakis described himself as a merchant well established in his native Spinalonga until he and his family were expelled from the islet. Not only were his house and store expropriated, but he was also forced to leave behind some of his furniture and merchandise, leaving him with a total loss of 4,300 francs. Seyidakis concluded his petition by noting that the government's policy of expropriation and expulsion made him lose his clientele, reducing a modest yet successful trader to a life of misery as a fishmonger in the streets of Iraklio.[73]

Reasoning that an equitable amount of indemnity fell somewhere between 35,136 francs, the figure set by the court in July 1906, and 127,750

Adaptability in Vulnerability 105

francs, the amount claimed by the Spinalongans, the French authorities launched their own investigation on the islet. On a late August day in 1906, Lucien Maurouard, the consul general of France, and Cyril Amiel, the commander of French troops in eastern Crete, headed to Spinalonga in the company of two French officers (figure 18). On the same boat also sailed two lawyers hired by the thirteen former residents of the islet. In the resulting report, Lucien Maurouard pointed out that the commission conducted its investigation on the basis of the estimated condition of the buildings in 1904, the year when the Spinalongans were expelled from the islet. This task was made difficult by the damage that Spinalonga's current inhabitants of around two hundred lepers had inflicted on the properties since then. Walled off from the rest of the world, the lepers extracted all the wood they could from the beams, door and window frames, and lintels of the unoccupied houses for personal use or to sell to smugglers. While attempt-

FIGURE 18. A view of Spinalonga as seen from the French torpedo boat *Flèche*, which carried the commission of inquiry to the islet. Part of the leper colony on the shore curiously awaits the surprise visitors, 1906. Source: French Foreign Ministry Archives in Nantes, 328 PO/1/148.

ing to come up with a fair assessment, the commission disregarded the claims by some of the former residents regarding financial injuries due to the loss of business connections and the means of livelihood. Although the commission acknowledged the legitimacy of such arguments, Maurouard noted that its limited expertise would prevent accurate calculations. The report concluded that the state owed the Spinalongans an indemnity of 106,043 francs. According to the list that contained the information about 284 property owners from Spinalonga, only 74 claimants resided in Crete as of 1906. They inhabited the parts of its eastern coast not too far from Spinalonga. The majority, however, had already emigrated farther afield: 116 to the island of Kos; 90 to Asia Minor, many among them to Bodrum; 2 to Rhodes; and 2 to Libya.[74]

Although the Ottoman defeat in the Balkan Wars (1912–13) settled the Crete question once and for all, the Spinalonga question still lacked closure. Despite numerous complaints and reports by the parties involved in the matter of expropriation and indemnity, the payment of compensation never materialized. In 1918, twelve years after the inquiry of the commission headed by Lucien Maurouard, a report sent to the French mission in Athens outlined the latest in the Spinalonga saga. In it, the French vice-consul in Hania noted that the European consuls had intervened in the protracted case in June 1914 and ordered the withdrawal of 106,043 francs from the Bank of Crete to be paid as indemnity to the Spinalongans. The funds were transferred to the register of the Italian Post in Hania. Because of the closure of the postal branch in Crete, they were placed with the Italian Ministry of Post and Telegraph in Rome, most of whose clerks happened to be on a summer leave of absence, delaying the examination of the indemnities until the fall. With the rapid escalation of World War I, however, the issue of compensating the poor inhabitants of a distant islet for their losses proved too minor of a concern for the European powers caught up in a continent-wide conflagration.[75] In terms of numbers, the expulsion of more than three hundred individuals from Spinalonga and the expropriation of their properties affected only a small fraction of Crete's Muslim population. Still, this is a telling episode that emblematizes the unsettling impact of an official policy on a fragile minority, particularly its poorer subsection living outside of larger towns in Crete.[76]

In his memoirs, Prince George, the high commissioner in Crete until 1906, recounted that Crete's leper community had historically inhabited the outlying neighborhoods of towns and cities. They formed settlements known as *meskinies* (leper villages, from Turkish *miskin*) in which they lived under unhygienic conditions. For the autonomous regime, the establishment of a leper asylum in Spinalonga signified more than a mere measure of public health. By confining the lepers from all around Crete to an islet, after expelling its long-established Muslim community, the government also sought a break with the Ottoman past. For the formulators of this policy, the complete isolation of the infected stood in sharp relief to the approach of the former regime. Prince George, who traced his noble lineage to Denmark, where his father George I had been a Danish prince prior to his consecration as the king of Greece in 1863, envisioned Crete as a polity that would be administered according to European principles of governance. The realm of public health was no exception.[77]

Such a vision regarding the creation of a leper colony had surfaced as early as the summer of 1898, when the European great powers had been seriously considering Prince George to take on the mantle of high commissioner. At that time, the Greek prince happened to be in Copenhagen visiting his grandparents. Professor Edvard Ehlers, a Danish dermatologist serving as the general secretary of the International Committee for the Prevention and Treatment of Leprosy, contacted the prince to express his desire to conduct research on leprosy in Crete, adding that a wealthy German doctor named Otto Cahnheim had earmarked a large fund to be used in a scientific study of the disease. Prof. Ehlers thought that Crete, with a high number of infections, would make a suitable laboratory for the investigation into the nature of leprosy.[78] Prince George's engagement with a European medical network adds more context to the establishment of a leper colony in Spinalonga.[79] Gone with the forcible transfer of lepers into Spinalonga and expulsion of its native residents were two social features of the long Ottoman presence in Crete: relatively unhindered existence of lepers in the vicinity of urban areas and an exclusively Muslim presence in an area with clearly set boundaries. In the case of Spinalonga, the autonomous regime achieved the former's isolation through the latter's expulsion.

FOUR

"CRETE OR DEATH"

Sounds of Protest in the Ottoman Empire

Protests triggered by the Cretan administration's declaration of union with Greece in October 1908 began to spread to all corners of the empire in early 1909. They peaked in the spring of 1910 in response to an explosive political move on the island: determined to see Crete united with Mother Greece, Christian members of the Cretan Assembly took a pledge of allegiance to the king of Greece. Against such a backdrop, a long opinion piece appeared in a June 1910 issue of *Le Jeune Turc*, a French-language daily from Istanbul.[1] Penned by *Giridi* (Cretan) Ahmed Saki (b. 1876, Rethimno), a journalist, lawyer, and legal scholar based in the capital, the article caught the attention of the Greek ambassador. He attached a clipping of the newspaper to his report sent to Athens. In the article, Ahmed Saki pointed out that "in the wake of the proclamation of our cherished constitution [July 1908], the Ottomans, saved from the tyrannical grip of a nefarious regime of absolutism," had felt hopeful for a better future. But two consecutive blows, Austria-Hungary's annexation of Bosnia-Herzegovina and Bulgaria's declaration of independence, had shattered the facade of optimism. They had also provoked a profound mistrust of the Western powers, discrediting their much-touted espousal of justice and sovereign rights of states. As deep of a scar as these incidents had opened in the Ottoman psyche, Saki considered them a wake-up call: "Awoken from a years-long lethargy, the

Ottomans realized that they cannot let Crete face a similar fate and become yet another territory to be lost for the weakness of the despotic [Hamidian] regime."[2]

What Ahmed Saki referred to was the Cretan government's declaration of union with Greece, announced a day after Austria-Hungary's annexation of Bosnia-Herzegovina on 6 October 1908 and two days after Bulgaria's proclamation of independence. He condemned Crete's government both for infringing on the empire's sovereign rights and for mistreating the island's Muslim minority. The Ottomans, the lawyer-journalist protested, demanded the recognition of their inviolable rights over Crete. They "desire to live, make progress, and march forward enjoying the exact same rights and privileges as other [Western] nations. . . . This is the psychology of the Ottoman nation."[3]

Partly financed by the Zionist Organization, *Le Jeune Turc* was edited by Sami (Shmuel) Hochberg, Vladimir (Ze'ev) Jabotinsky, and Celal Nuri. It championed the CUP. The newspaper's Jewish founders and editors promoted Zionism as an ideology supportive of Ottomanism, not as a separatist movement advocating for an independent Jewish homeland in Palestine. A popular publication, *Le Jeune Turc* sold more than ten thousand daily copies around the time Ahmed Saki's piece appeared in June 1910.[4] Such a relatively high circulation figure explains why his article drew the Greek ambassador's attention.[5] *Le Jeune Turc* became a conduit that carried Unionist worldviews to the literate public, especially to those not proficient in Turkish. Celal Nuri and Ahmed Saki, both tracing their roots to Crete, played instrumental roles in this regard, the former as editor and the latter as contributor. Moreover, Saki sought to strengthen the existing bonds between the island and the empire. In his capacity as the representative of the Muslim community of his native Rethimno, he kept the Ottomans abreast of Cretan affairs through his public appearances.[6]

The network within which these two personalities operated transcended the confines of a popular newspaper. Both Celal Nuri and Ahmed Saki belonged to a coterie of refugee activists based in Istanbul, who since late 1908 had been raising awareness about their native Crete through articles, conferences, and speeches at rallies. The work of this network is critical to understanding how the island emerged as one of the most burning topics in the public space from late 1908 onward. The pioneering activism of this group of displaced individuals nurtured a culture of protest in the postrevolutionary empire. They helped form a widespread perception of their native island in terms of "a matter of life and death."[7]

This chapter is structured in two parts, the first focusing on Istanbul and the second on the provinces. In the first section I zero in on a network of Cretan public figures in the capital. They include journalists, writers, and politicians who crafted a lexicon with which they introduced their native island to the broader population as a space indispensable for the empire's integrity. The core of what I call *Crete-speak* infused the script of mass rallies throughout the empire. This was an emotive discourse shaped by historical and political associations with the island. It depicted Crete as a site marked by violence, enshrined in the example of Ottoman soldiers martyred during its protracted conquest in the seventeenth century and decried in the case of atrocities against Muslim civilians in contemporary episodes of conflict. Some of the aspects of Crete-speak predated 1908, with antecedents that can be traced at least to the 1890s.[8] During the civil war of that decade multiple Young Turk publications in exile deployed an emotional language to cover the strife.[9] Under the heavy lid of Hamidian censorship on Cretan affairs, however, such coverage reached only a restricted readership. The novelty after 1908, therefore, lies, not in the uniqueness of the rhetoric forged, but in the opening of previously unavailable channels for its dissemination well beyond exilic and underground circles.

In rendering Crete relatable to other Ottomans, the Istanbul-based group of activists formulated a script highlighting the sacrifices at the time of its conquest in the seventeenth century and underscoring its geostrategic importance in the twentieth. If the fraught past of the island, laced with the blood of Muslim Ottoman martyrs, imbued it with symbolism, its strategic location in the Mediterranean made it indispensable for an empire looking to rejuvenate its navy.[10] The diasporic network of Cretan activists in Istanbul often used relatively unhindered press and increasingly politicized conference halls to address literate audiences. But their public outreach transcended the narrower bounds of largely bourgeois sites. They took a leading role in the organization of a massive Istanbul demonstration in early 1909. With the participation of tens of thousands of protesters, it passed down in history as the largest organized rally in the late Ottoman Empire. It also provided a blueprint for mass gatherings that proliferated farther afield in the following months.

After a brief discussion of this unprecedented event I explore the deeds of refugee protesters from less privileged social classes. This part of the chapter turns the spotlight onto the provinces. If figures like Ahmed Saki and Celal Nuri made up the intellectual dimension of a diasporic protest movement, mostly anonymous Cretans constituted its popular corps. Archival records documented their deeds in the streets but often omitted their names. Yet although their names are mostly absent in historical documents, I posit that it is still possible to locate the signs of their sonorous presence in the empire's streets and squares. I do this by tracing the characteristic sounds of Ottoman protest-scape to foreground the nonelite but resonant voices. A sonic approach allows for imagining how unnamed demonstrators experienced mass gatherings in their local settings. Sound in the form of speeches, ovation, and slogans, and sight with the pervasiveness of red, both materially through Ottoman flags and fezzes and figuratively through the imagery of blood, characterized the sensory landscape of most Crete rallies. I lend an ear to a wide array of textual sources in addition to many petitions stored in the Ottoman Archives. The reports by Austro-Hungarian, British, French, Greek, and Italian diplomats posted across the eastern Mediterranean yield fresh insights into the popular atmosphere in towns and cities. The coverage of open-air meetings in the multilingual Ottoman press illustrates the interplay between the printed word and street actions from early 1909 through 1911.

At its heart, this chapter intervenes in the study of crowds and mass politics by reflecting on soundscapes of protest. Foregrounding sensory clues in historical documents betokens more than a methodological novelty in the examination of mass protest. Perhaps the greatest analytical merit of a sensory approach lies in its potential to center quotidian acts of gathering in crowds rather than relatively abstract concepts such as nationalism. The scrutiny of the sensory dimensions of protest lays bare how simple acts of shouting slogans and insults undergirded a mass movement. In doing so, it foregrounds the experiences of people in the streets and squares of an empire during a transformative period in its history.

Scholars have written extensively about the activism of the displaced in late Ottoman history through the examples of emigrants from the Russian Empire.[11] A mainland emphasis in the historiography of migration and its attendant transformations has stimulated a robust body of work scrutinizing the linkages between continuous masses of land. In those accounts, the émigrés and refugees travel on railway tracks or on foot. Peregrinations by sea, on relatively comfortable steamships for some and in the cramped steerage deck of ships for most, have received far less attention.[12] This chapter is meant to serve as a reminder of the long history of the Mediterranean and its maritime routes in the cartographies of displacement. It fills a void in the historiography on displacement and activism by featuring an underexplored refugee community from an island. I posit that the examination of a displaced group of middle-class activists, held together by common ties to Crete, illuminates the making of diasporic networks in the late Ottoman Empire. More than filling a gap, this chapter also contributes to the scholarship, which has largely drawn on the perspectives of literate subjects of history. I do this by underscoring the activism of unnamed protesters in a cross section of hundreds of rallies about Crete throughout the Ottoman Empire. I argue that Crete-speak, largely forged in Istanbul, echoed in multiple venues of mass assembly from the Balkans to the Levant. By assigning origin to an empire-wide movement of protest, I acknowledge the key roles of middle-class, mostly intellectual, activists both in raising awareness and in shaping the terms of Crete-speak. I do, however, eschew imagining the provinces in terms of a center-periphery divide that reifies a connected imperial space into detachable constructs. An apt image here is that of an echo rippling from the capital through provinces, highlighting how Istanbul-born Crete-speak was appropriated according to local dynamics.

In the discussion of street protests I especially focus on the areas, such as the Izmir region and Asia Minor, that became new homes to tens of thousands of peasants and urban poor dislocated from Crete around the turn of the twentieth century. I also address other locales with no refugee settlements to underscore the breadth of popular mobilization. Crete rallies drew people from diverse walks of life. In reporting these events, however, European observers often singled out the prominence of lower-class Ottomans at the sites of assembly. Frequently taking a derogatory tone, such an emphasis illustrates their protest-phobic perceptions of popular classes. But such bias is at the same time illuminating for demonstrating the scope of activism beyond the narrower bounds of literate circles. Continuous coverage of mass gatherings by the press and thousands of petitions telegraphed from small towns to the capital offer further evidence of the protest movement's social dynamics. The theme of protest-phobia constitutes part of my discussion in this chapter and continues in the next, which deals with the boycott movement against Greece.

Ties Beyond the Sea: A Network of Islander Refugee Literati in Istanbul

On 5 January 1909, around two hundred people gathered in the convention hall of the school of law in Istanbul, half an hour's walk from Sultanahmed Square, where a massive Crete demonstration would be staged several days later.[13] The meeting was presided over by Mustafa Nuri, a senator and minister of the treasury. Among high-profile attendees were Edhem Pasha, a senator and legendary commander of armies on the Thessalian plain during the 1897 war against Greece, and Ali Galib, minister of post and telegraph and ambassador to Greece in the early 1890s. These individuals came together with the goal of weighing the pros and cons of possible reactions to the Cretan government's declaration of *enosis* (union) with Greece on 7 October 1908. With the recent example of an effective boycott against Austria-Hungary in mind, economic warfare waged in response to that empire's annexation of Bosnia-Herzegovina, some participants proposed a similar course of action against Greece. Deeming an aggressive strategy a premature option for the time being, the group instead reached a consensus on mounting a large rally in Sultanahmed Square. Several of its members were tasked to prepare for the event. Although this would not be the first Crete-related public demonstration in response to the declaration of *enosis*, its organizers intended it to be the largest that the empire had thus far seen.[14]

What made this meeting at the school of law especially conspicuous was the composition of its attendees. Nine among them hailed from relatively well-off families rooted in Crete's three principal cities: Hania, Iraklio, and Rethimno. Chairing the meeting as the most senior member, Mustafa Nuri (b. 1851, Iraklio) brought with him years of gubernatorial experience in various Ottoman provinces.[15] Among the other participants was his son, Celal Nuri (b. 1881, Gallipoli), an extraordinarily prolific writer and journalist. He also had a knack for public speaking, as indicated by the address he would deliver before thousands of protesters in the Sultanahmed rally four days later.[16] Another attendee, his cousin Yusuf Razi (b. 1870, Hania), worked for the illustrated periodicals *Resimli Kitap* (Illustrated Book) and *Şehbal* (Wing Feather). With a near-native fluency in French, he was Turkey correspondent of the famous Paris magazine *L'Illustration*. An engineer by training, he became known for his intimate appreciation for music and fine arts, probably thanks to the inspiration of his mother Leyla Saz, an acclaimed poet and musician.[17]

Two of the participants came from the ranks of the recently opened parliament. Ahmed Nesimi (b. 1876, Hania) was a deputy for Istanbul who went on to become a prominent member of the CUP. He reached the apex of his political career when he became the last Unionist minister of foreign affairs, serving from February 1917 to October 1918.[18] The other parliamentarian was Mehmed Ali (b. 1876, Iraklio), representative of Samsun. Another notable attendee was Mehmed Aziz Kavurzade (b. 1866, Hania), a distinguished legal scholar of his generation, renowned especially for his expertise in criminal law. He was not a stranger to the venue of the assembly, for he taught in the school of law.[19] And Ahmed Cevad (b. 1876, Rethimno), with a dazzlingly prolific publishing career lasting into the 1960s, was someone with many hats. He was a writer, journalist, educator, and recent transplant to Istanbul from Crete, where he had championed the rights of the Muslim minority.[20] During the meeting, Ali Zeki (b. ca. 1860s–1870s, Crete), who worked as a correspondent with the influential daily *Tanin*, read out the telegrams sent to that newspaper from Nazilli and Tekfurdağı, which communicated the inhabitants' concerns over Crete's future.[21]

A trio within this Istanbul-based Cretan contingent merit special recognition for their efforts in making Crete a legible geography for the public during late 1908 and early 1909. A brief elaboration on the roles played by Ali Zeki, Ahmed Cevad, and Mustafa Nuri is in order before I examine, in the second part of this chapter, the sounds rising from the streets and squares.

Two days after the assembly that was held in early January 1909 in the school of law, an evening conference took place in the same venue with the participation of more than a thousand people. This large congregation included students, representatives of multiple political associations, and journalists. The first speaker, Ali Zeki, gave the audience a crash course on the recent history of Crete. Covering the period from the time of European occupation in the 1890s to the present, he recounted the most important developments on the island. At the close of his informative lecture, he described Crete as an autonomous province with special administrative privileges (*eyalet-i mümtaze*) and an inseparable part of the empire, eliciting the enthusiastic applause of the audience.[22] A version of the verbal narrative garnished with Ali Zeki's personal reflections had previously appeared in print. From mid-December 1908 to early 1909, he had published in *Tanin* a four-part series of articles about Cretan history.[23] He had begun his installments by underlining the significance of publicizing the affairs of Crete for making the Ottomans mindful of its recent past. He provided a dramatic recounting of Crete's last decade as a time of injustice for its much-diminished Muslim population. In so doing, not only did Ali Zeki portray the condition of his fellow islanders in the bleakest terms, he also indicted the Hamidian regime for preventing their plight from being communicated to the Ottoman public.[24]

Ali Zeki remains a rather obscure figure, of whom little biographical details are known. Few literary specialists have written about him as a writer of short stories and novels.[25] The impact he left in politics is arguably deeper than the one in literature. That aspect of his life too remains unexplored. Particularly important here is his contribution to a growing anti-Greek discourse among CUP circles after 1908. Fluent in Greek, like other Cretan Muslims, Ali Zeki put his islander identity into invaluable service of *Tanin*. For this leading Unionist daily, he regularly provided translations from the Greek Ottoman press, focusing on articles critical of the CUP. His formative role was recognized by the famous writer Abdülhak Şinasi (Hisar) in 1921 when he paid homage to Ali Zeki in the literary criticism column of the magazine *Dergah* (Salon). Writing at the time of Greece's occupation of western Anatolia, Abdülhak Şinasi highlighted the political significance of Ali Zeki's translations for Turks ignorant of Greek: "Our naïve and well-meaning press forever remained oblivious of the scornfully antagonistic tone and content of Greek newspapers and magazines published in the capital and in the provinces." Noting the popularity of *Tanin* especially among military officers, he emphasized its influence to conclude that "Ali Zeki Bey helped lift the veil that covered our eyes."[26]

After this brief profile of a lesser-known but key figure, let us now revisit the evening conference at the school of law in January 1909. Following Ali Zeki's lecture on the recent past of Crete, Ahmed Cevad delivered an exposition of the diplomatic crisis that the island had triggered. He addressed the antecedents and current state of the Crete question. In his comprehensive account covering the island's history from the Venetian period onward, he underscored the immeasurable amount of martyrs' blood shed during its conquest, which lasted longer than a quarter century. His occasionally emotional speech was interrupted several times by a storm of applause from the audience. Using "Muslim" and "Turkish" interchangeably in identifying Crete's minority population, Ahmed Cevad dwelled on various "calamities and atrocities" that befell the Turks from 1896 onward.

Those sorrowful incidents demonstrated how misguided the Europeans were in viewing "Turks as cruel and bloodthirsty and Greeks as wronged and oppressed." The violence that intensified during the mid-1890s had caused the Muslim population of Crete to diminish to forty thousand, a sharp drop from its pre–civil war figure of one hundred thousand.[27]

"Conveyor" is an apt descriptor for Ahmed Cevad, considering how invested he was in the affairs of his native island and how he conveyed the condition of his people to the Ottoman public. When the organizers of the Istanbul rally in January 1909 proceeded to the Sublime Porte, it was Ahmed Cevad who conveyed the appreciation of his fellow islanders by reading out their telegram. Earlier, while in Crete after his 1905 escape from Libyan exile, a banishment endured in the company of several other Young Turks such as Yusuf Akçura, he often served as a conveyor of popular petitions, interceding on several occasions with French and Russian consuls for aggrieved Muslims.[28] The role of a conveyor held true beyond his ties with Crete. During the 1910s he published a great number of linguistic materials, some used as textbooks, to convey the grammar rules of Turkish, French, and Persian to school-age children. With his *Kırmızı Siyah Kitap* (The Red and Black Book), a groundbreaking book published in 1913, he became the conveyor of atrocity propaganda, communicating the grim details of a catastrophe that had befallen the Balkan Muslims.

With an article in a November 1908 issue of *Tanin*, Celal Nuri's father, Mustafa Nuri, had prefigured some of the themes in the speeches that Ali Zeki and Ahmed Cevad delivered at the school of law. Titled "The Cry of Muslim Cretans," Mustafa Nuri's piece communicated both the incrimination of the Hamidian administration (a theme addressed by Ali Zeki) and the misery of the Muslim islanders (a subject covered by Ahmed Cevad).[29] For Mustafa Nuri, who would begin to fill a seat in the senate as of December 1908, the history of his native island must have put in sharp relief the contrast between the seventeenth-century conquerors and the Hamidian regime.[30] The former had sacrificed their lives to make Crete Ottoman. The latter, on the other hand, with tyrannical indifference and cowardice, had abandoned Crete's Muslims, who were displaced and dispossessed for being failed by the government. Mustafa Nuri called Muslim Cretans "bloodstained victims" of the tragedy they endured under the tyranny of the Hamidian regime. Nevertheless, in a demonstration of abnegation and unselfishness, they overlooked "the ears callous to their resounding cries, the hands indifferent to their pleas for help, and the tongues silent of consoling words." In the remainder of his article Mustafa Nuri described another tyranny, this time at the hands of the Cretan government. He exclaimed that this could never be ignored or forgotten. Writing on behalf of all Muslim Cretans, he remarked that they would now submit to the attention of the public "the outcry of [our] protest and the things that [we] could neither pronounce nor write when [our] mouths were shut and pens bound."[31]

Mustafa Nuri's words heralded the outpouring of demonstrators who would soon begin to occupy town squares in the provinces with cries of "Crete or Death." Before looking into such scenes, I discuss the enormous Istanbul rally in January 1909, the largest organized one in late Ottoman history, prior to the famous Sultanahmed examples in 1919 against the Allied occupation of the empire.[32] This massive event in Istanbul offered a model for hundreds of mass gatherings throughout the empire from early 1909 through 1911.

An Organization to Inspire, a Rally to Remember

On the second Saturday of 1909, the people of Istanbul woke up to a morning that progressed into a day abuzz with crowds heading toward the city's largest square. The sun was shining brightly. As if to bless the masses for evincing a "lofty emotion of patriotism," mused the poet Halil Nihad, it warmed the dead of winter into a day reminiscent of spring.[33] From early in the morning, people throughout the environs of the capital, from the tranquil Princes' Islands to picturesque Bosphorus villages, proceeded to Sultanahmed Square, adjoining the seat of the parliament. Ottoman flags waving above the befezzed heads imaginably painted in red the site of assembly, the area known as the Hippodrome during Roman times (figure 19).[34] The report that the Greek ambassador transmitted to Athens estimated the number of demonstrators around fifteen thousand, likely a downplayed figure.[35] Describing the scene as "a real human sea" (*une véritable mer humaine*), the French-language daily *Stamboul* (Istanbul) wrote that it was impossible to make an exact count of the crowd, which reached at least twenty-five thousand.[36] The Austro-Hungarian ambassador gave no numerical information in his dispatch to Vienna but noted a huge mass of protesters. He went on to add that "Crete stands much closer to the Turkish heart than Bosnia and Eastern Rumelia," an underlined remark in ref-

FIGURE 19. A scene from the Crete rally in Istanbul's Sultanahmed Square. Source: *Servet-i Fünun* (The Wealth of Sciences), 28 January 1909 (15 Kanunusani 1324).

erence to the regions recently annexed by Austria-Hungary and Bulgaria, respectively.[37]

In October 1908, the autonomous government of Crete, an island officially under Ottoman suzerainty yet integrated into Greece in multiple ways, declared *enosis* (union) with Athens. This act was not recognized by the guarantor powers that had been overseeing the island's affairs for the past decade, namely Britain, France, Italy, and Russia. Nevertheless, it thrust the Crete question into the public eye in the Ottoman Empire. When the inhabitants of Istanbul gathered for protest in January 1909, the island's fate was still hanging in the balance. The crowd that assembled in the city's largest square heard the first speech from Mahruki Cafer Bey, a high-ranking civil servant. Describing Crete as an inseparable part of the empire, he emphasized the large number of troops who had perished during the long war with the Venetians in the mid-seventeenth century. He reminded the demonstrators, who waved red flags and punctuated his speech with storms of applause, that "every one of us certainly counts among our ancestors someone whose life was sacrificed for Crete."[38] Electrifying his address were the loud cries rising from the crowd that declared, "Crete belongs to Ottomans!"[39] In an emotional address Celal Nuri carried on the theme of martyrdom, summoning the memories of the countless martyrs from its conquest, which had lasted for a quarter century from 1645 to 1669. Their souls, Celal Nuri exclaimed, gathered above the massive crowd as though menacing to haunt them if the Ottomans acted like prodigal sons squandering a precious inheritance instead of righteous heirs.[40]

The planning for this rally sheds light on how displacement fueled activism in the late Ottoman Empire. It also indicates intergroup solidarities among refugees. One day before the demonstration, Rumeli Muhacirin-i İslamiyesi Cemiyeti (the Association of Rumelian Muslim Refugees) issued a statement in *Tanin*. It asked all the Muslim Balkan refugees to show up to the event in support of their Cretan coreligionists who had been "subjected to years-long atrocities."[41] At the rally, the representatives of various grassroots associations recounted lamentable stories about those who had fled the territories lost in the Balkans since 1878. Their accounts situated the Cretan ordeal within the broader experience of the displacement and dispossession of Muslims in the Ottoman world.[42] At the close of the demonstration, a segment of the crowd followed the rally's organizing committee to the Sublime Porte, where the grand vizier received its Cretan members. Following the meeting, Mehmed Aziz Kavurzade, a professor of law, thanked, on behalf of all Turkocretans, the crowd waiting in front of the seat of the government.[43] Finally, another Cretan, Ahmed Cevad, read aloud a message of appreciation that his fellow islanders had shared with him.[44]

This mass event in the imperial capital was not a spontaneous gathering but the outcome of meticulous planning by a group of activists. Standing at the helm of that network was a coterie of Cretan personalities, whom I have discussed in the previous section. In preparation to mount a rally, this vocal circle of public figures was aided by the constant front-page coverage of the island affairs in the Ottoman press. In this regard, *Tanin* played a conspicuous role as one of the most influential pro-CUP dailies, to which two Cretans, Ali Zeki and Mustafa Nuri, also contributed. Hüseyin Cahid, a leading member of the CUP, a parliamentarian representing Istanbul, and the editor-in-chief of *Tanin*, remarked how "a patriotic Greek Ottoman deputy" (*hamiyetli bir Rum mebusu*), who had watched the protesters from the windows of the parliament told him: "Come near and observe with pride the fruit of your articles."[45] Obviously, *Tanin* was just one among many other dailies offering steady coverage of the Crete question.[46]

The site of the massive Crete rally stands out for its symbolism as a venue next to the parliament building. The recent reopening of the parliament, after a thirty-year hiatus, signaled a new era of representative politics in the Ottoman Empire. Sounds of the protesting crowds in the square next to it were a reminder for the deputies of their responsibility to serve as the mouthpiece of the population. Indeed, the imagination of the parliament as the voice of the people remained a widespread vision throughout the era of constitutional monarchy. One example among many is provided by a telegram dispatched by the CUP club in Üsküdar, a district on the Asian side of the Bosphorus. Addressed to the chamber of deputies, the telegram identified that institution as vox populi and castigated the Hamidian regime for its "stagnant and deplorable policies" that severed Crete from the "affectionate embrace of the motherland."[47]

The ban on all Crete-related coverage and public assembly during the reign of Abdülhamid II further accentuates the novelty of sounds related to Crete. They were both symbolic, as in the case of the parliament channeling the people's voice, and palpable, as in the example of protesters' cries. Considering the waning of Ottoman sovereignty on the island despite the victorious war against Greece, a factor fueling the Young Turk opposition in exile, the blackout surrounding the Crete question under the Hamidian regime was no surprise. As Hüseyin Cahid remarked in a rather dramatic tone, prior to the 1908 Revolution the Ottomans had had their "eyes shut, ears plugged, tongues tied by the tyrannical government."[48]

Restrictions on the dissemination of accounts of historical events that the Hamidian regime deemed subversive covered school curricula as well.[49] A Unionist parliamentarian from Baghdad and frequent contributor to *Tanin*, Babanzade İsmail Hakkı, indicted the Hamidian regime for teaching Ottoman history in the fashion of presenting a "dull family tree." Bemoaning people's scant familiarity with the empire's rich history, he likened the civic-minded lessons of history to "nourishment of patriotism," of which the previous generations had been starved.[50]

If Crete functioned as a device through which speakers in the mass rallies imparted a patriotic sense of history to ordinary citizens, it also served a similar purpose in more formal settings. A case in point is offered by a prize ceremony that the British consul in Tripoli, Libya, observed in June 1910. In a report to the embassy, the consul communicated his amazement at the speedy progress of a new school, named Mahmud Şevket Pasha, under CUP patronage and the direction of military officer Hayri Efendi. Drawing lively participation from Tripoli's diverse communities, the award ceremony took place in the gardens near the military barracks. Three students showcased the high quality of education they had received through remarkably articulate addresses in Turkish, Arabic, and French. Quizzed by a teacher on history and geography, one of the boys spoke of "an island that is a burning subject of discussion at the present moment." On the blackboard he drew its map from memory and marked the major landmarks of Crete, which he described as an autonomous Ottoman province. Another student talked about its conquest in the seventeenth century. He emphasized the sacrifices of Tripolitan soldiers, suggesting the bonds imagined between the island and Libya. The gathering continued with patriotic songs. After a speech by the school director, it progressed well into the afternoon with a variety of festive activities.[51]

One of the intense crises during the initial years of the postrevolutionary empire, the Crete question occasioned a transformation of Ottomans' relationship with history, especially with places and events obscured by the long shadow of Hamidian censorship. The blackout that stifled any open discussion concerning the island's history gave way to rampant talk from late 1908 onward, be it under the roof of a school or in open-air protests. The uniqueness of Cretan history enabled the fashioning of a language to mobilize the emotions of the Ottomans, particularly those of the Muslim persuasion. Crete's capture in the seventeenth century, representing the final major Ottoman conquest, allowed for crafting a story about former glories. In that protracted war against the Venetians lay a tale of martyrdom and sacrifice. That the major powers of Europe had forced the Sublime Porte to withdraw its troops from the island despite a victorious war against Greece in 1897 reinforced the trope of Western prejudices against the Ottoman state. Finally, the displacement of tens of thousands of Muslims following the establishment of an autonomous regime under European tutelage in 1898 generated multiple accounts of victimhood.

Popular Sounds Echoing in the Ottoman Provinces

On the heels of the massive Istanbul demonstration in early January, a flurry of mass gatherings occurred in the provinces at a pace to justify dubbing the winter of 1909 the season of popular protest. During a later stage of Crete rallies, the newspaper *Stamboul* would pronounce on its front page that "at each intense phase of the Crete question, the provinces have been in a state of resolute agitation, more so than the capital."[52] Although much smaller than the tremendous Istanbul demonstration, provincial rallies showcase how a novel type of mass politics became a regular affair outside the capital, especially thanks to the efforts of the local CUP branches. At this point, it is worth underscoring the novelty of open-air political gatherings in the Ottoman Empire. As Noémi Lévy-Aksu remarks, the Hamidian administration, in power for more than three decades, prohibited popular rallies on political issues, an indication "of the intrusive state intervention into social and private life to which the new regime was expected to put an end."[53] Indeed, the core of the CUP's rhetoric rested on its claim to be the staunchest advocate of the popular will. One of its manifestations was protest rallies swelled by imperial citizens. Seeing that such gatherings were mostly organized with a push, gentle or otherwise, from local CUP branches, these events helped Unionists tap into and boost their skills of mobilization.[54]

The telegrams that rally organizers from various towns sent to *Tanin* are telling examples of the diffusion of a coherent narrative formulated by the Cretan network in Istanbul, a script evocative of violence and sacrifice. In those telegrams published by *Tanin* in January 1909, Ottoman patriots in Gallipoli, for instance, avowed the determination to sacrifice their lives to safeguard Crete. Muslim inhabitants of Lesbos pronounced the impossibility of ceding Crete to Greece so long as "the Mediterranean undulated with the blood of Ottoman martyrs." Another telegram reported an assembly of three thousand inhabitants in the Black Sea town of Inebolu and transmitted the eagerness of the populace to "shed [our] blood to the last drop" for the land "molded by the blood of [our] ancestors."[55]

Active involvement of the Cretans became a routine feature of rallies held in regions hosting sizable communities of the displaced since the late 1890s. Izmir and its environs stood out among such areas with a conspicuous refugee presence. Writing in June 1910, amid an intense bout of protest across the empire, Austro-Hungarian consul August Kral observed that "the agitation against Greece over the Cretan question orchestrated by the Turkish newspapers at the instigation of the Young Turk Committee provoked an extraordinary effervescence among the Muslim population, especially among the Cretan emigrants, who amount to about sixteen thousand souls."[56] Another hosting area for thousands of Cretans was the Libyan littoral, whose proximity to Crete made it one of the main destinations for refugee resettlement around the turn of the twentieth century.[57] In January 1909, during the early phase of Crete protests, the Italian consul in Tripoli detailed a rally with the islanders at the helm. It was led by H. Culchi (*sic*), an erstwhile employee in the Hania branch of Navigazione Generale Italiana, the leading Italian shipping company. The Arab inhabitants of Tripoli also attended the demonstration. A deputation, with Ottoman flags in hand, proceeded to the European consulates and submitted a note of protest. The document evoked the Islamic character of the island by mentioning "all of its soil tinged with the blood of [our] ancestors" and "the decline of the Muslim population from ninety thousand to thirty thousand due to the cruelties of the current Cretan government." The Italian consul noted that a recent issue of an Arabic-language newspaper (*El Kesciaf*) had mentioned the likelihood of starting a boycott against Greece. The local paper based this information on the reporting of Istanbul dailies, hinting at reverberations from the capital, which was seething from the massive Crete rally.[58]

Half a year later, in July 1909, a long article devoted primarily to publicizing the grim scenes of refugee resettlements in Libya appeared in *Siper-i*

Saika-i Hürriyet (Lightning Rod of Liberty) with the title "Cretan Refugees."[59] The Istanbul newspaper, issued under the direction of Ahmed Cevad, whom I discussed in the previous section, spotlighted the plight of Cretan refugees around Benghazi and Derna. It detailed the hardships caused by corrupt state officials' embezzlement of the funds allocated to the displaced. Describing the current misery of Muslim Cretans as "the evil fruit of the depravity of the tyrannical [Hamidian] regime," the article concluded on a hopeful note by assuring its readers of better times ahead. It maintained that the Crete question would be favorably resolved thanks to the effort of "all Ottomans, united together, raising a brave howl of 'Crete or Death' from deep in their hearts." This ardent remark that the anonymous author of the article specifically addressed to "[our] refugee brethren" was more than a mere rhetorical device. "Crete or Death" was indeed the rallying cry that epitomized a protest-scape that an island fostered throughout the empire.[60]

Speeches delivered in mass rallies from the Balkans to the Levant coalesced around several common themes, such as the geopolitical value of Crete to the Ottoman state and the centrality of martyrdom and anti-Muslim violence in its history. Public speakers harangued the crowds on the importance of Crete's commanding position in the Mediterranean and amplified its legacy of martyrdom. At the conclusion of rallies, petitions were telegraphed to various state departments in Istanbul that picked out the main features of speeches. One particular slogan, "Crete or Death," proved ubiquitous among the words of protest, delivered verbally by orators and crowds, or telegraphically by the organizing committees of demonstrations.[61] "No force is powerful enough to erase from our minds and hearts the patriotic rallying cry of 'Crete or Death' [*Ya Ölüm Ya Girit düstur-ı vatanperveranesi*]," the petitioners from Izmir exclaimed after a large demonstration in June 1910. The signatories from the empire's second-largest city included the mayor, the mufti, the chief rabbi, the deputy to the Greek Orthodox bishop, and the head of the Ottoman Navy League. The petition sent from the nearby small town of Seferihisar mentioned that villagers from its environs had joined the townspeople in "raising the gallant cry [*ref-i avaze-i hamaset*] of 'Crete or Death.'" About one hundred miles south in the town of Menteşe, the crowds marched behind the ulama, "holding Ottoman flags and shouting the patriotic slogan [*terane-i vatanperverane*] 'Crete or Death.'"[62]

Although not boasting as prominent a Cretan presence as Izmir or Tripoli, Salonica too resounded with the echoes of Crete-speak. The

French consul stationed in that principal port city of the Balkans reported that every conversation revolved around Crete. He added that the Salonican press, its Turkish-language titles in particular, discussed it at length, often through first-page articles. In an August 1909 dispatch to the embassy in Istanbul, the consul wrote about a rally in Salonica's central Tenth of July Square that drew more than ten thousand people. The event was held on a Saturday, a sabbatical intermission to the busy rhythm of this predominantly Jewish city, known as the Shabatopolis, bustling with commercial and maritime activity.⁶³ After an introduction by the mayor Ismail Hakkı Bey, seven orators took turns to deliver ten-minute speeches in Turkish, Albanian, Bulgarian, Greek, Judeo-Spanish, Serbian, and Romanian, all declaring the resolve to defend the empire's inviolable rights over Crete "to the last drop of their blood." With loud applause the audience responded to the speeches, whose multilingualism conveyed a statement about the unity of the Ottoman peoples. Some among the crowd were heard repeating after the speakers the phrase "We are prepared to die." At the conclusion of the addresses, a young man read aloud various petitions that the inhabitants of nearby towns and villages had telegraphed to express support.⁶⁴

Saadi Lévy's *Journal de Salonique* portrayed the rally enthusiastically. According to its front-page account, around fifteen thousand protesters had crowded the main square of Salonica, where, for days on end, two words had resonated like a refrain in the hearts of its patriotic citizens: *Crete* and *Death*. An hour before the demonstration, people had begun to come in droves into the main square, a huge space, but not large enough to contain the thousands who proceeded there to hear the fiery words of orators. The crowds loudly applauded all the speeches, which occasioned the phrase "Crete or Death." As if to communicate the clamor of that slogan, *Journal de Salonique* featured it in large bold fonts in three different paragraphs within the body of the text that covered the event.⁶⁵

In less than a year, Salonica's Tenth of July Square hosted another mass Crete protest in which various public figures delivered speeches in eight languages. The final address was given by Ismail Hakkı Efendi, a lawyer with Cretan roots, not to be confused with Ismail Hakkı Bey from the August 1909 rally in the same city. Haranguing the crowd in the name of all Muslim Cretans, Ismail Hakkı Efendi pronounced "in a rather sorrowful voice" the collective wish of "forty thousand persecuted Muslims in Crete":

the safeguarding of its ties to the Ottoman state, a message that the spectators received with a mix of applause and tears.⁶⁶

In its coverage of mass demonstrations, which by 1911 had become routine events, *Ahenk* (Harmony), a Turkish-language newspaper from Izmir, observed that every time people heard the word *Crete* they responded at once with "the patriotic and gallant sound of 'Crete or Death'" (*sada-i vatanperverane ve kahramanesi*). *Ahenk* featured this oft-repeated phrase in oversize fonts. A popular strategy of the period, this style recalls *Journal de Salonique*'s similar method of rendering the effect of shouting in the streets on paper.⁶⁷ Two years earlier, *Amaltheia*, a Greek Ottoman daily in Izmir and one of *Ahenk*'s main rivals, had reported about a rally organized by the city's Cretan community. The newspaper underscored the placards held by the protesters, which read "Crete or [Our] Blood."⁶⁸ This was a massive demonstration. The French consul reported that about fifteen thousand Cretans took part in it.⁶⁹

Among the speeches delivered, the Greek-language daily highlighted two: one by a rabbi, likely in Judeo-Spanish, and the other by Emrullah Efendi. The latter called for the expulsion of those Hellenic subjects sowing discord between Turks and Greeks. In the petition sent to the parliament, the protesters expressed determination to sacrifice their blood, children, and families for the island and the empire. *Amaltheia* added that many Jews and some Persian nationals had also attended the rally.⁷⁰

If *Ahenk* and *Journal de Salonique* used larger fonts to translate the sonic nature of rallies onto paper, *Amaltheia*'s editorial strategy brought out the multilingual content of sound in those events. The newspaper printed the phrase "Crete or [Our] Blood" both in Turkish with Greek letters and in Greek translation. It remains elusive whether the demonstrators inscribed the placards and raised their cries in Greek or Turkish, as the refugee community was largely constituted by native speakers of Greek who by this time were likely conversant in Turkish too. One thing is certain, though: openly anti-Greece, and occasionally also anti-Greek, words and sounds pervading the organized open-air assemblies were a novel phenomenon in Izmir. In her recent work on popular politics in Jordan, Jillian Schwedler underscores the core feature of protest as "people assembling in public to express some form of claim-making." I argue that this interpretation is applicable to the Ottoman case beyond the streets and allows for reimagining textual sources as sites of claim-making.⁷¹ Not only the Cretan protesters in Izmir's main square but also the single Turkish sentence in the *Amaltheia* article can be seen in terms of claim-making. Occupying several lines as if to interlope on the page of a prominent Greek-language daily, the chant "Crete or [Our] Blood" makes a claim on its pages. And in the streets where it was chanted, this intimidating slogan was perceived by many as a sonic interloper in Belle Époque Izmir, a city strongly marked by Greekness.[72]

The coverage of popular rallies by the two rival newspapers of Izmir in 1909 and 1911 leaves no uncertainty as to what became the typical repertoire of these events in this major port city. It is pertinent to recall here Ziad Fahmy's suggestion to heed latent sounds in textual and visual materials, which, if assessed critically, "can be as useful in reimagining some of the lost soundscapes of the past."[73] As shown in figures 20, 21, and 22, the editorial strategies to transmit sound in print within the Ottoman context point to the significance of Fahmy's remark about auditory clues in deceptively soundproof sources.

In addition to keeping the public up to date on the affairs of Crete, provincial newspapers notified readers of the rallies near them.[74] In reference to both the intense press coverage and continuous demonstrations, an editorial in *Yeni Edirne* noted in May 1910 that "everything that needs to be said about Crete has already been said, which in no way means that we will keep silent now. On the contrary, we will speak, nay, raise an outcry."[75] Notices posted in central locations functioned as neighborhood-level channels to relay announcements of open-air meetings to the townspeople. But perhaps more effective heralds than textual signs were town criers traversing the streets to proclaim important events to the population.[76] Their cries, amplified by the din of their drums, added to an auditory environment largely shaped by what I call the summoning Ottoman sound marks, including the *adhan* (Islamic call to prayer) and church bells that coexisted in most towns. In reporting on protest rallies, European diplomatic agents frequently mentioned the broadcasting function of the street crier, identifying him as a key figure in popular mobilization. For instance, in August 1909 the Portuguese consulate in Aleppo informed the Italian embassy in Istanbul of a Crete rally in that city. Its report highlighted that the local CUP branch tasked a street crier with summoning the population to the grand square by the medieval citadel.[77] A month later, the Italian consul in Benghazi reported that about six hundred Cretan refugees and a thousand Arabs answered the call of the street crier for a rally organized by

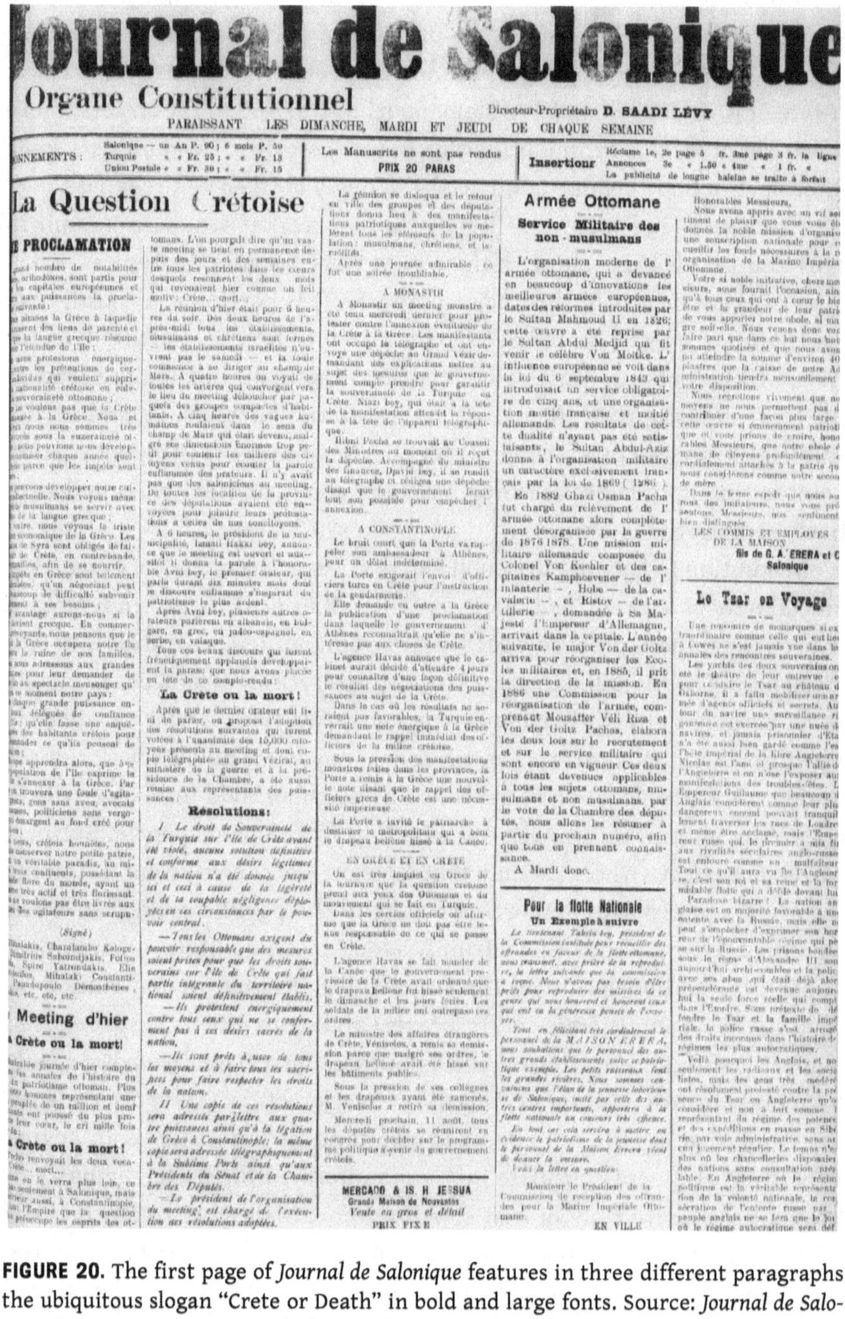

Journal de Salonique

Organe Constitutionnel

Directeur-Propriétaire D. SAADI LÉVY

PARAISSANT LES DIMANCHE, MARDI ET JEUDI DE CHAQUE SEMAINE

Les Manuscrits ne sont pas rendus

PRIX 20 PARAS

La Question Crétoise

PROCLAMATION

Meeting d'hier

La Crète ou la mort!

La Crète ou la mort!

La Crète ou la mort!

Résolutions:

A MONASTIR

A CONSTANTINOPLE

EN GRÈCE ET EN CRÈTE

MERCADO & IS. H. JESSUA

Grande Maison de Nouveautés

Vente en gros et détail

PRIX FIXE

Armée Ottomane

Service Militaire des non-musulmans

Pour la flotte Nationale

Un Exemple à suivre

Le Tsar en Voyage

FIGURE 20. The first page of *Journal de Salonique* features in three different paragraphs the ubiquitous slogan "Crete or Death" in bold and large fonts. Source: *Journal de Salonique*, 8 August 1909, National Library of France.

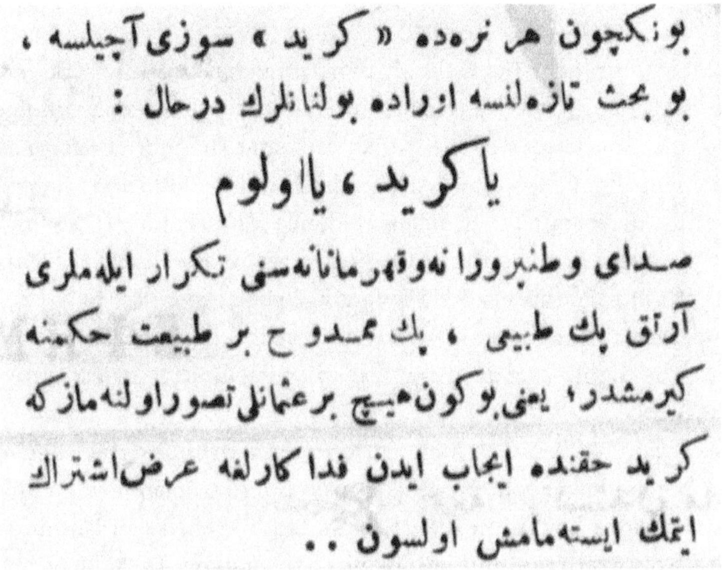

بونکچون هر نرده « کرید » سوزی آچیلسه ،
بو بحث تازه‌لنسه اوراده بولنانلرك درحال :

یا کرید ، یا اولوم

صدای وطنپرورانه وقهرمانانه‌سنی تکرار ایله‌ملری
آرتق پك طبیعی ، پك ممدوح بر طبیعت حکمنه
گیرمشدر ؛ یعنی بوکون هیچ بر عثمانلی تصور اولنه‌مازکه
کرید حقنده ایجاب ایدن فداکارلغه عرض اشتراك
ایتمك ایسته‌مامش اولسون ..

FIGURE 21. *Ahenk*'s rendering of the slogan "Crete or Death" (*Ya Girit, Ya Ölüm*) in oversize fonts. Source: *Ahenk*, 30 May 1911, Ahmet Piriştina City Archive and Museum.

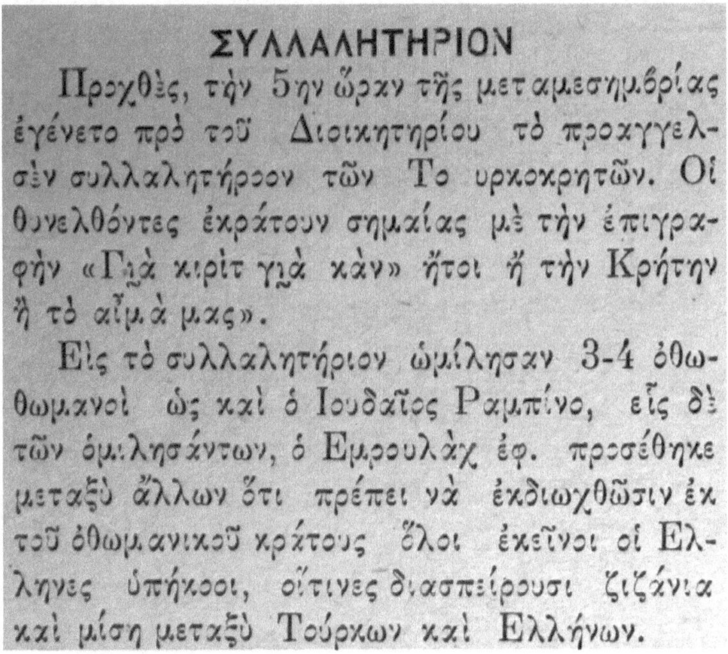

ΣΥΛΛΑΛΗΤΗΡΙΟΝ

Προχθὲς, τὴν 5ην ὥραν τῆς μεταμεσημβρίας ἐγένετο πρὸ τοῦ Διοικητηρίου τὸ προαγγελθὲν συλλαλητήριον τῶν Τουρκοκρητῶν. Οἱ συνελθόντες ἐκράτουν σημαίας μὲ τὴν ἐπιγραφὴν «Γιὰ κιρὶτ γιὰ κὰν» ἤτοι ἢ τὴν Κρήτην ἢ τὸ αἷμά μας».

Εἰς τὸ συλλαλητήριον ὡμίλησαν 3-4 ὀθωμανοί ὡς καὶ ὁ Ἰουδαῖος Ραμπῖνο, εἷς δὲ τῶν ὁμιλησάντων, ὁ Εμρουλλὰχ ἐφ. προσέθηκε μεταξὺ ἄλλων ὅτι πρέπει νὰ ἐκδιωχθῶσιν ἐκ τοῦ ὀθωμανικοῦ κράτους ὅλοι ἐκεῖνοι οἱ Ἕλληνες ὑπήκοοι, οἵτινες διασπείρουσι ζιζάνια καὶ μίση μεταξὺ Τούρκων καὶ Ἑλλήνων.

FIGURE 22. Another protest slogan featured in *Amaltheia*, "Crete or [Our] Blood" (*Ya Girit Ya Kan*), in Turkish with Greek characters and its Greek translation, 3 August 1909. Source: *Amaltheia*, National Library of Greece.

the local CUP branch. The military band provided the official soundtrack at the gathering while Benghazi's inhabitants produced an indigenous soundscape. To the ears of the Italian diplomat the mix of native sounds was ominous if not cacophonous: "hundreds of vagabond and idle men and children ... performing their macabre dance [*danza macabra*], waving flags, uttering prayers, and chanting liturgical songs" in the fashion of Marabout (*al-Murabitun*) celebrations. Also receiving special mention in the consul's unsympathetic observations were the Cretans who lingered in the cafes late into the night, long after the rally dispersed, uttering spiteful words against Greece.[78]

In addition to press and diplomatic sources, Ottoman state documents provide a good idea about provincial mass politics. There are hundreds of protest petitions housed in the Ottoman State Archives in Istanbul. Telegraphed from Crete rallies that took place throughout the empire between 1909 and 1911, they are usually classified under separate headings by point of origin. Given such categorization, a trove of documents bundled together under a single archival entry stands out. It comprises scores of petitions dated between 9 January 1910 and 2 June 1910 sent from multiple provinces. The reason for arranging together a large number of petitions for this five-month interval seems to be their common response to a specific incident during the perplexing Crete crisis: the oath taking by the Christian deputies of the Cretan Assembly in the name of George I, the king of Greece. This defiant act by the island's recalcitrant politicians suggested a clear gesture toward annexing the autonomous polity to Greece.[79] A map that I prepared from this database of petitions (figure 23) includes 233 locations where the Ottomans organized public meetings and gatherings over a period of five months in 1910. In the remainder of this section, I zero in on this period of five months to underscore the intensity and pervasiveness of Crete-inspired mass protest in the Ottoman Empire.

One noteworthy feature of this map is the high concentration of public gatherings in western Anatolia and Macedonia. This is a sign of especially well-organized local CUP networks in these regions. It was indeed the provincial CUP circles who did most of the heavy lifting and formed the logistical backbone of protest meetings. Mass demonstrations generally took place in town squares, where several notable personalities gave speeches in Turkish and other Ottoman languages widely spoken in the area. Press and archival reports frequently mention speeches delivered in Albanian,

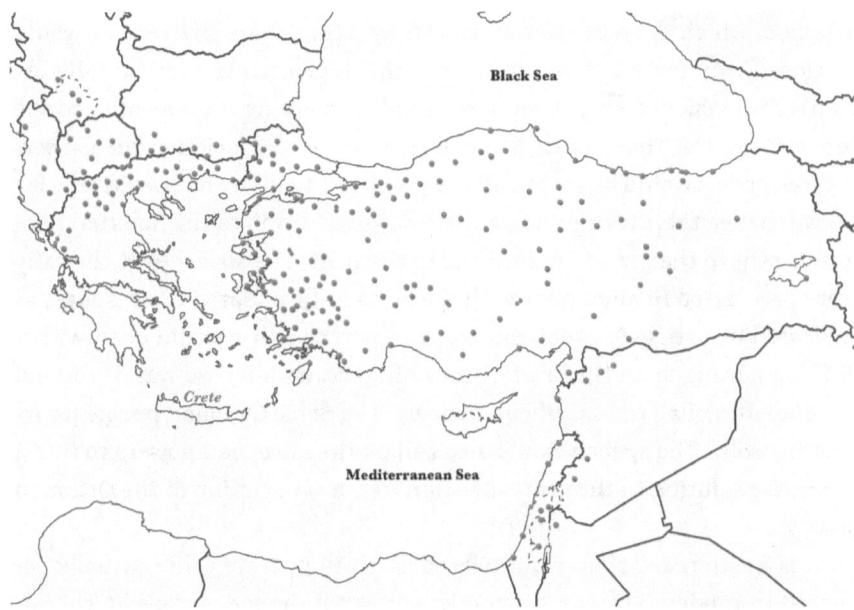

FIGURE 23. Locations of Crete-related public gatherings and protest rallies between 9 January 1910 and 2 June 1910. Outside the mapped area are one rally in Libya (Tripoli) and two in the Hijaz (Medina and Taif). Source: Drawn on protest petitions from Ottoman State Archives, HR. SYS. 512/2.

Arabic, Bulgarian, Greek, Ladino (Judeo-Spanish), Romanian, and Serbian. The gatherings concluded with the organizing committee's sending telegrams to various imperial institutions in the capital, such as the palace and parliament. These documents summarized the event by noting the number of participants and the main points of the speeches. They formulaically emphasized people's determination to defend, to the last drop of their blood, imperial sovereignty over Crete.

A nineteen-article program of a demonstration staged in Monastir in May 1910 outlines the details crafted by the rally organizing committee. The document provides a glimpse into the logistics of staging a mass protest in the Ottoman Empire. Its opening articles explained the purpose of the event as an expression of public reaction against the oath taking by the Christian Cretan deputies in the name of the king of Greece. They identified the venue of the assembly as Monastir's Liberty Square. This mass rally had a bearing on the commercial and social life of the city, as evidenced by article 5, which decreed that all the stores other than pharmacies would be closed two hours before the start of the demonstration.[80] The rally organizers envisioned this event in terms of connecting their locality to the broader empire. Thus article 6 stated that at the conclusion of the gathering, telegrams would be sent to all the provinces to invite fellow citizens far away to stage their own protests. This was in addition to the habitual telegrams sent to the grand vizirate and parliament. The speeches at the rally were precrafted in alignment with the already-formulated Crete-speak, as indicated by article 9, which mentioned that the event would open with a Turkish harangue on the brief history of Crete. Its purpose was to remind the audience of all the sacrifices made by "the noble Ottoman people for its pristine soil." The speech would also call on the European powers to find a definitive solution to the Crete question to the satisfaction of the Ottoman state.[81]

It is apt to recall that, from 1909 through 1911, Crete rallies usually occurred in tandem with an economic boycott of Greece. Article 10 threatened a fierce boycott against Hellenic merchandise and shipping unless, within five days of the official announcement by the rally organizing committee, the Greek government declared the oath of the Cretan deputies null and void. The CUP exerted a clear influence in the organization of the rally, as suggested by article 12. It stated that five men from each of the city's ethnoreligious communities would convene beforehand in the Union Club, where red and white ribbons would be fastened to their arms. The colors of the Ottoman flag would identify them as a task force responsible for ensuring the smooth unfolding of the event. Although more symbolic than taxing, the organizing committee involved the city's diverse communities in the planning of the demonstration. Article 14 set forth that the logistical costs would be defrayed by the collection of ten Ottoman liras from the Muslim community and five liras from each of the non-Muslim communities. The organizers intended this rally to have an impact beyond the actual day and event, as suggested by article 15. It specified that the speeches delivered at the gathering would be translated into all local languages to be broadcast by the press. Last, in a symbolic gesture to pay homage to the island that had given birth to the late Ottoman mass protest, article 19 concluded that a telegram would be sent to *Ümid* (Hope), a Turkish-language newspaper published in Hania.[82] Soon after the Monastir demonstration, *Ümid* ran an editorial to address the rallies triggered by the oath crisis.

Using a script now familiar to the protesting crowds, the author of the article declared Ottoman sovereign rights over the island to be founded on "the sacred blood of thousands of our ancestors."[83]

Propagated by the newspapers, embraced by the rally organizers, and declared by the orators and spectators, the outcry "Crete or Death" emblematized the soundscape of Ottoman mass politics. Despite the slogan's violent connotations, the Turkish-language press usually viewed these mass gatherings as evidence of civic consciousness.[84] Typical portrayal of the rallies as orderly events is unsettled by some earwitness accounts suggesting the utterance of unscripted and perilous phrases. A demonstration from Çandarlı, a small town north of Izmir, offers an intriguing case for prompting a months-long investigation by the state authorities. Amid a season of protest across the empire, what turned a small-town event in May 1910 into an episode involving several ministries began with a serious allegation. It was rumored that the district administrator of Çandarlı had sought to exploit the rally to plot a riot against the local Christians. In an unsigned piece published in the Greek-language daily *Armonia* (Harmony) of Izmir, the Greek Orthodox deputy bishop of Çandarlı claimed that the demonstrators were ignorant and armed drunkards. In the piece, which was later translated into Turkish during the official investigation, the clergyman claimed that those men repeatedly hurled vicious words like "We will f**k the infidels' mothers." And they did so in the presence of the district administrator. As the investigation deepened, an array of witnesses was summoned for deposition. A certain Andreas stated that nobody had insulted the Christians, nor had anyone borne arms. "Crete or Death" were the only words the crowd shouted. The miller Vasileios testified that on the day of the rally he was present only in the designated place for the gathering in front of the town hall, where he listened to the speeches on Crete. He heard no profanities targeting the Christians. The miller added that for the past several days he had overheard people speak in the neighborhood cafes about *Armonia*'s coverage of the alleged incident in the town. Hristos, a member of the municipal council, stated that he had arrived at the rally late but had heard nothing against the Christians either during or after the event. He said that on a recent visit to the nearby town of Bergama, those reading the newspaper had asked him about the veracity of its story, a detail attesting to the reverberations of this incident beyond the small town of Çandarlı.

Many more non-Muslim and Muslim residents of the town confirmed the earlier testimonies, eleven of them highlighting the chanting of the phrase "Crete or Death" during the rally. Their remarks underscored the slogan's pervasiveness in those years. In this sense, a small-town protest exemplified the most characteristic sonic feature of imperial mass politics. In the interrogations only one testimony of Çandarlı residents differed from the rest. Georgios, another member of the municipal council, echoed the statements of other witnesses. He also remarked that the orators at the rally spoke only of Crete, delivering no anti-Christian messages. But he went on to add that he had later heard from someone else, whose name he did not recall due to the passage of time, that several adults and some school-age children had shouted obscenities. He specified by telling the police what came to his ears: "Fuck the mothers of the *Yunanlıs* [Hellenes] and the *gavurs* [meaning 'infidels,' which, in theory, included Greek Ottomans too]."[85]

Incidents like this over the course of Crete demonstrations help contextualize the directives that the Ministry of Interior sent to several provincial administrators, urging them to be watchful for the maintenance of intercommunal peace.[86] Suggesting the room for spontaneous street action during the popular mobilization, the Çandarlı episode demonstrates the impracticality of policing the crowds. It indicates the anxieties that a deviation from the scripted soundscape of protest caused for state authorities, in the capital and in the provinces alike.

In the Çandarlı case the police kept asking what the earwitnesses had heard at the rally. Many of them responded that "Crete or Death" was the only slogan they had heard. The repetitiveness of the chant suggests how quickly it became a quotidian element of the imperial protest-scape, "much like any other sensory phenomenon experienced on a regular basis."[87] The process of the police interrogation inspires a different kind of interrogation, one to be conducted by historians. I ask what sounds are latent in the written documents from the archives and what they suggest in terms of people's experience with sonic stimuli in the Ottoman protest-scape. Answers might not be as straightforward as those extracted under a police investigation. But they nevertheless help enliven the past. The scrutiny of the soundscape of Crete demonstrations illustrates what the denizens of the past heard or expected to hear when they showed up at a rally or when they simply happened to be near the sites of assembly. Lending an ear to the description of characteristic sounds pervading empire-wide gatherings brings closer the distant and mostly undocumented universe of ordinary Ottomans.

Although rewarding for its novel insights, sonic pathways into the past may sometimes lead to cul-de-sacs. Aimée Boutin sums up the promises and illusions of searching for sound in the archives. In her sensory study of nineteenth-century Paris she observes that "the tense relationship between descriptions of sound perception and the historical question of how the street *really* sounded is irresolvable" but "it propels the research."[88] Indeed, it is crucial to recognize that the meanings of sounds are very much shaped by the particularities of their generation. As Mark Smith cautions, "The utmost care must be taken in using sensory evidence and . . . we should fear flirting with the seductive nature of that evidence."[89] Historicity of sounds dictates that they be scrutinized in accordance with their context-specific features. As this chapter has shown, the rallying cry "Crete or Death" was the sonic signature of mass gatherings in the Ottoman Empire. Following the Sultanahmed demonstration of early 1909, continual and organized protest became an ingrained practice in the Ottoman world, with an outpouring of rallies throughout the provinces. The magnitude of the Sultanahmed gathering was surpassed in the aftermath of World War I when better-known demonstrations for Turkish independence were held in the same location in 1919. Around that time in Damascus, Syrians too were raising the cry of independence. The streets of Damascus that had rung with the outcry of "Crete or Death" after 1909 now transformed into sites filled with leaflets bearing the title "Independence or Death."[90] The core of this ubiquitous slogan, whose earlier version was chanted most vehemently by Cretans, outlasted the empire. In its postimperial afterlife, the island was replaced by what animated popular protest in a new Middle East: desire for independence.

Necropolitical Echoes

This chapter started with a discussion of the key roles that a coterie of Istanbul-based Cretans played from late 1908 onward in crafting a lexicon to render their native island a relatable territory to the broader public. The narrative they helped forge manifested itself in areas well beyond the capital. It reached the broader public through a variety of channels such as publications, conferences, demonstrations, and mosque sermons. Schools, university halls, mosques, and theaters emerged as indoor sites where the tales of sacrifice found receptive ears. In July 1909, Léon Krajewski, the French vice-consul in Skopje (Üsküp), Macedonia, reported on the mobilizing function of mosques in relation to the Crete question. As the shops of Skopje closed at dusk, mosques turned into venues for the discussion of urgent worldly matters, in which preachers referenced sacrifices made and martyrs fallen for the island.[91] Certain secular spaces served a similar purpose. In the summer of 1910, for instance, an emotional play on Crete that was staged in a Cairo theater incited a spectator to deliver an impromptu speech electrifying the audience in British-controlled Egypt.[92]

From 1909 onward and peaking around the spring of 1910, Crete-speak, with its echoes of sacrifice and martyrdom, transcended walled spaces and spilled over into the streets and squares as people across the empire staged a slew of mass demonstrations. From 1909 through 1911 across a host of locales ranging from Albania to Libya, the ubiquitous slogan "Crete or Death" imbued the Ottoman protest-scape with necropolitical overtones. Through the imagery of death, which became an indispensable feature of popular mobilization, mass gatherings coalesced into a coherent movement. In regions with a sizable refugee population, those who had been displaced from the island a decade earlier became the driving force of rallies. Across provinces boasting a strong CUP network, especially in western Anatolia and Macedonia, a flurry of protest was sparked mostly by the initiative of resourceful Unionists.

Echoes of death emanating from both the capital and Unionist strongholds resonated in locations farther afield from the epicenters of protest. In September 1909, a mass meeting was held in the Islamic holy city of Mecca, one of the principal destinations for the annual hajj. The opening speech was delivered in Arabic by Abdullah Saraj, the Hanafi mufti of Mecca, who would serve as future prime minister of Transjordan from 1931 to 1933.[93] After stating people's readiness to sacrifice their blood for Crete, a message that by this point had become the staple of empire-wide rallies, he bemoaned that "the echoes from the lofty seat of the caliphate" had reached the Hijaz belatedly because of its remoteness. Saraj addressed those words to the governor of the province, who, near the podium, awaited his turn to speak. When the governor took the floor for an impromptu speech in Arabic, he stressed the significance of Crete and the inviolability of Ottoman sovereign rights that were rooted in a long-lasting war of conquest in the seventeenth century. *Şems-i Hakikat* (The Sun of Truth), a new daily from Mecca, published the full text of the third speech, redacted by the CUP's central committee and delivered in an articulate manner by the army physician major Hüsnü Akif. Following several remarks relating to Crete's history, the CUP member reiterated the determination of Muslim Ottomans to spill their "patriotic blood" (*hun-u hamiyet*) by fighting any force that would dare to sever the island from them. The physician major ended his harangue on a slogan-like ominous note by declaring, "Not a home but a grave alone can Crete be for the *Yunan* [Hellene]."[94]

During the period of intense protest inspired by Crete, no war with Greece broke out for Ottomans to shed blood for the island. Crete rallies, however, coincided with a fierce economic boycott of Greece. The language of blood and sacrifice that resounded throughout the empire in the demonstrations described in this chapter animated the contentious, and at times violent, boycott movement, which many contemporaries dubbed economic warfare. I devote the next chapter to its examination.

FIVE

RESETTLING the DISPLACED into HISTORY
Refugee Boycotters in the Ottoman Protest Movement

In June 1910, at a time of interminable protest about Crete throughout the Ottoman Empire, the representatives of the Greek Ottoman (*Rum*) community in the western Anatolian town of Akhisar dispatched an alarming telegram to the Ministry of Interior. In it, they complained about the antagonistic attitude of the local CUP branch, which doubled as the boycott committee in that town. Signatories to the note, including the board members of *Rum* schools and churches in Akhisar, informed the ministry that the committee had asked them to terminate the employment of two teachers and one church cantor. Their Hellenic nationality was cited as the reason. Against the uncompromising stance of the CUP branch, the board members were forced to discharge the three Hellenic subjects. The telegram implied that the Hellenic subjects were not the exclusive objects of the local Unionists. Under the pretext that the *personae non gratae* still resided in the town, the boycott was extended to all board members of Akhisar's Greek Ottoman community. A street crier announced to town residents the extension of boycotting even to those holding Ottoman nationality. The boycott committee put the stores owned by the board members under surveillance by placing two men in front of them. The vigilantes of the committee kept away customers, compelling the owners to close their shops. Soon after, the complaints of Greek Ottomans came to the attention of Mahmud Muhtar, governor of the Aydin province. In his communication with Istanbul on the matter of transgressive boycotting of the Greek Ottoman stores, the governor informed the Ministry of Interior that he had sent all necessary instructions to the district administrator for "the strict prevention of such infractions."[1]

This episode in Akhisar encapsulates several aspects of the anti-Greece boycott that first began in multiple locations across the empire in 1909 and had continued since then with only occasional respites. First, rallies and boycott often constituted two intertwined components of Crete-inspired protest and agitation in a late Ottoman town. A month before the boycott incident in Akhisar, a petition signed by the mayor of that town on behalf of four thousand people had mentioned the protesters exclaiming the formulaic slogan of "Crete or Death" with a vow that they would never allow this "precious island, which became a legitimate Ottoman possession by the blood of our ancestors, to be trampled under the cursed feet of those bloodthirsty [Christian Cretans]."[2] Second, as in the mounting of mass demonstrations, local CUP branches steered the boycott movement in the provinces. For instance, around the time of the Akhisar incident but far away in the eastern Black Sea city of Trabzon, it was at a meeting held in the Unionist club that a boycott committee was elected.[3] Third, although the boycotters officially targeted Greece with the ultimate goal of crippling its vibrant economic presence in the empire, the boycott's implementation frequently harmed the well-being of the Greek Ottoman population as well. In the Akhisar case, the ostensibly noneconomic friction between the boycott committee and the board members of the Greek Ottoman community over the employment of Hellenic subjects quickly took a commercial turn with an economic embargo against native Greek businesses. The announcement of the boycott to the public through a street crier accentuated the social dimension of this policy of shunning, while the placing of men in front of the stores to keep away customers made it a transgressive act.

In his 2014 monograph, Y. Doğan Çetinkaya presents a thorough analysis of economic boycotting in the Ottoman Empire, examining it as a social movement from its first manifestation against Austria-Hungary in late 1908 through the longer-lasting anti-Greece dimension.[4] Çetinkaya's study can be situated at the intersection of social and labor histories, like that of classical practitioner Donald Quataert, especially his work that foregrounded workers in the economic boycott against Austro-Hungarian merchandise in late 1908.[5] This was the first serious boycott movement in the empire but was much shorter than the boycott against Greece.[6] Çetinkaya's interventions relate to questions of periodization and working-class agency in late Ottoman history. Whereas scholars have traditionally identified World War I as the period during which Greek Ottomans saw a great injury to their economic power because of the policies pursued by the government under the CUP command, Çetinkaya rightly puts forward an earlier periodization, one that was heralded by the economic boycott six years before the outbreak of the Great War. In so doing, he exposes the antecedents of *milli iktisad* (the nationalized economy), a new model of political economy characterized by the state-sanctioned favoring of Turks in particular and Muslims in general to the detriment of others.[7] Through examples that show how various historical personalities followed a course of action independent of, and at times even in defiance of, the positions prescribed by official figures regarding the boycott policy, Çetinkaya highlights the roles of social actors in the development of Turkish nationalism in the late Ottoman Empire. My main contribution, and this is where my work is distinguished from the extant scholarship, lies in the centering of Cretan refugees in the examination of the boycott movement between 1909 and 1911, the most sweeping in Ottoman history. If those displaced from Crete only a decade earlier became the driving force of the boycott in their new homes, the widely propagated narrative about violence on the island served to inflame the passions of broader segments of the population, most of whom, unlike the refugee islanders, held no physical ties to Crete.

Of all places in the Ottoman Empire, Izmir hosted the most robust community of Hellenic subjects, the strongest both numerically and economically.[8] The economic ascendancy of the Hellenic diaspora in and around Izmir mirrored Greece's powerful maritime standing across the Aegean Sea. The statistics published in early 1909 by *Amaltheia*, the leading Greek-language Ottoman daily of Izmir, make evident the predominance of Greece in the region's transportation and commerce. According to the figures for the year 1908, of the annual total number of 3,055 steamers visiting the port of Izmir, 854 flew the Hellenic flag (28 percent), followed by 757 Ottoman (25 percent), and 320 British (10 percent).[9] This major port city at a prime commercial location, together with its hinterland, witnessed the most ferocious and rebellious manifestation of boycotting. The predominance of those with Hellenic nationality in the demographic composition of Izmir and the vibrancy of Hellenic commerce there partly explain the intensity of the boycott.[10]

The economic boycott of Greece occurred in multiple port cities, affecting even inland towns. This chapter pays special attention to the situation in Izmir.[11] It is an urban setting that uniquely and literally brought face to face, with frequently tense encounters, two diasporic communities: a Hellenic diaspora around forty thousand strong and a Cretan Muslim diaspora of almost equivalent numbers. I take the experience of displacement seriously to better historicize the ardent involvement of Cretans in the blacklisting of Hellenic subjects and businesses. The boycott pitted one diasporic group against another, and Cretans got involved in many physical confrontations with their antagonists. The commonality of Greek afforded a degree of intimacy to such fraught encounters. Unhealed traumas of exile, which, the refugees had all the reason to perceive, were initiated by Hellenic ambitions of *enosis*, likely functioned as an invisible engine animating their eagerness in the boycott.

With a focus on boycotters rather than boycotted, in this chapter I underscore the critical roles performed by a refugee community, most of whom settled in and around Izmir after being displaced from Crete.[12] In my analysis, I view the boycott as an act of violent protest that aimed for the economic displacement of Hellenic subjects from the Ottoman country. Such an objective, however, cannot be disentangled from the intended prospect of their ultimate departure from the empire given that the obstruction of a group's commercial activities functions as one of the common push factors for emigration.[13] The relationship between economic and physical displacement is also pertinent to the nature of Cretan refugee experiences. It is true that their displacement a decade earlier occurred under disparate circumstances. An analogy is still plausible, and for this it is worthwhile to recall chapter 1. In it I demonstrated how during the civil war the destruction of olive trees, the principal source of subsistence for many villagers, stimulated the forced migration. In a twist of history, violence swept tens of thousands of Cretans into locales with conspicuous Hellenic communities. During the boycott movement many refugees ruled the streets with a zeal and bravado to bring about the economic displacement of the Hellenic population. Many among them likely perceived those groups as guilty by association for their losses.

By paying special attention to Cretan refugee protesters, this chapter continues the discussion introduced in the previous one. Boycotters were the subject of many reports by domestic and foreign observers for their conspicuous deeds, but unlike those who forged a refugee network shaping the contours of Crete-speak, their names are all but lost to history. The mark they left in late Ottoman history was made through street action, at times characterized by intimidation and violence, rather than through articulate public conferences and sophisticated newspaper columns.

Refugee Protesters Displaced from History

In the months following the Constitutional Revolution of 1908, the political situation in Crete became a recurrent news item, drawing the attention of Ottomans, especially the Cretan diaspora. The fast pace of events put the island in the limelight on multiple occasions, especially after the declaration of union with Athens in October 1908. In one remarkable incident in the late summer of 1909 a pro-Athens group hoisted the flag of Greece in Hania, the island's administrative capital. The French consul in Izmir wrote in early August that this act caused no disturbances in the city, home to thousands of Cretan refugees (*crétois refugiés*). But unease was palpable in his report. He mentioned that two days earlier the Cretan Muslims had held a massive protest rally. About fifteen thousand Cretans had gathered in the city's main square with banners and flags. The consul's account of the demonstration typified many observations that his European peers made about similar events. Like them he saw popular mobilization on political matters primarily through the lens of public security. He too was particularly attentive to the possible risks that the popular excitement could pose to foreign nationals. He informed the French embassy that one day before the planned demonstration the consular corps in Izmir had urged the governor to take all necessary measures to prevent disorder. The consul was relieved to report that the rally had concluded without any disturbances. The only incident he found worth mentioning showcases the scope of agitation in one of the most cosmopolitan Ottoman cities. It involved a working-class French national named Barelier, in the employ of the shipping company Messageries Maritimes. The Frenchman was arrested by the police in Cordélio (Karşıyaka) for exclaiming in public that the Turks had already lost Crete and that the island would be soon handed to Greece.[14]

Two weeks later, the same consul penned a series of observations from the boycott-struck port city. In a note communicated to the embassy, he depicted the boycott in Izmir as a movement driven by lower-class Cretans. They were the voice and muscle of the boycott, while an unofficial committee, whose exact character and composition remained shrouded in mystery, operated as its brain.[15] The French consul provided a litany of deeds to feature Cretan emigrants (*crétois émigrés*) as a troublesome community with an "audacity truly unheard of." Growing bolder by the inertia of the authorities loath to displease popular opinion, the Cretans, most of whom were "shady characters" (*gens sans aveu*), would enter the cafés and pull down the portraits of the king of Greece. They would burst into stores, threateningly asking the owners to sack Hellenic nationals on their payroll. The consul wrote that two days earlier bands of Cretans from around the city had headed to the harbor, where they prevented ships hoisting the blue and white Greek flag from unloading their cargo.[16] That same day, incited by these colors featured on the awning of a shop, they menacingly requested its owner to modify the store's exterior, an example illustrating the chromatic effects of the boycott. The matter was not resolved until the storeowner, a Russian subject, solicited consular assistance and mounted a Russian flag at the entrance to ward off the unwelcome visitors. The consul alleged that in another color-provoked incident that occurred the following day, a group of vigilante boycotters tore off the clothes of women dressed in blue and white. Judging from similar incidents, which mostly remained at the level of verbal harassment, the French consul averred that "the streets have become the property of the Cretans, and the police, afraid to offend the popular national feeling, are reluctant to act."[17]

The coverage of the boycott by the Greek-language Izmir daily *Amaltheia* provided some weight to the French consul's claims. In August 1909, during an early phase of the boycott, the newspaper reported that a band of "Turkish Cretans" had paid a morning visit to the café Hermes on the seafront promenade. They gave the café's Hellenic proprietor twenty-four hours to take down the portraits of the king of Greece, adding that his failure to do so would lead them to literally take the matter into their own hands. Another Turkish Cretan group under the leadership of an islander who ran a coffeehouse across from the customhouse proceeded to the Hellenic-owned café Lambros to demand the removal of all the Hellenic insignia from the premises. They even asked that the color of the store's canopy be changed from Hellenic blue to Turkish red.¹⁸ In another incident, a group of boycotters paid a visit to the tobacco shop of a certain Karagiannis, situated across from the governor's office, threatening to close his shop.¹⁹ Although *Amaltheia* made several exclusive references to the leading roles of Turkish Cretans, it also mentioned that many Jews joined the boycotters. Not only did this detail point to a class-based solidarity between the two relatively marginal communities of the city, it harkened back to the periodic outbreaks of tension between Izmir's Greek and Jewish communities in previous years.²⁰ The newspaper reported that the peripatetic band of Turkish Cretan boycotters traversed the commercial center of Izmir, from Başdurak to Bit Pazarı to Basmane, making ominous stops at various greengrocers, flour shops, fabric stores, and wine shops, shouting threats at the owners to shut down their establishments.²¹

The staunch boycott in this prosperous city disrupted the daily life. Although the movement's chief target was Hellenic nationals, the Cretans as its zealous protagonists did not hesitate to confront and intimidate Muslims. Even those accustomed to being treated with more respect sometimes found themselves disciplined by the ardent islanders. An incident that involved a Greek Ottoman shop owner and two Muslim clerics indicates the sweeping nature of the boycott in the empire's second-largest city. On a late summer morning, two hodjas were sitting down in the coffeehouse Krini. They ordered coffee and continued chatting. Before they had the chance to sip their drinks, a group of Turkocretans entered the store and began to insult the hodjas for being there. Ignoring the protests of the owner, Ioannis Aksiotis, that he too was an Ottoman citizen, the boycotters drove the hodjas from Krini, spoiling their leisurely coffee hour. This confrontation presents a case in which neither bearing Ottoman citizenship nor wearing Islamic headgear guaranteed immunity from being boycotted.²²

In November 1911 the British consul in Izmir referred to Cretan Muslims in derogatory terms widely deployed against refugee populations by those speaking from a position of diplomatic or state authority. His remarks came two years after his French counterpart's observations mentioned above, a detail attesting to the longevity of the boycott. The British consul pointed out that Izmir was home to a sizable population of Cretan Muslims, composed of many "undesirable" characters, and that some men among them were "employed in the harbor as lightermen and others have figured as hooligans in the pay of the boycott committee."²³ He claimed that since the promulgation of the constitution in July 1908, these men "have been a constant source of trouble. They have been the leaders in all strikes connected with shipping, in all acts of violence connected with the Greek boycott." This time the Cretans appeared as the protagonists in diplomatic correspondence by virtue of being involved in anti-Italy agitation in response to that country's unprovoked invasion of Libya. In his report to Ambassador Gerard Lowther, the consul mentioned that the Ottoman authorities had requested him to persuade a British company, C. Whittall and Co., which held a majority share in an agricultural factory in Izmir, to fire two Italians employed in the harbor.[24] The firm, content with the longtime service of the Italians, appeared reluctant to dismiss them, yet it nevertheless informed the consul that it would comply in the case of a direct order from the authorities. It was at this point that the Cretans took the matter into their own hands. An islander named Süleyman, chief of the harbor lightermen, menaced Fritz Charnaud, an employee with the firm superintending the loading of steamers, upon which the matter was brought to the attention of the police chief. Eager to prevent an escalation, the harbormaster advised the superintendent to give the Italian workers leave for several days. The British consul concluded his report with a commentary on Izmir's Italian diaspora, a community more than fifty thousand strong. He emphasized the central roles some Italian laborers played in railway strikes. In his account, the Cretans served as the epitome of trouble and as a yardstick to gauge the undesirability of another underprivileged class in this teeming port city: "There are bad characters among the Italians who are quite as undesirable as the Cretans and would be better out of the country."[25]

The Italian diplomats stationed in Izmir had already joined the chorus of consular observers who viewed the city's Cretan refugees through stereotypes of timeless Islamic fanaticism. Such perceptions were further aggravated by a class-specific condescension given the less privileged socioeconomic backgrounds of many Cretan refugee boycotters. Writing in June 1910, during an intense period of protest across the empire as discussed in the previous chapter, the Italian consul reported on the commotion produced by the forced closure of Hellenic stores in Izmir, which stemmed from coercion by "hordes of Muslims [*orde di musulmani*], mostly Cretans." The consular dispatch to the Italian embassy noted that the authorities had interfered to prevent the deepening of the turmoil, arresting the leaders of the fierce boycott and issuing a proclamation that distinguished the permissible form of boycotting (voluntary abstention from economic transactions) from the illegal type (forcing customers away from Hellenic stores). In the narrative of the Italian diplomat, the main drivers of the boycott movement, both within Izmir and in its environs, were lower-class Muslims, especially those of Cretan background, pejoratively branded as "Muslim plebs" (*plebi musulmane*).[26]

The tension that enveloped Izmir in early June 1910 was the primary topic of the Austro-Hungarian consul's correspondence with Vienna, this time treated much more fully and with details provided by the enclosure of the entire issue of *Ittihad* (Unity), a leading Turkish-language newspaper published in Izmir. The consul August Kral underscored the incitement of pro-CUP newspapers in the city, which produced an especially strong impression among "Cretan emigrants" (*kretensischen Auswanderern*). Also informing the Habsburg foreign minister of the developments in the small towns farther inland, Kral noted the presence of agitated Muslims roaming the streets "in gangs [*rottenweise*]" with flags in their hands and threats in their mouths. As for the implementation of the boycott at the street level, August Kral corroborated the earlier observations by his European counterparts. He reported that the boycott against Hellenic shipping and stores was "initiated by fanatical Cretan gangs [*fanatisierte Kretenserbanden*] who traversed the bazaar and the adjacent neighborhoods, forcing all those businesses to shut down. Several merchants who resisted the initial onslaught of the gangs were mistreated, some seriously injured." Kral added that the panic in the streets proved short-lived and that the forcibly closed shops reopened the same day thanks to the intervention of the local authorities, an important detail also noted by the Italian consul above. The Austro-Hungarian diplomat concluded his report with a commentary on the social psychology of the crowd. He gave little credit to the collective agency of boycotters while simultaneously acknowledging the likelihood of uncontrollable mass action that would defy the directives of its orchestrators: "It is only to be hoped that in other similar cases the passions of the mob [*Pöbel*], once unleashed, prove no more powerful than the reins of those who occasionally stir them up to serve their own political purposes."[27] Beyond indicating the protest-phobia of Western officials, the singling out of Cretans as protagonists of the boycott suggests that they were perceived to embody a cohesive social unit. In a way, the dispersal caused by their displacement from Crete in the late 1890s morphed into cohesion by means of protest a decade later.

The portrayal of those refugees as fanatical in outlook and plebeian in background is common thread in the reports of European diplomats. Islam and a lower social class background made a dangerous amalgamation in the eyes of multiple contemporary observers. Such colonial viewpoints banished the Cretan refugees from history. In other words, once they were stereotyped by these double markers, no explanation was needed to parse their active involvement in the boycott movement against Greece, as if to suggest that history began with the recording of their anti-Greek and anti-European acts in 1909. Timeless identities sufficed to rationalize their deeds.

The banishment of Cretan refugees from history, I argue, was intertwined with their physical displacement from their native island. Incomplete but striking documentation of that link is provided by a list prepared by the French gendarmerie active in Crete as part of the European occupation during the late 1890s. It includes details such as name, profession, address, and additional remarks of 120 individuals who were arrested for being deemed dangerous and suspect by the French gendarmerie. Of these 120 detainees at the hands of the occupier's justice, 118 were Muslim, domiciled in Hania and its environs. The international authorities expelled 107 of them to Izmir in the fall of 1898. The breakdown by profession sheds light on the class backgrounds of the expellees, giving some historical context to the European diplomats' commentary on the ethnographic profile of refugee boycotters after 1909. The expelled Cretans were engaged in occupations that ran the gamut, such as coffeehouse keepers/workers (13), butchers (11), boatmen (8), fishermen (4), grocers (4), and the like. With 36 individuals, the unemployed constituted the largest category. Pithy remarks attached to the profiles of some expellees served not only to justify their deportation from the island but to exemplify the coding of undesirability and criminality attached to lower classes in colonial parlance. The adjective *dangerous* was dispensed generously to identify numerous individuals. As if a plain form were too weak to characterize some of them, the qualifier *very dangerous* was used. Among other noteworthy descriptions are "influential killer," "fanatical killer," "rabble-rouser" (*fomenteur de troubles*), "wielding a great influence," "militant politician," "fanatical politician,"[28] "total rogue" (*gredin fieffé*), "dangerous speaker," and "dangerous vagabond."[29] Given the impossibility of tracing the lives of those unwanted Cretans once they set foot in Izmir, it would be erroneous to draw a straightforward connection between their expulsion from Crete and the boycott a decade later. Equally unjustifiable, however, is the presumption that the scores of individuals who held the attention of the European occupiers would stand idle while a fierce boycott set off by a transnational crisis over Crete upended the socioeconomic life of Izmir.

A degree of occupational overlap between the expelled Cretans and the active boycotters can be located in Ottoman state documents as well. While a definitive matching is unfeasible, it is possible to profile the boycott as a social movement driven by economically underprivileged groups. For instance, in June 1910, the district administrator of Antalya, a coastal city some 250 miles southeast of Izmir boasting a sizable Cretan refugee population, reported that a band of protesters had launched a forceful boycott of Hellenic-owned stores. The Cretan refugee boycotters visited such establishments and, in an ominous manner, told the owners to close their shops. This group managed to mobilize a broader segment of Antalya's petty traders and merchants. More than a hundred people, including bakers, street vendors, and coffeehouse keepers/workers, took part in the boycott.[30]

Placing Refugee Protesters in History

During the decade that followed their forced exile in the late nineteenth century, the displaced and dispossessed of Crete maintained a relatively low-profile presence in the official documentation of both European diplomats and Ottoman administrators.[31] Occasional references to them in that time period would give way to frequent mentions of their deeds within the protest movement throughout the Ottoman Empire after the autonomous government of Crete announced its union with Greece in October 1908. What accounts for the most enthusiastic involvement of Cretan refugees in the boycott movement? The powerful presence of Hellenic nationals in the commercial life of Izmir largely explains the intensity of the boycott in that vibrant city. It also explains why the Cretans, more than any other distinct urban community, consistently held the attention of contemporary observers for their engagement in the protest movement. As we have seen, according to the leading diplomatic agents stationed in Izmir, the main reason for their fierceness lay in the ageless notion of Islamic fanaticism, a widespread conception in European commentaries on Ottoman society. Frequently, this old trope was further accentuated by unfavorable references to the underprivileged class background of refugee boycotters.

Even historians known for a deft examination of intercommunal relations in the Ottoman Empire occasionally reproduced oversimplified assessments of the imperial past. According to Vangelis Kechriotis, a pioneering scholar of late Ottoman history who revised the literature on Greek Ottomans, "This population [Cretan Muslims] without any resources and in a state of misery maintained an unreconcilable hatred against the Christian population due to the hardships they had suffered in Crete."[32] His emphasis on the memory of violence unfolding in Crete illuminates the lasting grip of displacement, while the suggestion of sweeping communal hatred obscures the motivation of refugee protesters. This verdict on the Cretan Muslim community rhymes with multiple oral testimonies of Asia Minor Greeks displaced from their homeland in the aftermath of World War I. In one such account provided by Nicholas Doumanis's insightful work, a Greek Orthodox interviewee from the Black Sea region reminisces about the friendly atmosphere of intercommunal life before World War I. He then adds how things deteriorated "when the Turk-Jews from Salonica and the Cretans arrived. They were fanatical Greek haters. They had some reason to be that way, as they were driven out by the Greeks, who forced them from their villages to our villages."[33]

As much as hatred is undeniably among primary motivators in a climate of tension, not only is it an elusive concept, but it may entrap us in a Huntingtonian framework when attributed to a large social group such as Cretan Muslims. Hatred as an explanation corroborates the way early twentieth-century European observers rendered the fierce anti-Greece boycott legible by viewing it as an outpouring of Islamic fanaticism and rage exhibited by a refugee community. Rather than resort to a shortcut of hatred that explains away the ferocity of Cretan refugees in boycotting Greece, I argue that it is essential to historicize their frequently aggressive activism by foregrounding their violent displacement from Crete, a story that I have narrated in the first two chapters. The refugees' enthusiasm in the protest movement was rooted not in age-old fanaticism or wholesale hatred but in a sense of injustice and loss, economic and beyond, born out of exile from Crete.[34] I suggest that the civil war that dispossessed and displaced them during the 1890s rekindled after 1908, morphing into a violent boycott against Hellenic nationals: first, up to the outbreak of the Balkan Wars (1912–13), with the goal of displacing them economically, and thereafter with the goal of displacing them physically. A tit-for-tat logic that had poisoned intercommunal relations in 1890s Crete found a novel channel of expression in the time of boycott, upending the socioeconomic life of places such as Izmir. In such settings individuals often found themselves chastised if they were perceived to be violating the hardening of intercommunal boundaries, as often happens in civil wars. In Kemer, for instance, a Cretan named Ali kept serving coffee to K. Sevastos, a Hellenic national, flouting the orders of the boycott committee based in that small coastal town near Antalya. The headstrong islander paid for his disobedience with a chair that landed on his head, forcing him to shut his coffee shop.[35]

Although the identification of a sense of injustice in historical actors is as elusive as the detection of hatred, especially in the absence of personal accounts left by those who experienced it, various documents help us catch glimpses of misfortune centered on loss, material or otherwise. Of such sources, I will provide two examples to hint at probable root causes of refugee actions in the anti-Greece boycott, one from the violence-torn Crete of the 1890s and the other from the restless Izmir of 1910.

The first one concerns one of the most dramatic episodes of the civil war in Crete, the evacuation of more than twenty-five hundred Muslim villagers in the southwestern district of Selinos, an incident related by the British consul Alfred Biliotti, a veteran diplomat of Levantine background whose many reports on the conflict in Crete during the 1890s point to an observer sensitive to the plight of civilians. Together with his Italian and Russian colleagues, Biliotti took part in the international military enterprise of bringing the entrapped group, under siege from insurgents heartened by the recently arrived Greek troops of occupation in southwestern Crete, to the safety of the shore. Biliotti reported that at least 104 Muslim villagers, including women and children, were massacred in this bloody episode of the civil war.[36] Describing the procession of hundreds of peasants for longer than ten miles as a "sorrowful march of the exiles," Biliotti spoke of the incident as a "wild, confused, and distressing scene, which certainly cannot be forgotten by those who witnessed it, nor realized by those who were not present."[37] Most of the refugees walked down to the port of the Selinos district with nothing but the clothes on their backs. "These refugees are in such a destitute state and are themselves so convinced of the impossibility of living in the future alongside of the Selinos Christians, that they wish to emigrate to Smyrna."[38]

We do not know under what circumstances these unfortunate people continued this sorrowful journey until they settled down in lands far off from their villages, nor do we know if they really ended up among upwards of thirty thousand displaced islanders in Izmir. As these refugees left no written records narrating their experiences of displacement and their trials and tribulations of building new lives in exile, it is impossible to fathom how they carried the trauma of losing almost everything but their own lives. The lack of such personal accounts is partly redressed by the availability of documents that lend themselves to imagining the emotional states that many Cretan refugees likely inhabited. One such document is a front-page piece published in March 1910 by *Köylü* (Peasant), a popular Turkish-language newspaper from Izmir.[39] Similar in tone and content to countless other articles that filled the pages of Ottoman publications around this time, the piece in *Köylü* portrayed the condition of the small Muslim population in Crete in the gloomiest terms possible, as a minority beset by "political and ethnic murders and aggressions." Especially indicative here is the long preface to this description of the situation of Muslims on the island, constituting a community of about thirty thousand members, slightly less populous than that of Cretan refugees in Izmir around 1910.[40]

The anonymous piece, penned as a first-person narrative, opens by mentioning a recently released song titled "Felek Yar Olmuyor Bana" (Fortune Favors Me Not), which, for the past two months, had gained immense popularity in Izmir. It gripped the bourgeois residents and the wider public alike, savored both in the comfort of affluent households and in the company of friends and strangers in coffeehouses. As the narrator sits one evening in a coffeehouse in Kemeraltı, the lively bazaar neighborhood of Izmir where many a fraught scene of boycott would transpire during the day, he begins to observe the clientele immersed in the quotidian socialization of the space, some in spirited conversation, some busy with cards and others with newspapers. His gaze scanning the mixed crew of customers lands on two Cretans seated at a table near the phonograph, their origins likely identifiable by the distinct outfit sported by the islanders. "Fortune Favors

Me Not" has been playing on the phonograph, and the narrator in *Köylü* observes one of the Cretans listen to it intently, heaving a sigh of sorrow. When they begin to converse among themselves, he wonders why they seem deeply moved by this tune. As one of them plunges into deep thought, cupping his jaw in his hand, the other one grabs a newspaper from the next table, perusing it with deep and frequent sighs. Growing increasingly intrigued about its content, whose anguishing effect on the reader seems to be aggravated by the melancholic song, the narrator subtly walks behind the Cretans' table and glances at a letter from Crete published in the newspaper, which is none other than *Köylü*. Overcome by curiosity about what ties the text of the letter and the tune together, he asks the reader about the evidently intimate connection between them. Putting down the newspaper on the table, one of the islanders stares at him and answers with a bitter smile: "Brother, our fate is left in the hands of fortune. But alas, fortune favors [us] not."[41]

What explains the oft-noted eagerness of the Cretan refugees to engage in the anti-Greece boycott? A definitive answer to this question would be misguided, given that it is challenging, to say the least, to demonstrate the reasoning behind decisions. They are often *just* taken without leaving documented justifications. Narratives that center the displaced, however, may lead us to perceptions of loss and exile as constitutive of collective action. Although intangible, the sense of injustice in being dislocated kindles collective action. In her influential ethnography on exile and memories of homeland among Hutu refugees in Tanzania in the wake of mass violence in Burundi, Liisa Malkki scrutinizes the issue of being a refugee in terms of a condition passed down from one generation to next so long as exile continued and homeland remained a distinct, yet distant possibility. Malkki draws on ethnography conducted fourteen years after the Hutu exodus from Burundi.[42] In the case of the Cretan refugees in Izmir and other locales, a decade had elapsed when they began to be widely noticed in diplomatic correspondence, Ottoman state documents, and local and imperial press coverage. Archival and printed sources suggest that a decade after their displacement, the descriptor of "refugee" remained widely used to characterize the identity of the islanders, severed from Crete physically yet attached to it emotionally.[43] In Malkki's analysis, there were major differences between the condition of what she categorizes as town refugees and camp refugees. Whereas the former "situated the impetus for change in the

Resettling the Displaced into History 153

hands of those Hutu people actually living in Burundi," for those hosted in the camp "the force of change was epicentered in exile. In sum, exile was an era of political empowerment."[44]

In the absence of camps for the displaced in the late Ottoman context, Cretan refugees resided in towns and cities, frequently mixing with other communities, and, in some cases, in suburban settlements that the state built for them especially during the early 1900s. If the displaced Cretans resembled the town refugees in Malkki's study in terms of settlement patterns, they harbored visions comparable to those of the camp refugees in terms of the empowerment of exile. I interpret the street action of those refugees through the prism of political empowerment. Recurrent commentaries about them in state documents and in the press illuminate their newfound prominence in exile and substitute for the lack of ethnographies. Cretan refugees performed the most active roles in the economic boycott against Greece, as though to prevent their home-island from being seized by that nation. In their hands, the boycott turned into a tool of displacement, a grassroots action to erase Hellenic subjects from the commercial life of a city. The erasure from economic life suggested a more radical prospect, disappearance with an exodus from Izmir. The political empowerment that Malkki referred to in her ethnography materialized under much different circumstances for the Cretan refugees, as their central involvement in the boycott can be seen as a process of their transformation from the displaced to the displacers. In other words, their relentless boycott in a city strongly marked by Greekness represented an action that restored them to history as agents of radically disruptive change.

When the Photograph Mobilizes

In late June 1910, Harry Lamb, the British consul in Salonica, reported that Hellenic steamers had stopped showing up in port. Under normal circumstances around ten vessels visited Salonica every week, but with the increasing ferocity of the boycott none had appeared recently.[45] He would write again at the end of summer to inform the embassy in Istanbul about the escalation of the anti-Greece boycott after several weeks of relative quiet in the principal port city of the Balkans. On the final Saturday in August, an Italian national was scheduled to load 110 cattle imported from Serbia onto a Hellenic steamer *Antigone* destined for Italy. The Italian businessman had secured a special permission from the boycott committee thanks to holding a contract with the shipping firm that predated the proclamation of the boycott. But an unpleasant surprise awaited him at the port. When *Antigone* anchored off the port of Salonica, a crowd of several hundred people composed of "Cretans, hodjas, and riffraff" assembled on the quay, "uttering threats against all and sundry who had anything to do with the boat." After Italian and Serbian consulates interceded with the acting governor, a police force was sent to disperse the protesters and the cattle were belatedly loaded only at the end of a tense day. Boatmen of Salonica also refused to do anything with the two other Hellenic steamers, one carrying Austrian timber and the other Russian petroleum from Batumi.[46]

The British consul enclosed the translation of a piece from the Turkish-language daily *Yeni Asır* (New Century) that illuminated the boycott dynamics. It explained why Hellenic ships were prevented from loading their third-party cargo despite the recent decision of the Istanbul boycott committee allowing those vessels to deliver non-Hellenic foreign goods. It was the doing of Kerim Agha, a public-spirited citizen according to the description of the newspaper. As the head of the guild of boatmen (*kayıkçılar kethüdası*) in Salonica, he had paid a visit to the office of *Yeni Asır* to communicate the decision to boycott Hellenic vessels regardless of the provenance of their cargo. Underlying his intransigence with everything Hellenic and the bypassing of the resolution of the Istanbul boycott committee was the news that a Muslim man had been murdered in Rethimno, Crete.[47]

Kerim Agha maintained active ties with a network of boatmen operating between multiple ports. In June 1910, a leading Salonica newspaper, *Rumeli* (Rumelia), wrote that a telegram had been sent to Kerim Agha from Beirut, acknowledging with praise the message received from him earlier.[48] In that message, addressed to the guild of boatmen in Beirut, Kerim Agha had urged them to boycott Greece. Around that time a major Crete rally was held in Beirut. Led by Sheikh Abdul Rahman Salam, a group of protesters walked in a procession through main streets of the city. The center of attention among the crowd was a man who brandished a sword in janissary costume. The British consul highlighted the Islamic character of the assembly by noting that one of the demonstrators flaunted a Quran. The consul reported that the governor appeared resolute to prevent any harm to the local economy, a sign of which was the arrest of Sharqawi, the influential leader of boatmen, for helping a Cretan Muslim damage the property of a boycotted coffeehouse owner.[49]

Malkki's ethnography on the Hutu refugees in Tanzania is pertinent here as well in terms of asking "how the accounts of atrocity come to assume thematic form."[50] The discussion of protest rallies in the previous chapter has shown that the themes of violence were central to the construction of a coherent narrative about Crete in the Ottoman public space. A distinctive trope in it was death, with the common slogan of mass demonstrations "Crete or Death" being one typical indicator. The formation of a necropolitical atmosphere fostered by Crete went beyond the level of discourse. It determined decisions too. Kerim Agha, who evidently wielded influence beyond the port workers of Salonica, made it obvious that his action was informed by the situation in Crete. His persistence fueled by the news of killings suggests the ripples of death from the island and illustrates the potency of death on the island to shape the course of the boycott in the empire. Through examples of death photography, this section examines the construction of a formulaic narrative of violence, which, I argue, lent necropolitical qualities to the Ottoman protest movement.

In late 1909, two postcards were mailed from Salonica to the attention of Minister of Interior Talat Bey, who was also serving as a parliamentary deputy for Edirne at the time. In the back of both postcards was an identical sentence wishing him success on the occasion of the parliament's convocation for its second year. The images on the front side of the postcards stood in stark contrast to the festive message of congratulations. One of them showed a dead man, Hüseyin Soubasaki, in baggy trousers worn by Cretan peasants, naked above the waist, and with a deep scar in his head, which left the headband wrapped around it soaked in blood. Standing around him were six men with arms folded and eyes fixed upon the dead man. In addition to the victim's name, domicile, and date of death, the French caption of the postcard noted that "he was treacherously murdered while working in his field." The Turkish caption that was later penciled in replaced "murdered" with "martyred." The other image showed the dead body of Osman Korasaki, photographed lying on the same bench, bearing the French caption "murdered inside his home." In this postcard too "murdered" was changed to "martyred" in the Turkish translation. The French caption in these postcards seems to indicate that they were originally intended for the attention of European audiences. That these postcards were addressed to a high-profile figure such as Talat Bey suggests that their senders sought out influential channels rather than the general public to communicate a message.[51]

Six months later, the illustrated monthly magazine *Resimli Kitap* (as mentioned in chapter 3, Cretan Yusuf Razi worked for this leading publication) featured these two images in its June 1910 issue. For Ottoman readers this was an eerily unusual sight to encounter when turning the pages of a popular publication. As Susan Sontag posited in her work on photography, "A photograph that brings news of some unsuspected zone of misery cannot make a dent in public opinion unless there is an appropriate context of feeling and attitude."[52] The validity of Sontag's observation regarding the role of affective climate in affording legibility to images is borne out by *Resimli Kitap*'s note that the photographs actually dated from August 1909. The magazine explained that the recent course of the Crete question, with the Christian deputies of the island's parliament taking an oath of allegiance to the king of Greece, had obligated it to release these pictures with almost a year's delay. Indeed, the images of the murdered Muslims from Crete appeared in *Resimli Kitap* during continuous Crete protests throughout the empire. Their publication, accompanied by a long caption in Turkish and French, demonstrates how the targeted audiences of ghastly images broadened from political figures to a wider public. One of the photographs in the magazine showed Hüseyin Soubasaki alone, without the six men surrounding his lifeless body in the postcard sent to Talat Bey six months earlier. Taken from a different angle, blood that had dripped onto the floor from the victim's scarred head added a gory detail that was lacking in the postcard. The Turkish caption underneath the image, entitled "Cretan Tragedies," noted that after the "martyred" Soubasaki was shot, "the murderers maimed his head and organs with knives and sticks." The opposite page of the magazine displayed the photograph of the second victim, Osman Korasaki, presenting it as "a tragic souvenir from Crete . . . to the mercy and humanity of the entire civilized world."[53] Unlike earlier cases of atrocity propaganda involving Muslim Ottoman dead, these examples were not etchings or printed engravings but photographs meant for the public eye. Qualitatively distinct documents with an effect of authenticity, they reached more people thanks to circulating in a setting of an extensive and relatively free press.[54] As Howard Brown observes in his discussion about the photographs of death proliferating amid the violence of the Paris Commune, "The initial psychological impact came from seeing graphic and irrefutable proof of the person's violent death."⁵⁵

Resimli Kitap was a popular publication with a circulation beyond Istanbul, yet we lack information about the exact locations where its pictures of death were seen by the populace. Nevertheless, the juxtaposition of its June 1910 issue with several petitions telegraphed by the organizers of mass rallies that occurred the same month offers a glimpse into the climate of protest under the shadow of death. "The blood we would gladly spill to break the greedy hands reaching toward our beloved Crete will prove our worthiness to our ancestors who fell on the way to Crete," exclaimed the petition sent to the Ministry of Interior from the central Anatolian town of Bozkır. Three hundred miles north, in the town of Çorum, a petition bearing the signatures of Turkish, Greek, and Armenian citizens declared, "We would rather die than live without Crete, the darling [*ciğerpare*] of all Ottomans." The petition following a rally in Urfa emphasized Crete's special position, a strategic one on the map of the Mediterranean and an emotional one in the hearts of Ottomans, and declared people's preparedness "to sacrifice their lives" to safeguard it. Exasperated by the grim news coming from the island, the petitioners from the Black Sea town of Ordu wrote, "No longer can we bear the savage tyranny unfolding [in Crete] before the eyes of the European powers."⁵⁶

In his work on death and the rituals surrounding it in late Ottoman history, Edhem Eldem discusses the shunning of postmortem photography among Muslims, a documented practice among certain Christian communities of the empire.⁵⁷ Similarly, Bahattin Öztuncay mentions the absence of the practice of postmortem photography among Muslim Ottomans by observing that "photographs of the deceased were nearly impossible."⁵⁸ Given the general avoidance of photographic documentation of Muslim bodies, the residents of the Macedonian city of Monastir must have found it disturbing to see the front page of a popular newspaper published in their city. On a May day in 1911, the Turkish-language newspaper *Süngü* (Bayonet) came out with an unusual photograph covering half of its front page (figure 24). The image featured a dead man seeming to be in his thirties, victim to a religiously motivated murder in his native Crete, according to the newspaper's presentation.⁵⁹ It is important to note that the photograph appeared in a newspaper wielding great influence in the region, a point also emphasized in a report that the Austro-Hungarian consul in Monastir sent to Aehrenthal, foreign minister of a European power with a special interest in Macedonia. The consul pointed out that fifteen thousand printed copies of the weekly *Süngü* were eagerly bought, especially by the Muslim population.[60] His remark that the town and village imams habitually read the newspaper aloud to illiterate but enthusiastic crowds indicates that *Süngü*'s circulation numbers would undercount the size of its actual audience. This observation also suggests the audial nature of engaging with textual materials in a largely illiterate society.

The text accompanying the image in *Süngü* offers important clues into the emotions elicited in the Ottomans of that era. Titled "A Blood-Stained Portrait!" the text above the photograph reads: "Lamentable martyr Çaponaki Musa Efendi, murdered in a monstrous manner by the vile thugs of Crete, and his five orphaned children, left bare and naked."[61] In this striking image, the unfortunate man, a cobbler by profession, lies dead in front of his five orphaned children, the oldest aged twelve and the youngest a newborn baby held by an unidentified man.[62] With the obvious exception of the baby, they all look into the camera, as if to gaze into the eyes of anyone, literate or illiterate, who sees the front page of the newspaper.

The longer text underneath the photograph is meant to amplify the visceral emotions prompted by the image, which seems to validate, at least for the publishers of *Süngü*, Susie Linfield's point that "there is no doubt that we approach photographs, first and foremost, through emotions."[63] The first paragraph indicts the so-called contemporary era of progress as an epoch of barbarism in the garb of enlightenment:

> Ye twentieth century! Ye red civilization! Ye guarantor states [of Crete]! May you feel ashamed before the bloodstained sight of this persecuted martyr lying lifeless in red blood and before his five orphans shedding tears of blood, helpless and whimpering. May you blush with shame before these innocent children, shivering and unprotected, who curse with their cries the cruelties of the present age that left them beleaguered as if in the Inquisition dungeons of bygone centuries.

In the remainder of the text, *Süngü* shifts its audience to an internal one in order to address all Ottomans: "Behold! . . . Do you see this persecuted man villainously martyred on the blazing and bloody slopes of that sorrowful island of Crete under the Mediterranean horizons that redden with

FIGURE 24. Front page of the Monastir newspaper *Süngü*. Source: *Süngü*, 18 May 1911.

Muslim Ottoman blood at the fall of dusk? . . . Today the Islamic buildings in Crete are all in decay and everything resembles a dilapidated cemetery [*mezaristan*]."⁶⁴ If through the use of vocative *Süngü* beseeches Europeans to see the death of Muslims, through the use of imperative it calls on the Ottomans to gaze at a tormented man. This image owes part of its visceral quality to an emotionally charged text inserted by the newspaper. What makes the photograph more than an ekphrastic example, however, are the facial expressions of the two little girls standing at the feet of their murdered father. Although staged, this image breaks free of the rigidity widely associated with death. The unimaginable shock evinced by the small children, frequently unruly subjects before the camera, makes this staged photograph relatively free of the stiffness that characterizes most pictures of the period taken with an eye toward public opinion.⁶⁵

A Generative Destruction: To Build from Ruins

In a July 1910 report to Vienna, the Austro-Hungarian ambassador Pallavicini discussed the economic boycott of Greece in port cities along the Mediterranean and the Black Sea. Noting the uninterrupted fierceness of the boycott despite the protests of European powers, Pallavicini observed that "the movement is much deeper and more widespread than the boycott against us," a reference to the first large-scale boycott in the Ottoman Empire launched in reaction to the annexation of Bosnia-Herzegovina in October 1908. The veteran ambassador observed that the orchestrators of the boycott were "no longer concerned with Crete alone, but rather bluntly admit that the purpose of the boycott is to replace the Hellenic ventures, in particular the shipping, with Ottoman ones." For Pallavicini, the reason for the much wider scope of the anti-Greece boycott lay in the large Hellenic diaspora carrying out superior retail trade in the Ottoman Empire and the intentional confusing of "Turkish Greeks" (*türkischer Griechen*) with those from the neighboring Greek Kingdom.⁶⁶

The Austro-Hungarian ambassador required no detailed intelligence reports to make a claim about the purpose of the boycott, for it would suffice to follow the front-page coverage of *Tanin*, arguably the most influential of pro-CUP dailies. Two weeks before Pallavicini's correspondence with Vienna, *Tanin* published a long first-page article with the title "Economic Warfare" (Harb-i İktisadi), a popular epithet to describe the ongoing boycott against Greece.⁶⁷ Authored by Babanzade Ismail Hakkı, a notable Unionist serving as a parliamentarian for Baghdad, the article conveyed two central points. First, treating the boycott as a component of the broader protest movement set off by the Crete question, Ismail Hakkı underscored its popular roots. He equated the phenomenon of boycott with a special type of warfare "declared through the influence of a patriotic voice emanating from the heart of the nation," a description that aptly corresponded to the sonic symbolism surrounding mass mobilization, as discussed in the preceding chapter. If the sites of boycott could be likened to a theater stage, the people represented the main cast, striking heavy blows against Greece's economic standing in the Ottoman Empire. "The government," Ismail Hakkı argued, "lacked the ability to command the people as if they were puppets on a string." The second point of the article concerned the possible long-term consequences of the boycott. Bemoaning the commanding sight of Hellenic flags on Ottoman seas and in front of Ottoman businesses, he predicted the eventual defeat of Greece in this economic warfare. Mindful of the insufficient capital and weaker entrepreneurship of the homegrown merchant class, he anticipated the impracticality of an immediate Ottomanization of Hellenic businesses in the wake of Greece's liquidation of its ventures on both land and sea. Nevertheless, he foretold a victory in the commercial field with a realistic albeit "partial conquest of this field of business" (*bu meydan-ı ticareti kısmen feth*).⁶⁸

In his *Tanin* editorial, Babanzade Ismail Hakkı drew an analogy between military and economic warfare. Among those constituting the muscle power of the boycott, such as porters, longshoremen, and lightermen, many lost their wages, an outcome that resembled the deaths of soldiers in war. Some others saw a drop in their revenues, recalling those injured in armed conflict. This militaristic analogy inevitably led the author to the theme of sacrifice. He argued that the sense of social responsibility, dictated by patriotism, necessitated standing in solidarity with "those assiduous and ferocious soldiers of economic warfare." Because the boycott was not orchestrated by the government, Ismail Hakkı continued, it behooved merchants and tradesmen to devise support mechanisms to compensate for the sacrificial losses of the working-class boycotters. The Baghdad deputy aimed to motivate Ottoman capitalists to perform this burdensome task with a promise of lucrative return on their investment, for they would be the ones to benefit most from the elimination of Hellenic businesses.⁶⁹

When Babanzade Ismail Hakkı wrote these lines in June 1910, he was most likely aware of a scheme worked out by Kerim Agha, the chief of the guild of boatmen in Salonica, a figure who had long held the attention of foreign observers in that city and that of the Ottoman public at large. That scheme was the subject of the report that the British consul Harry Lamb dispatched to the British embassy in Istanbul a week before the publication of Ismail Hakkı's article. Informing the British ambassador of the intensification of the boycott in Salonica, the consul transmitted him the text of a notice issued by the local boycott committee. In the translated document, the boycott committee acknowledged the possibility of mistakenly hurting "the interests of our (Greek) Ottoman fellow-countrymen" and announced the printing of certificates with the purpose of shielding non-Hellenic businessmen from the boycott. Merchants holding Ottoman nationality were asked to apply in writing to Kerim Agha, who would distribute them those documents at the cost of ten piastres.[70] A similar strategy was implemented by boycott committees operating in other cities.

Although we might not know what the certificates distributed by Kerim Agha in Salonica resembled, an example from Istanbul provides an idea about the content of such documents. In July 1910, *Şehbal*, one of the leading illustrated magazines from Istanbul, published a copy of a document, issued by the committee of economic warfare in Istanbul, that certified the participation of its holders in the boycott (figure 25). The Turkish inscription at the top of the paper stated that the purpose of the document was to "introduce to our populace the merchants who swore not to engage in any business transactions with the Hellenes."[71]

The labeling of the boycott as economic warfare accorded with the affective atmosphere surrounding the popularization of the Crete question in the Ottoman Empire. In chapter 4, I examined mass mobilization with an emphasis on its necropolitical and sacrificial climate, underlying the ubiquity of the chant "Crete or Death." In this chapter I have integrated a visual element into that discussion through a brief analysis of postmortem photography. I have demonstrated how the narrative of violence and atrocities committed against Muslim Cretans fueled the boycott by stimulating action against Hellenic interests. In so doing, I have posited a parallel between the actual deaths of islanders and the popular project of killing Greece's economic presence in the empire. It was not a coincidence that those who proved most effective and eager to strike the death blow to Greece's eco-

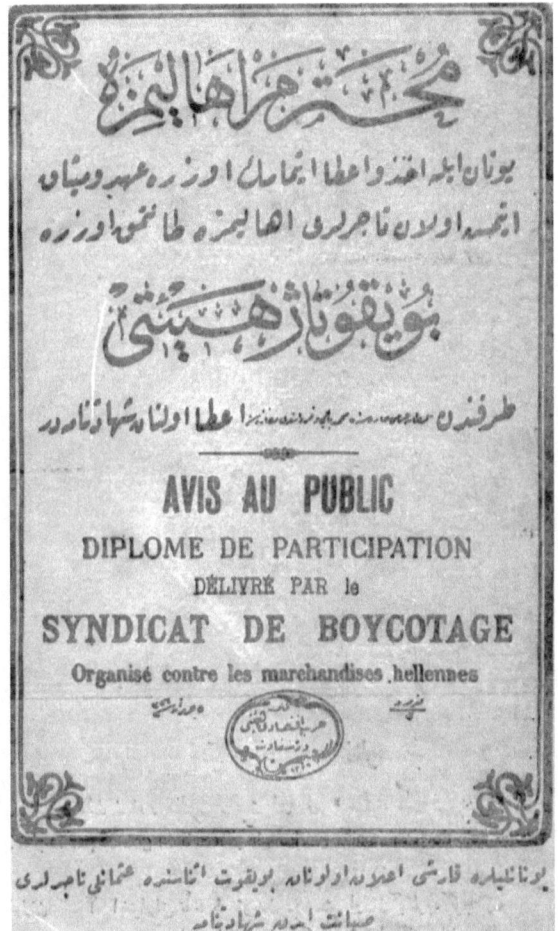

FIGURE 25. Certificate of participation in the anti-Greece boycott. Source: *Şehbal*, no. 23, 28 July 1910.

nomic interests were Cretan refugees. After all, of all Ottomans, they were the ones who, only a decade earlier, had been caught up in a civil war with all its attendant trauma of dispossession and displacement. The formulation of the boycott as economic warfare must have struck a chord for many of those refugees who owed their sorrowful emplacement on the Ottoman mainland to destructively violent strife on their home-island.

CONCLUSION
AGAINST VIOLENCE
Worse Than Refugeehood Is Death

Under the watch of *kaymakam* (district administrator) Ferid Bey, the late spring of 1914 witnessed a violent campaign of terrorizing Greek Orthodox residents of Foça, a prosperous small coastal town near Izmir. The operation, designed to force their flight to Greece, seemed to have unfolded in a spirit of division of labor. Armed bands from the environs of Foça performed the physical labor of bullying and intimidating. Ferid Bey tolerated their descent into the town. He then failed to mobilize the gendarmerie at his disposal to stop the robberies, abuse, and murder.[1]

A native of Iraklio, Crete, Ferid Bey (b. 1872) belonged in the generation of displaced middle-class islanders born around the third quarter of the nineteenth century. Multiple figures within that cohort held instrumental roles in the formulation of what I labeled Crete-speak in chapter 4. The condition of his home-island, its future uncertain and its past marked by mass displacement, likely fostered a fellowship of loss between Ferid Bey and the formulators and propagators of Crete-speak. He too was equipped with an advanced education as a graduate of *mekteb-i mülkiye* (the imperial academy of civil service). Like other displaced middle-class activists, he was proficient in French, Greek, and Turkish. A distinguishing and key feature in Ferid Bey's trajectory was his service in the commission tasked with the resettlement of the Cretan refugees in the Izmir region in 1899. That experience must have highlighted for him the plight of his co-islanders as they embarked on an unfamiliar land.²

The case of Ferid Bey as the principal representative of the state in Foça in 1914 represents a turnabout, a transformation from a victim of dislocation to its perpetrator. As his position shifted from the displaced to the displacer, he began to resemble the refugee boycotters of Cretan origin more closely, despite clear differences in social class. Personal history of displacement alone, as in the cases of Ferid Bey and the nameless boycotters, cannot really account for all the decisions of actors marked by displacement. That biography nevertheless illuminates their emergence as the principal figures driving the process of weakening, or at times even eliminating, the power of *Yunan*, and to a lesser degree *Rum*, in the empire. The refugee boycotters of Izmir, aiming to displace the city's Greeks economically, a gambit that would certainly trigger a total displacement, operated within the same historical plot, albeit in a different register, as Ferid Bey in nearby Foça. However distinct in social origin and incomparable in experiences of dislocation from Crete, a connected examination of these protagonists yields a fuller picture about the lasting impact of displacement across class lines. In this book I have sought to bring together renowned public figures and anonymous members of crowds to steer clear of a narrative neatly divisible into elites and ordinary people.³ The anti-Greece boycott provides a useful setting to jettison binary framings of late Ottoman history through the prism of elites or nonelites, both of which generate distinct categories out of a past that hardly lends itself to parsing.

The question of violence and displacement characterizing the case of Foça in 1914 is relevant well beyond a small town. This was a matter of empire on the eve of World War I. This was an issue that was prominently debated in the Ottoman parliament. In the second sitting of the chamber on 6 July 1914, fourteen Greek Ottoman deputies presented an interpellation. They asked the Interior Ministry to inform the parliament of the measures to restore tranquility on and around the coast of western Asia Minor.⁴ Their motion came in response to a humanitarian crisis generated by what Emre Erol has labeled "organized chaos," a policy of scaring away the Greek Orthodox in droves from their towns and villages, a strategy implemented by actors at the local and imperial level.⁵

Before Talat Bey (later Pasha), the interior minister, proceeded to address the matter, the charged question electrified the hall of deputies. Emmanouil Emmanouilidis, a deputy for Aydın speaking on behalf of Greek Ottoman representatives, remarked that the very fact of being able to raise the matter confirmed that freedom of speech existed in the parliament. His apologetic wording, however, failed to prevent the escalation of emotions among his Turkish colleagues. Parenthetical notes dotting the text of this debate in the published minutes provide a glimpse into the parliamentary soundscape composed of indistinct murmurs and agitated outcries rising against Emmanouilidis's speech. For instance, Rıza Bey, a deputy for Bursa, voiced his irritation: "Do we have to listen to this for hours on end?"[6]

Emphasizing that he was not a *Yunan* deputy but an Ottoman, Emmanouilidis implored his colleagues to lend an ear to him even for half an hour as he talked about 150,000 Greek Orthodox forced away from their homeland. Emmanouilidis traced the root of the mass flight to the phenomenon of boycotting. He acknowledged the complete freedom that private individuals enjoyed in economic transactions. Worth recalling here is that the Unionist proponents of anti-Greece boycotting made a similar point frequently after 1909 as they framed the economic warfare as a grassroots action steered by the people rather than an official entity. Things turned sour quickly, Emmanouilidis continued, when a movement that was born with avowed economic goals morphed into a radical political project. It quickly became a propaganda campaign that tethered the material amelioration of Turkish/Muslim Ottomans to the economic decline of the Greek Orthodox. At this point of Emmanouilidis's speech, a parenthetical remark in the parliamentary minutes recorded the collective cries of "No" from the mouths of multiple deputies. If the boycott movement that sowed discord among the Ottoman communities had been nipped in the bud at its earlier stage, Emmanouilidis asserted, he would not be addressing the parliament about the mass flight of Greeks from Asia Minor. As if to deaden the loud chorus of discontent in the parliament, he underscored his loyalty to the principles of Ottomanism, steering clear of a narrative of wholesale friction at the societal level. Emmanouilidis emphasized that many Muslims decried the aggressive boycott and carried on business with Greek Ottomans. It was through the deployment of thugs (*sopacı*) that the influential boycotters sought to discipline the boycott-breakers. "The job of those thugs," the Aydın deputy remarked, "involved more than violent physical action. They represented an executive force to wage economic warfare."[7]

In Emmanouilidis's telling, the physical violence surrounding the economic boycott coexisted with, or perhaps was born out of, an accusatory discourse in the public sphere that tarred Greek Ottomans with the brush of Hellenism, depicting them as the agents of Hellenic interests in the empire. Interior Minister Talat Bey's urging the parliamentarians to listen with calm seemed to have made little impact as Ziya Bey, a deputy for Izmit, complained, "How can we stay silent before such words?" and Hüseyin Fazıl Efendi, a deputy for Aintab, protested, "But is this going to last until the evening?"[8] Having dwelled on the antecedents of the mass flight of the Greek Orthodox from Asia Minor, Emmanouilidis finally arrived at the core of the interpellation introduced by his fellow Greek Ottoman deputies. He claimed that the government had resettled the Muslim refugees from the Balkans in *Rum* villages across Asia Minor, a policy likely to produce tension between the natives and the displaced given the anti-Greek climate that he had referred to earlier in his speech. While more than one hundred thousand Greeks had departed the empire during the past several months, tens of thousands of them had recently departed the inland towns and villages of Asia Minor, with thirty-five thousand of them living in limbo as refugees in Izmir. They hoped for the provision of security to return home while fearing a forced exile, as in the case of those who crossed the sea to wind up on the opposite shore. The climate of fear produced by the resettlement of Muslim refugees in Greek locales and by armed assaults on the region's Greek inhabitants, two anomalies that Emmanouilidis expected to end with Talat Bey's recent investigative trip to the region, still pushed many to emigrate. Warning that the threat of violence could be as effective a device in driving displacement as actual violence, Emmanouilidis mentioned letters he had received from trusted contacts in Izmir that conveyed the fear that prevented the Greeks from venturing into their fields outside the relative safety of towns.[9]

Emmanouilidis's description of the forced migration of Thracian and Asia Minor Greeks contains several parallels with the story of displacement that I narrated in chapter 1, hinting at similarities between large-scale episodes of dislocation two decades apart. During the civil war in Crete, the atmosphere of panic and uncertainty had doomed tens of thousands, who escaped a real possibility of death in the countryside, to a life of bare survival in the island's coastal cities. In his response to Emmanouilidis,

Talat Bey harkened back not to the Cretan example but to the still bleeding wound of the Balkan defeat. After all, he hailed from Edirne, a Balkan city liberated from the Bulgarian occupation only a year earlier. The interior minister began by citing the atrocities that had befallen the Muslim populations during the Balkan Wars, labeling them "a veritable stain in the history of civilization," a rejoinder to Emmanouilidis, who had used similar wording to describe the events leading up to the Greek exodus.

For Talat Bey, the mass flight of Greeks represented a clear case of the displaced turning into the displacer. In the devastating aftermath of the Balkan Wars, "a flood of displacement" (*seyl-i muhaceret*) sent hundreds of thousands of Muslims to Anatolia, with fresh memories of unspeakable brutalities.[10] "The influx of so many desperate and angry people," as Michael Reynolds notes on the basis of Russian diplomatic sources, "had injected a dangerous anti-Christian element into the empire's politics."[11] Talat Bey stated that the combined force of the mobilization of these traumatized refugees and the ensuing emergence of an emotive atmosphere (*hissiyat*) pregnant with intercommunal tension incapacitated the government. In so saying, not only did he concede the limits of state power but he instrumentalized the refugees to shirk the government's responsibility to safeguard the well-being of its citizens.

Regarding the specific examples of Thrace and Asia Minor, Talat Bey acknowledged the mass flight of Greeks but rejected the accusation that the state tolerated, let alone encouraged it. As for the example of the Greek emigration from Edirne, he remarked that during the short-lived Bulgarian occupation of this Thracian city, some of its Greek inhabitants committed cruelties against their neighbors, poisoning intercommunal relations and making the previous coexistence untenable after the city was retaken by Enver Bey in July 1913. Drawing on his observations from an investigative tour in the region, Talat Bey related that the Greek villagers cited the pressure they were subjected to as the reason for emigration, a claim denied by the local authorities, who tied the flight to a profound fear of retribution that seized them. As for the example of Foça and the anti-Greek violence there mentioned by Emmanouilidis, Talat Bey confirmed the cases of plunder and murder, adding that he had inquired into the incidents and had ordered the dismissal of *kaymakam* Ferid Bey for dereliction of duty.[12] Finally, regarding the question of the boycott, Talat Bey insisted that the central government disapproved of its forceful and violent implementation. He noted that scores of individuals, civil servants and plain civilians alike, had been convicted in extraordinary courts and that the policemen failing to prevent, or worse, eager to tolerate the excesses of the boycott had been dismissed. This was a candid confession of official involvement in the campaign of intimidation, popularly dubbed economic warfare.[13]

The story of displacement that I have told in *Island and Empire* is, at the same time, a story of replacement. Muslim displacement from Crete during the late 1890s, the anti-Greece boycott after 1909, the removal of the Greek Orthodox from Asia Minor, including the case of Foça—all point to a process of replacement that hinged on displacement. As discussed in chapter 1, the first case of displacement involved not just the departure of Muslims but the vanishing of the socioeconomic landscape that had defined Ottoman Crete. With fields and other real estate owned by Muslims shifting hands, the island's land tenure changed dramatically. Christian islanders replaced Muslims as predominant landowners. In the case of the anti-Greece boycott between 1909 and 1911, at least some of the violent boycott-mongers saw a promise in the movement of economic warfare, the seeds of material revival of Turkish Ottomans at the expense of Greeks. This was also one of the claims made by Emmanouilidis during the parliamentary debate in July 1914. The cultivation of a climate of fear and terror between the end of the Balkan Wars and the start of World War I represented the further radicalization of the earlier boycott. Ethnic replacement intensified through the resettlement of Balkan refugees in heavily Greek Orthodox areas in Asia Minor, again a point that Emmanouilidis made in explaining the driving force behind the mass flight of his coreligionists.

"A Victim of Exile" against "the Injustice of Expulsion"

The previous section covered a debate that Emmanouil Emmanouilidis and his fellow Greek Ottoman parliamentarians initiated in July 1914. Perhaps the exchange was short, lasting only minutes, yet it touched upon manifold processes such as boycott, war, mass expulsion, and resettlement, all of which cast a long shadow in late Ottoman and modern Middle Eastern history. The remainder of this conclusion offers some reflections on the question of violence and displacement through the story of Hüseyin Nesimi (b. 1868, Hania, Crete), whom I introduced in chapter 1 as the coauthor of a voluminous book detailing the atrocities that befell Muslim islanders during the civil war in Crete. I pivot to his case through the medium of another parliamentarian.

On 24 April 2021, Garo Paylan, the single Armenian deputy in the Turkish national assembly, posted a photograph of Hüseyin Nesimi as part of his tweet commemorating the 106th anniversary of the Armenian genocide, a process of forced removal and mass killing that erased most of the Armenian presence in the Ottoman Empire. "Hüseyin Nesimi Bey, the *kaymakam* of Lice, was slain for opposing the expulsion [*tehcir*] and massacres [*katliamlar*] of Armenians," began Paylan's tweet to around half a million followers and beyond. "With his example in mind, I bow with respect before the memory of all public officials who refused to become complicit in the crime at the cost of their lives. May this land [Turkey] become the country not of Talat Pashas but Hüseyin Nesimi Beys."[14] That Hüseyin Nesimi's assassination was widely believed to have been ordered by Dr. Mehmed Reşid (b. 1873), the governor of Diyarbakır province, perhaps deepened the sympathy that Paylan, himself a parliamentary representative of the city of Diyarbakır, expressed for Nesimi.[15] The statement was short, containing only 280 characters, yet it involved a plea for coming to terms with the mass violence that cast a lingering shadow over the modern history of Turkey and that of the Middle East more broadly.

Paylan's brief text called for paying homage to the *kaymakam* of Lice, a meaningful appeal given the obscurity surrounding Hüseyin Nesimi's name. In the 1954 edition of the biographical encyclopedia of the graduates of *mekteb-i mülkiye*, Nesimi, an alumnus of 1888, receives only a short mention that reads, "It has been ascertained that he passed away and no other records about him have been found."[16] The 1968 edition of the same encyclopedia devotes a longer entry to him that includes a portrait photograph and a copy of a letter that he sent as a seventeen-year-old student in Istanbul to a newspaper published in Crete, in which he encouraged his fellow islanders to give utmost importance to the education of children.[17] The encyclopedia does not dwell on the death of Nesimi but includes the official story that he was martyred by *çetes* (paramilitary gangs) during the pursuit of outlaws. It also adds the alternative narrative offered by his son, that he was martyred by a *çete* following his disagreement with CUP policies. Both versions identify the culprits to be an undefined armed band, an ambiguity that befits Nesimi's historical legacy enveloped in "silences [that] are inherent in history because any single event enters history with some of its constituting parts missing. Something is always left out while something else is recorded."[18] Nesimi was condemned to obscurity and oblivion through a layered silencing occurring within the realms of historiography and official national memory. Nesimi's writings and deeds have eluded the scrutiny of historians. His legacy in the public realm has remained hidden while his body has lain in an unmarked grave near the spot where a Circassian gendarmerie force, reporting to the governor of the Diyarbakır province, Dr. Mehmed Reşid, took his life in 1915.[19] As Rosie Bsheer notes, "Erasure is not simply a countermeasure to the making of history: it is History."[20]

In his 1918 book titled *Osmanlı Vilayat-ı Şarkiyesi* (Eastern Ottoman Provinces), Ali Emiri (b. 1857, Diyarbakır), a renowned bibliophile with a long career in state service, referred to Hüseyin Nesimi as a "persecuted martyr" (*şehid-i mazlum*), killed for defying the governor's orders, one life sacrificed to save many Armenian lives.[21] Ali Emiri's remarks merit further quoting as they historicize the *kaymakam*'s righteous deeds, prompting us to consider them within the context of bearing witness to mass violence in his native Crete two decades earlier:

> Behold the supreme degree of purity adorning the conscience of true Muslims. As a native of Crete, Nesimi Bey saw the injustice and persecution endured by the Muslims there. He was a victim of exile [*vatan mağduru*], severed from his homeland together with his fellow Muslim islanders. In view of this, he, nevertheless, sacrificed his own life to spare the Armenians the injustice of expulsion [*tehcir mağduriyeti*], the bitter taste of which he had experienced. May God have mercy upon his soul.[22]

There is perhaps a hint of astonishment in Ali Emiri's commentary about a Muslim victim of displacement striving to rescue non-Muslims from a comparable tragedy (the word *tehcir* suggests that Ali Emiri imagined Nesimi as a *muhacir*). The tone of surprise in his words would accord with the gist of historiography on displacement. Characteristic works in such scholarship feature a diasporic prototype and reproduce a model of prominent individuals hardened by forced migration. In such accounts, displacement, as firsthand experience or as legacy, plays a formative role in setting off processes of a radicalization that makes staunch ideologues, and sometimes perpetrators, out of exilic figures. Dr. Mehmed Reşid fits the stereotype. As underscored by Uğur Ümit Üngör, the recognition of vindictive feelings and memories of ethnically targeted persecution allows for more historically informed analyses of perpetrators.[23] In many ways, Mehmed Reşid was a product of Tsarist violence in the Caucasus. Together with several other influential figures such as Yusuf Akçura and Ahmed Agayef/Ağaoğlu from Russia, he contributed to the amplification of Turkish nationalism in the late Ottoman Empire.[24]

A caveat is in order here. The fatal encounter between Hüseyin Nesimi and Dr. Reşid, two Unionists, the former with roots in Crete and the latter in the Russian Caucasus, could easily lend itself to the recounting of a Manichean narrative, in which life stories and motivations of complex personalities are distilled into an ultimate clash between good and evil. It would be more straightforward to relate the fateful confrontation between these two figures through stark contrasts, typifying one of them as victim and the other as perpetrator. A more nuanced profile, however, can be drawn by showcasing the parallels between them. This would accentuate certain Unionist tenets held in common by the two personalities, who were sharply divided in their responses to the Armenian question during the final years of the empire.

Perhaps the most striking feature common to their worldviews was the indictment of the West for what they perceived as its long-held policy of brutality and hypocrisy toward the non-Western world in which the Ottomans held a special place.[25] The fraught history of the waning of the Ottoman rule over Crete following the European intervention there provided much fodder to the Young Turks, both in European and Egyptian exile before 1908 and in government after then, for calling out European Ottomanophobia. By their accounts, Crete became a byword for European encroachment on the empire's sovereign rights. Later, in 1919, Dr. Reşid decried how "serial gunfire put down the independence protests of the Irish. . . . The rifles stopped short the action of the free and ancient Morocco against the enemy assaults, while the freedom of Iran and the rights of Egypt were violated . . . and all of this clothed in the garb of civilization and humanity! Is this humanity? Is this civilization?"[26] On his part, Hüseyin Nesimi exclaimed in his detailed and sorely overlooked 1914 book *Sahib Zuhur* that "the European powers have committed much oppression and savagery, ranging from the actions of the English in India, Africa, and beyond; the French in Tunisia and Algeria; and the Belgians in Congo. Heaps rose of the amputated hands of the Congolese resisting forced labor, dumdum bullets and machine gun fire decimated the innocent tribes of the Sahara, a war was waged against the Chinese to force on them an addiction to opium."[27] Through the listing of such crimes Nesimi expressed disdain for the highest stage of Western modernity as "a so-called humanity!" (*zehi insaniyet!*) and branded the European collectivity "a Crusader's assemblage that we call Europe" (*Avrupa dediğimiz mecmua-i salib*).[28]

Educated in elite public institutions and au courant with world affairs, Dr. Reşid and Hüseyin Nesimi epitomized the quintessential late Ottoman administrator-cum-intellectual. They expressed a pronounced sense of mission to save the state perceived to be besieged by external and internal foes.[29] For them, the external threat materialized in the form of the Western onslaught, carried out not only by dreadnoughts and machine guns but through missionaries and merchants, before which the Ottomans stood as the last bastion of the East. Both Dr. Reşid and Hüseyin Nesimi fit the typology of the hyperpolitical and West-suspicious Young Turks, who, in the words of Cemil Aydın, deemed "the Ottoman Empire a member not of the club of empires but of the victimized East and Muslim world."[30] "The West," Nesimi exclaimed, "is the shameless enemy and the restless adversary of the East."[31]

As for the identification of internal threats besetting the state, some common ground existed between the two Unionists, yet I had better briefly address the difference that divided them sharply, in fact lethally. Insisting on the necessity of implementing "strong measures" against Armenian Ottomans, Dr. Reşid remarked that "the lack of action before the preparations and cruel deeds of the Armenians would amount to a suicide for our nation and state."[32] In his memoirs that rather read as a text of self-defense, he acknowledged the violations under his watch against the Armenians of the Diyarbakır province in 1915 but absolved himself of direct responsibility by ascribing the misdeeds to a host of groups such as refugees, tribes, Armenian bands, and the local population eying opportunities to plunder Armenian property, an explanation reminiscent of Talat Bey's distribution of the blame for the human rights abuses against Asia Minor's Greek Orthodox in 1914.[33]

Hüseyin Nesimi thought differently about Armenian Ottomans. In his 1914 book *Sahib Zuhur*, he asserted that there was no nationalities question in Eastern Anatolia, a remark suggesting that Armenians and Kurds lived in relative harmony: "It is undeniable that the two communities [Christians and Muslims in the Ottoman East], who have been working for centuries in solidarity within the realm of economy, be it in the fields or in the markets, harbor mutual feelings of respect for their national and religious ethos."[34] He argued that it was the Armenians from the Caucasus who disrupted the peace enjoyed by Anatolian Armenians, a noteworthy claim considering that it came from a diasporic figure like Nesimi. Careful not to paint Armenian Ottomans with the brush of separatism that he saved for the Caucasus revolutionaries alone, Nesimi wrote that "he could not think of any Armenian willing for the dissemination of Caucasus currents across a region where they lived most tranquilly and happily, as it would only spell a terrible blow to their national existence." Identifying Russia as the chief instigator of the "Caucasus currents," keeping alive the hopes for Armenian autonomy with its deceptive assurances, he harkened back to history by recalling how "the promises made to Crimean Tatars drove them to their pit of death."[35] He remarked that "the failure to learn from history would be calamitous," having in mind the example of Crimean Tatars, whose legacy of autonomy was smothered under Russian subjugation. For Nesimi, faith in Russian promises would send Armenian Ottomans to "fall from an illustrious position of prestige, thrusting them under the enemy's feet and putting an end to their life and erasing their identity." Expressing nothing but praise for Armenian Ottomans, describing them as "civilized and intelligent," he nevertheless issued words of warning for "our beloved fellow citizens [Armenians]" that "trading the joy of living for the chasing of imaginary visions" would bring about a calamity leading to a grave.[36]

In envisioning history as the repository of lessons for future generations, Hüseyin Nesimi exemplified a generation of educated Ottomans with a heightened degree of political sensibility. The origin of such powers bestowed on the knowledge of the past obviously predated the late nineteenth century. But the regarding of history as a guiding beacon gained much traction during Nesimi's lifetime with the higher volume and wider reach of publications propagating such conviction (figure 26). In Nesimi's interpretation of the recent past, history functioned as a tool for guidance or for prophecy. If he summoned history as a counsel in the case of Armenian Ottomans, urging them not to pursue a misguided course of action, he invoked it with a prophetic effect in the example of Greek Ottomans.

The discussion of the Armenians occupies a mere seven pages in *Sahib Zuhur*, his tome of 434 pages examining various challenges facing the Otto-

FIGURE 26. In this front-page illustration of *Kalem* (Pen), a leading satirical magazine, History, represented as a wise elderly man, almost like a prophet, exhorts the grand vizier Kıbrıslı Kamil Pasha to seek guidance from the past. "The peace, my son, the peace. . . . Remember 1877 (1293)." Source: *Kalem*, no. 4, 25 September 1908.

man Empire. Tens of pages, on the other hand, are devoted to the coverage of the Greeks. While a telling difference by itself, a more substantial way of appraising the difference between these populations in terms of threats to the state is through the content rather than the number of pages. Identifying Greeks as the group posing the most serious internal danger to the survival of the empire, Nesimi considered the epicenter of this threat to be coastal Asia Minor, the region that saw the fiercest implementation of the anti-Greece boycott from 1909 onward. "Particularly around the coastal areas of Anatolia resides a *Yunan* element awaiting the commands from Ethniki Etaireia [the National Society]," Nesimi warned. He saw the secret revolutionary society founded in 1894 in Athens, an organization that actively pushed for Crete's annexation to Greece during the civil war on his native island, as the mastermind of Hellenic irredentism in the Ottoman Empire.[37]

Regarding the external root of the menace facing the Ottoman state, Nesimi likened the Armenian and Greek cases, with the former based in the Caucasus and the latter in Greece. In terms of the reception of foreign propaganda, however, these native populations stood qualitatively apart from each other. "There is ample evidence," Nesimi remarked, "that this harmful element [*Yunanlıs*] would manage to corrupt the *Rum* of Anatolia."[38] Once again, the historical record held up a mirror to the present, but with implications distinct from the Armenian case. According to Nesimi, thanks to the activities of Ethniki Etaireia, the Christian inhabitants of southern Albania, who had until recently preserved their language and customs, underwent a process of cultural Hellenization. And Crete, where the Muslims had constituted until the late eighteenth century half of its population, finally became part of Greece. If the vigorous irredentism of Greece had succeeded in replacing the Muslim strength in Crete, measured not only in numbers but in economic and cultural impact, with a Christian supremacy, who could deny that Ethniki Etaireia had the ability to perform a similar feat in Anatolia?[39] The Greek Orthodox Patriarchate of Constantinople, Nesimi went on to argue, operated in league with this society that championed the cause of greater Greece, undermining the ties of Greek Ottomans to the empire through bishops and priests who resembled the executive arm of a clandestine government rather than religious figures.[40] Here it is important to recall that the perception of the Greek Orthodox religious establishment as anti-Ottoman had already taken root among many prominent Unionists after 1908. Such views helped foster an atmosphere of hostility against the native *Rum* at the time of boycott and protest. That Nesimi expressed no negative sentiments about the Armenian patriarchate, the second major Christian clerical establishment in the empire, also fit well into the public discourse of certain CUP figures who frequently praised the Ottoman patriotism of Armenian priests, juxtaposing them against their Greek Orthodox counterparts.[41]

In the final two chapters of *Island and Empire* I discussed how the displaced activists from distinct social classes animated the Ottoman protest movement with words and meanings linked to Crete. The lexicon of an island, comprising such characteristic themes as atrocity, martyrdom, dispossession, and displacement, pervaded the mass mobilization. While an island is an insular space in the literal sense of the word, the type of insularity I have explored highlights Crete's strong ties to the broader imperial geography. It suggests connectivity, not obscurity. Cretan Ottomans were deeply invested in the affairs of their homeland, and it was only natural that they would seek to amplify, in words and deeds, Crete's significance beyond an insular setting. In that regard, Hüseyin Nesimi constructed a narrative in *Sahib Zuhur* as if Crete were a lighthouse shining the rough seas navigated by the imperial vessel. Lodged in the history of Crete were signposts that he urged his audience to notice and take seriously. The depiction of Crete as having an outsized impact, with events unfolding there commanding an influence well beyond its shores, was perhaps expected of Nesimi and his co-islanders. In no way did such thinking, however, remain the prerogative of Cretans. For instance, in February 1897, only weeks before the breakout of the Greco-Ottoman War, Abidin (Dino) Pasha (d. 1906), the governor of the province of the Aegean Islands (Cezair-i Bahr-i Sefid), warned in his correspondence with the Yıldız Palace that "God forbid, should Greece, the nemesis of our state and religion fixing its covetous gaze on Crete, attain its goal, it will turn its avaricious glare first to the Aegean islands and later to Macedonia and Epirus." The experienced statesman saw a trendsetting quality in the example of Crete. He anticipated that separatist currents in the empire would be either restrained or incited depending on the progression of the Cretan question.[42]

Only days before the start of the 1897 war, the domino effect that Crete was imagined to wield and the attribution of suspect loyalties to the Greek Orthodox population found another expression. This time the sentiment was displayed in an even more official capacity, with the Ottoman Council of Ministers referring to the perilous ripples that Crete's loss would send across the islands much closer to Anatolia.[43] The fear of ripple effects that Crete could produce across the regions inhabited by Greek Ottomans only grew in later years, with frequent references in the Unionist press. One representative example among many alarmist pieces was *Tanin*'s warning in early 1909, coinciding with the start of mass Crete rallies throughout the empire, that the island's loss to Athens would ultimately lead the entire Anatolian coast to turn into "a colony of Greece" (*Yunan müstemlekesi*).[44]

The Long Shadow of Civil War

Island and Empire has narrated dispossession in 1890s Crete and protest and boycott in the post-1908 Ottoman Empire as threads weaving a story of displacement from an island to the mainland. In the final two chapters, I have suggested that the refugee protesters, most of them from peasant or urban lower-class backgrounds, saw in their confrontation with the *Yunan* an extension of the civil war that had displaced them from Crete a decade earlier. The refugee protesters obviously knew that their displacement was not caused by *Yunan* inhabitants of Asia Minor, against whom they mounted an opposition and with whom they stood on an intimate footing thanks to their being native speakers of Greek. We might lack written evidence as to whether they shared the concerns voiced by multiple statesmen and journalists that certain areas such as the Aegean islands and Asia Minor could become a second Crete. Absence of written evidence, however, does not suggest evidence of absence. Thanks to knowledge of Greek and familiarity with the urban environment of Izmir, where a fraction of the population championed or condoned a resurgent Greece, a segment of lower-class Cretan refugees certainly perceived an element of menace in the visual (Greek flag and blue-white national colors) and audible (pro-Athens chatter and exclamations) manifestations of Hellenism. In this book I have argued that they engaged such threats, real or imagined, through the strength of their muscles, as they implemented a violent boycott of Greek stores, and of their lungs, as they shouted the loudest slogans in the rallies. I suggest that the evidence lay in the streets. Its most direct and authoritative form, however, eludes the historian. Nevertheless, multiple contemporary sources underscore the active involvement of the Cretan refugees in the protest movement in a manner to set them apart from other identifiable social groups. Much commented on in historical documents, such eagerness suggests that unaddressed injustices of displacement still haunted them a decade later. Dispossession and dislocation caused by the devastating violence in Crete presented, at least for some, a motivation for making the Greeks pay in kind.

The case of Hüseyin Nesimi encapsulates the lasting grip of history, leading me to posit that the woes of civil war and displacement energized his Hellenophobia. He was divided in terms of social class from the street boycotters of Cretan background, who dominated the movement in the prosperous port city of Izmir. The experience of dislocation from the home-island, however, united him with them. The case of Nesimi, "a victim of exile," in Ali Emiri's poignant description, helps historicize the activism of the displaced in the Ottoman world. His example illuminates the long shadow cast by civil war, an elusive matter in the case of street protesters, making a foray into their motivations more challenging. Hüseyin Nesimi advanced one of the most striking assertions of a bond between an island and empire when he wrote, "Ethniki Etaireia, striving to accomplish its objectives, would turn Anatolia into an arena of atrocity reminiscent of Crete."[45] In *Sahib Zuhur*, he reproduced the ubiquitous imagery of the blood of martyrs in popular rallies that painted the history of Crete red, by asserting that "the island of Crete has been molded by blood."[46] In his possibly most antagonistic description of the *Rum* of Asia Minor, he argued that "the *Rum* in general identify as *Yunan* and wish for the bad fortune of the Ottoman nation [*millet-i Osmaniye*]," a statement excluding the great majority of Greek Ottomans from the imperial family.[47]

I am reluctant to envision Nesimi as a stand-in for the Muslims displaced from Crete. I rather imagine him as an administrator-cum-intellectual in possession of literary tools and cultural capital, which allowed him to foreground Crete in his narrative of the empire. Nesimi's interpretation of conflict is steeped in history. His framework identifies Greek nationalism and European imperialism as the leading factors to explain violence in Crete, avoiding the facile trope of ancient hatreds between Christians and Muslims. Nesimi's distrust and hostility toward the Greeks, first and foremost related to those from his native island but also beyond them, do not imply a primordial condition. Those sentiments are historical. They are rooted in a chronicle of strife that began to take shape from the late eighteenth century onward. Against the backdrop of violence, "the exemplary affection and strikingly warm coexistence between the two communities [Crete's Christians and Muslims] retained, until recent times, its impact despite all the mutual killings [*mukatelat*] and fights."[48]

I have argued that during the late nineteenth century, the Ottoman Turkish word *mukatelat* (from the Arabic verb *qatala*) conveyed the idea of civil war. The expression summons the image of a society with its constituent elements locked up in an internecine fight. In this sense, *mukatelat* accorded with the terms that multiple contemporary observers used during the 1890s in English (civil war), French (*la guerre civile*), German (*Bürgerkrieg*), and Greek (*emfylion*). With this word Nesimi described the episodes of intercommunal clashes in Crete while drawing broader lessons for the Ottoman state. His handling of two scales of analysis, an island and empire, parallels the essence of my approach in *Island and Empire*. I posit that not only does civil war terminology explain the Cretan case better than such common notions as revolt or revolution, but it prompts us to reframe our histories of violence in the late Ottoman Empire.

Despite the great strides scholarship has made toward nuanced analyses, fanaticism and feelings of pure revenge are still enduring factors that masquerade as causes of interethnic violence in the Ottoman world. The case of occasionally aggressive activism of Cretan refugee protesters in cities like Izmir is no exception. I have argued that violence needs to be historicized not only in its manifestation (in this case, Crete in the 1890s) but in its legacies (mainland empire post-1908). I have proposed locating the eagerness of refugee boycotters under the long shadow cast by civil war. There is an extensive literature on the politics of civil war with an emphasis on factionalism and fighting to take over the state. In this book I have chosen to focus on its sociocultural dimensions. And in this regard the element of intercommunal intimacy has relevance. As Stathis Kalyvas remarks, "[The violence of civil wars] often takes place where there is a record of closeness and peaceful interaction between victims and victimizers, even on the individual level."[49] Understanding the assertive collective action of Cretan refugees requires taking seriously the sense of injustice caused by the dispossession and displacement of the Cretan civil war. But this alone is insufficient. It is also essential to consider the degree of intimacy shared with the Greeks, common language being one of its most significant components. I suggest that such tension between antagonism and closeness also illuminates Hüseyin Nesimi's fixation with the peril that Greece, and by extension many domestic (*Rum*) and foreign (*Yunan*) Greeks, posed to the Ottoman Empire. For refugee boycotters and displaced intellectuals alike, the civil war that raged during the 1890s smoldered as the trauma of exile from Crete lingered. If the former represented the street element of a lingering civil war, the latter featured the elite corps.

Civil wars show humans at their worst—and best. They are ferocious conflicts in which neighbors turn against neighbors. They are also occasions for rescue, attempted by righteous individuals, sometimes at the risk of death. In chapter 1, I mentioned several such examples from the fiercest phase of violence in Crete. It would be opportune to conclude *Island and Empire* by paying homage to Hüseyin Nesimi, whose remarkable life was cut short at the age of forty-seven while he was trying to save as many Armenian Ottoman civilians as possible from deportation, a criminal act of expulsion and murder performed in the name of the fatherland (*vatan*).

There are many passionate sections in reference to the persecution of Muslims in Nesimi's book *Girit Hailesi*, written during the late 1890s when the embers of the civil war in Crete were still burning. But one part stands out. This is a passage that the author would republish more than fifteen years later in the preface to his *Sahib Zuhur*. It holds a plea for redress regardless of the victim's identity. And the words become more meaningful considering how Hüseyin Nesimi spent his last breath: "I had remarked in *Girit Hailesi* that the Omnipotent, grieved by all the terrible murders committed for the sake of the fatherland, will in the end restore its absolute justice [on earth]."[50]

ABBREVIATIONS USED IN NOTES

ASDMAE   Archivio Storico Diplomatico del Ministero degli Affari Esteri (Italian Diplomatic Archives)

BNA   British National Archives

BOA   Devlet Arşivleri Başkanlığı Osmanlı Arşivi (Ottoman State Archives)

CADC   Centre des archives diplomatiques (French Foreign Ministry Archives in La Courneuve)

CADN   Centre des archives diplomatiques (French Foreign Ministry Archives in Nantes)

EEKP   *Episimos Efimeris tis Kritikis Politeias* (Official Gazette of the Cretan State)

HHStA   Haus-, Hof- und Staatsarchiv (Family, Court and State Archives of the Austrian State Archives)

IAPAK   Istoriko Arheio tou Panepistimiou Kritis (Historical Archives of University of Crete)

MMZC   *Meclis-i Mebusan Zabıt Ceridesi* [Minutes of the Ottoman Chamber of Deputies]

YDIA   Ypiresia Diplomatikou kai Istorikou Arheiou (Hellenic Foreign Ministry Archives)

NOTES

Introduction: No Refugee Is an Island

1. Translation mine. For an alternative translation, see Nazım Hikmet, *Selected Poetry*, trans. Randy Blasing and Mutlu Konuk (New York: Persea Books, 1986), 125.

2. This paragraph draws on observations from the following archives: Haus-, Hof- und Staatsarchiv (Family, Court and State Archives of the Austrian State Archives, hereafter HHStA), PA XII, Liasse XXVIII, 279, Vice-Consul Berinda to Julius von Pinter, Iraklio, 6 August 1896; Devlet Arşivleri Başkanlığı Osmanlı Arşivi (Ottoman State Archives, hereafter BOA), Y.A.RES. 81/7, Foreign Minister to Sublime Porte, 6 August 1896 (25 Temmuz 1312); British National Archives (hereafter BNA), FO 421/155, Alfred Biliotti to Marquess of Salisbury, Iraklio, 7 August 1896; Archivio Storico Diplomatico del Ministero degli Affari Esteri (Italian Diplomatic Archives, hereafter ASDMAE), 144, Augusto Medana to Alberto Pansa, Hania, 8 August 1896.

3. H. H. Munro (Saki), "The Jesting of Arlington Stringham," in *The Short Stories of Saki* (1911; repr., New York: Viking Press, 1930), 150.

4. Akin to various diplomatic questions throughout what Holly Case aptly describes as "the extremely long nineteenth century (1770–1970)," the Crete question too was "linked to the possibility of a broader European conflict in the minds of many querists." *The Age of Questions: Or, A First Attempt at an Aggregate History of the Eastern, Social, Woman, American, Jewish, Polish, Bullion, Tuberculosis, and Many Other Questions over the Nineteenth Century, and Beyond* (Princeton, NJ: Princeton University Press, 2018), xiv, 104.

5. Célestin Albin, *L'île de Crète: Histoire et souvenirs* (Paris: Sanard et Dérangeon, 1898), 147–62; Mustafa Yavuz, *Demokratik İhtilaller Çağında Girit* (Istanbul: Belge Yayınları, 2017), 205–47.

6. At an initial stage, Austria-Hungary and Germany also took part in the military intervention. Both withdrew from Crete in early 1898, fixing the number of states in

the European coalition at four. In March 1898, Frank Lascelles, British ambassador to Germany, reported that Emperor Wilhelm II had told him on multiple occasions that Germany had no interests in the Mediterranean. BNA, ADM121/53, F. Lascelles to the Marquess of Salisbury, 16 March 1898.

7. Titus 1:12–13, *Greek-English New Testament* (Stuttgart: Deutsche Bibelgesellschaft, 1979).

8. Aristotelis Korakas Collection, Istoriko Arheio tou Panepistimiou Kritis (Historical Archives of University of Crete, hereafter IAPAK), Aristotelis Korakas to Christian inhabitants of the Candia province, 15 February 1897 (3 February 1897).

9. BOA, Y. PRK. A. 11/35, Muslim Community of Rethimno to Sublime Porte, Ottoman Foreign Ministry, Embassies of Great Britain, France, Italy, Russia, Germany, and Austria, 19 February 1897.

10. ASDMAE 145, Italian Consulate to Tommaso Catalini, Hania, 31 January 1895.

11. BNA, FO 195/2345, A. C. Wratislaw to Edward Grey, Hania, 21 April 1910.

12. BOA, İ.MTZ.GR 32/1248, Turhan Pasha to Sultan, 1 November 1897 (20 Teşrinievvel 1313).

13. Mustafa Nuri, "Girit Müslümanlarının Suzişli Bir Feryadı," *Tanin*, 9 November 1908 (27 Teşrinievvel 1324).

14. Nikos Kazantzakis in a radio interview with Pierre Sipriot, Paris, 6 May 1955, https://www.historical-museum.gr/webapps/kazantzakis-pages/en/life/talkforcrete.php.

15. Leonidas Kallivretakis, "A Century of Revolutions: The Cretan Question between European and Near Eastern Politics," in Paschalis M. Kitromilides, ed., *Eleftherios Venizelos: The Trials of Statesmanship* (Edinburgh: Edinburgh University Press, 2006), 11–35; John S. Koliopoulos and Thanos M. Veremis, *Modern Greece: A History since 1921* (Chichester: Wiley-Blackwell, 2010), 46–47; Pınar Şenışık, *The Transformation of Ottoman Crete: Revolts, Politics and Identity in the Late Nineteenth Century* (London: I. B. Tauris, 2011).

16. Tobie Meyer-Fong, *What Remains: Coming to Terms with Civil War in 19th Century China* (Stanford, CA: Stanford University Press, 2013), 10.

17. Antonios N. Giannaris, *Peri tēs Katastaseōs tēs en Krētē Geōrgias kai Emporias: Syntomos kai Praktikē Meletē* (Hania, 1906), 12–13.

18. Titled "Turkish Civil War, 1919–22," a recent essay offers a reappraisal of the Turkish War of Independence. See Mesut Uyar, "Türk İç Savaşı, 1919–22," *Toplumsal Tarih*, no. 347 (November 2022): 12–15. Uyar emphasizes the reluctance of Turkish historians to employ the concept of civil war in understanding the rival struggles between various factions in post–World War I Anatolia. For one exception that he cites, see Sina Akşin, *İstanbul Hükümetleri ve Milli Mücadele III: İç Savaş ve Sevr'de Ölüm* (İstanbul: Türkiye İş Bankası Yayınları, 2010). In his study focusing on the South Marmara region during this time period, Ryan Gingeras argues that "the War of Independence was in fact a civil war without a clear, binary set of protagonists and antagonists." *Sorrowful Shores: Violence, Ethnicity, and the End of the Ottoman Empire, 1912–1923* (Oxford: Oxford University Press, 2009), 169. For a recent study utilizing the terminology of civil war to examine European interventions in the Levant during the earlier phase of the Eastern Question, see Ozan Ozavci, *Dangerous Gifts: Imperialism, Security, and Civil Wars in the Levant, 1798–1864* (Oxford: Oxford University Press, 2021).

19. David Armitage, *Civil Wars: A History in Ideas* (New York: Vintage, 2017), 13–14.

20. İpek K. Yosmaoğlu, *Blood Ties: Religion, Violence, and the Politics of Nationhood in Ottoman Macedonia, 1878-1908* (Ithaca, NY: Cornell University Press, 2014), 16–17.

21. It remains uncertain whether the language of conflict used by Macedonia's inhabitants included the term *civil war*.

22. The terminology of civil war to describe intercommunal violence in Crete has an old history. During his travels in Crete in the 1830s a British army officer described the village of Dafnes near Iraklio as a place that offered "a most heart-rending example of the sad effects of civil war!" C. Rochfort Scott, *Rambles in Egypt and Candia*, vol. 2 (London: Henry Colburn, 1837), 266.

23. Centre des archives diplomatiques (French Foreign Ministry Archives in Nantes, hereafter CADN), 328 PO/1/152, Evmenios to Ottoman Administration of Crete, Moni Preveli, 9 June 1896 (28 May 1896). The question of civil war has generated a vast scholarship in Greece, a country with a painful period of civil strife in the twentieth century. Greek historians have mostly used the term *emfylios polemos* or just *emfylios* to describe the civil war in Greece between 1946 and 1949. Although less common, the phrase *emfylios sparagmos* has also been employed. Giorgos Margaritis, *Istoria tou Ellēnikou Emfyliou Polemou, 1946-1949* (Athens: Vivliorama, 2001).

24. BNA, ADM 121/53, Muslim Representatives in Hania to Captain Custance, enclosed in Evan MacGregor (Permanent Secretary to the Admiralty) to Foreign Office, 22 March 1897.

25. Nikos Kazantzakis, *The Fratricides* (1955; repr., New York: Simon and Schuster, 1964). The original Greek title of Kazantzakis's novel is *Oi Aderfofades*, with a literal meaning "Brother-Eaters."

26. "Girit Havadisi," *Meşveret*, 23 July 1896 (12 Safer 1314).

27. Arheio G. I. Hatzigrigoraki (G. I. Hatzigrigorakis Archives—Archives of the Russian Vice-Consulate), Bishop of Rethimno to Muslim Notables, Arkadi Monastery, 21 May 1898 (9 May 1898). The English translation of the letter that the British consul Alfred Biliotti shared with the Marquess of Salisbury rendered the Greek phrase *emfylios sparagmos* as "civil war." BNA, ADM 121/53, Alfred Biliotti to Marquess of Salisbury, Hania, 2 June 1898.

28. Armitage, *Civil Wars*, 12.

29. Stathis N. Kalyvas, *The Logic of Violence in Civil War* (Cambridge: Cambridge University Press, 2006), 333.

30. Earlier European travelers to Crete mentioned such stark regional variations, sometimes in derogatory contrasts. "The name of the Sfakiot is . . . a by-word amongst the lowland Cretans, for talents perverted, and for unscrupulous intrigue, theft, and cruelty. . . . In stature, in activity, and hardihood, he is the counterpart of our Scotch Highlander, and in past days might have resembled him in other respects; but now, in respect to character and principles, he is the very reverse." T. A. B. Spratt, *Travels and Researches in Crete*, vol. 1 (London: John van Voorst, 1865), 53–54.

31. Ussama Makdisi, "Diminished Sovereignty and the Impossibility of 'Civil War' in the Modern Middle East," *American Historical Review* 120, no. 5 (2015): 1739–40.

32. Christine M. Philliou, *Biography of an Empire: Governing Ottomans in an Age of Revolution* (Berkeley: University of California Press, 2011), xvii.

33. According to Akçam's coverage of the nineteenth century, one of the salient features of the period seems to be "the hatred that the Muslim population felt toward the Christians," which was progressively exacerbated by the involvement of European powers in Ottoman affairs. Taner Akçam, *A Shameful Act: The Armenian Genocide and the Question of Turkish Responsibility* (New York: Metropolitan Books, 2006), 35. For a glaring application of the "clash of civilizations" thesis into the late nineteenth and early twentieth centuries in which undifferentiated populations turn into religiously motivated fanatical killers, see Benny Morris and Dror Ze'evi, *The Thirty-Year Genocide: Turkey's Destruction of Its Christian Minorities, 1894-1924* (Cambridge, MA: Harvard University Press, 2019).

34. Bedross der Matossian, *The Horrors of Adana: Revolution and Violence in the Early Twentieth Century* (Stanford, CA: Stanford University Press, 2022), 5.

35. Max Bergholz, *Violence as a Generative Force: Identity, Nationalism, and Memory in a Balkan Community* (Ithaca, NY: Cornell University Press, 2016), 321.

36. For conversion from Christianity into Islam in Crete, see Nuri Adıyeke, "Multidimensional Complications of Conversion to Islam in Ottoman Crete," in Antonis Anastasopoulos, ed., *The Eastern Mediterranean under Ottoman Rule: Crete, 1645-1840* (Rethymno: Crete University Press, 2009), 203–9; Molly Greene, *A Shared World: Christians and Muslims in the Early Modern Mediterranean* (Princeton, NJ: Princeton University Press, 2000),103–9.

37. Barbara F. Walter, *How Civil Wars Start: And How to Stop Them* (New York: Crown, 2022), 205.

38. Mahmood Mamdani, *When Victims Become Killers: Colonialism, Nativism, and the Genocide in Rwanda* (Princeton, NJ: Princeton University Press, 2001), 141.

39. Admiral Sir Reginald H. Bacon, *A Naval Scrap-Book (First Part, 1877-1900)* (London: Hutchinson, 1925), 47.

40. Theodore George Tatsios, *The Megali Idea and the Greek-Turkish War of 1897: The Impact of the Cretan Problem on Greek Irredentism, 1866-1897* (Boulder, NY: East European Monographs, 1984), 93.

41. Ayşe Nükhet Adıyeke and Nuri Adıyeke, *Osmanlı Dönemi Kısa Girit Tarihi* (İstanbul: Türkiye İş Bankası Kültür Yayınları, 2021); Robert Holland and Diana Markides, *The British and the Hellenes: Struggles for Mastery in the Eastern Mediterranean, 1850-1960* (Oxford: Oxford University Press, 2006); Davide Rodogno, *Against Massacre: Humanitarian Interventions in the Ottoman Empire, 1815-1914* (Princeton, NJ: Princeton University Press, 2012); Tatsios, *Megali Idea*.

42. "Greece and Crete," *New York Times*, 16 February 1897.

43. "Apografē tou Plēthysmou en Etei 1900," *Episimos Efimeris tis Kritikis Politeias* (Official Gazette of the Cretan State, hereafter *EEKP*), vol. 2 (annex), 24 March 1904 (11 March 1904).

44. I. K. Sfakianakis, President of the Assembly of Cretans, to Foreign Ministers of the Four Great Powers of Europe, Akrotiri, 27 December 1897 (15 December 1897), in *Krētika: Ētoi Syllogē tōn Diplōmatikōn Eggrafōn tēs Epanastatikēs Syneleuseōs, tēs Syneleuseōs tōn Krētōn, tou Ektelestikou, tōn Nauarhōn k.l.p. & tōn Egkykliōn tēs Syneleuseōs kai tou Ektelestikou meta Sēmeiōseōn Istorikōn—26 Iouniou 1897-9 Dekemvriou 1898* (Hania: Proodos, E. D. Frantzeskaki, 1901), 41–44.

45. BNA, ADM 121/53, Alfred Biliotti to the Marquess of Salisbury, Hania, 30 December 1897. Paul Blanc, the French consul general, who was related to the British consul

through Biliotti's wife, also emphasized the profound sense of attachment to land evinced by both Christian and Muslim islanders. According to Blanc, such sentiment was caused by insularity, that is, inhabiting a land with natural boundaries surrounded by the sea. Centre des archives diplomatiques (French Foreign Ministry Archives in La Courneuve, hereafter CADC) 153 CPCOM/74, Paul Blanc to Théophile Delcassé, Hania, 23 March 1899.

46. BNA, ADM 121/53, Alfred Biliotti to the Marquess of Salisbury, Hania, 30 December 1897. Biliotti was a fascinating character hailing from an Italian-speaking Levantine family from Rhodes. English was Biliotti's fourth language after French and Greek. Turkish was his fifth. See David Barchard, "The Fearless and Self-Reliant Servant: The Life and Career of Sir Alfred Biliotti (1833–1915), an Italian Levantine in British Service," *Studi Micenei ed Egeo-Anatolici* 48 (2006): 5–53.

47. BNA, ADM 121/53, Alfred Biliotti to the Marquess of Salisbury, Hania, 11 March 1897.

48. BNA, FO 421/229, Foreign Office to Acting Consul General Graham, Foreign Office, 10 October 1906.

49. Laura Robson, *States of Separation: Transfer, Partition, and the Making of the Modern Middle East* (Oakland: University of California Press, 2017), 7.

50. Ibid., 7–18.

51. Arie M. Dubnov and Laura Robson, *Partitions: A Transnational History of Twentieth-Century Territorial Separatism* (Stanford, CA: Stanford University Press, 2019), 25.

52. Rodogno, *Against Massacre*, 219.

53. BOA, İ. MTZ. GR. 31/1234, Interim Governor of Crete Müşavir İsmail to Yıldız Başkitabet Dairesi, Hania, 26 August 1897 (14 August 1313).

54. The Ottoman governor envisioned the exchange as a project to be ideally implemented in cooperation with the European coalition. For bilateral exchange projects after the Balkan Wars, see Stephen P. Ladas, *The Exchange of Minorities: Bulgaria, Greece and Turkey* (New York: Macmillan, 1932); Yannis G. Mourelos, "The 1914 Persecutions and the First Attempt at an Exchange of Minorities between Greece and Turkey," *Balkan Studies* 26 (1985): 384–413; Umut Özsu, *Formalizing Displacement: International Law and Population Transfers* (Oxford: Oxford University Press, 2015), 1–5.

55. "Kavala Muhabir-i Mahsusamızdan," *Yeni Edirne*, 11 June 1910 (29 Mayıs 1326).

56. A variation of this grim chant retained a place in the Greek nationalist mythos as well. Mark Mazower points out that "collective death haunted the Greek revolutionary imagination. The slogan 'Freedom or Death' was a pledge to die rather than surrender, but it was also a warning that not to fight was itself tantamount to a living death." *The Greek Revolution: 1821 and the Making of Modern Europe* (New York: Penguin Press, 2021), 185. This grim outcry in different phrasings was popular with other political projects at the height of nationalism. For instance, in 1919 D'Annunzio occupied the strategic port city of Fiume with the goal of annexing it to Italy. His motto was "Italy or death." Dominique Kirchner Reill, *The Fiume Crisis: Life in the Wake of the Habsburg Empire* (Cambridge, MA: Belknap Press of Harvard University Press, 2020), 5.

57. "Kavala Muhabir-i Mahsusamızdan," *Yeni Edirne*, 11 June 1910 (29 Mayıs 1326).

58. Helen Gardikas Katsiadakis, *Greece and the Balkan Imbroglio: Greek Foreign Policy, 1911-1913* (Athens: Syllogos pros Diadosin Ofelimon Vivlion, 1995), 33–40.

59. BNA, FO 421/267, Report of the House of Commons Debate on Crete, 15 June 1910.

60. "Hindistan İslamları ve Donanma İanesi," *Tearüf-i Müslimin*, 21 July 1910 (8 Temmuz 1326). For more on Abdürreşid İbrahim (b. 1857 in Tara, Omsk Oblast), one of the leading names associated with this publication, see Nadir Özbek, "From Asianism to Pan-Turkism: The Activities of Abdürreşid İbrahim in the Young Turk Era," in Selçuk Esenbel and Inaba Chiharu, eds., *The Rising Sun and the Turkish Crescent: New Perspectives on the History of Japanese Turkish Relations* (Istanbul: Boğaziçi University Press, 2003), 86–104.

61. CADN, 166 PO/E/294, Adolphe-Ernest Ronssin to French Foreign Ministry, Calcutta, 6 October 1912.

62. Beginning in October 1908, the coverage of Cretan affairs became a daily feature in the Unionist press. For instance, in a series of detailed articles, Ali Zeki narrated the island's recent history around the theme of oppression endured by Crete's Muslim minority. See Ali Zeki, "Girit Hakkında Mülahazat," in the multiple issues of *Tanin*, a leading pro-CUP daily from Istanbul, dated 15, 17, and 21 December 1908, 3 January 1909.

63. Ahmed Hamdi, "Ya Eyyuhel Müminin! Cahidu fi Sebilillah," *Yozgat*, 18 January 1911 (5 Kanunusani 1326).

64. Kafkasyalı Doktor Karabey, "Girit'in Kaybolmasına Alem-i İslam Ne Diyecek?," *Hikmet*, 11 May 1910 (28 Nisan 1326). This is how he signed the *Hikmet* article. In Azerbaijani history he is known as Qara bəy Qarabəyov or Qarabəyli. *Hikmet* was published by Şehbenderzade Ahmed Hilmi (b. 1865, Plovdiv), a prolific intellectual who had a falling-out with the CUP around 1911.

65. Hüseyin Nesimi and Mehmet Behçet, *Girit Hailesi*, vol. 2/1 (Hania, 1896), 117.

66. Ali Haydar Emir, "Rotamız: Kıble Lodos!," *Şura-i Ümmet* (Council of Ummah), 27 January 1910 (14 Kanunusani 1325).

67. BOA, HR. SYS. 512/2, Konya Vilayeti Mektubi Kalemi to Dahiliye Nezareti, 4 June 1910 (22 Mayıs 1326).

68. BOA, HR. SYS. 512/2, Petition to the Sultan after a Protest Rally in Izmir, 2 June 1910 (20 Mayıs 1326).

69. Hüseyin Cahid, "Neyin Cezasını Çekiyoruz?," *Tanin*, 10 October 1908 (27 Eylül 1324).

70. Hüseyin Cahid, "Girit'e Dair," *Tanin*, 14 November 1908 (1 Teşrinisani 1324).

71. Reşat Kasaba, *A Moveable Empire: Ottoman Nomads, Migrants, and Refugees* (Seattle: University of Washington Press, 2009), 11.

72. Ibid., 11–12.

73. Triggered by the violent Russian imperial expansion, the dislocation of massive Muslim populations from the Caucasus into the Ottoman territories constitutes an immense demographic upheaval during the nineteenth century. For a discussion about its transformative effects in a local context, see Oktay Özel, "Migration and Power Politics: The Settlement of Georgian Immigrants in Turkey, 1878–1908," *Middle Eastern Studies* 46, no. 4 (2010): 477–96.

74. For several informative works, see Eyal Ginio, *The Ottoman Culture of Defeat: The Balkan Wars and Their Aftermath* (New York: Oxford University Press, 2016); Justin McCarthy, *Death and Exile: The Ethnic Cleansing of Ottoman Muslims, 1821–1922* (Princeton, NJ: Darwin Press, 1995); Bilal N. Şimşir, *Rumeli'den Türk Göçleri* (Ankara: Türk Tarih Kurumu, 1989); Alexandre Toumarkine, *Les migrations des populations musulmanes balkaniques en*

Anatolie (1876–1913) (Istanbul: Isis Press, 1995); Keith David Watenpaugh, *Bread from Stones: The Middle East and the Making of Modern Humanitarianism* (Oakland: University of California Press, 2015).

75. For an investigation of the linkages between war and mass mobilization during World War I, see Mehmet Beşikçi, *The Ottoman Mobilization of Manpower in the First World War: Between Voluntarism and Resistance* (Leiden: Brill, 2012).

76. Houri Berberian, *Roving Revolutionaries: Armenians and the Connected Revolutions in the Russian, Iranian, and Ottoman Worlds* (Oakland: University of California Press, 2019); Lale Can, *Spiritual Subjects: Central Asian Pilgrims and the Ottoman Hajj at the End of Empire* (Stanford, CA: Stanford University Press, 2020); David E. Gutman, *The Politics of Armenian Migration to North America, 1885–1915* (Edinburgh: Edinburgh University Press, 2019); Ilham Khuri-Makdisi, *The Eastern Mediterranean and the Making of Global Radicalism, 1860–1914* (Berkeley: University of California Press, 2010); Devi Mays, *Forging Ties, Forging Passports: Migration and the Modern Sephardi Diaspora* (Stanford, CA: Stanford University Press, 2020).

77. Peter Gatrell, Anindita Ghoshal, Katarzyna Nowak, and Alex Dowdall, "Reckoning with Refugeedom: Refugee Voices in Modern History," *Social History* 46, no. 1 (2021): 71.

78. For a study bridging the areas of citizenship and empire studies, two fields that for long remained largely separated, see Julia Phillips Cohen, *Becoming Ottomans: Sephardi Jews and Imperial Citizenship in the Modern Era* (Oxford: Oxford University Press, 2014).

79. Pamela Ballinger, *The World Refugees Made: Decolonization and the Foundation of Postwar Italy* (Ithaca, NY: Cornell University Press, 2020).

80. Liisa H. Malkki, "Speechless Emissaries: Refugees, Humanitarianism, and Dehistoricization," *Cultural Anthropology* 11, no. 3 (1996): 388.

81. Isa Blumi, *Ottoman Refugees, 1878–1939: Migration in a Post-imperial World* (London: Bloomsbury, 2013); Ella Fratantuono, "Producing Ottomans: Internal Colonization and Social Engineering in Ottoman Immigrant Settlement," *Journal of Genocide Research* 21, no. 1 (2019): 1–24; Vladimir Hamed-Troyansky, "Circassian Refugees and the Making of Amman, 1878–1914," *International Journal of Middle East Studies* 49, no. 4 (2017): 605–23; Khatchig Mouradian, *The Resistance Network: The Armenian Genocide and Humanitarianism in Ottoman Syria, 1915–1918* (East Lansing: Michigan State University Press, 2021).

82. Peter Gatrell, *The Making of the Modern Refugee* (Oxford: Oxford University Press, 2013), 10.

83. The birth and development of Turkish nationalism constitutes one of the dominant themes in the scholarship surrounding the famous figures with a story of displacement. Benjamin C. Fortna, *The Circassian: A Life of Eşref Bey, Late Ottoman Insurgent and Special Agent* (Oxford: Oxford University Press, 2016); François Georgeon, *Aux origines du nationalisme turc: Yusuf Akçura (1876–1935)* (Paris: ADPF, 1980); James H. Meyer, *Turks across Empires: Marketing Muslim Identity in the Russian-Ottoman Borderlands, 1856–1914* (Oxford: Oxford University Press, 2014); A. Holly Shissler, *Between Two Empires: Ahmet Ağaoğlu and the New Turkey* (London: I. B. Tauris, 2003); Erik-Jan Zürcher, "The Young Turks: Children of the Borderlands?," in Kemal H. Karpat and Robert W. Zens, eds., *Ottoman Borderlands: Issues, Personalities, and Political Changes* (Madison: Center of Turkish Studies, University of Wisconsin, 2003), 276–85.

84. R. Murray Schafer, *The Soundscape: Our Sonic Environment and the Tuning of the World* (Rochester, VT: Destiny Books, 1994), 8–9, 137.

85. Alain Corbin, *Village Bells: Sound and Meaning in the 19th-Century French Countryside* (New York: Columbia University Press, 1998), ix–xx.

86. Mark M. Smith, *Sensing the Past: Seeing, Hearing, Smelling, Tasting, and Touching in History* (Berkeley: University of California Press, 2007), 4–5. For a more recent work by the same author analyzing the American Civil War from a sensory perspective, see *The Smell of Battle, the Taste of Siege: A Sensory History of the Civil War* (Oxford: Oxford University Press, 2015).

87. Jan Plamper, "Sounds of February, Smells of October: The Russian Revolution as Sensory Experience," *American Historical Review* 126, no. 1 (2021): 141.

88. A case in point is the Austro-Hungarian vice-consul in Kale-i Sultaniye, who reported about a Crete rally in that town as a forced gathering. HHStA, Konstantinopel GesA 456, 19 May 1910.

89. For an overview of Ottoman historiography on the popular involvement in politics, see Eleni Gara, Christoph K. Neumann, and M. Erdem Kabadayı, eds., *Popular Protest and Political Participation in the Ottoman Empire: Studies in Honor of Suraiya Faroqhi* (Istanbul: Bilgi University Press, 2011), 1–37.

90. Two monographs stand out with their emphasis on the increasing power of the public and the collective in the late Ottoman Empire: Michelle Campos, *Ottoman Brothers: Muslims, Christians, and Jews in Early Twentieth Century Palestine* (Stanford, CA: Stanford University Press, 2010), and Bedross Der Matossian, *Shattered Dreams of Revolution: From Liberty to Violence in the Late Ottoman Empire* (Stanford, CA: Stanford University Press, 2014).

91. Y. Doğan Çetinkaya, *The Young Turks and the Boycott Movement: Nationalism, Protest and the Working Classes in the Formation of Modern Turkey* (London: I. B. Tauris, 2014) and especially "Patterns of Social Mobilisation in the Elimination of the Greek Orthodox Population, 1908–1914," *Low Countries Journal of Social and Economic History / Tijdschrift voor Sociale en Economische Geschiedenis* 10, no. 4 (2013): 55.

92. Ali Sipahi notes the scarcity of scholarly works on the politics of crowds in the Ottoman Empire, arguing that *"the era of crowds* for the Ottomans" traces its beginnings to the late 1890s. "Deception and Violence in the Ottoman Empire: The People's Theory of Crowd Behavior during the Hamidian Massacres of 1895," *Comparative Studies in Society and History* 62, no. 4 (2020): 817. Emphasis in the original.

93. Antonis Hadjikyriacou, "Envisioning Insularity in the Ottoman World," *Princeton Papers: Interdisciplinary Journal of Middle Eastern Studies*, no. 18 (2017): xi.

94. E. J. Hobsbawm, *Bandits* (1969; repr., New York: Pantheon Books, 1981).

Chapter 1: Fear and Trembling in the Mediterranean

1. In August 1895, the recently appointed governor of Crete, Alexandros Karatheodoris, wrote to Istanbul of "the frostiness and mutual hatred" among Christians and Muslims in the aftermath of several killings in the district of Selino in southwestern Crete. These murders sent dreadful echoes to Hania, the island's seat of administration. The governor highlighted an incident in which an elderly Christian man was murdered near Hania. That the unfortunate man was found with two liras in his pockets and two donkeys at the site of murder suggested the ethnopolitical nature of the crime. BOA, Y.A.HUS 334/45, Cipher from Alexandros Karatheodoris (Governor of Crete) to Grand Vizirate, 12 August 1895 (31 Temmuz 1311).

2. In May 1896, the British newspaper *The Standard* reported that 25,000 Ottoman liras recently put at the disposal of the governor fell significantly short of alleviating the island's financial troubles given that Crete cost the state 400,000 Ottoman liras per year. The budgetary hardships were inseparable from security concerns as the island's gendarmerie had overdue salaries for about eighteen months. "The Cretan Insurrection," *The Standard*, 26 May 1896. The clipping of the piece also appeared in BOA, HR.SYS. 492/1.

3. BNA, FO 421/153, Alfred Biliotti to the Marquess of Salisbury, Hania, 13 March 1896. After Karatheodoris's recall, a young British diplomat, Charles Eliot, who soon published his famous *Turkey in Europe* (London: Arnold, 1900), secured an interview with him in Istanbul. Not a boasting type, Karatheodoris gave due credit to the previous grand vizier Cevad Pasha, whose strong support had ensured the successful meetings of the Cretan Assembly. When the Assembly's resolutions were conveyed to the Sublime Porte, however, he was no longer the grand vizier, and the central government rejected the islanders' proposals *in toto* without explanation. A government, Karatheodoris maintained, that "checks every effort of its officials to work in its interest, and which never takes any action except with the apparently deliberate intention of injuring itself" drove him to a point where he became convinced of the futility of battling with the high bureaucracy. BNA, FO 421/154, Philip Currie to the Marquess of Salisbury (very confidential, memorandum by Charles Eliot), Istanbul, 14 April 1896.

4. BNA, FO 421/149, Alfred Biliotti to the Earl of Kimberley, Hania, 12 March 1895.

5. L'Alliance Philantropique Musulmane de Crète, *Un coup d'oeil aux événements crétois* (Paris: L. Lhen, 1897), 18. This short book first came out in Paris in French and was released the same year in Crete in Turkish as Girit Muhibb-i İnsaniyet Cemiyet-i İslamiyesi, *Girit Vekaiyine Atf-ı Nazar* (Hania: Yusuf Kenan Matbaası, 1897).

6. HHStA, PA XII, Liasse XXVIII, 282, Julius von Pinter to Agenor von Goluchowski, Hania, 19 February 1897; BOA, BEO 911/68288, 16 February 1897 (14 Ramazan 1314). Upon expressing his deepest regret at having fled his post, Berović was granted an imperial pardon three years later. See BOA, BEO 1538/115295, 23 August 1900 (26 Rebiyülahir 1318). Berović's arrival in Crete too had stood in stark contrast to Karatheodoris's. In the spring of 1895, Karatheodoris was warmly received by the civil and military authorities in Crete, the bishop, Christian and Muslim notables, and the municipal body: BNA, FO 421/150, Alfred Biliotti to Earl of Kimberley, Hania, 1 April 1895. In the summer of 1896, the ceremonial welcome given to Berović presented a clear contrast. His reception by Abdullah Pasha, whom he succeeded, almost bordered on disrespect, and not a single Christian deputy showed up to meet him. More than anything, the scene reflected how radically the overall situation in Crete had changed within a year. BNA, ADM 116/82, Charles C. Drury to M. Culme-Seymour, Hania, 1 July 1896.

7. HHStA, PA XII, Liasse XXVIII, 282, Julius von Pinter to Agenor von Goluchowski, Hania, 19 February 1897.

8. BNA, FO 421/154, Philip Currie to the Marquess of Salisbury (very confidential, memorandum by Charles Eliot), Istanbul, 14 April 1896.

9. Victor Bérard, *Les affaires de Crète* (Paris: Armand Colin, 1900), 199.

10. Spratt, *Travels and Researches*, 2:164.

11. Manos Perakis, "Return to Ottoman Sovereignty and De-Ottomanization of Christians on Crete (1889–1895)," *Cretica Chronica* 36 (2016): 93–118.

12. Ibid.

13. Only one recent monograph in English has examined this eventful period in the island's history by drawing on a rich array of Ottoman archival documents, offering an analysis that views the turbulence in Crete as a series of revolts by Christian insurgents against the Ottoman state. Şenışık, *Transformation of Ottoman Crete*.

14. In an April 1897 correspondence with the Austro-Hungarian foreign minister, Julius von Pinter enclosed a map of Crete showing the number of Ottoman and international troops stationed in the vicinity of the main cities. HHStA, PA XII, Liasse XXVIII, 285, Julius von Pinter to Agenor von Goluchowski, Hania, 2 April 1897.

15. BOA, Y. A. HUS 336/79, Cipher from Alexandros Karatheodoris to Sublime Porte, 15 September 1895 (3 Eylül 1311).

16. ASDMAE 144, M. Marefoschi to Chargé d'Affaires at Italian Embassy in Istanbul, Hania, 26 September 1895.

17. BOA, Y. A. HUS 326/14, Governor's Office to Grand Vizier, Hania, 16 March 1895 (4 Mart 1311).

18. BNA, FO 421/151, Alfred Biliotti to the Marquess of Salisbury, Hania, 27 August 1895.

19. Zahid R. Chaudhary, *Afterimage of Empire: Photography in Nineteenth-Century India* (Minneapolis: University of Minnesota Press, 2012), 56.

20. BNA, FO 421/151, Alfred Biliotti to the Marquess of Salisbury, Hania, 12 September 1895.

21. Similar complaints had started to circulate in late 1895 and multiplied in the early months of 1896. Alexandros Skouzes Collection, IAPAK, Dorotheos Klonaris to Parthenias Kelaidis, 29 May 1896.

22. BNA, FO 421/152, Alfred Biliotti to the Marquess of Salisbury, Hania, 9 November 1895.

23. BNA, FO 421/152, Alfred Biliotti to the Marquess of Salisbury, Hania, 24 November 1895. Biliotti obtained some of the details in his report from one of the village elders, who negotiated with the Ottoman commander. The villager later went to Hania and, apparently, had a conversation with the consul.

24. IAK, Archives of the Revolutionary Reform Committee of Crete, II, Proclamation by Epitropi, Fres (Apokoronas, Crete), 14 November 1895 (2 November 1895).

25. Accompanying the insurgency in Crete's mountains were demonstrations mounted by diaspora Greek communities and those supportive of their cause. BOA, HR. SYS. 522/14, Ottoman Consulate in Naples to Tevfik Pasha, Minister of Foreign Affairs, Naples, 4 March 1897.

26. IAK, Archives of the Revolutionary Reform Committee of Crete, II, Proclamation by Epitropi, Fres, 14 November 1895 (2 November 1895).

27. At the time of its founding, the core of the committee consisted of thirteen individuals, including politicians, lawyers, and other professionals. Charles C. Drury, the commanding officer of the British battleship HMS *Hood* in Cretan waters, observed that "these persons have made politics their calling to the great detriment of the island." BNA, ADM 116/82, Charles C. Drury to M. Culme-Seymour, Hania, 6 June 1896.

28. IAK, Archives of the Revolutionary Reform Committee of Crete II, Proclamation by Epitropi, Apokoronas, Crete, 25 March 1896 (13 March 1896).

29. Ibid.

30. BNA, FO 421/155, Alfred Biliotti to Marquess of Salisbury, Hania, 23 July 1896; BOA, Y.PRK.ASK. 112/106, Cipher telegram from Abdullah Pasha, General Commander of Crete, 18 July 1896 (7 Safer 1314).

31. BNA, ADM 116/82, Charles C. Drury to M. Culme-Seymour, Hania, 31 July 1896.

32. BNA, FO 421/155, Alfred Biliotti to the Marquess of Salisbury, Hania, 30 July 1896.

33. The atmosphere of fear reported by Biliotti and other observers in the summer of 1896 was largely shaped by serious clashes in May 1896 in the streets of Hania, claiming lives from both Christian and Muslim populations.

34. Born in 1858 in a village in the southwestern district of Selinos, Kriaris took active part in all major armed struggles against the Ottoman state, including the violent episodes in 1878 and 1889. A short autobiography can be found in his book containing a vast collection of Cretan folk songs and poetry. Aristidis Kriaris, *Plērēs Syllogē Krētikōn dēmōdōn asmatōn: Ērōikōn, istorikōn, polemikōn, tou gamou, tēs tavlas, tou horou klp klp. Kai apasōn tōn krētikōn paroimiōn distihōn kai ainigmatōn meth' ermēneutikōn yposēmeiōseōn* (Athens: A. Frantzeskaki and A. Kaitatzi Press, 1920).

35. By "beys" Kriaris refers to the powerful land-holding class of Muslim Cretans commanding strong influence in the island's politics.

36. Alexandros Skouzes Collection, IAPAK, Aristides Kriaris to Alexandros Skouzes, letter, Hania, 25 April 1896 (13 April 1896).

37. L'Alliance Philantropique Musulmane de Crète, *Coup d'oeil*, 19, in Turkish translation as Girit Muhibb-i İnsaniyet Cemiyet-i İslamiyesi, *Girit Vekaiyine Atf-ı Nazar*, 28.

38. For a discussion of Cretan politics, with a focus on the notions of majority and minority, under the Halepa regime, see Andreas Kalokairinos, "Defining the 'Majority' in the General Assembly of Cretans between 1878 and 1889: The Transition from Religious towards Political Disputes," in *Proceedings of the 12th International Congress of Cretan Studies*, Iraklio, 21–25 September 2016, 1–12, https://12iccs.proceedings.gr/en/proceedings/category/38/34/989.

39. CADN, 328 PO/1/152, Muslim Cretan Deputies to Paul Blanc, Hania, 12 July 1896 (30 Haziran 1312).

40. *Diplōmatika Eggrafa: Krētē* (Athens: Ethnikou Typografeiou, 1898), Christian Cretan Deputies to European Consuls, Hania, 15 July 1896 (3 July 1896).

41. Ibid.

42. Ibid.

43. Ibid.

44. Ibid.

45. The text of the resolutions passed at Klima and Krapi was soon published in Athens in 1895. *Ypomnēma tōn Hristianōn tēs Krētēs Ypovlēthen eis tas Eurōpaikas Kyvernēseis ypo tou Synathroisthentos Laou en Klēma kai Krapē tē 3 kai 10 Septemvriou 1895* (Athens: N. Tarousopoulou, 1895). Abdullah Pasha, the general commander of Crete, transmitted the Turkish translation of this booklet to the Yıldız Palace in July 1896. BOA, Y. MTV. 143/102, Abdullah Pasha to Mabeyn-i Hümayun Başkitabeti, 9 July 1896 (27 Haziran 1312). Earlier, a Greek-language original copy of the booklet was also sent to Istanbul. BOA, Y. PRK. TKM 37/68, 11 June 1896 (29 Zilhicce 1313).

46. CADN, 328 PO/1/152, Muslim Cretan Deputies to European Consuls, Hania, 22 July 1896.

47. Ibid.

48. Şenışık notes that she disagrees "with the scholars who argued that the mother tongue of the Cretan Muslims was Greek. It seems to me that further examination is necessary to provide a definitive conclusion on the language of the Cretan Muslims." Multiple contemporary accounts, including the memorandum of Muslim deputies referenced here, contradict this claim. Şenışık, *Transformation of Ottoman Crete*, 67.

49. Kalyvas, *Logic of Violence*, 330.

50. Antonis Trakakis, "Oi Seliniōtes Tourkoi kai ta Hōria tōn," *Kritiki Estia* 53–64 (1955–56).

51. Ayşe Nükhet Adıyeke, *Osmanlı İmparatorluğu ve Girit Bunalımı, 1896-1908* (Ankara: Türk Tarih Kurumu, 2000); Theoharis Detorakis, *Istoria tēs Krētēs* (Iraklio: Mystis, 1990).

52. "These revolts," Pınar Şenışık writes, "threatened the survival of the Ottoman administration" in Crete. Şenışık, *Transformation of Ottoman Crete*, 231. And for Leonidas Kallivretakis, the word *revolution* best reflected the nature of periodic bouts of violence in Crete during the nineteenth century. Despite layers of cultural complexity inscribed to the island's character following centuries of Arab and Venetian rule, a primordial Greek identity appears to be imparted to Crete: "The island of Crete was the last Greek region to be subjugated by the Ottoman Turks." Kallivretakis, "Century of Revolutions," 11.

53. CADN, 328 PO/1/152, Evmenios to Ottoman Administration of Crete, Moni Preveli, Crete, 9 June 1896 (28 May 1896). Crowded by civil and military authorities, both Ottoman and European, the cities, especially the capital Hania, made it easier to prevent unlawful conduct among the troops. In the countryside, however, it was usually easier for the soldiers to act with impunity. The Ottoman central government repeatedly drew the attention of the local administration to the importance of ensuring that no assaults take place on the Christian population and European soldiers in the cities. For instance, see BOA, İ.MTZ.GR. 31/1199, Encümen-i Mahsus-ı Vükela, 23 March 1897 (11 Mart 1313).

54. BNA, ADM 121/53, Muslim Representatives of Hania to Captain Custance, enclosed in Evan MacGregor (Permanent Secretary to the Admiralty) to Foreign Office, 22 March 1897.

55. BNA, ADM 121/53, Commander Noel to Captain Custance, Suda Bay, 8 February 1897.

56. In her memoirs of the strife in Anatolia during the Turkish War of Independence after World War I, the famous novelist Halide Edib wrote about a series of "civil wars" (*iç savaşlar*) and "bloodshed between brothers" (*kardeşler arasında kan dökülüyordu*). Originally published in English in 1928 with the title *The Turkish Ordeal*, the book's Turkish version, not a translation but a rewrite by the author, came out in 1962. By that time, *iç savaş* (literally "internal war") had already become common usage in Turkish. Halide Edib Adıvar, *Türkün Ateşle İmtihanı* (İstanbul: Çan Yayınları, 1962), 136.

57. BOA, İ.MTZ.GR. 30/1116, Girit Valisi Corci ve Girit Kumandanı Abdullah'tan Yıldız Saray-ı Hümayunu Başkitabet Dairesi'ne Şifreli Telgraf, Hania, 1 August 1896 (20 Temmuz 1312).

58. BOA, İ.MTZ.GR. 31/1204, Encümen-i Mahsus-ı Vükela, 5 April 1897 (24 Mart 1313).

59. *İslam ve Hıristiyan beyninde bir mukatele* (a fatal clash between Muslims and Christians) is used in BOA, Y. PRK. MYD. 17/57, Bahrisefid Boğaz Muhafızlığı Vekaletinden

Şifre, 25 May 1896 (13 Mayıs 1312). *Mukatele* could also correspond to intrareligious clashes with fatalities. One telegram reported the killing of four in the clashes between the Christians of two villages. BOA, Y. PRK. MYD. 20/56, Mirliva Şakir Paşa'dan Şifre, Hania, 5 December 1897 (23 Teşrinisani 1313).

60. HHStA, PA XII, Liasse XXVIII, 280, Julius von Pinter to Agenor von Goluchowski, Hania, 28 August 1896.

61. Ibid.

62. Ibid.

63. Perakis, "Return to Ottoman Sovereignty," 101–2.

64. For a discussion of irredentism in Greece, see Georgios Michalopoulos, "Political Parties, Irredentism and the Foreign Ministry: Greece and Macedonia, 1878–1910" (PhD diss., University of Oxford, 2013).

65. IAK, Archives of the Revolutionary Reform Committee of Crete II, Letter from Student Committee for the Defense of Crete to Epitropi, Athens, 13 June 1896 (1 June 1896).

66. Several European consuls and admirals expressed the belief that Hellenic troops in Crete further complicated the already-arduous task of pacifying the island. The British rear-admiral Robert Harris stated that the Greeks had to leave Crete at once, for "every day lost in accomplishing this object is a day gained to the Greeks in establishing their propaganda of annexation." BNA, ADM 121/53, Rear-Admiral R. H. Harris to Admiral J. O. Hopkins, Suda Bay, 1 April 1897.

67. *Megalē Stratiōtikē kai Nautikē Egkyklopaideia*, vol. 4 (Athens, 1929), 193–94.

68. Distances that I include here would be misleading if assessed by today's measures. As we are reminded by someone intimately familiar with the highlands and foothills of Crete, "Thirty miles, in some parts, meant three days (or nights) of scrambles up rocks and breakneck, treacherous descents of landslides. Only in the rare plains is the reckoning normal." Patrick Leigh Fermor, foreword to George Psychoundakis, *The Cretan Runner: His Story of the German Occupation* (1955; repr., New York: NYRB, 2015), 22.

69. Aristotelis Korakas Collection, IAPAK, Aristotelis Korakas to Christian inhabitants of the Candia province, 15 February 1897 (3 February 1897).

70. Aristotelis Korakas Collection, IAPAK, Aristotelis Korakas to Muslim inhabitants of the Candia province, 15 February 1897 (3 February 1897).

71. Aristotelis Korakas Collection, IAPAK, Aristotelis Korakas to Papadiamantopoulos (aide-de-camp of the king of Greece), Neapolis, Crete, 9 March 1897 (25 February 1897).

72. Lefteris Alexiou, "Penēnta Hronia Prin: Prosfygia, Sfagē, Leuteria," *Nea Hronika*, newspaper series starting on 29 March 1948, quoted in Manolis E. Detorakis, "Koinōnikes Epiptōseis sto Diamerisma Ērakleiou stē Metapoliteutikē Epanastasē, 1895–8," in Theoharis Detorakis and Alexis Kalokerinos, eds., *Ē Teleutaia Fasē tou Krētikou Zētēmatos* (Iraklio: Etairia Krētikōn Historikōn Meletōn, 2001), 115–16.

73. CADN, 328 PO/1/63, Petition to French Vice-Consul, Rethimno, 28 August 1896 (16 August 1896).

74. The choice of words presents an interesting detail in this petition. In referring to their belligerent compatriots (*oi Othōmanoi sympolitai ēmōn*, meaning "our Ottoman compatriots") the petitioners used the word *Ottoman* instead of the more common term

Turkish or Turkocretan, perhaps a choice that reflects their close association of native Muslims with the Ottoman authorities. The word *Ottoman* was also used in the telegram they wired, bearing ninety signatures, to the Ottoman governor of Crete, bemoaning injustices and hardships the Christians endured, "whereas the Ottomans live off the properties they looted of us."

75. Ypiresia Diplomatikou kai Istorikou Arheiou (Hellenic Foreign Ministry Archives, hereafter YDIA), A.A.K./Δ, Christian Villagers to Ottoman Administration in Rethimno, Rethimno, 11 June 1896 (30 May 1896).

76. ASDMAE 144, Augusto Medana to Alberto Pansa, Hania, 8 August 1896.

77. Ibid.

78. ASDMAE 144, Augusto Medana to Alberto Pansa, Hania, 17 August 1896.

79. BNA, ADM 121/53, Alfred Biliotti to the Marquess of Salisbury, Hania, 16 June 1898.

80. BNA, FO 195/1939, Alfred Biliotti to Philip Currie, Hania, 12 November 1896.

81. Ibid. The account in this paragraph is based on the enclosed testimonies of Mathaios Zahariadis, the investigator from Iraklio, and Dimitris Kokkinakis, an inhabitant of Anopolis and eyewitness to the carnage on that August night.

82. Hüseyin Nesimi and Mehmet Behçet, *Girit Hailesi*, vol. 2/2 (Hania, 1897), 9–30.

83. BOA, Y.A.HUS. 366/105, Ottoman Administration in Iraklio, 17 February 1897 (15 Ramazan 1314). About the same incident, Muslims in Rethimno sent a telegram to the grand vizierate, foreign ministry, and European embassies. They hoped that "the great powers of Europe, as protectors of humanity and civilization, would not allow the extermination of Muslim Cretans, who are deeply rooted in the island in terms of their property ownership" (hami-i insaniyet ve medeniyet olan Avrupa devlet-i muazzaması cezirede mülken en ziyade alakadar olan bunca nüfus-u İslamiye'nin külliyen mahv-u itlafına). BOA, Y. PRK. A. 11/35, Telegram from Rethimno Muslims, 20 February 1897 (18 Ramazan 1314).

84. Georgios Mitsotakis Collection, Istoriko Mouseio Kritis (Historical Museum of Crete), 2α/35, Petition from Iraklio Muslims to Russian Vice-Consul Georgios Mitsotakis, February 1897.

85. HHStA, PA XII, Liasse XXVIII, 286, Julius von Pinter to Agenor von Goluchowski, Hania, 13 July 1897. For the breakdown of figures by village, see Nesimi and Behçet, *Girit Hailesi*, vol. 2/2.

86. Nesimi and Behçet, *Girit Hailesi*, vol. 2/2, 27.

87. BNA, ADM 121/53, Letter dated 4 March 1897, enclosed in Alfred Biliotti to the Marquess of Salisbury, Hania, 17 March 1897.

88. BOA, Y. MTV. 175/107, 31 March 1898 (8 Zilkade 1315).

89. Jason De León, *The Land of Open Graves: Living and Dying on the Migrant Trail* (Oakland: University of California Press, 2015), 17–18.

90. Hüseyin Nesimi and Mehmet Behçet, *Girit Müslümanlarının Numune-i Felaketi* (Hania: Yusuf Kenan Matbaası, 1897), 20.

91. BNA, ADM 121/53, Alfred Biliotti to the Marquess of Salisbury, Hania, 20 July 1897.

92. HHStA, PA XII, Liasse XXVIII, 286, Julius von Pinter to Agenor von Goluchowski, Hania, 13 July 1897.

93. Jeffrey S. Kopstein and Jason Wittenberg, *Intimate Violence: Anti-Jewish Pogroms on*

the *Eve of the Holocaust* (Ithaca, NY: Cornell University Press, 2018), 3, 103–4. For a discussion about the clergy as perpetrators or bystanders during the Rwandan genocide, see Mamdani, *When Victims Become Killers*, 139–42.

94. BNA, ADM 121/53, Alfred Biliotti to the Marquess of Salisbury, Hania, 22 February 1897; BOA, Y. MTV. 151/88, Cipher from Ferik Ibrahim Edhem Pasha, 18 February 1897 (6 Şubat 1312).

95. BNA, ADM 121/53, Alfred Biliotti to the Marquess of Salisbury, Hania, 20 July 1897.

96. BNA, ADM 121/53, Alfred Biliotti to the Marquess of Salisbury, Hania, 22 February 1897.

97. BOA, HR. SFR. 3 463/4, Foreign Minister Tevfik Pasha to Anthopoulo Pasha, Ottoman Ambassador in London, Sublime Porte, 28 September 1897.

98. CADN, 328 PO/1/152, Hadjimihalis Giannaris to the population of Kydonia, Alikianou, 29 May 1897 (17 May 1897).

99. Ibid. Documents from the Archives of the Defense Committee of Archanes, one of the richest and largest villages in Crete near Iraklio, show how the destruction of Muslim properties was done with a view to bar an eventual return of their owners to the country. "In order to prevent the Turks' repatriation, their properties need to be devastated with determination, leaving not even a single olive tree.... We are imploring you, in the name of Christianity and fatherland, for which our brothers have spilled their blood, to begin, without delay, the destruction of olive groves and other properties owned by the Turks. The operation needs to be systematic and has to start immediately." Archives of the Defense Committee of Archanes, 29 March 1898, quoted in M. Detorakis, "Koinōnikes Epiptōseis," 129–30.

100. ASDMAE 144, Augusto Medana to Alberto Pansa, Hania, 8 December 1897.

101. Arnold J. Toynbee, *The Western Question in Greece and Turkey: A Study in the Contact of Civilisations* (London: Constable, 1922), 37.

102. According to estimates from 1903, the share of olive oil in the total value of agricultural production was 55 percent, a telling figure especially in light of the massive destruction of olive trees during the civil war. Manos Perakis, "An Eastern Mediterranean Economy under Transformation: Crete in the Late Ottoman Era," *Journal of European Economic History* 40, no. 3 (2011): 521.

103. Giannaris, *Perē tēs Katastaseōs*, 12–13. For a discussion about massive destruction of trees during the American Civil War, see Megan Kate Nelson, *Ruin Nation: Destruction and the American Civil War* (Athens: University of Georgia Press, 2012), 103–59.

Chapter 2: Sheltering Mountain

1. This sartorial detail recalls Fatma Kassem's point about the displaced Palestinian women who, by continuing to don traditional dress, "are maintaining the memory of their origin; it is a reminder of the place they come from." *Palestinian Women: Narrative Histories and Gendered Memory* (London: Zed Books, 2011), 180–81.

2. "Epistolai ek tēs Doulēs: Ē Tourkikē Kyvernēsis kai oi Prosfyges Tourkokrētes," *Nea Erevna*, 7 March 1902 (22 February 1902).

3. Native islander aspects of the encounter between the reporter and the displaced are reflected in the rendering of the man's question about the location of refugee relief in the Cretan dialect of Greek: "Kateheis kyrie, na mas edeiksēs pou moirazoune tsi pa-

rades gia tsi mouatzirides; Giati rōtoumene da epada sta spēthia, ma de katemene ēnta mas elene."

4. Ibid. Later in 1909, a Greek-language newspaper from Izmir would report that during the month of Ramadan a *hodja* was heard denigrating the Cretan refugees in that city as nominal Muslims. "Antidrastikoi Hotzai en Smyrnē," *Amaltheia*, 23 October 1909. Many a Cretan resettled in Bodrum would be derided or teased by the mainland Muslims as "half-infidel." Fatma Mansur, *Bodrum: A Town in the Aegean* (Leiden: E. J. Brill, 1972), 7.

5. "Girit Havadisi," *Meşveret*, 23 July 1896 (12 Safer 1314).

6. BNA, FO 421/154, the Marquess of Salisbury to the Marquess of Dufferin, Foreign Office, 11 June 1896.

7. Following the riot, 164 Muslims were arrested and handed over to British authorities. Seventeen of them were sentenced to death, four sentenced to twenty years' penal servitude, two sentenced to one year of imprisonment, one acquitted, and 120 released. See Ron Phillips, "Candia 6th September 1898 (25th August 1898)," in Theoharis Detorakis and Alexis Kalokerinos, eds., *Ē Teleutaia Fasē tou Krētikou Zētēmatos* (Iraklio: Etairia Krētikōn Historikōn Meletōn, 2001), 463.

8. Rüştü Çelik, *Kandiye Olayları: Girit'in Osmanlı Devletinden Kopuşu* (Istanbul: Kitap Yayınevi, 2012).

9. The text of the constitution of the Cretan state can be found in *EEKP*, 16 April 1899.

10. J. R. McNeill, *The Mountains of the Mediterranean World: An Environmental History* (Cambridge: Cambridge University Press, 1992), 12.

11. A famous account of this latest episode from Cretan history was told by George Psychoundakis, a resister shepherd from the village of Asi Gonia in western Crete. His description of a hideout cave near the village of Fourfouras in central Crete among the peaks of Mount Ida, at an elevation of 2,456 meters, provides a clear idea of the island's geography: "This cave lies on the very edge of a sheer precipice, among the last wooded peaks of the mountain. . . . It is a very peculiar cave, hard of access even for shepherds: you have to approach from above, and tread with care in order to avoid going headlong over those sheer and enormous precipices; you advance to the right behind a needle of rock, like a mountain goat, climbing first up and many times down, before finding the cave. From there all the villages of the Amari are spread out below you in a panorama. The cave has a large opening but does not go very deep, but in spite of this, it is invisible from all sides, owing to the narrowness of the precipice." Psychoundakis, *Cretan Runner*, 122.

12. For a discussion about sheltering mountains in the context of southern Italy, see Marco Armiero, *A Rugged Nation: Mountains and the Making of Modern Italy, Nineteenth and Twentieth Centuries* (Cambridge: White Horse Press, 2011), 53–86. John Lawrence Tone's point that "mountains provided a last refuge to the guerillas" applies to the case of Crete as well. *The Fatal Knot: The Guerilla War in Navarre and the Defeat of Napoleon in Spain* (Chapel Hill: University of North Carolina Press, 1994), 10.

13. Bacon, *Naval Scrap-Book*, 47–48.

14. CADN, 328 PO/1/50, Paul Blanc to F. A. Bourée, Hania, 1 October 1897.

15. BOA, İ.MTZ.GR 32/1248, Turhan Pasha to Sultan, 1 November 1897 (20 Teşrinievvel 1313).

16. Ibid.

17. BNA, FO 421/153, Alfred Biliotti to the Marquess of Salisbury, Hania, 24 December 1895.

18. Ibid. While mountains widely represent the abode of peril in the imagination of states, they are frequently perceived as sites of refuge by antistate forces. A case in point is the Kurdish conflict in Turkey. Salih Can Açıksöz, *Sacrificial Limbs: Masculinity, Disability, and Political Violence in Turkey* (Oakland: University of California Press, 2020), 15–44.

19. BNA, FO 421/153, Alfred Biliotti to the Marquess of Salisbury, Hania, 24 December 1895. Emphasis mine.

20. Rodogno, *Against Massacre*, 185–211.

21. Selim Deringil, "'The Armenian Question Is Finally Closed': Mass Conversions of Armenians in Anatolia during the Hamidian Massacres of 1895–1897," *Comparative Studies in Society and History* 51, no. 2 (2009): 344–71. For a discussion of the Armenian revolutionaries' occupation of the Ottoman Bank in Istanbul in August 1896, by which point the Crete conflict had greatly intensified, see Edhem Eldem, "26 Ağustos 1896 'Banka Vak'ası' ve 1896 'Ermeni Olayları,'" *Tarih ve Toplum* 5 (2007): 113–46.

22. A series of reports from foreign missions indicates the Ottomans' anxieties. See Sinan Kuneralp, ed., *Ottoman Diplomatic Documents on "The Eastern Question": Crete and Turco-Greek Relations (1869–1896)* (Istanbul: Isis Press, 2012), 442, 474, 483. According to the Sublime Porte, the coverage of Cretan affairs in European press always pointed an accusatory finger at the Muslims. In an attempt at better image management, the Ottoman state considered signing a contract with Reuters. BOA, İ.MTZ.GR 31/1224, Yıldız Palace Secretariat, 19 August 1897.

23. BOA, Y.A.HUS 359/123, Ottoman Embassy to Foreign Ministry, Rome, 20 September 1896 (8 Eylül 1312).

24. BOA, HR.SYS. 522/4, Ottoman Consulate to Foreign Minister Tevfik Pasha, Naples, 4 March 1897.

25. BOA, Y.A.HUS. 370/83, Ottoman Embassy to Foreign Ministry, London, 12 March 1897. For the British papers' reporting on Armenian and Cretan issues, see BOA, Y.A.HUS. 355/46, 20 July 1896, BOA Y.A.HUS. 361/73, 19 October 1896.

26. ASDMAE 150, Augusto Medana to Alberto Pansa, Hania, 9 August 1898.

27. Petition to Russian colonel Fyodor Schostak by the Christian inhabitants of the villages Atsipopoulo, Gallos, Prines, Armeni, and Kastellos in ASDMAE 150, Augusto Medana to Alberto Pansa, Hania, 9 August 1898.

28. Ibid.

29. CADN, 328 PO/1/152, Muslim Cretan Deputies to Paul Blanc, Hania, 22 July 1896.

30. BOA, Y.PRK.UM 36/35, Cipher telegram from Berović to the Yıldız Palace, Hania, 14 November 1896 (2 Teşrinisani 1312).

31. Christian General Administrative Councilors to N. Gennadis, Hania, 2 November 1896, in *Diplōmatika Eggrafa*.

32. Revolutionary assemblies and committees established across Crete varied by their visions of autonomy or annexation to Greece. For a discussion of their differences, see Stratis Papamanusakis, "Krētē 1897–1898: Apo tēn Epanastasē sto Kratos," in Theoharis Detorakis and Alexis Kalokerinos, eds., *Ē Teleutaia Fasē tou Krētikou Zētēmatos* (Iraklio: Etairia Krētikōn Historikōn Meletōn, 2001): 187–218. Alfred Biliotti reported that

while earlier assemblies aimed for extensive administrative reform, the Revolutionary/Insurrectionary Assembly strove for union with Greece and was under the heavy influence of Greek agents. BNA, FO 421/155, Alfred Biliotti to the Marquess of Salisbury, Hania, 22 August 1896.

33. Assembly of Cretans to Canevaro, Melidoni, 29 October 1897 (17 October 1897), in *Krētika: Ētoi Syllogē*, 7–13.

34. Nikolas Stavrakis, *Statistikē tou Plēthysmou tēs Krētēs meta Diaforōn Geōgrafikōn, Istorikōn, Arhaiologikōn, Ekklēsiastikōn ktl. Eidēseōn peri tēs Nēsou* (Athens, 1890), 67. Grand Vizier Rıfat Pasha claimed that the census underrepresented the Muslims while overcounting the Christians. See BOA, Y.E.E. 114/93, Grand Vizier Rıfat Pasha to Yıldız Palace, 21 March 1897. Ayşe Nükhet Adıyeke questioned the reliability of these figures by citing the results of the Ottoman provincial yearbook (*salname*) from 1876, according to which the Muslims made up 40 percent of the island's total population instead of 26 percent as recorded by the 1881 census. See Adıyeke, *Osmanlı İmparatorluğu*, 80–83. From the numbers provided by Kemal Karpat, Muslims constituted 30 percent of Crete's population during the early 1890s. See Kemal H. Karpat, *Ottoman Population, 1830–1914: Demographic and Social Characteristics* (Madison: University of Wisconsin Press, 1985), 155.

35. *Krētika: Ētoi Syllogē*.
36. Ibid.
37. Ibid.
38. Ibid.
39. CADN, 166 PO/E/244, Paul Blanc to Paul Cambon, Hania, 12 February 1898. Underlined in the original.

40. Ibid. Without losing sight of a taint of prejudice against the Muslims, it is worthwhile to consider Blanc's remarks as a reminder of the connection between the Cretan and Armenian questions. Rewinding the historical record to early 1896, we encounter an Ottoman garrison in its darkest hour, under siege by the Cretan insurgents in the western inland town of Vamos. An Ottoman relief force from Salonica finally saved the besieged troops after they hovered for weeks on the brink of starvation, with more than a hundred soldiers perishing in clashes during the operation. In the aftermath of the Vamos debacle, Charles Drury, the commanding officer of the British battleship HMS *Hood*, pointed out that among the 2,400-strong troops from the Aleppo Army Corps, another detachment recently sent to the island, were many soldiers who were rumored to have been present in the killings of Armenians in Zeitun in southern Anatolia. Deeply frightened by this rumor, the Christians spoke of soldiers selling in the bazaars items they had plundered from their Armenian victims. It was even heard that a soldier had tried to sell a pair of earrings from which dangled the flesh of the Armenian woman he had killed and robbed. See BNA, ADM 116/82, Charles C. Drury to M. Culme-Seymour, Hania, 5 June 1896. Hearing the same story, British consul Biliotti asked that such jewelry be purchased for him, but none was found. See BNA, FO 421/155, Alfred Biliotti to the Marquess of Salisbury, Hania, 14 June 1896.

41. BOA, İ.MTZ.GR 32/1248, Turhan Pasha to Sultan, 1 November 1897 (20 Teşrinievvel 1313).

42. Ibid.

43. BNA, ADM 121/53, Marquess of Salisbury to Edmund Monson, Foreign Office, 13 October 1897.

44. BNA, ADM 121/53, Colonel R.B. Mainwaring to President of Committee of Archanes, Iraklio, 11 July 1898.

45. Robert Hastings Harris (Admiral Sir), *From Naval Cadet to Admiral: Half-a-Century of Naval Service and Sport in Many Parts of the World* (London: Cassell, 1913), 231–32.

46. BNA, ADM 121/53, Alfred Biliotti to the Marquess of Salisbury, Hania, 11 March 1897.

47. Ibid.

48. For more on R. A. H. Bickford-Smith, including a discussion of his pan- and phil-Hellenic sentiments, see Maria Christina Chatziioanou, "Like a Rolling Stone, R. A. H. Bickford-Smith (1859–1916) from Britain to Greece," *British School at Athens Studies* 17 (2009): 39–48. Bickford-Smith is especially known for his work on Greece in the early 1890s. See R. A. H. Bickford-Smith, *Greece under King George* (London: Richard Bentley and Son, 1893).

49. A popular word in the Orientalist imagination, *houri* entered several European languages with the meaning of a voluptuous, alluring woman.

50. R. A. H. Bickford-Smith, *Cretan Sketches* (London: Richard Bentley and Son, 1898), 205–7.

51. BNA, ADM 121/53, Captain H. H. Hallett to Admiralty, Suda Bay, 13 August 1898.

52. BNA, ADM 121/53, Alfred Biliotti to the Marquess of Salisbury, Hania, 30 December 1897.

53. Ibid.

54. BNA, ADM 121/53, Alfred Biliotti to the Marquess of Salisbury, Iraklio, 16 December 1898.

55. Ibid.

56. ASDMAE 150, Augusto Medana to Alberto Pansa, Hania, 9 December 1898.

57. BNA, ADM 121/53, Alfred Biliotti to the Marquess of Salisbury, Iraklio, 15 December 1898.

58. CADC, 153 CPCOM/74, Paul Blanc to Théophile Delcassé, Hania, 23 March 1899.

59. Ibid.

60. Ibid. For a discussion of Muslim emigration from Bulgaria during the late nineteenth century, see Anna M. Mirkova, "'Population Politics' at the End of Empire: Migration and Sovereignty in Ottoman Eastern Rumelia, 1877–1886," *Comparative Studies in Society and History* 55, no. 4 (2013): 955–85.

61. Sunil S. Amrith, *Crossing the Bay of Bengal: The Furies of Nature and the Fortunes of Migrants* (Cambridge, MA: Harvard University Press, 2013), 141.

62. Barchard, "Fearless and Self-Reliant Servant," 20. As pointed out by Barchard, likely thanks to some of Biliotti's impartial reports, "Lord Salisbury and other observers in London were well aware of the existence of violence by Christian Cretans." Ibid., 22.

63. BNA, FO 881/7359, Alfred Biliotti to the Marquess of Salisbury, Hania, 26 May 1899.

64. CADC, 153 CPCOM/74, Paul Blanc to Théophile Delcassé, Hania, 15 May 1900.

65. Ibid.

66. *EEKP*, vol. 2 (annex), 24 March 1904 (11 March 1904). Across the more fertile east-

ern Crete, forty-five exclusively or majority-Muslim settlements were deserted, while ninety-six lost more than half their population from 1881 to 1900. See Nikos Andriotis, "Les querelles ethnoreligieuses en Crète et l'intervention des puissances européennes (seconde moitié du XIXe siècle)," in Anastassios Anastassiadis, ed., *Voisinages fragiles: Les relations interconfessionnelles dans le Sud-Est européen et la Méditerranée orientale, 1854–1923. Contraintes locales et enjeux internationaux* (Athens: EFA, 2013), 197–211.

67. IAK, Archives of the Cretan Gendarmerie, "Petition by Merchants and Other Residents of Arkalohori to the Cretan Gendarmerie," Arkalohori, May 1908.

68. Ibid.

69. BNA, FO 421/229, Acting Consul-General Ronald Graham to Edward Grey, Hania, 31 August 1906.

70. BNA, FO 421/246, Arthur Peel to Edward Grey, Hania, 3 June 1908.

71. According to the census carried out in 1900, only fifty-one people lived in Larani, twenty-eight Muslims and twenty-three Christians. *EEKP*, vol. 2 (annex), 24 March 1904 (11 March 1904): 25.

72. CADN, 328 PO/1/148, Muslims of Larani to Vice-Consul of France in Iraklio, Iraklio, 3 October 1907.

73. BNA, FO 421/238, Acting Consul General Wyldbore Smith to Edward Grey, Hania, 10 October 1907.

74. CADN, 328 PO/1/148, Muslims of Larani to Vice-Consul of France in Iraklio, Iraklio, 3 October 1907.

75. BNA, FO 421/217, Memorandum by Mr. Parker on the Situation in Crete, Foreign Office, 2 October 1905.

76. BNA, FO 421/228, C. des Graz to Edward Grey, Rome, 16 July 1906.

77. BNA, FO 421/229, Foreign Office to Acting Consul General Graham, 10 October 1906.

78. BNA, FO 421/228, Esme Howard to Edward Grey, Hania, 27 July 1906. Davide Rodogno mentions other similar examples such as transferring part of the Muslim Cretan population to Tunisia, a thought entertained by the French admiral Pottier. See Rodogno, *Against Massacre*, 219.

79. The question of ethno-religious unmixing has been generally studied in the context of the disintegration of empires following World War I. See Rogers Brubaker, "Aftermaths of Empire and the Unmixing of Peoples: Historical and Comparative Perspectives," *Ethnic and Racial Studies* 18, no. 2 (1995): 189–218.

80. BOA, İ. MTZ. GR. 31/1234, Interim Governor of Crete Müşavir İsmail to Yıldız Başkitabet Dairesi, Hania, 26 August 1897 (14 August 1313).

81. BNA, ADM 121/53, Alfred Biliotti to the Marquess of Salisbury, Hania, 30 April 1897.

82. BOA, İ. MTZ. GR. 31/1234, Interim Governor of Crete Müşavir İsmail to Yıldız Başkitabet Dairesi, Hania, 26 August 1897 (14 August 1313).

Chapter 3: Adaptability in Vulnerability

1. According to the census of 1900, 11,659 Muslims resided in Iraklio, constituting half of the city's total population. *EEKP*, vol. 2 (annex), 24 March 1904 (11 March 1904).

2. "Dēlōsis tou Dēmarhou Ērakleiou," *Kiryks*, 1 July 1908 (18 June 1908).

3. CADC, 153 CPCOM/74, Paul Blanc to Théophile Delcassé, Hania, 15 May 1900.

4. CADC, 153 CPCOM/74, Paul Blanc to Théophile Delcassé, Hania, 23 March 1899.

5. Nükhet Varlık, *Plague and Empire in the Early Modern Mediterranean World: The Ottoman Experience, 1347-1600* (New York: Cambridge University Press, 2015), 72-88.

6. Adıyeke, *Osmanlı İmparatorluğu*. A more recent revised monograph narrates the condition of the Muslim minority during the period of autonomy in terms of a theme of persecution. See Adıyeke and Adıyeke, *Osmanlı Dönemi*, 336. Mount Lebanon is another autonomous Ottoman province whose history has been widely told through the prism of persecution. For a critique of such approaches in the context of Lebanese Ottoman emigration, see Andrew Arsan, *Interlopers of Empire: The Lebanese Diaspora in Colonial French West Africa* (Oxford: Oxford University Press, 2014), 23-30; Akram Fouad Khater, *Inventing Home: Emigration, Gender, and the Middle Class in Lebanon, 1870-1920* (Berkeley: University of California Press, 2001), 49-52. For a study of Muslims of Iraklio as Greek subjects from the end of the Balkan Wars to the exchange of populations between Greece and Turkey, see Melike Kara, *Girit Kandiye'de Müslüman Cemaati, 1913-1923* (Istanbul: Kitap Yayınevi, 2008).

7. Elektra Kostopoulou, "The Muslim Millet of Autonomous Crete: An Exploration into Its Origins and Implications" (PhD diss., Boğaziçi University, 2009), 315-16.

8. For a discussion of the popularity of *Erotokritos* among Muslim Cretans, see Johann Strauss, "*Aretos yani Sevda*: The Nineteenth Century Ottoman Translation of the 'Erotokritos,'" *Byzantine and Modern Greek Studies* 16 (1992): 189-201. The Cretan cuisine includes various snail recipes. It is a well-known fact among the community of Cretan origin in Turkey that Muslim islanders too enjoyed eating those shelled gastropods. Most of the Muslims in the Ottoman Empire, however, shunned the eating of snails, widely perceiving it as a culinary taboo. This is one of the particularities of Cretan Muslims, a feature that distinguishes them from many of their coreligionists in the Ottoman world.

9. *EEKP*, vol. 2 (annex), 24 March 1904 (11 March 1904): ιαʹ.

10. Devin E. Naar, *Jewish Salonica: Between the Ottoman Empire and Modern Greece* (Stanford, CA: Stanford University Press, 2016), 13. For an examination of the Muslim communities in autonomous Bulgaria that eschews state-centric accounts of Muslim persecution, see Milena B. Methodieva, *Between Empire and Nation: Muslim Reform in the Balkans* (Stanford, CA: Stanford University Press, 2021). A study of Bosnian Muslim experiences under the Austro-Hungarian Empire provides some parallels to the Cretan case. See Leyla Amzi-Erdogdular, "Alternative Muslim Modernities: Bosnian Intellectuals in the Ottoman and Habsburg Empires," *Comparative Studies in Society and History* 59, no. 4 (2017): 912-43.

11. Having received no satisfactory response to its proposals for the appointment of a Greek Orthodox Ottoman subject as the top administrator of Crete, the Sublime Porte refused to recognize Prince George's government. In 1900, for instance, the Ottoman government requested the post offices in the empire to cross off the stamps that bore the images of Prince George on the letters originating from Crete. BOA, DH. MKT. 2395/113, 12 August 1900 (29 Rebiülahir 1318).

12. BNA, ADM 121/53, Alfred Biliotti to the Marquess of Salisbury, Hania, 24 December 1898. Prince George had previously come to the island in a quite different capacity,

as the commander of Hellenic torpedo boats. Around that extraordinary time, in February 1897, the British rear-admiral Robert Harris reported about a visit Prince George paid to him, together with the captain of the Hellenic vessel *Sfaktiria*, making "no secret of their intention to acts of hostility with a view to insurrection." BNA, ADM 121/53, Rear-Admiral Harris to Admiralty, Hania, 24 February 1897.

13. BNA, ADM 121/53, Alfred Biliotti to the Marquess of Salisbury, Hania, 24 December 1898.

14. CADN, 166 PO/E/243, Paul Blanc to M. Bapst (French chargé d'affaires in Istanbul), Hania, 28 December 1898.

15. BNA, ADM 121/53, Alfred Biliotti to the Marquess of Salisbury, Iraklio, 7 January 1899.

16. "Ē Doksologia yper tēs A. V. Y. toy Ē gemonas ēmōn en tō tourk. Temenei Haniōn," *Anagennisis*, 17 January 1899 (4 January 1899).

17. CADN, 328 PO/1/152, Muslim Cretan Deputies to European Consuls, Hania, 22 July 1896.

18. BNA, FO 881/7392, Alfred Biliotti to the Marquess of Salisbury, Hania, 18 May 1899.

19. Ibid.

20. "Ē Ypodohē tēs A. V. Y. en Ē rakleiō," *Anagennisis*, 21 May 1899 (9 May 1899).

21. BNA, FO 881/7392, Alfred Biliotti to the Marquess of Salisbury, Hania, 18 May 1899. According to the 1900 census, 157 Muslims and 95 Christians inhabited the village of Gazi. *EEKP*, vol. 2 (annex), 24 March 1904 (11 March 1904): 21.

22. According to the 1900 census, 625 Muslims resided in the district of Ierapetra. *EEKP*, vol. 2 (annex), 24 March 1904 (11 March 1904): 30.

23. IAK, Archives of the Directorate of Education and Religion, 9 December 1901 (26 November 1901).

24. "Diatagma peri egkriseōs tou Katastatikou tou Gymnastikou Syllogou Halepas," *EEKP*, 30 December 1899 (17 December 1899).

25. "Diatagma peri egkriseōs tou Katastatikou tou en Rethymnē Gymnastikou Syllogou," *EEKP*, vol. 1, 26 March 1900 (13 March 1900).

26. A renowned teacher and scholar, the president of the Gymnastic Society authored a geography textbook that was assigned in the island's primary schools. See Emmanouil Generalis, *Epitomos Geōgrafia tēs Nēsou Krētēs* (Hania: I Proodos; E. D. Frantzeskaki, 1900).

27. "Diatagma peri egkriseos tou Katastatikou tou en Rethymnē Gymnastikou Syllogou," *EEKP*, vol. 1, 26 March 1900 (13 March 1900). Emphasis is mine.

28. For a discussion about the popularization of modern conceptions of masculinity in the early twentieth-century Ottoman Empire, see Murat C. Yıldız, "'What Is a Beautiful Body?' Late Ottoman 'Sportsman' Photographs and New Notions of Male Corporeal Beauty," *Middle East Journal of Culture and Communication* 8 (2015): 192–214.

29. Throughout the nineteenth century, several words in the Cretan vernacular referred to the island's Muslim population. Used interchangeably, the descriptors "Muslim," "Mohammedan," "Turkish," and "Ottoman" all denoted the same segment of Crete's population.

30. "Diatagma peri egkriseōs diorganismou tou syndesmou tōn Hristianōn kai Othōmanidōn Krēssōn," *EEKP*, vol. 1, 5 August 1901 (23 July 1901).

31. Errieta K. Manou was the spouse of Konstantinos Manos, who chaired the Gymnastic Society of Halepa.
32. "Diatagma peri egkriseōs diorganismou tou syndesmou tōn Hristianōn kai Othōmanidōn Krēssōn," *EEKP*, vol. 1, 5 August 1901 (23 July 1901).
33. "Syndesmos Hristianōn kai Othōmanidōn Krēssōn," *Nea Erevna*, 15 November 1901 (2 November 1901).
34. "Syndesmos Hristianōn kai Othōmanidōn Krēssōn," *Nea Erevna*, 4 April 1902 (22 March 1902).
35. "Syndesmos Krēssōn," *Nea Erevna*, 20 May 1902 (7 May 1902).
36. See, for example, the issue dated 1 March 1906 (16 February 1906).
37. *Anagennisis*, 28 July 1907 (15 July 1907).
38. "Yper tou Ethnikou Stolou kai tēs Eth. Amynēs," *Nea Erevna*, 24 June 1904 (11 June 1904). For a detailed look at education during the period of autonomy, see Antonis Hourdakis, *Ē Paideia stēn Krētikē Politeia (1898–1913)* (Athens: Gutenberg, 2002).
39. Ibid.
40. Ibid.
41. "Yper tōn Tameiōn tou Ethnikou Stolou kai tēs Ethnikēs Amynēs," *Nea Erevna*, 12 August 1904 (30 July 1904).
42. "Yper tou Ethnikou Stolou," *Nea Erevna*, 8 February 1905 (26 January 1905).
43. Ibid.
44. "Yper tou Ethnikou Stolou," *Nea Erevna*, 1 March 1906 (16 February 1906). Also emphasized in the official accounts regarding Crete's ancient history was the significance of the mastery over the seas. In a textbook authored by Ioannis Kondilakis on the history and geography of the island, Minos, the legendary king of Crete, was referred to as "the ruler of the waves" (*Minos O Thalassokrator*). Ioannis Kondilakis, *Istoria kai Geōgrafia tēs Krētēs* (Athens: D. K. Kokkinaki, 1903), 21–23. Once the autonomous regime described Crete as a major sea power in ancient times, it set out to translate its distant glory into a present might.
45. "Yper tou Ethnikou Stolou," *Nea Erevna*, 1 March 1906 (16 February 1906).
46. For contributions made by numerous schools, see the following issues of *Nea Erevna*: 29 July 1904 (16 July 1904), 9 November 1904 (27 October 1904), 23 November 1904 (10 November 1904).
47. "Yper tou Ethnikou Stolou," *Nea Erevna*, 12 August 1904 (30 July 1904).
48. Ibid.
49. CADN, 328 PO/1/133, Speech by Emmanouil Angelakis, Ierapetra, 23 November 1898.
50. Emmanouil Angelakis began to compile an autobiography in 1930, an undertaking that took up about twenty years. See Emmanouil Angelakis, *Apomnēmonevmata 1856–1906* (Athens: Estia, 2004).
51. CADN, 328 PO/1/133, Speech by Emmanouil Angelakis, Ierapetra, 23 November 1898.
52. Ibid.
53. BNA, FO 881/7452, Proclamation by Admirals G. Bettolo, G. H. Noel, N. Skrydloff, E. Pottier, Suda, 10 December 1898.

208 *Notes to Chapter 3*

54. *EEKP*, vol. 2 (annex), 24 March 1904 (11 March 1904).

55. Proclamation of Prince George to Inhabitants of Sphakia Province, in BNA, FO 421/195, Acting Consul General James McGregor to the Marquess of Lansdowne, Hania, 12 June 1902.

56. "Oi Fonoi tōn Sfakiōn," *Patris*, 9 June 1902 (27 May 1902).

57. Charalambos Pologeorgis, "Ē Tetraplē Dolofonia," *Patris*, 12 June 1902 (30 May 1902).

58. BOA, HR. SFR. 1. 127/60, circular from Tevfik Pasha to Ottoman Ambassadors in European Capitals, 3 July 1902.

59. BNA, FO 421/228, Esme Howard to Edward Grey, Hania, 27 June 1906.

60. CADN, 328 PO/1/148, E. Monaco to Lucien Maurouard, Hania, 22 August 1906.

61. BNA, FO 421/238, Arthur Peel to Edward Grey, Hania, 6 August 1907.

62. BNA, FO 421/237, Consul General Arthur Peel to Edward Grey, Hania, 24 April 1907.

63. Ibid. Elektra Kostopoulou also notes that Crete served as a model for the expanding Greece under Venizelos. See "The Island That Wasn't: Autonomous Crete (1898–1912) and Experiments of Federalization," *Journal of Balkan and Near Eastern Studies* 18, no. 6 (2016): 557. For a study on the absorption of Muslim communities into the enlarging Greece, see Stefanos Katsikas, *Islam and Nationalism in Modern Greece, 1821–1940* (New York: Oxford University Press, 2021).

64. "Oi Mousoulmanoi Sympolitai," *Kiryks*, 17 May 1908 (4 May 1908).

65. BNA, FO 421/237, Arthur Peel to Edward Grey, Hania, 14 March 1907.

66. CADN, 328 PO/1/148, Petition of Spinalonga Residents to Cretan Government, 5 July 1903.

67. Drs. Ehlers and Cahnheim, "La lèpre en Crète," no. 1, 161. Authors' copy to king of Greece (Leipzig: Johann Ambrosius Barth, n.d.), originally published in *Lepra Bibliotheca Internationalis* 2, nos. 1 and 3 (1901).

68. CADN, 328 PO/1/148, Petition of Spinalonga Residents to Cretan Government, 5 July 1903.

69. Précis of Judgment of Court of Appeal on the Spinalonga Claims, Hania, 4 December 1906, in BNA, FO 421/237, Arthur Peel to Edward Grey, Hania, 14 March 1907.

70. CADN, 328 PO/1/148, French Vice-Consul to French Consul A. Drouin, Iraklio, 18 October 1904.

71. BNA, FO 421/215, Esme Howard to the Marquess of Lansdowne, Hania, 18 May 1905.

72. Précis of Judgment of Court of Appeal on the Spinalonga Claims, Hania, 4 December 1906, in BNA, FO 421/237, Arthur Peel to Edward Grey, Hania, 14 March 1907.

73. CADN, 328 PO/1/148, Petition by Hasan Seyidakis to Commander of French Troops of Occupation in Eastern Crete, Iraklio, 30 July 1906.

74. CADN, 328 PO/1/148, Report of Commission of Inquiry for Claims of Spinalonga Muslims, Hania, 10 September 1906.

75. CADN, 328 PO/1/148, French Vice-Consul to French Minister in Athens, Hania, 15 February 1918.

76. For more on Spinalonga and leprosy during the Ottoman times and beyond, see Aytek Soner Alpan, "'Meskinides' ve Nüfus Mübadelesi Üzerine," *Toplumsal Tarih* (August 2021): 50–54; Maria Sorou, "Ē Spinalogka tōn Othōmanikōn Hronōn," *Kritika Hronika* 33 (2013): 121–54.

77. Prince George of Greece, *The Cretan Drama: The Life and Memoirs of Prince George of Greece, High Commissioner in Crete (1898-1906)*, ed. A. A. Pallis (New York: Robert Speller and Sons, 1959), 63–67.

78. Ibid. Ehlers's interest in researching leprosy in Crete should be considered within the context of his earlier work about the subject on another island. See Edward Ehlers, "On the Conditions under Which Leprosy Has Declined in Iceland and the Extent of Its Former and Present Prevalence," in *Prize Essays on Leprosy* (London: New Sydenham Society, 1895), 151–87.

79. The medico-political control of an illness like leprosy and the civilizational language inherent in such a project fit the expressed worldview of various figures that associated the Ottoman rule in Crete with backwardness. Well before the proclamation of autonomy in late 1898, the vocabulary of civilization against barbarity constituted the discursive core of the struggle against the Ottoman regime. For instance, in June 1896, the Central Cretan Committee in Athens asserted that only through union with Greece could the island embark on the path of progress and civilization. See IAK, Archives of the Revolutionary Reform Committee of Crete, II, Central Cretan Committee in Athens, Athens, 27 June 1896 (14 June 1896). Soon after the withdrawal of Ottoman troops from Crete, Emmanouil Angelakis, referenced earlier in this chapter, proclaimed that the principal aspiration behind the entire struggle against the former regime was the desire to achieve moral and material perfection like other civilized peoples. See CADN, 328 PO/1/133, Speech by Emmanouil Angelakis, Ierapetra, 23 November 1898.

Chapter 4: "Crete or Death"

1. See Orhan Koloğlu, "Celal Nuri'nin *Jeune Turc* Gazetesi ve Siyonist Bağı," *Tarih ve Toplum*, no. 108 (December 1992): 46–48; Ozan Ozavci, "A Jewish 'Liberal' in Istanbul: Vladimir Jabotinsky, the Young Turks and the Zionist Press Network, 1908–1911," in Abigail Green and Simon Levis Sullam, eds., *Jews, Liberalism, Antisemitism: A Global History* (Cham, Switzerland: Palgrave Macmillan, 2020), 289–314.

2. YDIA, A/6, Ambassadorial Report to Foreign Ministry, Istanbul, 16 June 1910 (3 June 1910).

3. Ibid.

4. Koloğlu, "Celal Nuri'nin *Jeune Turc* Gazetesi," 46–48.

5. Italian diplomats too shared with their superiors clippings from *Le Jeune Turc*'s multiple issues.

6. Cihan Özgün, "II. Meşrutiyetin İlk Yıllarında Türk Basınında Girit Diplomasisi Üzerine Bazı Tespitler," in Tuncay Ercan Sepetcioğlu and Olcay Pullukçuoğlu Yapıcı, eds., *Ege Araştırmaları I: Batı Anadolu'da Giritliler* (İzmir: Ege Üniversitesi Basımevi, 2019), 179.

7. For one of many examples of this phrase, see the first-page article in the leading Turkish-language newspaper from Edirne. "Girit Meselesi Dolayısıyla Miting," *Yeni Edirne*, 12 May 1910 (29 Nisan 1326).

8. Prior to the 1890s, Namık Kemal, a hero of many Young Turks, had depicted Crete's Muslims in similar words. In an 1884 letter to Ebuzziya Tevfik, he likened the Crete question to a seven-headed dragon, "one head cut off only to sprout seven more." See İ. Hakkı Uzunçarşılı, "Namık Kemal'in Abdülhamid'e Takdim Ettiği Arizalarla Ebuzziya Tevfik Bey'e Yolladığı Bazı Mektuplar," *Türk Tarih Kurumu Belleten* 11, no. 42 (April 1947): 282.

9. For instance, when the newspaper *Girit* (Crete) of Geneva published a letter sent from Hania, it spoke of the island's Muslims in a manner to stimulate the sentiments of its readers. They implored the Sublime Porte "with burning hearts and weeping eyes" to safeguard them. For that state they had always "gladly shed the last drop of their blood." In vain, however, they had anticipated the protection of "the cursed regime," which left them no choice but to beg the European powers, "in the name of civilization," for "humanity, mercy, compassion, and kindness." *Girit*, "Girit Mektubu," 1 April 1897. For several other examples in this regard, see "En Crète," *Mechveret* (Consultation), 1 April 1897; "Girit Kimindir?," *Hürriyet* (Liberty), 1 September 1897; "Yine Girit," *Doğru Söz* (Righteous Word), 14 June 1906.

10. Serhat Güvenç, *Osmanlıların Drednot Düşleri: Birinci Dünya Savaşı'na Giden Yolda* (Istanbul: Türkiye İş Bankası Kültür Yayınları, 2011).

11. Georgeon, *Aux origines du nationalisme turc*; Meyer, *Turks across Empires*; Shissler, *Between Two Empires*.

12. For a discussion of transoceanic routes of Middle Eastern migrants and their ensuing activism, see Stacy Fahrenthold, "Transnational Modes and Media: The Syrian Press in the *Mahjar* and Emigrant Activism during World War I," *Mashriq and Mahjar* 1, no. 1 (2013): 34–63; Akram Fouad Khater, "Becoming 'Syrian' in America: A Global Geography of Ethnicity and Nation," *Diaspora: A Journal of Transnational Studies* 14, nos. 2/3 (2005): 299–331. For a recent collected work in which several essays address displacement from Crete, see Ayşe Nükhet Adıyeke and Tuncay Ercan Sepetcioğlu, eds., *Geçmişten Günümüze Girit: Tarih, Toplum, Kültür* (Uluslararası Sempozyum bildiri kitabı) (Ankara: Gece Kitaplığı, 2017).

13. "Mekteb-i Hukuk'taki İctima ve Girit Meselesi," *Tanin*, 6 January 1909 (24 Kanunuevvel 1324).

14. "Girit Hakkında Bir İctima-i Mühim," *İkdam* (Perseverance), 6 January 1909 (24 Kanunuevvel 1324). At the meeting, it was also decided to send telegrams to Manisa and Bartın to convey appreciation for the smaller rallies organized in these Anatolian towns.

15. Sinan Kuneralp, *Son Dönem Osmanlı Erkan ve Ricali (1839-1922): Prosopografik Rehber* (Istanbul: İsis, 1999), 110.

16. For an exploration of Celal Nuri's ideas, see the recently published book by York Norman, *Celal Nuri: Young Turk Modernizer and Muslim Nationalist* (London: I. B. Tauris, 2021).

17. Nezih Neyzi, *Kızıltoprak Hatıraları* (Istanbul: İletişim Yayınları, 1993); Ercüment Ekrem Talu, "Yusuf Razi Bey," TTOK Belleten, Şubat 1947.

18. Kuneralp, *Son Dönem Osmanlı Erkan*, 5. Ahmed Nesimi's brother, Ekmel Bey, served as a deputy in the Cretan parliament in the early 1900s during the period of autonomy. See Ali Zeki, "Girit Hakkında Mülahazat II," *Tanin*, 17 December 1908 (4 Kanunuevvel 1324).

19. Ali Adem Yörük, "Kapitülasyonların Kaldırılması Sürecine Dair Bibliyografik Bir Deneme: 1909-1927 Yılları Arasında Yazılmış Kapitülasyon Kitapları," *Türk Hukuk Tarihi Araştırmaları*, no. 5 (Spring 2008): 115–18. This article about late Ottoman and early Republican books on the topic of capitulations includes a discussion about Mehmed Aziz's work on foreign concessions and privileges in the empire. Still more evidence of Cretan

intellectual networks in Istanbul is indicated by the fact that the book was published by the Ahmed Saki Bey Printing House.

20. There are no English monographs on the life and work of Ahmed Cevad (Emre). For a recent MA thesis, see Nisa İçen, "Ahmet Cevat Emre Hayatı ve Eserleri (1876–1961)" (MA thesis, Muğla Sıtkı Koçman Üniversitesi, 2021).

21. "Mekteb-i Hukuk'taki İctima ve Girit Meselesi," *Tanin*, 6 January 1909 (24 Kanunuevvel 1324).

22. "Mekteb-i Hukuk'ta Konferans," *Şura-i Ümmet*, 8 January 1909 (26 Kanunuevvel 1324). For a related discussion about the term *eyalet-i mümtaze*, see Aimee M. Genell, "Autonomous Provinces and the Problem of 'Semi-sovereignty' in European International Law," *Journal of Balkan and Near Eastern Studies* 18, no. 6 (2016): 533–49.

23. They appeared in *Tanin* under the title "Girit Hakkında Mülahazat" on 15 December 1908 (2 Kanunuevvel 1324), 17 December 1908 (4 Kanunuevvel 1324), 21 December 1908 (8 Kanunuevvel 1324), and 3 January 1909 (21 Kanunuevvel 1324).

24. Ali Zeki, "Girit Hakkında Mülahazat," *Tanin*, 15 December 1908 (2 Kanunuevvel 1324).

25. Fikret Uslucan, "Edebiyat Tarihimizin Unuttuğu Bir İsim: Ali Zeki Bey ve Bir İmla Eleştirisi," *Journal of Turkish Studies* 2, no. 2 (2007): 690–96.

26. Abdülhak Şinasi, "Alev Muharriri Ali Zeki Bey ve Romancılık," *Dergah*, 15 April 1921 (15 Nisan 1337): 12–13.

27. "Mekteb-i Hukuk'ta Konferans," *Şura-i Ümmet*, 8 January 1909 (26 Kanunuevvel 1324).

28. Ahmet Cevat Emre, *İki Neslin Tarihi* (Istanbul: Hilmi Kitabevi, 1960), 89–95.

29. Mustafa Nuri, "Girit Müslümanlarının Feryadı," *Tanin*, 20 November 1908 (7 Teşrinisani 1324).

30. His son, Celal Nuri, later mentioned the conquerors by name in his speech delivered at the Istanbul protest rally in January 1909 and swore that today's Ottomans would follow the example set by "those great Ottomans, the Köprülü [a family that nurtured several grand viziers to the imperial administration during the seventeenth century]." "Dünkü Miting," *Tanin*, 10 January 1909 (28 Kanunuevvel 1324).

31. Mustafa Nuri, "Girit Müslümanlarının Feryadı," *Tanin*, 20 November 1908 (7 Teşrinisani 1324). Mustafa Nuri's taking on the role of a veteran representative of Turkocretans is consistent with another duty that he would soon come to perform. A notice issued in *Hürriyet* in March 1909 informed the public of the establishment of an association called Girit Cemiyet-i Osmaniyesi (Cretan Ottoman Association), headed by the senator Mustafa Nuri. *Hürriyet* began to be published in Istanbul in early 1909 as the semiweekly newspaper of this civil society organization. This publication, too, should be seen as part of the active network of notable Cretans in Istanbul. The newspaper was published by the Ahmed Saki Bey Printing House. *Hürriyet* featured, among other authors, articles by Celal Nuri and Ahmed Saki. "Girit Cemiyet-i Osmaniyesi," *Hürriyet*, 11 March 1909 (26 Şubat 1324). In the spring of 1909, *Hürriyet* merged with another Istanbul newspaper, *Siper-i Saika*, taking the name *Siper-i Saika-i Hürriyet* (Lightning Rod of Liberty). The director of the merged newspaper was Ahmed Cevad, who published in it opinion pieces on Crete in addition to articles on domestic and international affairs.

32. One of the most memorable speeches in those rallies was delivered by Halide Edib.

See Elizabeth F. Thompson, *Justice Interrupted: The Struggle for Constitutional Government in the Middle East* (Cambridge, MA: Harvard University Press, 2013), 91–96; Tahsin Yıldırım, *İşgal, Feryad ve Direniş: Milli Mücadelede İstanbul Mitingleri* (Istanbul: Ketebe, 2019).

33. Halil Nihad, "Girit İçin," *Aşiyan*, 21 January 1909 (8 Kanunusani 1324).

34. "Girit Meselesi," *Şura-i Ümmet*, 10 January 1909 (28 Kanunuevvel 1324). The Ottoman parliament had resumed its sessions only recently, after being prorogued by Sultan Abdülhamid II thirty years earlier.

35. YDIA, KZ#98.2, Gryparis to Hellenic Ministry of Foreign Affairs, Istanbul, 9 January 1909. On the exaggerated end, *Şura-i Ümmet* wrote that more than two hundred thousand protesters attended the demonstration; "Girit Meselesi," 10 January 1909 (28 Kanunuevvel 1324).

36. "Pro Candia: Le meeting de Sultan-Ahmed," *Stamboul*, 11 January 1909.

37. HHStA, PA XII, Liasse XXVIII, 294, Pallavicini to Aehrenthal, Istanbul, 15 January 1909.

38. "Dünkü Miting," *Tanin*, 10 January 1909 (28 Kanunuevvel 1324).

39. "Girit Meselesi," *Şura-i Ümmet*, 10 January 1909 (28 Kanunuevvel 1324).

40. "Dünkü Miting," *Tanin*, 10 January 1909 (28 Kanunuevvel 1324).

41. "Girit İçin Miting," *Tanin*, 8 January 1909 (26 Kanunuevvel 1324).

42. BNA, FO 421/255, Gerard Lowther to Edward Grey, Istanbul, 14 January 1909.

43. "Pro Candia: Le meeting de Sultan-Ahmed," *Stamboul*, 11 January 1909.

44. "Girit Meselesi," *Şura-i Ümmet*, 10 January 1909 (28 Kanunuevvel 1324).

45. Hüseyin Cahid, "Büyük Bir Gün, Büyük Bir Millet," *Tanin*, 10 January 1909 (28 Kanunuevvel 1324).

46. *Yeni Gazete* (New Gazette) sarcastically mocked *Tanin* for "exhibiting the modesty of passing off the articles published for months by its striving [*mücahidekari*, a pun on the name Hüseyin Cahid] editor as the source of the eagerness demonstrated by the Ottoman people." In its response to *Yeni Gazete*, *Tanin* divulged the name of that *hamiyetli mebus*. It was Pantelis Kosmidis, an Istanbul deputy. "Girit ve Tanin," *Tanin*, 12 January 1909 (30 Kanunuevvel 1324).

47. "Girit Meselesi," *Tanin*, 31 July 1909 (18 Temmuz 1325).

48. Hüseyin Cahid, "Neyin Cezasını Çekiyoruz?," *Tanin*, 10 October 1908 (27 Eylül 1324).

49. On education in the late Ottoman Empire, see Benjamin C. Fortna, *Imperial Classroom: Islam, the State, and Education in the Late Ottoman Empire* (Oxford: Oxford University Press, 2002); Selçuk Akşin Somel, *The Modernization of Public Education in the Ottoman Empire, 1839–1908: Islamization, Autocracy and Discipline* (Leiden: Brill, 2001).

50. İsmail Hakkı, "Tarih ve Osmanlılar," *Ikdam*, 2 October 1908 (19 Eylül 1324).

51. BNA, FO 195/2336, Justin Alvarez to Gerard Lowther, Tripoli, 26 June 1910.

52. "Les meetings de protestations," *Stamboul*, 14 May 1910.

53. Noémi Lévy-Aksu, "Freedom versus Security: Regulating and Managing Public Gatherings after the Young Turk Revolution," in Noémi Lévy-Aksu and François Georgeon, eds., *The Young Turk Revolution and the Ottoman Empire: The Aftermath of 1908* (London: I. B. Tauris, 2017), 215. In the post-1908 period, the novelty of popular protests should be considered in tandem with the proliferation of publications on political issues thanks to the relative press freedom in that period. See Ipek K. Yosmaoğlu, "Chasing the Printed

Word: Press Censorship in the Ottoman Empire, 1876–1913," *Turkish Studies Association Journal* 27, nos. 1/2 (2003): 15–49.

54. In a report sent to Rome, the Italian consul in Ioannina mentioned that the military officers stationed in that city near the Greek border exchanged two visits with the Greek Orthodox archbishop to ensure the participation of the representatives of the Greek Ottoman community in a planned rally. The consul went on to claim that Colonel Sabit Bey had threatened that "the Greeks, who in the present circumstances have not proven themselves good Ottoman patriots," would be expelled from the province. ASDMAE 215, Augusto Stranieri to Italian Minister of Foreign Affairs, Ioannina, 20 August 1909.

55. "Girit ve Vilayat," *Tanin*, 12 January 1909 (30 Kanunuevvel 1324).

56. HHStA, PA XII, Liasse XXVIII, 297, August Kral to Aehrenthal, Izmir, 11 June 1910.

57. In April 1900, the Italian vice-consul in Benghazi had informed his superior in Tripoli of the arrival of around five thousand Cretan refugees in the eastern Cyrenaica region of Libya. ASDMAE 156, Mancinelli Scotti to Enrico Chicco, Benghazi, 30 April 1900. For a discussion about the Ottoman state's attempts to harness the agricultural and martial capabilities of Cretan refugees on the eastern Libyan coast, see Fredrick Walter Lorenz, "The 'Second' Egypt: Cretan Refugees, Agricultural Development, and Frontier Expansion in Ottoman Cyrenaica, 1897–1904," *International Journal of Middle East Studies* 53, no. 1 (2021): 89–105.

58. ASDMAE 215, Giulio Pestalozza to Minister of Foreign Affairs, Tripoli, 16 January 1909.

59. Interestingly, the article picked out the word *mülteci* over its much more common synonym *muhacir* during this period. Today, *mülteci* is the most widely used word in Turkish for "refugee."

60. "Girit Mültecileri," *Siper-i Saika-i Hürriyet*, 1 August 1909 (19 Temmuz 1325).

61. A recent article has discussed Crete protests in 1910 through the lens of history of emotions. Pınar Şenışık, "Politics of Emotions in the Late Ottoman Empire: 'Our Beloved Crete,'" *Journal of Balkan and Near Eastern Studies* 24, no. 2 (2022): 365–85. In it the author notes in passing the predominance of death-infused slogans in those rallies.

62. BOA, HR.SYS. 512/2, 24 June 1910.

63. CADN, 166 PO/E/251, French Consul to Maurice Bompard (French Ambassador), Salonica, 8 August 1909. For the moniker *Shabatopolis*, see Naar, *Jewish Salonica*, 30.

64. CADN, 166 PO/E/251, French Consul to Maurice Bompard (French Ambassador), Salonica, 8 August 1909.

65. "La question crétoise," *Journal de Salonique*, 8 August 1909.

66. "Girit İçin Taşralarda Mitingler," *Tanin*, 16 May 1910 (4 Mayıs 1326).

67. "Girit İçin Miting," *Ahenk*, 30 May 1911 (17 Mayıs 1327).

68. "Syllalētērion," *Amaltheia*, 3 August 1909.

69. CADC, 153 CPCOM/75, French Consul to French Foreign Ministry, Izmir, 3 August 1909.

70. "Syllalētērion," *Amaltheia*, 3 August 1909.

71. Jillian Schwedler, *Protesting Jordan: Geographies of Power and Dissent* (Stanford, CA: Stanford University Press, 2022), 7.

72. In her classical work, Sia Anagnostopoulou has emphasized the strong imprint of

Greeks (*Rum* as well as *Yunan*) in the cultural and economic life of Izmir. *Mikra Asia, 19os ai.-1919: Oi Ellēnorthodokses Koinotētes. Apo to Millet tōn Rōmiōn sto Ellēniko Ethnos* (Athens: Ellinika Grammata, 1997), 140, 333–34.

73. Ziad Fahmy, *Street Sounds: Listening to Everyday Life in Modern Egypt* (Stanford, CA: Stanford University Press, 2020), 17.

74. Robert Darnton's remark that throughout most of recorded history "books had audiences rather than readers" can be extended to include newspapers and magazines. Robert Darnton, *The Kiss of Lamourette: Reflections in Cultural History* (New York: W. W. Norton, 1990), 168–69. In the Ottoman Middle East, reading aloud such publications was "an old practice that converted a text of any kind to the property of a circle of listeners." Ami Ayalon, *The Press in the Arab Middle East: A History* (New York: Oxford University Press, 1995), 156–57.

75. "Girit," *Yeni Edirne*, 26 May 1910 (13 Mayıs 1326).

76. The calls of street criers in the enlistment process were ominous sounds for many Ottomans during World War I. See Yiğit Akın, *When the War Came Home: The Ottomans' Great War and the Devastation of an Empire* (Stanford, CA: Stanford University Press, 2018), 55. For a discussion about the place of street hawkers in the soundscape of modern Egypt, see Ziad Fahmy, "An Earwitness to History: Street Hawkers and Their Calls in Early 20th-Century Egypt," *International Journal of Middle East Studies* 48, no. 1 (2016): 129–34.

77. ASDMAE 215, Portuguese Consulate to Guglielmo Imperiali, Aleppo, 16 August 1909.

78. ASDMAE 215, Vincenzo Bernabei to Marquis Imperiali di Francavilla, Benghazi, 4 September 1909.

79. During the spring of 1910, the consular correspondence of European diplomats in Crete exposed the escalating tension surrounding the oath question. In May, at a time when the popular rallies enveloped the Ottoman provinces, British consul Albert Wratislaw apprised the British Foreign Office of his communication to pro-Greece figures in the Cretan Assembly. The consul sought to break their determination to bar the Muslim Cretan deputies to sit in the chamber without taking an oath of allegiance to the king of Greece. He warned them that their obstinacy "might thereby create a very grave situation entailing the intervention of the Powers," a position shared by his Continental colleagues but ineffective in exacting a compromise from the pro-Athens deputies. BNA, FO 195/2345, A. C. Wratislaw to Edward Grey, Hania, 17 May 1910.

80. In its correspondence with the embassy, the Italian consulate in Monastir noted that the town crier had implored the shop owners to close their stores two hours ahead of the rally if they did not want to pay a penalty of one Ottoman lira. ASDMAE 216, Consulate to Mayor des Planches, Monastir, 14 May 1910.

81. Once again, we learn from the report of the Italian consulate that Mehmed Hasib, the editor of *Neyyir-i Hakikat* (Bright Light of Truth), an influential pro-CUP newspaper published in Monastir, delivered the Turkish oration.

82. The select articles of the rally program described in this paragraph are based on the files in BOA, HR.SYS. 512/2, 24 June 1910.

83. *Ümid*, "Tahlif Meselesi Münasebetiyle Mitingler," 25 May 1910 (12 Mayıs 1326).

84. For instance, *Yeni Edirne*'s correspondent reported from Kavala that a large number of people, including those from nearby villages present in the town for the

market day, gathered in an open space, which featured the familiar protest mise-en-scène, complete with red Ottoman flags and "Crete or Death" placards. At the conclusion of the rally, people "dispersed in perfect calm" (*kemal-i sükun ile dağıldılar*). *Yeni Edirne*, "Kavala Muhabir-i Mahsusamızdan," 11 June 1910 (29 Mayıs 1326).

85. BOA, DH.İD. 113/1, 20 September 1910. As part of the official investigation, a certain Nikolaki Efendi translated the *Armonia* piece into Turkish. He transcribed the expletive in a parenthesis with the two letters denoting the f-word (س ك). In the interrogation records, the obscenity in its full form appeared several times.

86. BOA, DH.ŞFR. 663/40, 9 June 1910; BOA, DH.ŞFR. 663/43, 9 June 1910; BOA, DH.ŞFR. 663/45, 10 June 1910.

87. Plamper, "Sounds of February," 146.

88. Aimée Boutin, *City of Noise: Sound and Nineteenth-Century Paris* (Urbana: University of Illinois Press, 2015), 4.

89. Mark M. Smith, *A Sensory History Manifesto* (University Park: Pennsylvania State University Press, 2021), 24.

90. James L. Gelvin, *Divided Loyalties: Nationalism and Mass Politics in Syria at the Close of Empire* (Berkeley: University of California Press, 1998), 150–53.

91. CADN, 166 PO/E/251, Léon Krajewski to French Chargé d'Affaires in Istanbul, Skopje, 2 July 1909. Krajewski's report was also communicated to Paris. Krajewski showed an avid interest in the ethnographic landscape of locations in which he served as a diplomat. He is best known for a long report he compiled in 1904 on the traditions of Yazidis while he was stationed in Mosul as vice-consul. See CADN, 166 PO/E/293.

92. Khuri-Makdisi, *Eastern Mediterranean*, 74.

93. In late 1908, Abdullah Saraj was elected deputy to represent Mecca in the Ottoman parliament. However, Saraj ended up not going to Istanbul. Hasan Kayalı, *Arabs and Young Turks: Ottomanism, Arabism, and Islamism in the Ottoman Empire, 1908–1918* (Berkeley: University of California Press, 1997), 110–11.

94. "Miting," *Şems-i Hakikat*, 6 September 1909 (24 Ağustos 1325).

Chapter 5: Resettling the Displaced into History

1. BOA, DH. MUİ. 107/39, Representatives of Akhisar Greek-Ottoman Community to Ministry of Interior, 24 June 1910 (11 Haziran 1326). The Greek Orthodox of Akhisar also informed the Patriarchate, which in turn conveyed the complaint to the Ministry of Justice and Religious Affairs. BOA, DH. MUİ. 110/38, 26 June 1910 (17 Cemazeyilahir 1328).

2. Petition to Sadaret, BOA, HR. SYS. 512/2, 20 May 1910 (7 Mayıs 1326).

3. HHStA, PA XXXVIII, Konsulate, 349, Consul to Aehrenthal, Trabzon, 27 May 1910. The Austro-Hungarian consul made no secret of his astonishment that among the seven-member boycott committee two members were from Trabzon's Greek Ottoman community. Greek Ottomans' participation in the anti-Greece boycott is a fascinating topic that merits a detailed analysis mindful of local factors in shaping the decisions of historical actors. For a general discussion of the boycott in Trabzon, see Selim Ahmetoğlu, *Devrim Günlerinde Trabzon: II. Meşrutiyet, İttihatçılık ve Toplumsal Dönüşüm, 1908-1914* (Istanbul: Timaş, 2022), 176–85.

4. Çetinkaya, *Young Turks*.

5. Donald Quataert, *Social Disintegration and Popular Resistance in the Ottoman Empire*,

1881-1908: Reactions to European Economic Penetration (New York: New York University Press, 1983), 121-45.

6. Y. Doğan Çetinkaya, *1908 Osmanlı Boykotu: Bir Toplumsal Hareketin Analizi* (İstanbul: İletişim, 2004).

7. The classical monograph on *milli iktisad* as a concept and policy is Zafer Toprak's influential *Türkiye'de 'Milli İktisat' 1908-1918* (Ankara: Yurt Yayınları, 1982). While acknowledging the formative importance of intellectual debates and soul-searching after the Young Turk Revolution, Toprak devotes an overwhelming part of his book to the discussion of wartime economic policies between 1914 and 1918. The author has the following remarks to make for the period preceding World War I: "Although in the aftermath of the revolution, the Muslim-Turkish element began to get engaged in commerce, opening stores and establishing companies, until the First World War they showed little presence in the field of joint-stock companies, which required large capital. The liberal atmosphere in the early years after the revolution benefited non-Muslims" (55). Once the magnitude of economic losses suffered especially by Hellenes and, to a smaller extent, Greek Ottomans in this period is considered, the portrayal of the epoch as a lucrative time for non-Muslims needs to be reassessed.

8. According to the information provided by Hüseyin Rıfat, Hellenic nationals living in Izmir in 1914 numbered around forty-five thousand. The American consulate estimated that those holding Hellenic nationality constituted the largest group of foreign subjects in the city, around forty thousand out of the total number of sixty thousand foreigners. See Erkan Serçe, ed., *İzmir ve Çevresi Nüfus İstatistiği, 1917* (İzmir: Akademi Kitabevi, 1998), vii.

9. "Limenikē Kinēsis," *Amaltheia*, 27 January 1909. For an economic portrait of the city with a focus on its Greek communities, see Elena Frangakis-Syrett, "The Economic Activities of the Greek Community of Izmir in the Second Half of the Nineteenth and Early Twentieth Centuries," in Dimitri Gondicas and Charles Issawi, eds., *Ottoman Greeks in the Age of Nationalism: Politics, Economy, and Society in the Nineteenth Century* (Princeton, NJ: Darwin Press, 1999), chap. 1.

10. For an illuminating examination of the economic boycott at the local level through the case of Izmir, see Evangelia Ahladi, "İzmir'de İttihatçılar ve Rumlar: Yunan-Rum Boykotu, 1908-1911," *Kebikeç* 26 (2008): 175-200.

11. An article about the Cretan Muslim migration to the Izmir area makes a crucial point about the necessity of probing the links between Crete and Izmir to better understand the boycott movement in that city. Pınar Şenışık, "Cretan Muslim Immigrants, Imperial Governance and the 'Production of Locality' in the Late Ottoman Empire," *Middle Eastern Studies* 49, no. 1 (2013): 92-106.

12. According to official Ottoman estimates in 1899, the total number of Cretan Muslims who were settled in the entire Aydın province exceeded thirty thousand. BOA, Y.PRK.MYD. 22/55, 14 October 1899.

13. Dawn Chatty, *Displacement and Dispossession in the Modern Middle East* (Cambridge: Cambridge University Press, 2010), 11-20.

14. CADC, 153 CPCOM/75, French Consul to French Foreign Ministry, Izmir, 3 August 1909.

15. The opaque nature of the boycott committee was not specific to Izmir. Boycott

committees first emerged in the Ottoman Empire at the time of the economic boycott against Austro-Hungary in late 1908. The pioneering organizations based in Istanbul and Salonica quickly expanded across the empire through the establishment of local branches with the initiative of mostly lower-ranking CUP members. As also noted by Çetinkaya, the boycott committee maintained an unofficial character since "its main body of operations was at the fringes of what was lawful." Çetinkaya, *Young Turks*, 111. In late December 1908, an announcement by the Izmir Boycott Committee published in the weekly newspaper *Kave* (Kaveh), the official mouthpiece of that committee, recognized the pioneering roles of the Istanbul and Salonica organizations by acknowledging that Smyrnaeans had lagged behind during the earlier weeks of the boycott campaign. "İzmir Boykotaj Cemiyeti'nden," *Kave*, 31 December 1908 (18 Kanunuevvel 1324).

16. Donald Quataert also emphasized the leading roles played by port workers in many locales along the Ottoman coast. In January 1909, during a later stage of the Austro-Hungarian boycott, local CUP figures in alliance with porters and boatmen assumed the leadership of the boycott movement in multiple ports such as Beirut, Tripoli, Trabzon, and Izmir. Quataert, *Social Disintegration*, 141.

17. CADN, 166 PO/E/251, French Consul to French Ambassador, Izmir, 20 August 1909.

18. "To boikotaz," *Amaltheia*, 18 August 1909. Another case reported by *Kurşun* (Bullet), a Turkish-language newspaper published in Monastir, shows that storefront battles were not confined to Izmir. An article titled "Blue and White Store Signs" accused the proprietors of stores with blue-and-white signage of being anti-Ottoman. *Kurşun* perceived in such signs insolent gestures against the sovereignty of the Ottoman state, whose authentic colors were red and white. "Mavi Beyaz Levhalar," *Kurşun*, 17 April 1911 (4 Nisan 1327). According to the information given by the Austro-Hungarian consul in Monastir, *Kurşun*'s circulation figures amounted to around eight thousand copies daily. HHStA, PA XXXVIII, Konsulate, 396, Freiherr von Bornemisza to Aehrenthal, Monastir, 8 June 1911.

19. "O Emporikos apokleismos," *Amaltheia*, 19 August 1909.

20. Dina Danon mentions the resentment that the strong Jewish support for the Ottoman troops during the 1897 war with Greece over Crete caused in the city's Greeks. The resulting friction led to a boycott of Jewish businesses in Izmir. *The Jews of Ottoman Izmir: A Modern History* (Stanford, CA: Stanford University Press, 2020), 14.

21. "O Emporikos apokleismos," *Amaltheia*, 19 August 1909.

22. "O Emporikos apokleismos," *Amaltheia*, 25 August 1909.

23. The influential boycott committee of Izmir had been issuing a weekly publication whose title serves to deepen the chromatic symbolism surrounding the anti-Greece boycott. Named *Alsancak* (Red Standard), the pages of the weekly were printed in red typeface. *Alsancak*'s mission statement on the upper half of its front page next to a large Ottoman standard in red read: "Authentic [öz] Ottoman newspaper, published once a week for the time being, which defends the honor and glory of the Red Standard by smashing the blue and white ideals and by breaking the heads harboring Hellenic ideas." *Alsancak*, 15 May 1911 (2 Mayıs 1327).

24. The origin of the Whittall family in Izmir dates to the early nineteenth century. Hugh Whittall, *The Whittalls of Turkey, 1809-1973* (n.p., 197?).

25. BNA, FO 195/2383, Henry Barnham to Gerard Lowther, Izmir, 10 November 1911.

26. ASDMAE 216, Italian Consulate to Mayor des Planches, Izmir, 10 June 1910.

27. HHStA, PA XII, Liasse XXVIII, 297, August Kral to Aehrenthal, Izmir, 11 June 1910.

28. Rather than referring to someone engaged in formal politics, the word *politician*, which is repeated several times in the list, points to characters with an imagined or real capacity to influence and mobilize others at the grassroots level. The individuals who were labeled "politicians" were in reality engaged in occupations such as coffeehouse owner/worker, miller, merchant, and clerk.

29. CADN, 328 PO/1/133, Commander of Gendarmerie Detachment of Crete, Hania, 17 November 1898.

30. In his correspondence with Istanbul on this matter, Arifi Pasha, the governor of Konya province, assured the Ministry of Interior that he strongly urged the local authorities in Antalya to take necessary measures to prevent the repetition of such a transgressive boycott. BOA, DH. MUİ. 108/9, Cipher telegram from the governor of Konya to the Ministry of Interior, 26 June 1910.

31. During the time between their displacement from Crete in the late 1890s and their emergence as active boycotters and protesters after 1908, the islanders were generally mentioned in the official correspondence for resettlement-related reasons in Libya, Syria, and Asia Minor. For two such examples, see ASDMAE 158, Cretan Emigrants to Italian Ambassador, Tripoli of Syria, 11 October 1907; BOA Y.PRK.ASK. 167/126, 18 March 1901 (27 Zilkade 1318).

32. Vangelis Kechriotis, "Experience and Performance in a Shifting Political Landscape: The Greek-Orthodox Community of Izmir/Smyrna at the Turn of the 20th Century," *Bulletin of the Centre for Asia Minor Studies* 17 (2011): 80.

33. Nicholas Doumanis, *Before the Nation: Muslim-Christian Coexistence and Its Destruction in Late Ottoman Anatolia* (Oxford: Oxford University Press, 2013), 66. For more testimonies regarding the Cretans in Anatolia, see 71, 136–42.

34. Also pertinent here is the point Peter Gatrell makes about refugees that "the past has been a means to express their predicament and a channel for articulating and validating the possibilities of collective action. . . . A sense of history was often close to the surface of refugees' self-expression." Gatrell, *Making of the Modern Refugee*, 12.

35. "Apokleismos Katastēmatos," *Amaltheia*, 6 September 1909.

36. BNA, ADM 121/53, Alfred Biliotti to the Marquess of Salisbury, Hania, 22 February 1897.

37. BNA, ADM 121/53, Alfred Biliotti to the Marquess of Salisbury, Hania, 11 March 1897.

38. BNA, ADM 121/53, Alfred Biliotti to the Marquess of Salisbury, Hania, 11 March 1897, 11:45 a.m.

39. As with many other Turkish newspapers that appeared after the July Revolution, the use of plain language constituted one of the core elements of *Köylü*'s mission statement. This characteristic was also signaled by the newspaper's name pointing at its self-proclaimed goal of championing the interests of less privileged social classes, including workers and small tradesmen. Its owner, Mehmed Refet, later published another Izmir newspaper, *Alsancak*, in 1911, a weekly that functioned as the mouthpiece of the boycott committee in that city. For more on *Köylü*, see Zeki Arıkan, "Dilde Sadeleşme Akımı ve *Köylü* Gazetesi," *Kebikeç* 4 (1996): 129–48.

40. "Felek Yar Olmuyor Bana," *Köylü*, 23 March 1910 (10 Mart 1326).

41. Ibid.

42. Liisa H. Malkki, *Purity and Exile: Violence, Memory, and National Cosmology among Hutu Refugees in Tanzania* (Chicago: University of Chicago Press, 1995), 228.

43. Two will suffice among a large number of examples in Turkish sources that spoke of Cretans, ten years after their exile, as refugees. While an Ottoman Interior Ministry document used the common word *muhacir*, an Istanbul newspaper issued by several intellectuals with a Cretan background chose the less common word *mülteci* in referring to their displaced compatriots. DH. MUİ. 108–1/9, 27 June 1910, and "Girit Mültecileri," *Siper-i Saika-i Hürriyet*, 1 August 1909 (19 Temmuz 1325).

44. Malkki, *Purity and Exile*, 228–30.

45. BNA, FO 195/2358, Harry Lamb to Gerard Lowther, Salonica, 28 June 1910.

46. Ibid.

47. BNA, FO 195/2358, Harry Lamb to Gerard Lowther, Salonica, 1 September 1910.

48. "Boykotaj," *Rumeli*, 20 June 1910 (7 Haziran 1326).

49. BNA, FO 195/2342, British Consulate to British Embassy, Beirut, 23 June 1910.

50. Malkki, *Purity and Exile*, 94.

51. BOA, DH. MUI. 40–1/56, 10 January 1910 (28 Zilhicce 1327). For an account of the Soubasaki murder, see ASDMAE 215, V. Lebrecht to Marquis Imperiali di Francavilla, Hania, 9 September 1909. There are examples from various other settings regarding the earlier use of graphic postcards to generate awareness and mobilize public opinion. For instance, Poale-Zion, a socialist Zionist party, published a postcard using the photograph of child victims of the Ekaterinoslav pogrom of 1905 in the Russian Empire. See Shlomo Lambroza, "The Pogroms of 1903–1906," in John D. Klier and Shlomo Lambroza, eds., *Pogroms: Anti-Jewish Violence in Modern Russian History* (Cambridge: Cambridge University Press, 1992), 229. Obviously, pictorial representation of atrocities predates the age of the camera. See Barbara Donagan, "Atrocity, War Crime, and Treason in the English Civil War," *American Historical Review* 99, no. 4 (1994): 1137–66; Cengiz Kırlı, "Tyranny Illustrated: From Petition to Rebellion in Ottoman Vranje," *New Perspectives on Turkey* 53 (2015): 3–36.

52. Susan Sontag, *On Photography* (1977; repr., New York: Picador, 2014), 17. For a rich discussion of photography's role in "making a dent in public opinion" in the context of the atrocities in King Leopold's Congo, see Kevin Grant, "Christian Critics of Empire: Missionaries, Lantern Lectures, and the Congo Reform Campaign in Britain," *Journal of Imperial and Commonwealth History* 29, no. 2 (2001): 27–58. For an examination of how illustrated magazines introduced novel reading practices in the late Ottoman Empire, see Ahmet A. Ersoy, "Ottomans and the Kodak Galaxy: Archiving Everyday Life and Historical Space in Ottoman Illustrated Journals," *History of Photography* 40, no. 3 (2016): 330–57.

53. *Resimli Kitap*, no. 21, June 1910 (Haziran 1326), 734–35.

54. For a discussion related to the Russo-Ottoman War of 1877–78, see Martina Baleva, "Das Imperium schlägt zurück: Bilderschlachten und Bilderfronten im Russisch-Osmanischen Krieg 1877–1878," in Martina Baleva, Ingeborg Reichle, and Oliver Lerone Schultz, eds., *Image Match: Visueller Transfer, "Imagescapes" und Intervisualität in globalen Bild-Kulturen* (Munich: Wilhelm Fink, 2012).

55. Howard G. Brown, *Mass Violence and the Self: From the French Wars of Religion to the Paris Commune* (Ithaca, NY: Cornell University Press, 2018), 207.

56. BOA, HR.SYS. 512/2, 24 June 1910.

57. Edhem Eldem, *İstanbul'da Ölüm: Osmanlı-İslam Kültüründe Ölüm ve Ritüelleri* (İstanbul: Osmanlı Bankası Arşiv ve Araştırma Merkezi, 2005), 256.

58. See Bahattin Öztuncay, "The Origins and Development of Photography in Istanbul," in Zeynep Çelik, Edhem Eldem, and Bahattin Öztuncay, *Camera Ottomana: Photography and Modernity in the Ottoman Empire, 1840–1914* (Istanbul: Koç University Press, 2015), 99.

59. *Süngü*, 18 May 1911 (5 Mayıs 1327), in YDIA. I came across this image while sifting through the documents housed in the Hellenic Foreign Ministry Archives in Athens. Attached to the report that the Greek consul in Monastir relayed to his superiors in the foreign ministry was the entire first page of *Süngü*. This photograph is likely the first of its kind in the sense that a Turkish-language newspaper, published within the empire, featured a large front-page image of a dead Muslim Ottoman who was presented as a martyr. The photograph had also appeared a week earlier in the Istanbul weekly *Mecmua-i Ebuzziya* (Ebuzziya's Magazine) on 11 May 1911 (12 Cemazeyilevvel 1329), but not on the front page.

60. HHStA, PA XXXVIII, Konsulate, 396, Freiherr von Bornemisza to Aehrenthal, Monastir, 8 June 1911.

61. *Süngü*, 18 May 1911 (5 Mayıs 1327), in YDIA.

62. BOA, HR.SFR. 3 628/29. These details come from an archival document on the murder in Crete. Prepared by the representatives of the Muslim community of Hania, the document is dated 28 April 1911 (15 Nisan 1327).

63. Susie Linfield, *The Cruel Radiance: Photography and Political Violence* (Chicago: University of Chicago Press, 2010), 22.

64. *Süngü*, 18 May 1911 (5 Mayıs 1327), in YDIA.

65. For a discussion on staged photographs in nineteenth-century southeastern Europe, see Martina Baleva, "Revolution in the Darkroom: Nineteenth-Century Portrait Photography as a Visual Discourse of Authenticity in Historiography," trans. Thomas Cooper, *Hungarian Historical Review* 3, no. 2 (2014): 363–90.

66. HHStA, PA XII, Liasse XXVIII, 297, Pallavicini to Aehrenthal, Istanbul, 9 July 1910. Underlined in the original.

67. For instance, speaking of the boycott as economic warfare declared by the Ottoman nation, the Boycott Committee of Salonica announced in September 1909 the lifting of the measure for the time being. "Boykotaj Kalktı," *Tanin*, 3 September 1909 (21 Ağustos 1325). Speaking of an economic boycott in militaristic terms had earlier examples in history. For instance, during the anti-American boycott in late Qing China, one Chinese writer remarked: "The Chinese boycott against the American treaty today is also a war in everything but military form. If the battle is won, the prestige [of the Chinese] will not be lower than that of Japan." Guanhua Wang, *In Search of Justice: The 1905–1906 Chinese Anti-American Boycott* (Cambridge, MA: Harvard University Press, 2001), 149.

68. Babanzade İsmail Hakkı, "Harb-i İktisadi," *Tanin*, 23 June 1910 (10 Haziran, 1326).

69. Ibid.

70. BNA, FO 195/2358, Harry Lamb to Gerard Lowther, Salonica, 18 June 1910. Kerim Agha ventured out of the port of Salonica and visited the city's shops, asking their owners to display on the windows a paper certifying their lack of connection to Greece.

The band of fee collectors daubed the word *boycott* on the stores of those who did not obtain the required papers. When the owner of a big draper's store proceeded to erase the stigma, Kerim Agha, accompanied by a few others and "attended by a considerable crowd of roughs," entered the store and hurled threats at its proprietor. In another neighborhood, the agents of the boycott committee paid a visit to a Jewish grocery store, where they smashed the bottles of Hellenic liquor and beat the protesting owner. Three people involved in the incident were later arrested, an action that met with the approval of the Ottoman newspapers that otherwise supported the boycott. BNA, FO 195/2358, Harry Lamb to Gerard Lowther, Salonica, 28 June 1910.

71. *Şehbal*, no. 23, 28 July 1910 (15 Temmuz 1326).

Conclusion: Against Violence

1. Emre Erol, *The Ottoman Crisis in Western Anatolia: Turkey's Belle Epoque and the Transition to a Modern Nation State* (London: I. B. Tauris, 2016), 176–77.

2. As important as it is to emphasize Ferid Bey's islander background marked by displacement, the traumatic experience of his imprisonment during the first Balkan War in 1912 should also be acknowledged. This happened while he served as the *kaymakam* of Tikveş at the time of the town's occupation by Serbian forces. For more on Ferid Bey, see Emre Erol, *Foçateyn: Foça'nın Büyük Dönüşümü* (Istanbul: İletişim Yayınları, 2023), 177–84.

3. For a discussion about ahistorical and imprecise connotations of "ordinary" as an analytical category, see Yanni Kotsonis, "Ordinary People in Russian and Soviet History," *Kritika: Explorations in Russian and Eurasian History* 12, no. 3 (2011): 739–54.

4. *Meclis-i Mebusan Zabıt Ceridesi* (hereafter MMZC), İ: 26, C: 2, 606.

5. Erol, *Ottoman Crisis*, 187–89.

6. *MMZC*, İ: 26, C: 2, 607.

7. Ibid., 607–8.

8. Ibid., 609.

9. Ibid., 610.

10. Ibid., 611. For a reappraisal of the impact of the Balkan Wars, see Ginio, *Ottoman Culture of Defeat*; Ramazan Hakkı Öztan, "Point of No Return? Prospects of Empire after the Ottoman Defeat in the Balkan Wars (1912–13)," *International Journal of Middle East Studies* 50, no. 1 (2018): 65–84.

11. Reynolds observes that "the refugees had their blood shed, homes burned, and families expelled from their birthplaces because as Muslims they were judged to be without legitimate claim to their birthlands in an age of nation-states." Michael A. Reynolds, *Shattering Empires: The Clash and Collapse of the Ottoman and Russian Empires, 1908-1918* (Cambridge: Cambridge University Press, 2011), 38–39.

12. The dismissal of Ferid Bey did not spell the end of his career as a civil servant. In January 1915, about half a year after his removal from Foça, he was appointed as *kaymakam* to Karamürsel, a town with a significant Greek Orthodox population on the eastern shores of the Marmara Sea. Emre Erol, "Eski Foça'nın 'Kara Haziran'ı," *Toplumsal Tarih* 248 (August 2014), 90.

13. *MMZC*, İ: 26, C: 2, 611–13.

14. For Garo Paylan's tweet dated 24 April 2021, see https://twitter.com/garopaylan/status/1385957136497324036.

15. Hilmar Kaiser, *The Extermination of Armenians in the Diarbekir Region* (Istanbul: Bilgi University Press, 2014), 391–413. In his memoirs, Dr. Mehmed Reşid claimed that Hüseyin Nesimi had been killed by an Armenian band that operated with the goal of rescuing the expelled Armenians. Mehmed Reşid, "Mülahazat: Ermeni Meselesi ve Diyarbekir Hatıraları (1919)," in Nejdet Bilgi, ed., *Dr. Mehmed Reşid Şahingiray: Hayatı ve Hatıraları* (İzmir: Akademi, 1997), 86–87. Abidin Nesimi, a socialist thinker and writer, described his father's death as a crime perpetrated by the gendarmerie band led by Harun the Circassian, who was connected to Dr. Reşid. In Abidin Nesimi's telling, the question of whether the governor of Diyarbakır gave the killing order or the murder was perpetrated without his approval remains unanswered. See *Yılların İçinden* (Istanbul: Gözlem Yayınları, 1977), 38–46.

16. Mücellidoğlu Ali Çankaya, *Mülkiye Tarihi ve Mülkiyeliler, 1859-1949*, vol. 2 (Ankara: Örnek Matbaası, 1954).

17. Mücellidoğlu Ali Çankaya, *Yeni Mülkiye Tarihi ve Mülkiyeliler*, vol. 3 (Ankara: Mars Matbaası, 1968–69).

18. Michel-Rolph Trouillot, *Silencing the Past: Power and the Production of History* (Boston: Beacon Press, 1995), 49.

19. Neither his three-volume *Girit Hailesi*, coauthored with Mehmed Behçet at the time of the Cretan civil war, nor *Sahib Zuhur*, another extensive book released one year before his assassination, has appeared in print as a critical edition. In 2016, an abridged version of *Sahib Zuhur* came out in plain and simplified Turkish, a welcome effort, though unfortunately beset by multiple translation mishaps. The publication was dedicated to "righteous civil servants who lost their lives while resisting the massacre of 1915," a sentiment resonating with Garo Paylan's tweet five years later. In its preface, Oral Çalışlar, a journalist and public intellectual, mentioned his visit to Diyarbakır, in the company of Mıgırdiç Margosyan (d. 2022), a renowned Armenian-Turkish writer and native of that city, in search of Hüseyin Nesimi's unmarked grave. See Oral Calışlar and Serpil Calışlar Ekici, eds., *Hüseyin Nesimi: Sahib Zuhur* (Istanbul: Everest, 2016), 9. In his memoirs, Tarık Ziya Ekinci notes that Hüseyin Nesimi was killed near the village of Karaz, then part of the Lice district. The grave's presence was known by the villagers, who named the location *Tırba Kaymekam* (the *kaymakam*'s shrine). Tarık Ziya Ekinci, *Lice'den Paris'e Anılarım* (İstanbul: İletişim, 2010), 43. In her important book on the Ottomans who defied the killing orders and saved Armenian lives, Burçin Gerçek notes that the memory of Hüseyin Nesimi is still cherished by the inhabitants of Lice. See *Akıntıya Karşı: Ermeni Soykırımında Emirlere Karşı Gelenler, Kurtaranlar, Direnenler* (İstanbul: İletişim, 2016), 70–76.

20. Rosie Bsheer, *Archive Wars: The Politics of History in Saudi Arabia* (Stanford, CA: Stanford University Press, 2020), 5.

21. Ali Emiri, *Osmanlı Vilayat-ı Şarkiyesi* (Istanbul: Evkaf-ı İslamiye Matbaası, 1918), 97.

22. Ibid., 97.

23. "Circassian families like his [Mehmed Reşid's], whose parents' generations had been massacred and expelled, had intimate knowledge of Armenian nationalist activism in the Caucasus and, like the Balkan Muslims, were traumatized. The same would have been true for the three dozen Circassian militiamen that Reshid had employed." Uğur Ümit Üngör, *The Making of Modern Turkey: Nation and State in Eastern Anatolia, 1913-1950* (Oxford: Oxford University Press, 2011), 106.

24. In his work on Mehmed Reşid, Hans-Lukas Kieser argues that "it is within the circles of Turkish-speaking Muslims from Russia . . . [that] Turkism was born." Hans-Lukas Kieser, "From 'Patriotism' to Mass Murder: Dr. Mehmed Reşid (1873–1919)," in Ronald Grigor Suny, Fatma Müge Göçek, and Norman M. Naimark, eds., *A Question of Genocide: Armenians and Turks at the End of the Ottoman Empire* (Oxford: Oxford University Press, 2011), 127.

25. In this regard, their views reflect the common Unionist perception of European major powers, which was expressed in multiple publications prior to the Young Turk Revolution of 1908. M. Şükrü Hanioğlu, *Preparation for a Revolution: The Young Turks, 1902–1908* (Oxford: Oxford University Press, 2001), 178–79. Also relevant here is the emergence of "increasingly radical, younger leaders who believed that diplomatic history had taught a single lesson: only military power could preserve the empire." Mustafa Aksakal, *The Ottoman Road to War in 1914: The Ottoman Empire and the First World War* (Cambridge: Cambridge University Press, 2008), 9.

26. Reşid, "Mülahazat," 93.

27. Hüseyin Nesimi, *Sahib Zuhur* (İstanbul: Şems Matbaası, 1914), 80.

28. Ibid., 87, 93.

29. Both experienced the punishment of the Hamidian state at a young age. At the start of his forced journey into the Libyan exile in 1897, Mehmed Reşid, aged twenty-four, together with seventy-five of his companions, answered the whistle of the *Şeref Vapuru* (Steamer of Dignity) by crying out, "Long live the fatherland, down with the tyranny." See Mehmed Reşid, "Taşkışla Hatıraları (1897)," in Nejdet Bilgi, ed., *Dr. Mehmed Reşid Şahingiray: Hayatı ve Hatıraları* (İzmir: Akademi, 1997), 63. *Girit Hailesi*, the book that Hüseyin Nesimi coauthored with Mehmed Behçet around the age of thirty, was deemed harmful and banned by the Ottoman government. BOA, Y. MTV. 175/107, 31 March 1898 (8 Zilkade 1315).

30. Cemil Aydın, *The Idea of the Muslim World: A Global Intellectual History* (Cambridge, MA: Harvard University Press, 2017), 105.

31. H. Nesimi, *Sahib Zuhur*, 7.

32. Reşid, "Mülahazat," 101.

33. Ibid., 111–13.

34. H. Nesimi, *Sahib Zuhur*, 123.

35. Ibid., 124.

36. Ibid., 125. In an alternative reading one could perhaps interpret Nesimi's words as a veiled threat rather than a friendly warning. Even if we put aside for a while Nesimi's opposition to Armenian deportations, which ended in his tragic death a year after the writing of *Sahib Zuhur*, his tone in the section about Armenians would not allow for the making of a convincing argument about the insinuation of a threat in his writing.

37. Around 1896 Ethniki Etaireia boasted fifty-six branches in Greece and eighty-three among Greek communities abroad. During the Cretan civil war it operated as "a state within a state," enjoying great popularity among the noncommissioned officers. See Douglas Dakin, *The Unification of Greece, 1770–1923* (New York: St. Martin's Press, 1972), 150; Giannis Gianoulopoulos, *Ē Evgenēs mas Tyflōsis: Eksōterikē Politikē kai Ethnika Themata apo tēn Ētta toy 1897 eōs tē Mikrasiastikē Katastrofē* (Athens: Vivliorama, 1999), 47; Stefanos Katsikas and Anna Krinaki, "Reflections on an 'Ignominious Defeat': Reappraising the

Effects of the Greco-Ottoman War of 1897 on Greek Politics," *Journal of Modern Greek Studies* 38, no. 1 (2020): 115–22.

38. Hüseyin Nesimi, *Sahib Zuhur*, 148.

39. Ibid., 148–50.

40. Ibid., 253.

41. One prominent name among such Unionists is Hüseyin Cahid, who, in his editorial column of the daily *Tanin*, wrote in the context of elections in November 1908, a time of fierce debates on the issue of representation in the parliament, that "while the chief Armenian clergy walked side by side in partnership with their Muslim counterparts, indicating their cooperation and upright intentions, the chief Greek clergy encouraged and provoked the ignorant masses for a protest march onto the Sublime Porte, stirring them up against the government and law, which would only cause disturbances in the country." Hüseyin Cahid, "Yaşasın Asker," *Tanin*, 23 November 1908 (10 Teşrinisani 1324). Another bone of contention between the CUP and Greek Orthodox Patriarchate emerged in the context of the introduction of universal conscription in 1909. See Uğur Z. Peçe, "The Conscription of Greek Ottomans into the Sultan's Army, 1908–1912," *International Journal of Middle East Studies* 52, no. 3 (2020): 440–43.

42. BOA, Y. PRK. UM. 37/1, Cezair-i Bahr-i Sefid Vilayeti'nden Şifre, 26 February 1897 (14 Şubat 1312).

43. BOA, İ. MTZ. GR. 31/1204, Encümen-i Mahsus-ı Vükela, 5 April 1897 (24 Mart 1313). A comparable concern characterized the opinion expressed by the interior minister Memduh Pasha in April 1909. See BOA, Y. EE. 88/39, 27 April 1909 (14 Nisan 1325).

44. Safvet, "Girit Adası," *Tanin*, 9 January 1909 (27 Kanunuevvel 1324).

45. H. Nesimi, *Sahib Zuhur*, 150.

46. Ibid., 279.

47. Ibid., 253.

48. Ibid., 273.

49. Kalyvas, *Logic of Violence*, 11.

50. H. Nesimi, *Sahib Zuhur*, preface.

BIBLIOGRAPHY

Archives
Ahmet Piriştina Kent Arşivi ve Müzesi (Ahmet Piriştina City Archive and Museum), Izmir
Archivio Storico Diplomatico del Ministero degli Affari Esteri (Italian Diplomatic Archives), Rome
Arheio G. I. Hatzigrigoraki (G. I. Hatzigrigorakis Archives—Archives of the Russian Vice Consulate), Rethimno
British National Archives, Kew Gardens
Centre des archives diplomatiques (French Foreign Ministry Archives), La Courneuve
Centre des archives diplomatiques (French Foreign Ministry Archives), Nantes
Devlet Arşivleri Başkanlığı Osmanlı Arşivi (Ottoman State Archives), Istanbul
Dimosia Vivliothiki Rethimnou (Archives of the Public Library of Rethimno)
Dimotiki Vivliothiki Hanion (Archives of the Municipal Library of Hania)
Haus-, Hof- und Staatsarchiv (Family, Court and State Archives of the Austrian State Archives), Vienna
Istanbul Üniversitesi Nadir Eserler Kütüphanesi (Istanbul University Rare Documents Library)
Istoriko Arheio Kritis (Historical Archives of Crete), Hania
Istoriko Arheio tou Panepistimiou Kritis (Historical Archives of University of Crete), Rethimno
Istoriko Mouseio Kritis (Archives of Historical Museum of Crete), Iraklio
Vikelaia Vivliothiki (Archives of Vikelaia Library), Iraklio
Ypiresia Diplomatikou kai Istorikou Arheiou (Hellenic Foreign Ministry Archives), Athens

Periodicals
Ahenk (Izmir)
Alsancak (Izmir)
Amaltheia (Izmir)
Anagennisis (Rethimno)
Aşiyan (Istanbul)
Dergah (Istanbul)
Doğru Söz (Cairo)
Episimos Efimeris tis Kritikis Politeias (Hania)
Girit (Geneva)
Hikmet (Istanbul)
Hürriyet (Istanbul)
Hürriyet (London)
Ikdam (Istanbul)
Le Jeune Turc (Istanbul)
Journal de Salonique (Salonica)
Kalem (Istanbul)
Kave (Izmir)
Kiryks (Hania)
Köylü (Izmir)
Kurşun (Monastir)
Mechveret (Paris)
Mecmua-i Ebuzziya (Istanbul)
Meşveret (Paris)
Nea Erevna (Hania)
New York Times (New York)
Patris (Hania)
Resimli Kitap (Istanbul)
Rumeli (Salonica)
Siper-i Saika-i Hürriyet (Istanbul)
Stamboul (Istanbul)
The Standard (London)
Süngü (Monastir)
Şehbal (Istanbul)
Şems-i Hakikat (Mecca)
Şura-i Ümmet (Istanbul)
Tanin (Istanbul)
Tearüf-i Müslimin (Istanbul)
Ümid (Hania)
Yeni Edirne (Edirne)
Yeni Gazete (Istanbul)
Yozgat (Yozgat)

Parliamentary Minutes
Meclis-i Mebusan Zabıt Ceridesi [Minutes of the Ottoman Chamber of Deputies]

Published Primary Sources
Albin, Célestin, *L'île de Crète: Histoire et souvenirs* (Paris: Sanard et Dérangeon, 1898).
L'Alliance Philantropique Musulmane de Crète, *Un coup d'oeil aux événements crétois* (Paris: L. Lhen, 1897).
Angelakis, Emmanouil, *Apomnēmonevmata 1856–1906* (Athens: Estia, 2004).
Bacon, Admiral Sir Reginald H., *A Naval Scrap-Book (First Part, 1877–1900)* (London: Hutchinson, 1925).
Bérard, Victor, *Les affaires de Crète* (Paris: Armand Colin, 1900).
Bickford-Smith, R. A. H., *Cretan Sketches* (London: Richard Bentley and Son, 1898).
Bickford-Smith, R. A. H., *Greece under King George* (London: Richard Bentley and Son, 1893).
Diplōmatika Eggrafa: Krētē (Athens: Ethnikou Typografeiou, 1898).
Cevat (Emre), Ahmet, *İki Neslin Tarihi* (Istanbul: Hilmi Kitabevi, 1960).
Calışlar, Oral, and Serpil Calışlar Ekici, eds., *Hüseyin Nesimi: Sahib Zuhur* (Istanbul: Everest, 2016).
Çankaya, Mücellidoğlu Ali, *Yeni Mülkiye Tarihi ve Mülkiyeliler*, vol. 3 (Ankara: Mars Matbaası, 1968–1969).
———, *Mülkiye Tarihi ve Mülkiyeliler, 1859–1949*, vol. 2 (Ankara: Örnek Matbaası, 1954).
Edib (Adıvar), Halide, *Türkün Ateşle İmtihanı* (İstanbul: Çan Yayınları, 1962).
Ehlers, Edward, "On the Conditions under Which Leprosy Has Declined in Iceland and the Extent of Its Former and Present Prevalence," in *Prize Essays on Leprosy* (London: New Sydenham Society, 1895).
Ehlers, Edward, and Dr. Cahnheim, "La lèpre en Crète," authors' copy to king of Greece (Leipzig: Johann Ambrosius Barth, n.d.), originally published in *Lepra Bibliotheca Internationalis* 2, nos. 1 and 3 (1901).
Ekinci, Tarık Ziya, *Lice'den Paris'e Anılarım* (İstanbul: İletişim, 2010).
Eliot, Charles. *Turkey in Europe* (London: Arnold, 1900).
Emiri, Ali, *Osmanlı Vilayat-ı Şarkiyesi* (Istanbul: Evkaf-ı İslamiye Matbaası, 1918).
Fermor, Patrick Leigh, foreword to George Psychoundakis, *The Cretan Runner: His Story of the German Occupation* (1955; repr., New York: NYRB, 2015).
Generalis, Emmanouil, *Epitomos Geōgrafia tēs Nēsou Krētēs* (Hania: I Proodos; E. D. Frantzeskaki, 1900).
Giannaris, Antonios N., *Peri tēs Katastaseōs tēs en Krētē Geōrgias kai Emporias: Syntomos kai Praktikē Meletē* (Hania, 1906).
Girit Muhibb-i İnsaniyet Cemiyet-i İslamiyesi, *Girit Vekaiyine Atf-ı Nazar* (Hania: Yusuf Kenan Matbaası, 1897).
Greek-English New Testament (Stuttgart: Deutsche Bibelgesellschaft, 1979).
Harris, Robert Hastings (Admiral Sir), *From Naval Cadet to Admiral: Half-a-Century of Naval Service and Sport in Many Parts of the World* (London: Cassell, 1913).
Hikmet, Nazım, *Selected Poetry*, trans. Randy Blasing and Mutlu Konuk (New York: Persea Books, 1986).

Karpat, Kemal H., *Ottoman Population, 1830-1914: Demographic and Social Characteristics* (Madison: University of Wisconsin Press, 1985).

Kazantzakis, Nikos, *Fratricides* (1955; repr., New York: Simon and Schuster, 1964).

———, Radio interview with Pierre Sipriot, Paris, 6 May 1955, Historical Museum of Crete (IMK), https://www.historical-museum.gr/webapps/kazantzakis-pages/en/life/talk forcrete.php.

Kondilakis, Ioannis, *Istoria kai Geōgrafia tēs Krētēs* (Athens: D. K. Kokkinaki, 1903).

Krētika: Ētoi Syllogē tōn Diplōmatikōn Eggrafōn tēs Epanastatikēs Syneleuseōs, tēs Syneleuseōs tōn Krētōn, tou Ektelestikou, tōn Nauarhōn k.l.p. & tōn Egkykliōn tēs Syneleuseōs kai tou Ektelestikou meta Sēmeiōseōn Istorikōn—26 Iouniou 1897-9 Dekemvriou 1898 (Hania: Proodos, E. D. Frantzeskaki, 1901).

Kriaris, Aristidis, *Plērēs Syllogē Krētikōn dēmōdōn asmatōn: Ērōikōn, istorikōn, polemikōn, tou gamou, tēs tavlas, tou horou klp klp. Kai apasōn tōn krētikōn paroimiōn distihōn kai ainigmatōn meth' ermēneutikōn yposēmeiōseōn* (Athens: A. Frantzeskaki and A. Kaitatzi Press, 1920).

Krētē 1898-1899: Fōtografikes Martyries apo to Prosōpiko Lefkōma tou Prigkipa Geōrgiou (Iraklio: Panepistimiakes Ekdoeseis Kritis, 2009).

Kuneralp, Sinan, ed., *Ottoman Diplomatic Documents on "The Eastern Question": Crete and Turco- Greek Relations (1869-1896)* (Istanbul: Isis Press, 2012).

———, *Son Dönem Osmanlı Erkan ve Ricali (1839-1922): Prosopografik Rehber* (Istanbul: İsis, 1999).

Megalē Stratiōtikē kai Nautikē Egkyklopaideia, vol. 4 (Athens, 1929).

Munro, H. H. (Saki), "The Jesting of Arlington Stringham," in *The Short Stories of Saki* (1911; repr., New York: Viking Press, 1930).

Nesimi, Abidin, *Yılların İçinden* (Istanbul: Gözlem Yayınları, 1977).

Nesimi, Hüseyin, *Sahib Zuhur* (İstanbul: Şems Matbaası, 1914).

Nesimi, Hüseyin, and Mehmet Behçet, *Girit Hailesi*, vol. 2/1 (Hania, 1896).

———, *Girit Hailesi*, vol. 2/2 (Hania, 1897).

———, *Girit Müslümanlarının Numune-i Felaketi* (Hania: Yusuf Kenan Matbaası, 1897).

Neyzi, Nezih, *Kızıltoprak Hatıraları* (Istanbul: İletişim Yayınları, 1993).

Prince George of Greece, *The Cretan Drama: The Life and Memoirs of Prince George of Greece, High Commissioner in Crete (1898-1906)*, ed. A. A. Pallis (New York: Robert Speller and Sons, 1959).

Psychoundakis, George, *The Cretan Runner: His Story of the German Occupation* (1955; repr., New York: NYRB, 2015).

Reşid, Mehmed, "Mülahazat: Ermeni Meselesi ve Diyarbekir Hatıraları (1919)," in Nejdet Bilgi, ed., *Dr. Mehmed Reşid Şahingiray: Hayatı ve Hatıraları* (İzmir: Akademi, 1997).

———, "Taşkışla Hatıraları (1897)," in Nejdet Bilgi, ed., *Dr. Mehmed Reşid Şahingiray: Hayatı ve Hatıraları* (İzmir: Akademi, 1997).

Scott, C. Rochfort, *Rambles in Egypt and Candia*, vol. 2 (London: Henry Colburn, 1837).

Serçe, Erkan, ed., *İzmir ve Çevresi Nüfus İstatistiği, 1917* (İzmir: Akademi Kitabevi, 1998).

Sontag, Susan, *On Photography* (1977; repr., New York: Picador, 2014).

Spratt, T. A. B., *Travels and Researches in Crete*, vols. 1 and 2 (London: John van Voorst, 1865).

Stavrakis, Nikolas, *Statistikē tou Plēthysmou tēs Krētēs meta Diaforōn Geōgrafikōn, Istorikōn, Arhaiologikōn, Ekklēsiastikōn ktl. Eidēseōn peri tēs Nēsou* (Athens, 1890).

Toynbee, Arnold J., *The Western Question in Greece and Turkey: A Study in the Contact of Civilisations* (London: Constable, 1922).

Trakakis, Antonis, "Oi Seliniōtes Tourkoi kai ta Hōria tōn," *Kritiki Estia* 53–64 (1955–56).

Uzunçarşılı, İ. Hakkı, "Namık Kemal'in Abdülhamid'e Takdim Ettiği Arizalarla Ebuzziya Tevfik Bey'e Yolladığı Bazı Mektuplar," *Türk Tarih Kurumu Belleten* 11, no. 42 (April 1947): 237–97.

Ypomnēma tōn Hristianōn tēs Krētēs Ypovlēthen eis tas Eurōpaikas Kyvernēseis ypo tou Synathroisthentos Laou en Klēma kai Krapē tē 3 kai 10 Septemvriou 1895 (Athens: N. Tarousopoulou, 1895).

Secondary Sources

Açıksöz, Salih Can, *Sacrificial Limbs: Masculinity, Disability, and Political Violence in Turkey* (Oakland: University of California Press, 2020).

Adıyeke, Ayşe Nükhet, *Osmanlı İmparatorluğu ve Girit Bunalımı, 1896–1908* (Ankara: Türk Tarih Kurumu, 2000).

Adıyeke, Ayşe Nükhet, and Nuri Adıyeke, *Osmanlı Dönemi Kısa Girit Tarihi* (İstanbul: Türkiye İş Bankası Kültür Yayınları, 2021).

Adıyeke, Ayşe Nükhet, and Tuncay Ercan Sepetcioğlu, eds., *Geçmişten Günümüze Girit: Tarih, Toplum, Kültür* (Uluslararası Sempozyum bildiri kitabı) (Ankara: Gece Kitaplığı, 2017).

Adıyeke, Nuri, "Multi-dimensional Complications of Conversion to Islam in Ottoman Crete," in Antonis Anastasopoulos, ed., *The Eastern Mediterranean under Ottoman Rule: Crete, 1645–1840* (Rethymno: Crete University Press, 2009), 203–9.

Ahladi, Evangelia, "İzmir'de İttihatçılar ve Rumlar: Yunan-Rum Boykotu, 1908–1911," *Kebikeç* 26 (2008): 175–200.

Ahmetoğlu, Selim, *Devrim Günlerinde Trabzon: II. Meşrutiyet, İttihatçılık ve Toplumsal Dönüşüm, 1908–1914* (Istanbul: Timaş, 2022).

Akçam, Taner, *A Shameful Act: The Armenian Genocide and the Question of Turkish Responsibility* (New York: Metropolitan Books, 2006).

Akın, Yiğit, *When the War Came Home: The Ottomans' Great War and the Devastation of an Empire* (Stanford, CA: Stanford University Press, 2018).

Aksakal, Mustafa, *The Ottoman Road to War in 1914: The Ottoman Empire and the First World War* (Cambridge: Cambridge University Press, 2008).

Akşin, Sina, *İstanbul Hükümetleri ve Milli Mücadele III: İç Savaş ve Sevr'de Ölüm* (İstanbul: Türkiye İş Bankası Yayınları, 2010).

Alpan, Aytek Soner, "'Meskinides' ve Nüfus Mübadelesi Üzerine," *Toplumsal Tarih* (August 2021): 50–54.

Amrith, Sunil S., *Crossing the Bay of Bengal: The Furies of Nature and the Fortunes of Migrants* (Cambridge, MA: Harvard University Press, 2013).

Amzi-Erdogdular, Leyla, "Alternative Muslim Modernities: Bosnian Intellectuals in the Ottoman and Habsburg Empires," *Comparative Studies in Society and History* 59, no. 4 (2017): 912–43.

Anagnostopoulou, Sia, *Mikra Asia, 19os ai.—1919: Oi Ellēnorthodokses Koinotētes. Apo to Millet tōn Rōmiōn sto Ellēniko Ethnos* (Athens: Ellinika Grammata, 1997).

Andriotis, Nikos, "Les querelles ethnoreligieuses en Crète et l'intervention des puissances européennes (seconde moitié du XIXᵉ siècle)," in Anastassios Anastassiadis, ed., *Voisinages fragiles: Les relations interconfessionnelles dans le Sud-Est européen et la Méditerranée orientale, 1854-1923. Contraintes locales et enjeux internationaux*, 197–211 (Athens: EFA, 2013).

Arıkan, Zeki, "Dilde Sadeleşme Akımı ve *Köylü* Gazetesi," *Kebikeç* 4 (1996): 129–48.

Armiero, Marco, *A Rugged Nation: Mountains and the Making of Modern Italy, Nineteenth and Twentieth Centuries* (Cambridge: White Horse Press, 2011).

Armitage, David, *Civil Wars: A History in Ideas* (New York: Vintage, 2017).

Arsan, Andrew, *Interlopers of Empire: The Lebanese Diaspora in Colonial French West Africa* (Oxford: Oxford University Press, 2014).

Ayalon, Ami, *The Press in the Arab Middle East: A History* (New York: Oxford University Press, 1995).

Aydın, Cemil, *The Idea of the Muslim World: A Global Intellectual History* (Cambridge, MA: Harvard University Press, 2017).

Baleva, Martina, "Das Imperium schlägt zurück: Bilderschlachten und Bilderfronten im Russisch-Osmanischen Krieg 1877-1878," in Martina Baleva, Ingeborg Reichle, and Oliver Lerone Schultz, eds., *Image Match: Visueller Transfer, "Imagescapes" und Intervisualität in globalen Bild-Kulturen* (Munich: Wilhelm Fink, 2012).

———, "Revolution in the Darkroom: Nineteenth-Century Portrait Photography as a Visual Discourse of Authenticity in Historiography," trans. Thomas Cooper, *Hungarian Historical Review* 3, no. 2 (2014): 363–90.

Ballinger, Pamela, *The World Refugees Made: Decolonization and the Foundation of Postwar Italy* (Ithaca, NY: Cornell University Press, 2020).

Barchard, David, "The Fearless and Self-Reliant Servant: The Life and Career of Sir Alfred Biliotti (1833–1915), an Italian Levantine in British Service," *Studi Micenei ed Egeo-Anatolici* 48 (2006): 5–53.

Berberian, Houri, *Roving Revolutionaries: Armenians and the Connected Revolutions in the Russian, Iranian, and Ottoman Worlds* (Oakland: University of California Press, 2019).

Bergholz, Max, *Violence as a Generative Force: Identity, Nationalism, and Memory in a Balkan Community* (Ithaca, NY: Cornell University Press, 2016).

Beşikçi, Mehmet, *The Ottoman Mobilization of Manpower in the First World War: Between Voluntarism and Resistance* (Leiden: Brill, 2012).

Blumi, Isa, *Ottoman Refugees, 1878-1939: Migration in a Post-imperial World* (London: Bloomsbury, 2013).

Boutin, Aimée, *City of Noise: Sound and Nineteenth-Century Paris* (Urbana: University of Illinois Press, 2015).

Brown, Howard G., *Mass Violence and the Self: From the French Wars of Religion to the Paris Commune* (Ithaca, NY: Cornell University Press, 2018).

Brubaker, Rogers, "Aftermaths of Empire and the Unmixing of Peoples: Historical and Comparative Perspectives," *Ethnic and Racial Studies* 18, no. 2 (1995): 189–218.

Bsheer, Rosie, *Archive Wars: The Politics of History in Saudi Arabia* (Stanford, CA: Stanford University Press, 2020).

Campos, Michelle, *Ottoman Brothers: Muslims, Christians, and Jews in Early Twentieth Century Palestine* (Stanford, CA: Stanford University Press, 2010).
Can, Lale, *Spiritual Subjects: Central Asian Pilgrims and the Ottoman Hajj at the End of Empire* (Stanford, CA: Stanford University Press, 2020).
Case, Holly, *The Age of Questions: Or, A First Attempt at an Aggregate History of the Eastern, Social, Woman, American, Jewish, Polish, Bullion, Tuberculosis, and Many Other Questions over the Nineteenth Century, and Beyond* (Princeton, NJ: Princeton University Press, 2018).
Chatty, Dawn, *Displacement and Dispossession in the Modern Middle East* (Cambridge: Cambridge University Press, 2010).
Chatziioanou, Maria Christina, "Like a Rolling Stone, R. A. H. Bickford-Smith (1859–1916) from Britain to Greece," *British School at Athens Studies* 17 (2009): 39–48.
Chaudhary, Zahid R., *Afterimage of Empire: Photography in Nineteenth-Century India* (Minneapolis: University of Minnesota Press, 2012).
Cohen, Julia Phillips, *Becoming Ottomans: Sephardi Jews and Imperial Citizenship in the Modern Era* (Oxford: Oxford University Press, 2014).
Corbin, Alain, *Village Bells: Sound and Meaning in the 19th-Century French Countryside* (New York: Columbia University Press, 1998).
Çelik, Rüştü, *Kandiye Olayları: Girit'in Osmanlı Devletinden Kopuşu* (Istanbul: Kitap Yayınevi, 2012).
Çetinkaya, Y. Doğan, *1908 Osmanlı Boykotu: Bir Toplumsal Hareketin Analizi* (Istanbul: İletişim, 2004).
——, "Patterns of Social Mobilisation in the Elimination of the Greek Orthodox Population, 1908–1914," *Low Countries Journal of Social and Economic History / Tijdschrift voor Sociale en Economische Geschiedenis* 10, no. 4 (2013): 46–65.
——, *The Young Turks and the Boycott Movement: Nationalism, Protest and the Working Classes in the Formation of Modern Turkey* (London: I. B. Tauris, 2014).
Dakin, Douglas, *The Unification of Greece, 1770–1923* (New York: St. Martin's Press, 1972).
Danon, Dina, *The Jews of Ottoman Izmir: A Modern History* (Stanford, CA: Stanford University Press, 2020).
Darnton, Robert, *The Kiss of Lamourette: Reflections in Cultural History* (New York: W. W. Norton, 1990).
De León, Jason, *The Land of Open Graves: Living and Dying on the Migrant Trail* (Oakland: University of California Press, 2015).
Der Matossian, Bedross, *The Horrors of Adana: Revolution and Violence in the Early Twentieth Century* (Stanford, CA: Stanford University Press, 2022).
——, *Shattered Dreams of Revolution: From Liberty to Violence in the Late Ottoman Empire* (Stanford, CA: Stanford University Press, 2014).
Deringil, Selim, "'The Armenian Question Is Finally Closed': Mass Conversions of Armenians in Anatolia during the Hamidian Massacres of 1895–1897," *Comparative Studies in Society and History* 51, no. 2 (2009): 344–71.
Detorakis, Manolis E., "*Koinōnikes Epiptōseis sto Diamerisma Ērakleiou stē Metapoliteutikē Epanastasē 1895–8*," in Theoharis Detorakis and Alexis Kalokerinos, eds., *Ē Teleutaia Fasē tou Krētikou Zētēmatos* (Iraklio: Etairia Krētikōn Historikōn Meletōn, 2001).
Detorakis, Theoharis, *Istoria tēs Krētēs* (Iraklio: Mystis, 1990).

Donagan, Barbara, "Atrocity, War Crime, and Treason in the English Civil War," *American Historical Review* 99, no. 4 (1994): 1137–66.

Doumanis, Nicholas, *Before the Nation: Muslim-Christian Coexistence and Its Destruction in Late Ottoman Anatolia* (Oxford: Oxford University Press, 2013).

Dubnov, Arie M., and Laura Robson, *Partitions: A Transnational History of Twentieth-Century Territorial Separatism* (Stanford, CA: Stanford University Press, 2019).

Eldem, Edhem, *İstanbul'da Ölüm: Osmanlı-İslam Kültüründe Ölüm ve Ritüelleri* (Istanbul: Osmanlı Bankası Arşiv ve Araştırma Merkezi, 2005).

——, "26 Ağustos 1896 'Banka Vak'ası' ve 1896 'Ermeni Olayları,'" *Tarih ve Toplum* 5 (2007): 113–46.

Erol, Emre, "Eski Foça'nın 'Kara Haziran'ı," *Toplumsal Tarih* 248 (August, 2014).

——, *Foçateyn: Foça'nın Büyük Dönüşümü* (Istanbul: İletişim Yayınları, 2023).

——, *The Ottoman Crisis in Western Anatolia: Turkey's Belle Epoque and the Transition to a Modern Nation State* (London: I. B. Tauris, 2016).

Ersoy, Ahmet A., "Ottomans and the Kodak Galaxy: Archiving Everyday Life and Historical Space in Ottoman Illustrated Journals," *History of Photography* 40, no. 3 (2016): 330–57.

Fahmy, Ziad, "An Earwitness to History: Street Hawkers and Their Calls in Early 20th-Century Egypt," *International Journal of Middle East Studies* 48, no. 1 (2016): 129–34.

——, *Street Sounds: Listening to Everyday Life in Modern Egypt* (Stanford, CA: Stanford University Press, 2020).

Fahrenthold, Stacy, "Transnational Modes and Media: The Syrian Press in the *Mahjar* and Emigrant Activism during World War I," *Mashriq and Mahjar* 1, no. 1 (2013): 34–63.

Fortna, Benjamin C., *The Circassian: A Life of Eşref Bey, Late Ottoman Insurgent and Special Agent* (Oxford: Oxford University Press, 2016).

——, *Imperial Classroom: Islam, the State, and Education in the Late Ottoman Empire* (Oxford: Oxford University Press, 2002).

Frangakis-Syrett, Elena, "The Economic Activities of the Greek Community of Izmir in the Second Half of the Nineteenth and Early Twentieth Centuries," in Dimitri Gondicas and Charles Issawi, eds., *Ottoman Greeks in the Age of Nationalism: Politics, Economy, and Society in the Nineteenth Century*, chap. 1 (Princeton, NJ: Darwin Press, 1999).

Fratantuono, Ella, "Producing Ottomans: Internal Colonization and Social Engineering in Ottoman Immigrant Settlement," *Journal of Genocide Research* 21, no. 1 (2019): 1–24.

Gara, Eleni, Christoph K. Neumann, and M. Erdem Kabadayı, eds., *Popular Protest and Political Participation in the Ottoman Empire: Studies in Honor of Suraiya Faroqhi* (Istanbul: Bilgi University Press, 2011).

Gatrell, Peter, *The Making of the Modern Refugee* (Oxford: Oxford University Press, 2013).

Gatrell, Peter, Anindita Ghoshal, Katarzyna Nowak, and Alex Dowdall, "Reckoning with Refugeedom: Refugee Voices in Modern History," *Social History* 46, no. 1 (2021): 70–95.

Gelvin, James L., *Divided Loyalties: Nationalism and Mass Politics in Syria at the Close of Empire* (Berkeley: University of California Press, 1998).

Genell, Aimee M., "Autonomous Provinces and the Problem of 'Semi-sovereignty' in European International Law," *Journal of Balkan and Near Eastern Studies* 18, no. 6 (2016): 533–49.

Georgeon, François, *Aux origines du nationalisme turc: Yusuf Akçura (1876-1935)* (Paris: ADPF, 1980).
Gerçek, Burçin, *Akıntıya Karşı: Ermeni Soykırımında Emirlere Karşı Gelenler, Kurtaranlar, Direnenler* (İstanbul: İletişim, 2016).
Gianoulopoulos, Giannis, *Ē Evgenēs mas Tyflōsis: Eksōterikē Politikē kai Ethnika Themata apo tēn Ētta toy 1897 eōs tē Mikrasiastikē Katastrofē* (Athens: Vivliorama, 1999).
Gingeras, Ryan, *Sorrowful Shores: Violence, Ethnicity, and the End of the Ottoman Empire, 1912-1923* (Oxford: Oxford University Press, 2009).
Ginio, Eyal, *The Ottoman Culture of Defeat: The Balkan Wars and Their Aftermath* (New York: Oxford University Press, 2016).
Grant, Kevin, "Christian Critics of Empire: Missionaries, Lantern Lectures, and the Congo Reform Campaign in Britain," *Journal of Imperial and Commonwealth History* 29, no. 2 (2001): 27-58.
Greene, Molly, *A Shared World: Christians and Muslims in the Early Modern Mediterranean* (Princeton, NJ: Princeton University Press, 2000).
Gutman, David E., *The Politics of Armenian Migration to North America, 1885-1915* (Edinburgh: Edinburgh University Press, 2019).
———, "Travel Documents, Mobility Control, and the Ottoman State in an Age of Global Migration, 1880-1915," *Journal of the Ottoman and Turkish Studies Association* 3, no. 2 (2016): 347-68.
Güvenç, Serhat, *Osmanlıların Drednot Düşleri: Birinci Dünya Savaşı'na Giden Yolda* (Istanbul: Türkiye İş Bankası Kültür Yayınları, 2011).
Hadjikyriacou, Antonis, "Envisioning Insularity in the Ottoman World," *Princeton Papers: Interdisciplinary Journal of Middle Eastern Studies*, no. 18 (2017): vii-xix.
Hamed-Troyansky, Vladimir, "Circassian Refugees and the Making of Amman, 1878-1914," *International Journal of Middle East Studies* 49, no. 4 (2017): 605-623.
Hanioğlu, M. Şükrü, *Preparation for a Revolution: The Young Turks, 1902-1908* (Oxford: Oxford University Press, 2001).
Hobsbawm, E. J., *Bandits* (1969; repr., New York: Pantheon Books, 1981).
Holland, Robert, and Diana Markides, *The British and the Hellenes: Struggles for Mastery in the Eastern Mediterranean 1850-1960* (Oxford: Oxford University Press, 2006).
Hourdakis, Antonis, *Ē Paideia stēn Krētikē Politeia (1898-1913)* (Athens: Gutenberg, 2002).
İçen, Nisa, "Ahmet Cevat Emre Hayatı ve Eserleri (1876-1961)" (MA thesis, Muğla Sıtkı Koçman Üniversitesi, 2021).
Kaiser, Hilmar, *The Extermination of Armenians in the Diarbekir Region* (Istanbul: Bilgi University Press, 2014).
Kallivretakis, Leonidas, "A Century of Revolutions: The Cretan Question between European and Near Eastern Politics," in Paschalis M. Kitromilides, ed., *Eleftherios Venizelos: The Trials of Statesmanship*, 11-35 (Edinburgh: Edinburgh University Press, 2006).
Kalokairinos, Andreas, "Defining the 'Majority' in the General Assembly of Cretans between 1878 and 1889: The Transition from Religious towards Political Disputes," in *Proceedings of the 12th International Congress of Cretan Studies*, Iraklio, September 21-25, 2016, 1-12, https://12iccs.proceedings.gr/en/proceedings/category/38/34/989.
Kalyvas, Stathis N., *The Logic of Violence in Civil War* (Cambridge: Cambridge University Press, 2006).

Kara, Melike, *Girit Kandiye'de Müslüman Cemaati, 1913-1923* (Istanbul: Kitap Yayınevi, 2008).
Kasaba, Reşat, *A Moveable Empire: Ottoman Nomads, Migrants, and Refugees* (Seattle: University of Washington Press, 2009).
Kassem, Fatma, *Palestinian Women: Narrative Histories and Gendered Memory* (London: Zed Books, 2011).
Katsiadakis, Helen Gardikas, *Greece and the Balkan Imbroglio: Greek Foreign Policy, 1911-1913* (Athens: Syllogos pros Diadosin Ofelimon Vivlion, 1995).
Katsikas, Stefanos, *Islam and Nationalism in Modern Greece, 1821-1940* (New York: Oxford University Press, 2021).
Katsikas, Stefanos, and Anna Krinaki, "Reflections on an 'Ignominious Defeat': Reappraising the Effects of the Greco-Ottoman War of 1897 on Greek Politics," *Journal of Modern Greek Studies* 38, no. 1 (2020): 109-30.
Kayalı, Hasan, *Arabs and Young Turks: Ottomanism, Arabism, and Islamism in the Ottoman Empire, 1908-1918* (Berkeley: University of California Press, 1997).
Kechriotis, Vangelis, "Experience and Performance in a Shifting Political Landscape: The Greek-Orthodox Community of Izmir/Smyrna at the Turn of the 20th Century," *Bulletin of the Centre for Asia Minor Studies* 17 (2011).
Khater, Akram Fouad, "Becoming 'Syrian' in America: A Global Geography of Ethnicity and Nation," *Diaspora: A Journal of Transnational Studies* 14, nos. 2/3 (2005): 299-331.
———, *Inventing Home: Emigration, Gender, and the Middle Class in Lebanon, 1870-1920* (Berkeley: University of California Press, 2001).
Khuri-Makdisi, Ilham, *The Eastern Mediterranean and the Making of Global Radicalism, 1860-1914* (Berkeley: University of California Press, 2010).
Kieser, Hans-Lukas, "From 'Patriotism' to Mass Murder: Dr. Mehmed Reşid (1873-1919)," in Ronald Grigor Suny, Fatma Müge Göçek, and Norman M. Naimark, eds., *A Question of Genocide: Armenians and Turks at the End of the Ottoman Empire* (Oxford: Oxford University Press, 2011).
Kırlı, Cengiz, "Tyranny Illustrated: From Petition to Rebellion in Ottoman Vranje," *New Perspectives on Turkey* 53 (2015): 3-36.
Koliopoulos, John S., and Thanos M. Veremis, *Modern Greece: A History since 1921* (Chichester: Wiley-Blackwell, 2010).
Kologlu, Orhan, "Celal Nuri'nin *Jeune Turc* Gazetesi ve Siyonist Bağı," *Tarih ve Toplum*, no. 108 (December 1992): 46-48.
Kopstein, Jeffrey S., and Jason Wittenberg, *Intimate Violence: Anti-Jewish Pogroms on the Eve of the Holocaust* (Ithaca, NY: Cornell University Press, 2018).
Kostopoulou, Elektra, "The Island That Wasn't: Autonomous Crete (1898-1912) and Experiments of Federalization," *Journal of Balkan and Near Eastern Studies* 18, no. 6 (2016): 550-66.
———, "The Muslim Millet of Autonomous Crete: An Exploration into Its Origins and Implications" (PhD diss., Boğaziçi University, 2009).
Kotsonis, Yanni, "Ordinary People in Russian and Soviet History," *Kritika: Explorations in Russian and Eurasian History* 12, no. 3 (2011): 739-54.
Ladas, Stephen P., *The Exchange of Minorities: Bulgaria, Greece and Turkey* (New York: Macmillan, 1932).
Lambroza, Shlomo, "The Pogroms of 1903-1906," in John D. Klier and Shlomo Lambroza,

eds., *Pogroms: Anti-Jewish Violence in Modern Russian History*, 195–247 (Cambridge: Cambridge University Press, 1992).

Lévy-Aksu, Noémi, "Freedom versus Security: Regulating and Managing Public Gatherings after the Young Turk Revolution," in Noémi Lévy-Aksu and François Georgeon, eds., *The Young Turk Revolution and the Ottoman Empire: The Aftermath of 1908*, chap. 9 (London: I. B. Tauris, 2017).

Linfield, Susie, *The Cruel Radiance: Photography and Political Violence* (Chicago: University of Chicago Press, 2010).

Lorenz, Fredrick Walter, "The 'Second' Egypt: Cretan Refugees, Agricultural Development, and Frontier Expansion in Ottoman Cyrenaica, 1897–1904," *International Journal of Middle East Studies* 53, no. 1 (2021): 89–105.

Makdisi, Ussama, "Diminished Sovereignty and the Impossibility of 'Civil War' in the Modern Middle East," *American Historical Review* 120, no. 5 (2015): 1739–52.

Malkki, Liisa H., *Purity and Exile: Violence, Memory, and National Cosmology among Hutu Refugees in Tanzania* (Chicago: University of Chicago Press, 1995).

———, "Speechless Emissaries: Refugees, Humanitarianism, and Dehistoricization," *Cultural Anthropology* 11, no. 3 (1996): 377–404.

Mamdani, Mahmood, *When Victims Become Killers: Colonialism, Nativism, and the Genocide in Rwanda* (Princeton, NJ: Princeton University Press, 2001).

Mansur, Fatma, *Bodrum: A Town in the Aegean* (Leiden: E. J. Brill, 1972).

Margaritis, Giorgos, *Istoria tou Ellēnikou Emfyliou Polemou, 1946–1949* (Athens: Vivliorama, 2001).

Mays, Devi, *Forging Ties, Forging Passports: Migration and the Modern Sephardi Diaspora* (Stanford, CA: Stanford University Press, 2020).

Mazower, Mark, *The Greek Revolution: 1821 and the Making of Modern Europe* (New York: Penguin Press, 2021).

McCarthy, Justin, *Death and Exile: The Ethnic Cleansing of Ottoman Muslims, 1821–1922* (Princeton, NJ: Darwin Press, 1995).

McNeill, J. R., *The Mountains of the Mediterranean World: An Environmental History* (Cambridge: Cambridge University Press, 1992).

Methodieva, Milena B., *Between Empire and Nation: Muslim Reform in the Balkans* (Stanford, CA: Stanford University Press, 2021).

Meyer, James H., *Turks across Empires: Marketing Muslim Identity in the Russian-Ottoman Borderlands, 1856–1914* (Oxford: Oxford University Press, 2014).

Meyer-Fong, Tobie, *What Remains: Coming to Terms with Civil War in 19th Century China* (Stanford, CA: Stanford University Press, 2013).

Michalopoulos, Georgios, *Political Parties, Irredentism and the Foreign Ministry: Greece and Macedonia, 1878–1910* (PhD diss., Oxford University, 2013).

Mirkova, Anna M., "'Population Politics' at the End of Empire: Migration and Sovereignty in Ottoman Eastern Rumelia, 1877–1886," *Comparative Studies in Society and History* 55, no. 4 (2013): 955–85.

Morris, Benny, and Dror Ze'evi, *The Thirty-Year Genocide: Turkey's Destruction of Its Christian Minorities, 1894–1924* (Cambridge, MA: Harvard University Press, 2019).

Mouradian, Khatchig, *The Resistance Network: The Armenian Genocide and Humanitarianism in Ottoman Syria, 1915–1918* (East Lansing: Michigan State University Press, 2021).

Mourelos, Yannis G., "The 1914 Persecutions and the First Attempt at an Exchange of Minorities between Greece and Turkey," *Balkan Studies* 26 (1985): 384–413.

Naar, Devin E., *Jewish Salonica: Between the Ottoman Empire and Modern Greece* (Stanford, CA: Stanford University Press, 2016).

Nelson, Megan Kate, *Ruin Nation: Destruction and the American Civil War* (Athens: University of Georgia Press, 2012).

Norman, York, *Celal Nuri: Young Turk Modernizer and Muslim Nationalist* (London: I. B. Tauris, 2021).

Ozavci, Ozan, *Dangerous Gifts: Imperialism, Security, and Civil Wars in the Levant, 1798–1864* (Oxford: Oxford University Press, 2021).

———, "A Jewish 'Liberal' in Istanbul: Vladimir Jabotinsky, the Young Turks and the Zionist Press Network, 1908–1911," in Abigail Green and Simon Levis Sullam, eds., *Jews, Liberalism, Antisemitism: A Global History* (Cham, Switzerland: Palgrave Macmillan, 2020).

Özbek, Nadir, "From Asianism to Pan-Turkism: The Activities of Abdürreşid İbrahim in the Young Turk Era," in Selçuk Esenbel and Inaba Chiharu, eds., *The Rising Sun and the Turkish Crescent: New Perspectives on the History of Japanese Turkish Relations*, 86–104 (Istanbul: Boğaziçi University Press, 2003).

Özel, Oktay, "Migration and Power Politics: The Settlement of Georgian Immigrants in Turkey, 1878–1908," *Middle Eastern Studies* 46, no. 4 (2010): 477–96.

Özgün, Cihan, "II. Meşrutiyetin İlk Yıllarında Türk Basınında Girit Diplomasisi Üzerine Bazı Tespitler," in Tuncay Ercan Sepetcioğlu and Olcay Pullukçuoğlu Yapıcı, eds., *Ege Araştırmaları I: Batı Anadolu'da Giritliler* (İzmir: Ege Üniversitesi Basımevi, 2019).

Özsu, Umut, *Formalizing Displacement: International Law and Population Transfers* (Oxford: Oxford University Press, 2015).

Öztan, Ramazan Hakkı, "Point of No Return? Prospects of Empire after the Ottoman Defeat in the Balkan Wars (1912–13)," *International Journal of Middle East Studies* 50, no. 1 (2018): 65–84.

Öztuncay, Bahattin, "The Origins and Development of Photography in Istanbul," in Zeynep Çelik, Edhem Eldem, and Bahattin Öztuncay, *Camera Ottomana: Photography and Modernity in the Ottoman Empire, 1840–1914* (Istanbul: Koç University Press, 2015).

Papamanusakis, Stratis, "Krētē, 1897–1898: Apo tēn Epanastasē sto Kratos," in Theoharis Detorakis and Alexis Kalokerinos, eds., *Ē Teleutaia Fasē tou Krētikou Zētēmatos* (Iraklio: Etairia Krētikōn Historikōn Meletōn, 2001).

Peçe, Uğur Z., "The Conscription of Greek Ottomans into the Sultan's Army, 1908–1912," *International Journal of Middle East Studies* 52, no. 3 (2020): 433–48.

Perakis, Manos, "An Eastern Mediterranean Economy under Transformation: Crete in the Late Ottoman Era," *Journal of European Economic History* 40, no. 3 (2011): 483–525.

———, "Return to Ottoman Sovereignty and De-Ottomanization of Christians on Crete (1889–1895)," *Cretica Chronica* 36 (2016): 93–118.

Philliou, Christine M., *Biography of an Empire: Governing Ottomans in an Age of Revolution* (Berkeley: University of California Press, 2011).

Phillips, Ron, "Candia 6th September 1898 (25th August 1898)," in Theoharis Detorakis and Alexis Kalokerinos, eds., *Ē Teleutaia Fasē tou Krētikou Zētēmatos* (Iraklio: Etairia Krētikōn Historikōn Meletōn, 2001).

Plamper, Jan, "Sounds of February, Smells of October: The Russian Revolution as Sensory Experience," *American Historical Review* 126, no. 1 (2021): 140–65.

Quataert, Donald, *Social Disintegration and Popular Resistance in the Ottoman Empire, 1881–1908: Reactions to European Economic Penetration* (New York: New York University Press, 1983).

Reill, Dominique Kirchner, *The Fiume Crisis: Life in the Wake of the Habsburg Empire* (Cambridge, MA: Belknap Press of Harvard University Press, 2020).

Reynolds, Michael A., *Shattering Empires: The Clash and Collapse of the Ottoman and Russian Empires, 1908–1918* (Cambridge: Cambridge University Press, 2011).

Robson, Laura, *States of Separation: Transfer, Partition, and the Making of the Modern Middle East* (Oakland: University of California Press, 2017).

Rodogno, Davide, *Against Massacre: Humanitarian Interventions in the Ottoman Empire, 1815–1914* (Princeton, NJ: Princeton University Press, 2012).

Schafer, R. Murray, *The Soundscape: Our Sonic Environment and the Tuning of the World* (Rochester, VT: Destiny Books, 1994).

Schwedler, Jillian, *Protesting Jordan: Geographies of Power and Dissent* (Stanford, CA: Stanford University Press, 2022).

Shissler, A. Holly, *Between Two Empires: Ahmet Ağaoğlu and the New Turkey* (London: I. B. Tauris, 2003).

Sipahi, Ali, "Deception and Violence in the Ottoman Empire: The People's Theory of Crowd Behavior during the Hamidian Massacres of 1895," *Comparative Studies in Society and History* 62, no. 4 (2020): 810–35.

Smith, Mark M., *Sensing the Past: Seeing, Hearing, Smelling, Tasting, and Touching in History* (Berkeley: University of California Press, 2007).

——, *A Sensory History Manifesto* (University Park: Pennsylvania State University Press, 2021).

——, *The Smell of Battle, the Taste of Siege: A Sensory History of the Civil War* (Oxford: Oxford University Press, 2015).

Somel, Selçuk Akşin, *The Modernization of Public Education in the Ottoman Empire, 1839–1908: Islamization, Autocracy and Discipline* (Leiden: Brill, 2001).

Sorou, Maria, "Ē Spinalogka tōn Othōmanikōn Hronōn," *Kritika Hronika* 33 (2013): 121–54.

Strauss, Johann, "*Aretos yani Sevda*: The Nineteenth Century Ottoman Translation of the 'Erotokritos,'" *Byzantine and Modern Greek Studies* 16 (1992): 189–201.

Şenışık, Pınar, "Cretan Muslim Immigrants, Imperial Governance and the 'Production of Locality' in the Late Ottoman Empire," *Middle Eastern Studies* 49, no. 1 (2013): 92–106.

——, "Politics of Emotions in the Late Ottoman Empire: 'Our Beloved Crete,'" *Journal of Balkan and Near Eastern Studies* 24, no. 2 (2022): 365–85.

——, *The Transformation of Ottoman Crete: Revolts, Politics and Identity in the Late Nineteenth Century* (London: I. B. Tauris, 2011).

Şimşir, Bilal N., *Rumeli'den Türk Göçleri* (Ankara: Türk Tarih Kurumu, 1989).

Tatsios, Theodore George, *The Megali Idea and the Greek-Turkish War of 1897: The Impact of the Cretan Problem on Greek Irredentism, 1866–1897* (Boulder, NY: East European Monographs, 1984).

Thompson, Elizabeth F., *Justice Interrupted: The Struggle for Constitutional Government in the Middle East* (Cambridge, MA: Harvard University Press, 2013).

Tone, John Lawrence, *The Fatal Knot: The Guerilla War in Navarre and the Defeat of Napoleon in Spain* (Chapel Hill: University of North Carolina Press, 1994).

Toprak, Zafer, *Türkiye'de 'Milli İktisat' 1908-1918* (Ankara: Yurt Yayınları, 1982).

Toumarkine, Alexandre, *Les migrations des populations musulmanes balkaniques en Anatolie (1876-1913)* (Istanbul: Isis Press, 1995).

Trouillot, Michel-Rolph, *Silencing the Past: Power and the Production of History* (Boston: Beacon Press, 1995).

Uslucan, Fikret, "Edebiyat Tarihimizin Unuttuğu Bir İsim: Ali Zeki Bey ve Bir İmla Eleştirisi," *Journal of Turkish Studies* 2, no. 2 (2007): 690-96.

Üngör, Uğur Ümit, *The Making of Modern Turkey: Nation and State in Eastern Anatolia, 1913-1950* (Oxford: Oxford University Press, 2011).

Uyar, Mesut, "Türk İç Savaşı 1919-22," *Toplumsal Tarih*, no. 347 (November 2022): 12-15.

Varlık, Nükhet, *Plague and Empire in the Early Modern Mediterranean World: The Ottoman Experience, 1347-1600* (New York: Cambridge University Press, 2015).

Walter, Barbara F., *How Civil Wars Start: And How to Stop Them* (New York: Crown, 2022).

Wang, Guanhua, *In Search of Justice: The 1905-1906 Chinese Anti-American Boycott* (Cambridge, MA: Harvard University Press, 2001).

Watenpaugh, Keith David, *Bread from Stones: The Middle East and the Making of Modern Humanitarianism* (Oakland: University of California Press, 2015).

Whittall, Hugh, *The Whittalls of Turkey, 1809-1973* (n.p., 197?).

Yavuz, Mustafa, *Demokratik İhtilaller Çağında Girit* (Istanbul: Belge Yayınları, 2017).

Yıldırım, Tahsin, *İşgal, Feryad ve Direniş: Milli Mücadelede İstanbul Mitingleri* (Istanbul: Ketebe, 2019).

Yıldız, Murat C., "'What Is a Beautiful Body?' Late Ottoman 'Sportsman' Photographs and New Notions of Male Corporeal Beauty," *Middle East Journal of Culture and Communication* 8 (2015): 192-214.

Yosmaoğlu, İpek K., *Blood Ties: Religion, Violence, and the Politics of Nationhood in Ottoman Macedonia, 1878-1908* (Ithaca, NY: Cornell University Press, 2014).

———, "Chasing the Printed Word: Press Censorship in the Ottoman Empire, 1876-1913," *Turkish Studies Association Journal* 27, nos. 1/2 (2003): 15-49.

Yörük, Ali Adem, "Kapitülasyonların Kaldırılması Sürecine Dair Bibliyografik Bir Deneme: 1909-1927 Yılları Arasında Yazılmış Kapitülasyon Kitapları," *Türk Hukuk Tarihi Araştırmaları*, no. 5 (Spring 2008): 115-18.

Zürcher, Erik-Jan, "The Young Turks: Children of the Borderlands?," in Kemal H. Karpat and Robert W. Zens, eds., *Ottoman Borderlands: Issues, Personalities, and Political Changes*, 276-85 (Madison: Center of Turkish Studies, University of Wisconsin, 2003).

INDEX

Abdullah Pasha, 50, 193n6, 195n45
Abdülhak Şinasi (Hisar), 115
Abdülhamid II (sultan), 3, 6, 13, 15, 23, 36, 64–65, 68, 70, 74, 90, 120, 212n34. *See also* Hamidian censorship
Abdürreşid İbrahim, 190n60
Abidin (Dino) Pasha, 177
adhan, 127
Adıyeke, Ayşe Nükhet, 202n34
Aegean Islands (*also Cezair-i Bahr-i Sefid*), 177–78
Aehrenthal, Alois Lexa von, 158
Agioi Deka, 54
Agios Vasileios, 49
Ahenk (newspaper), 126, 129
Ahmed Agayef (Ağaoğlu), 172
Ahmed Cevad, 114–16, 120, 124, 211n31
Ahmed Hilmi (Şehbenderzade), 190n64
Ahmed Nesimi, 114, 210n18
Ahmed Saki (Giridi), 108–9, 111, 211n31
Akçam, Taner, 188n33
Akhisar, 138–39, 215n1
Albania, 33, 176
Aleppo, 127
Alexiou, Lefteris, 53

Algeria, 16, 21, 172
Ali Emiri, 171, 179
Ali Galib, 113
Ali Haydar Emir, 21
Ali Talat Mollazade, 93
Ali Zeki, 114–16, 120, 190n62
Alsancak (newspaper), 217n23, 218n39
Amaltheia (newspaper), 126–27, 129, 140, 143, 144
Amari, 200n11
Amiel, Cyril, 105
Amrith, Sunil, 79
Anagennisis (newspaper), 90, 94–95
Angelakis, Emmanouil, 97–99, 207n50, 209n79
Anopolis, 55, 198n81
Antalya, 148, 150, 218n30
Apokoronas, 38, 40–41
Archanes, 75, 199n99
Argyroupoli, 40
Arifi Pasha, 218n30
Arkalohori, 81–82
Armenian Ottomans: as foil for Greek Ottomans, 224n41; genocide of, 170–72, 181, 222n19, 222n23; Hamidian

240 Index

Armenian Ottomans (*cont.*)
massacres of 40, 42, 69–70, 201n21, 202n40; Hüseyin Nesimi's views on, 173–77, 223n36; Mehmed Reşid's views on, 173, 222n15; participation in Crete protests of, 157
Armitage, David, 8, 11
Armonia (newspaper), 133, 215n85
Asi Gonia, 200n11
Association of Christian and Ottoman Women (*Syndesmos tōn Hristianōn kai Othomanidōn Krissōn*), 93–94
Athens, 42, 51–52, 92, 96, 176, 195n45, 209n79, 220n59
Austria-Hungary: annexation of Bosnia-Herzegovina by 23, 108–9, 117, 119; intervention in Crete of, 2, 185n6; Ottoman boycott against, 113, 139, 160, 216n15, 217n16
Austrian Lloyd, 34, 53
autonomy. *See* Cretan State *and* Pact of Halepa (1878)
Axelos Efendi, 56
Aydın, 216n12
Aydın, Cemil, 173
Azerbaijan, 21

Babanzade İsmail Hakkı, 121, 161–62
Bacon, Reginald, 67
Balkan Wars, 17, 25, 102, 106, 150, 168–69
Ballinger, Pamela, 26
Bartın, 210n14
Battle of Navarino, 13
Batumi, 154
Beirut, 154, 217n16
Benghazi, 124, 127, 130, 213n57
Bérard, Victor, 34
Bergama, 133
Bergholz, Max, 12
Berović, Corci (Pasha), 34, 50, 72, 193n6
Bickford-Smith, R. A. H., 76–77, 203n48
Biliotti, Alfred: background of, 189n46; commentary on rumors and panic, 43–44, 202n40; internal displacement of Muslims and, 15–16, 54–55, 76–77, 79–80, 150; observations on atrocities against Muslims, 57–58, 60, 203n62; remarks on intercommunal tension, 39–40; views on insurgency, 69, 201n32; views on religious coexistence, 91–92; views on Turhan Pasha, 33–34
Black Sea, 149, 160
Blanc, Paul: insularity and, 188n45; views on insurgency 67–68; views on Muslim emigration, 78–80, 87, 89; views on Ottoman troops, 73–74, 202n40
Bodrum, 106, 200n4
Bombay, 20
borderland, 12
Bosnia-Herzegovina, 12, 23, 108–9, 113, 160
Boutin, Aimée, 135
boycott: breakers of, 144, 150, 166, 220n70; chromatic tension during, 143–44, 217n18, 217n23; displacement and, 141, 147–53, 164–69; of Greece (and Yunan), 23–24, 139–41, 143–45; of Greek Ottomans (*Rum*), 138–39, 144, 160, 162, 165–67; historiography on, 139–40, 149; nationalism and, 160–62, 166, 169; nationality and, 143–45, 153–54; network of boatmen and, 154–55; participation of Greek Ottomans in, 215n3; refugees as protagonists of, 30–31, 140–48, 153, 165, 218n30
Bozkır, 21, 157
Britain: appeals of Muslim Cretans for protection to, 77–82; House of Commons debate on Crete, 19–20; intervention in Crete of (*See* intervention); occupation of Cyprus of, 67; riot in Iraklio and, 65, 70; trade in Izmir of, 140, 144–45
Brown, Howard, 156
Bsheer, Rosie, 171
Bulgaria, 17, 23, 78–80, 108–9, 119, 168
Byron Society, 70

Cahnheim, Otto, 107
Calcutta, 20

Index 241

Canevaro, Felice Napoleone, 72
capitulations, 210n19
Case, Holly, 185n4
Caucasus, 172, 174, 176, 190n73, 222n23
Celal Nuri, 109–11, 113, 119, 211n30, 211n31
census, 15, 72, 80, 88, 98, 202n34
Central Cretan Committee in Athens, 209n79
Cevad Pasha, 193n3
Cezair-i Bahr-i Sefid (*also* Aegean Islands), 177
Chaudhary, Zahid, 39–40
China, 7, 173, 220n67
civil war: acts of interreligious rescue in, 58, 60, 181; atrocities during, 54–60; blurred lines between civilians and insurgents in, 8–9, 51; contemporary observers of, 9–10, 49–53, 80, 196n56; environmental destruction of, 34, 60–62, 199n99; exilic legacy of, 149–53, 162–63, 178–81; internal displacement during, 1–2, 29, 37, 53–54, 70–71; intimacy, shared culture and, 10–11, 48, 58, 97–98, 199n3; petitions of civilians during, 53–56, 60, 77–78, 197n74, 198n83; psychology of, 43–45, 57; rumors during, 12, 39–40, 202n40; significance of terminology of, 4, 8–9, 11–13, 37, 49–50, 186n18, 187n22, 187n23
Committee of Union and Progress (CUP): Cretan activists in Istanbul and, 109, 114–15, 120; indictment of Europe and, 223n25; indictment of the Hamidian regime and, 15, 22–23, 223n29; organization of protest and, 23–24, 27, 121–23, 127, 130–32, 136–39, 146, 160–61, 166, 214n81, 216n15, 217n16
Congo, 172, 219n52
Corbin, Alain, 26
Cretan Assembly, 36, 45–47, 82, 108, 130, 193n3, 214n79
Cretan question: Armenian question and, 40, 42, 69–70, 177, 201n21, 201n25, 202n40; description of 3–4, 209n8; diplomacy of, 65–67, 185n4; impact in Ottoman public space of, 115–24, 132, 136, 156, 161–62; impact on world Muslims of, 20–21; as a means to refashion the Ottoman Empire, 24
Cretan State (1898–1913): creation of a leper colony and, 102–7; donation campaign for Greek navy under, 94–96, 207n44; historiography on, 87–88, 205n6; multireligious civic engagement under, 81, 92–94; Muslim allegiance to, 86–87, 90–92, 97; security concerns of the minority under, 81–83, 98–102
Cretans: as diasporic middle class in Istanbul, 108–111, 211n31; imagined traits of, 5–7, 52, 78–80, 87; internecine fighting among, 6, 34, 192n1, 195n33; language of, 47–48, 90–91, 196n48, 206n29; nomenclature of, 48, 73, 197n74; rural vs urban divide among, 29, 39, 53, 72–73, 80–81, 88, 98, 100–101, 187n30, 196n53
Crete: conversion to Islam in, 12, 78; domino effect of, 177–78; as geography of affect for Ottomans, 23, 108–10, 114–17, 121–25, 139, 157–58, 210n9; geostrategic significance of 13, 21; global Muslim solidarities with, 19–21; idea of minority (*ekalliyet*) in, 45, 47, 74–75; as imagined space, 7, 11, 21, 188n45; Ottoman conquest of, 22, 115, 119; political instability in, 33–34, 44, 193n2; question of Ottoman troops in, 13–15, 65, 68–75; reform requests of Christians in, 38–39, 42–43, 46–47, 193n3. *See also* protest
Crete-speak, 110, 112, 124, 132, 136, 142, 164, 190n62
Crimean Tatars, 174
crowds: mobilization of, 19–20, 23–24, 30, 72, 117–20, 154, 192n92, 220n70; nationalism and, 27–28, 111; peasant formation of, 1–2, 82; perception of,

crowds (cont.)
  112, 124–25, 130, 145–46; policing of, 133–34; psychology of, 44, 146; public celebrations and, 89–91; public opinion and, 27–28; soundscape of, 120, 124–26
Custance, R. N., 49
Cyprus, 67
Çalışlar, Oral, 222n19
Çandarlı, 133–34
Çaponaki, Musa Efendi, 158
Çetinkaya, Doğan Y., 139–40, 217n15
Çorum, 157

Dafnes, 187n22
Damascus, 135
D'Annunzio, Gabriele, 189n56
Danon, Dina, 217n20
Darnton, Robert, 214n74
De León, Jason, 57
death: display of corpses, 1–2; martyrdom, 22, 110, 115, 119, 122–24, 136, 155–56, 158, 170–71, 177, 179, 220n59; mobilizing power of, 1–2, 123–25, 153–55, 189n56; postmortem photography, 155–60, 219n51, 220n59; as slogan in protest rallies, 19, 30, 124–26, 128–29, 133–36, 139, 214n84
Delcassé, Théophile, 78
Deliahmetakis, Mustafa, 86–87, 89, 92
Denmark, 107
Dergah (periodical), 115
Derna, 124
Dionysios (bishop), 11
displacement: Cretan connection with protest, 1–4, 111–12, 146–49, 218n34; displaced as displacer of Greek Orthodox, 141, 153, 165, 167–68; European intervention in Crete and, 4, 15–16; eviction of Muslim Cretans from Spinalonga, 102–107; of Greek Orthodox from Asia Minor, 164–69; as a policy of conflict resolution in Crete, 4–5, 75–80, 83–85
Diyarbakır, 170–71, 173, 222n19

Dorotheos (bishop), 40
Doumanis, Nicholas, 149
Drury, Charles C., 194n27, 202n40
Dubnov, Arie, 17

Eastern question, 3, 42, 65
Eastern Rumelia, 78–80, 117, 119
Ebuzziya Tevfik, 209n8
Edhem Pasha, 113
Edirne, 78–79, 168
Egypt, 20, 43, 136, 172
Ehlers, Edvard, 107, 209n78
ekalliyet, 46, 74
Ekinci, Tarık Ziya, 222n19
El Kesciaf (newspaper), 123
Eldem, Edhem, 157
Eliot, Charles, 193n3
Emmanouilidis, Emmanouil, 165–69
empowerment of exile, 153
Enver Bey (later Pasha), 168
Epirus, 177
Episimos Efimeris tis Kritikis Politeias (newspaper), 93
Epitropi (Central Revolutionary Reform Committee of Crete, also known as *cemiyet* and committee): emergence of 38–39, 194n27; mission and role of, 40–43, 47, 52; Ottoman troops and, 41; use of guerilla tactics by, 69
Erol, Emre, 165
Erotokritos, 88, 205n8
Ethniki Etaireia, 176, 179, 223n37
Evmenios (bishop), 10–11, 49–50
eyalet-i mümtaze, 114

Fahmy, Ziad, 127
fatalism, 78–80, 87–89
Ferid Bey: dismissal of, 168; experience during the Balkan Wars of, 221n2; reappointment of, 221n12; role in the displacement of Greek Orthodox of, 164–65
Fermor, Patrick Leigh, 197n68
Fiume, 189n56
Foça, 164–65, 168–69

France, 78, 82, 103–106, 147, 172; intervention in Crete of (*See* intervention)

Gallipoli, 123
Gatrell, Peter, 26, 218n34
Gazi, 92
Generalis, Emmanouil, 93, 206n26
George I (king of Greece), 65, 107
Gerasimidou, Anna, 94
Gerçek, Burçin, 222n19
Germanos (metropolitan), 96
Germany, 2, 185n6
Gerola, Giuseppe, ix–x
Giannaris, Antonios, 62
Giannaris, Hatzimihalis, 60–62
Gingeras, Ryan, 186n18
Girit (newspaper), 210n9
Girit Cemiyet-i Osmaniyesi (Cretan Ottoman Association), 211n31
Girit Hailesi (Cretan Tragedy) (Hüseyin Nesimi and Mehmet Behçet), 181, 222n19, 223n29
Graham, Ronald, 81–82
Great Powers of Europe: appeals of Cretans to, 15, 45–47, 56, 60–61, 71, 77–78, 82, 99–100, 103–4, 198n83; appointment of Prince George as high commissioner by, 65, 89, 107; as guarantor states of Crete, 98, 119; Ottoman criticism of, 158, 172–73
Greece: 1897 war with the Ottoman Empire, 13, 22, 29, 67–69, 122, 217n20; boycott against, 123, 132, 139–43, 149, 153–54, 160–63, 166, 169, 215n3, 217n23, 220n70; donation campaign in Crete for, 94–96; *enosis* (union) of Crete with, 15, 19, 42–43, 46–47, 53, 93, 102, 108–9, 113, 119, 141, 148, 156, 176–78, 201n32, 209n79, 214n79; exchange of populations and, 17; intervention in Crete of (*See* intervention); protest against, 123, 126, 130–32
Greek Orthodox in Crete (*See* Cretans)
Greek Orthodox Patriarchate, 176, 215n1, 224n41

Greek Ottomans: boycott against, 138–40, 144, 160, 162, 165–66, 176–77, 216n7; hostility against, 115–16, 126–27, 133–34, 149, 164–69, 224n41; Hüseyin Nesimi's views on, 174, 176–79, 181; participation in anti-Greece boycott, 215n3; participation in protest rallies, 19, 120, 124–25, 133–34, 157, 213n54; tension after the Balkan Wars and, 167
Greek Revolution, 189n56, 48
Gymnastic Society of Halepa, 93, 207n31
Gymnastic Society of Rethimno, 93

Hadjikyriacou, Antonis, 29
hajj, 136
Halepa, 92–94. *See also* Pact of Halepa
Halide Edib, 196n56, 211n32
Halil Nihad, 117
Hallett, H. H., (Captain), 77
Hamidian censorship, 5, 23, 56–57, 85, 115–16, 120–21, 124
Hania (Canea/Hanya): civic engagement in, 92–94, 96–97; deportation of Muslim civilians by French gendarmerie in, 147–48; European troops in, 14, 36, 68, 196n53; fire in 1897 in, 34–35, 60; flag incident in 1909 in, 142; the Great Powers' division of, 17–18; impact of rural insurgency in, 39, 40–42, 192n1; *mukatele* in, 50, 195n33; Muslim reaction to violence and, 99–100; panic in, 43–44, 202n40; refugees in, 58–59, 64, 75; share of Muslim properties in, 100–101; size of Muslim population in, 98; visit of Prince George to, 90–91
harb-i iktisadi (*also* economic warfare), 85, 160–63, 166, 169, 220n67
Harris, Robert, 197n66, 205n12
Hasan Pasha, 1–2
Hasan Tahsin Pasha, 45
Hellenic Foreign Ministry Archives, 220n59
Hellenophobia, 137, 179
Hijaz, 131, 136

244 *Index*

Hikmet (newspaper), 21, 190n64
Historical Archives of Crete, 29
Hobsbawm, Eric, 29
Hochberg, Sami (Shmuel), 109
House of Commons, 19–20
Howard, Esme, 84, 100, 104
Hünkar Camii, 90–91
Hürriyet (also *Siper-i Saika-i Hürriyet*) (newspaper), 123–24, 211n31
Hüseyin Cahid, 23, 120–21, 212n46, 224n41
Hüseyin Fazıl Efendi, 167
Hüseyin Naimbeyzade, 90–92
Hüseyin Nesimi: assassination of, 31, 222n15; critique of European imperialism and, 172–73; description of massacres of Muslim Cretans and, 56–57; emphasis on Crete's importance and, 21, 177; as an exilic figure, 169–78; grip of civil war on, 178–81; historical memory of, 170, 222n19; obscurity surrounding, 170–71; *Sahib Zuhur* and, 172–74, 177, 179, 181; views on Armenians, 173–74, 223n36; views on Greeks (*Rum* and *Yunan*), 176–77, 179–181
Hüseyin Rıfat, 216n8
Hüsnü Akif, 137

Ibrahim (sultan), 90
Ierapetra, 53, 92, 97, 206n22
India: British colonialism in, 172; ripples from Crete in, 19–20; migration from, 79; Sepoy Mutiny in, 39–40
Inebolu, 123
intervention: of Great Powers in Crete, 2–4, 13–18, 36, 46, 64–68, 83, 200n7, 214n79; of Greece in Crete, 51–52, 67–68, 197n66
Ioannina, 213n54
Iraklio (Candia/Kandiye): civil war in, 34, 50–51, 54; evicted Spinalonga Muslims in, 104, 106; Gerola's photograph in, ix-x; mayor of, 86–87; Muslim refugees in, 1–2, 54–56, 64; Muslims after the Balkan Wars in, 205n6; riot in 1898 in, 65, 70; share of Muslim properties in, 100–101; size of Muslim population in, 98, 204n1; survivors of Sitia massacres in, 56–57; visit of Prince George to, 91–92
Iran, 172
Ismail Hakkı Bey, 125
Istanbul: boycott committee in, 154, 162–63, 216n15; Cretan refugees in, 63–64; diasporic activists in, 108–17, 122–23, 135, 210n19; popularity of its press among Indian Muslims, 20; protest rally in, 117–20, 211n30, 211n31
istibdal. *See mübadele*
Italy, ix, 26, 69–70, 100, 106, 123, 130, 145–46, 153–54, 189n56, 200n12; intervention in Crete of (*See* intervention)
Ittihad (newspaper), 146
Izmir (Smyrna): boycott in, 140–41, 143–46, 148–51, 216n11, 216n15, 217n16, 217n23, 218n39; Greek Orthodox refugees in, 167; protest rallies in, 20, 124, 126–27, 133, 142; refugee protesters in, 25–26, 112, 123, 141–53, 165, 178–80; size of Hellenic (*Yunan*) population in, 216n8; size of Muslim Cretan population in, 123

Jabotinsky, Vladimir (Ze'ev), 109
Jews: cemetery in Prague, 1; in Greece, 89; participation in protest, 126, 144; tension with Greek Orthodox, 144, 149, 217n20; violence against, 57, 82, 219n51, 220n70
Jordan, 126
Joseph, Franz, 56
Journal de Salonique (newspaper), 125–26, 128

Kale-i Sultaniye, 192n88
Kalem (periodical), 175
Kalokairinos, Lysimachus, 65
Kalyvas, Stathis, 11, 48, 180
Kambos, 10
Kampoi, 41
Kandanos, 16, 60, 75–77

Karabey Karabekof, 21, 190n64
Karatheodoris, Alexandros (Pasha): convening of the general assembly and, 36; governorship of and challenges against, 45, 193n3; intercommunal tension and, 38–40, 192n1; tenure in Crete of, 33–34, 193n6; termination of governorship of, 46–47; views on insurgency, 69
Karşıyaka (Cordélio), 142
Kasaba, Reşat, 24–25
Kassem, Fatma, 199n1
Kavala, 19–20, 24, 214n84
Kave (newspaper), 216n15
Kazantzakis, Nikos, 7, 10
Kechriotis, Vangelis, 149
Kemer, 150
Kemeraltı, 151
Kerim Agha, 154–55, 162, 220n70
Kıbrıslı Kamil Pasha, 175
Kırmızı Siyah Kitap (The Red and Black Book) (Ahmed Cevad), 116
Kieser, Hans-Lukas, 223n24
Kiryks (newspaper), 86, 102
Kissamos, 11, 40, 96
Klima, 195n45
Kondilakis, Ioannis, 207n44
Kopstein, Jeffrey, 57
Korakas, Aristotelis, 6, 52–53
Korakas, Michail, 52
Korasaki, Osman, 155–56
Kos, 106
Kosmidis, Pantelis, 212n46
Kostaros, 51
Kostopoulou, Elektra, 88, 208n63
Köprülü (grand viziers), 211n30
Köylü (newspaper), 151–52, 218n39
Krajewski, Léon, 136, 215n91
Kral, August, 123, 146
Krapi, 38, 195n45
Kriaris, Aristidis, 44–45, 195n34
Kurds, 40, 173–74, 201n18
Kurşun (newspaper), 217n18
Kydonia, 60–62, 96

Lamb, Harry, 153–54, 162
Larani, 1, 82, 204n71
Lasithi, 103–4
Lausanne Treaty, 89
Le Jeune Turc (newspaper), 108–9, 209n5
League of Nations, 16
Lefka Ori (*also* White Mountains), 38, 60
leprosy: leper colony in Spinalonga, 102–106; *meskinies*, 107; public health and, 107
Lesbos, 123
Lévy, Saadi, 125
Lévy-Aksu, Noémi, 122
Leyla Saz, 113
Libya: education and historical consciousness in, 121–22; invasion of and protest, 145; as place of exile, 116, 223n29; protest rallies in, 123, 127, 130–31; resettlement of refugees in, 106, 123–24, 213n57, 218n31
Lice (district in Diyarbakır), 170, 222n19
L'Illustration (periodical), 113
Linfield, Susie, 158
Lloyd, G. A., 19
Loghadis (Greek Ottoman consul), 70
Lowther, Gerard, 145

Macedonia, 8, 130, 136, 157–58, 177, 187n21
Madras, 20
Mahmud Muhtar, 138–39
Mahmud Şevket Pasha, 121
Mahruki Cafer Bey, 119
Mainwaring, Rowland, 75
Makdisi, Ussama, 11
Malkki, Liisa, 26, 152–53, 155
Mamdani, Mahmood, 13
Manisa, 210n14
Manos, Konstantinos, 93, 207n31
Manou, Errieta K., 94, 207n31
Marabout (*al-Murabitun*), 130
Margosyan, Mıgırdiç, 222n19
Marquess of Salisbury, 65, 69, 75–77, 187n27
Maurouard, Lucien, 105–6

Mazower, Mark, 189n56
McNeill, J. R., 66
Mecca, 136–37
Mecmua-i Ebuzziya (periodical), 220n59
Medana, Augusto, 54, 61, 70–71
Medina, 131
Mehmed Ali (parliamentarian), 114
Mehmed Aziz Kavurzade, 114, 120
Mehmed Behçet, 57, 223n29
Mehmed Hasib, 214n81
Mehmed Refet, 218n39
Mehmed Reşid: assassination of Hüseyin Nesimi and, 170–71, 222n15; critique of colonialism and, 172–73; as diasporic nationalist prototype, 171–72, 222n23, 223n24; as political exile, 223n29; views on Armenian Ottomans, 173
mekteb-i mülkiye, 164, 170
Melidoni, 72
Menteşe, 124
Messageries Maritimes, 142
Meşveret (newspaper), 10–11, 64
Meyer-Fong, Tobie, 7
Milan, 69
milli iktisad, 140, 216n7
Moires, 54
Monastir (Manastır): atrocity propaganda in, 157–59, 220n59; boycott in 217n18; protest rally in, 131–33, 214n80, 214n81
Moroni, 54
Mount Ida, 200n11
Mount Lebanon, 205n6
mountains: as characteristic of Crete, 6–7, 61, 99; as refuge to fighters, 29, 60, 64–69, 74–75, 83, 85, 200n11, 200n12, 201n18; as sites of political assembly, 38–39, 47
Mouriziana, 61
muhacir and *mülteci*. *See* refugees
mukatelat, 50, 180; singular use of, 50, 196n59
Munro, H. H. (Saki), 3
Muslim Philanthropic Alliance of Crete, 34

Muslims (also Turkocretans) in Crete. *See* Cretans
Mustafa Nuri, 6–7, 113, 116–17, 120, 211n31
mübadele (also *istibdal*), 17, 84–85
müstemleke (also pl. *müstemlekat*), 21, 178
Müşavir İsmail, 17, 84

Naar, Devin, 89
Namık Kemal, 209n8
Naples, 69–70
Navigazione Generale Italiana, 123
Nazım Hikmet, 1, 31–32
Nazilli, 114
Nea Erevna (newspaper), 63, 85, 94, 96
Nesimi, Abidin, 222n15
New Testament, 5–6
Neyyir-i Hakikat (newspaper), 214n81
Noel, F. C. M., 50–51

olive trees, 2, 7–8, 29, 34, 40, 51, 61–62, 78, 84, 141, 199n99, 199n102
Ordu, 157
Osmanlı Vilayat-ı Şarkiyesi (Eastern Ottoman Provinces) (Ali Emiri), 171
Ottoman Council of Ministers, 177–78
Ottoman Navy League, 124
Ottoman parliament: Cretan members of, 114; debate on Greek Orthodox displacement in, 165–69; protest petitions and, 126, 131–32, 155; protest rally and, 117, 120; suspension of, 3, 36
Ottoman State Archives, 130–31
Ottomanophobia, 13, 69–70, 172, 201n22
Öztuncay, Bahattin, 157

Pact of Halepa (1878), 3, 24, 36, 43, 45–47, 195n38
Palaiochora, 48–49, 58
Pallavicini, Johann Markgraf von, 160
Papadiamantopoulos (aide-de-camp to George I of Greece), 53
Paris, 135, 156–57, 193n5
partition, 16–18
Patris (newspaper), 99
Paylan, Garo, 170, 222n19

peasants: insurgency and, 8–10, 29, 41, 51, 66; mobilization of, 1–2, 36–39; as movers of history, 85, 148–53, 178
Peel, Arthur, 82
Perakis, Manos, 37
Philliou, Christine, 11–12
Pinter, Julius von, 35, 50–51, 56, 194n14
Plamper, Jan, 27
Platanias, 9
Poale-Zion, 219n51
Pologeorgis, Charalambos, 99–100
Pombia, 52
Preveli Monastery, 9
Prince George: appointment as high commissioner of Crete, 65, 205n11; interaction with Muslim Cretans, 89–92; intervention in Crete and, 52, 205n12; policy against leprosy and, 106–7; reaction to violence, 99; repatriation of Muslim Cretans and, 80; Theriso uprising against, 83
protest: European perceptions of, 112, 130, 143–47, 192n88; mapping of, 130–31; mass rallies of, 19–20, 23, 117–37, 139, 142, 154, 157; necropolitical qualities of, 135–37, 155; peasant mobilization and, 1–2, 38–39; planning of, 113, 119, 131–33; social class and, 110–12, 164–65, 178–79; soundscape of, 27, 111, 120–31, 133–35; unruliness of, 133–34
protest-phobia, 112, 146
Psychoundakis, George, 200n11

Quataert, Donald, 139, 217n16
Queen Victoria, 77–80

refugees: descriptor and terminology of, 31–32, 152, 213n59, 219n43; historiography on, 24–26, 191n83; perceptions of, 63–64, 76, 200n4, 205n8; as protagonists in boycotts and rallies, 5, 24–26, 30–31, 111, 119, 140–49; social class and, 31–32, 110–12, 164–65, 178–79
Resimli Kitap (periodical), 20, 113, 156–57

Rethimno (Resmo): civic engagement in, 93; civil war in, 34, 38, 40–41, 53–54, 70–72, 198n83; distant ripples of violence in, 154; perceptions of civil war in, 6, 11; refugees in and from, 63–64; share of Muslim properties in, 100–101; size of Muslim population in, 98
Reuters, 201n22
Revolutionary assemblies of Cretans, 15, 72–73, 201n32
Reynolds, Michael, 168, 221n11
Rhodes, 16, 106, 189n46
Rıfat Pasha, 202n34
Rıza Bey, 166
rizitika, 48–49
Robson, Laura, 16–17
Rodogno, Davide, 17, 204n78
Rome, 70, 75, 100, 106
Rumeli (newspaper), 154
Rumeli Muhacirin-i İslamiyesi Cemiyeti (Association of Rumelian Muslim Refugees), 119
Russia, 27, 34, 70–71, 81–82, 111, 143, 168, 172, 174, 190n73, 219n51, 223n24; intervention in Crete of (*See* intervention)
Russian Revolution, 27
Russo-Ottoman War of 1877–78, 25, 46, 175
Rwandan Genocide, 13, 198n93

Sahara, 172–73
Sahib Zuhur (Hüseyin Nesimi), 172–74, 177, 179, 181, 222n19, 223n36
Salam, Sheikh Abdul Rahman, 154
Salonica: boycott in, 153–55, 162, 216n15, 220n67, 220n70; protest rallies in, 124–26; refugee protesters in, 25–26; reputation as Shabatopolis, 125; Tenth of July Square in, 125–26
Samos, 34, 46, 74
Saraj, Abdullah, 136, 215n93
Sarakina, 58–60
Schostak, Fyodor, 70–71
Schwedler, Jillian, 126
Scutari (İşkodra), 34
Seferihisar, 124

Selinos, 16, 39–40, 48–49, 76, 150–51, 195n34
Sempronas, 61
sensory history, 26–28, 111, 134–35
Serbia, 153–54, 221n2
Servet-i Fünun (periodical), 118
Seyidakis, Hasan, 104
Sfaka, 58
Sfakianakis, Amvrosios, 57
Sfakianakis, Ioannis, 72–73
Sharqawi (leader of Beiruti boatmen), 154–55
Singapore, 20
Sipahi, Ali, 192n92
Sitia, 11, 16, 55–58
Skouzes, Alexandros, 44
Smith, Mark, 26–27, 135
snails, 64, 88, 205n8
Sontag, Susan, 156
Soubasaki, Hüseyin, 155–56, 219n51
Sphakia, 49, 99
Spilia, 96
Spinalonga, 30, 89, 102–107. *See also* Cretan State *and* leprosy
Splantzia Square, 90
Spratt, T. A. B., 34, 187n30
Stamboul (newspaper), 117, 122
street criers (*also* town criers), 127, 138–39, 214n76, 214n80
Suda Bay, 3, 13–14, 49, 65, 67, 90
Sultanahmed Square, 113, 117–18, 135
Süngü (newspaper), 157–60, 220n59
Şehbal (periodical), 113, 162–63
Şems-i Hakikat (newspaper), 137
Şenışık, Pınar, 194n13, 196n48, 196n52, 213n61, 216n11
Şeref Vapuru (Steamer of Dignity), 223n29

Taif, 131
Talat Bey (later Pasha), 155–56, 165, 167–70, 173
Tanin (newspaper), 23, 114–16, 119–23, 160–61, 178, 212n46, 224n41
Tearüf-i Müslimin (newspaper), 20–21
Tekfurdağı, 114

Tevfik Pasha, 69–70
The Fratricides (Kazantzakis), 10, 187n25
The New York Times (newspaper), 13
The Standard (newspaper), 193n2
The Turkish Ordeal (Türkün Ateşle İmtihanı) (Halide Edib), 196n56
Theological School of Halki, 49
Theriso uprising, 83, 100
Thessaly, 13, 23, 80
Tittoni, Tommaso, 83
Toprak, Zafer, 216n7
Toynbee, Arnold, 61
Trabzon, 139, 215n3, 217n16
Trakakis, Antonis, 48–49
Treaty of Berlin, 3, 23, 67
Tripoli (Libya), 121, 123, 131, 213n57, 217n16
Tunisia, 21, 172, 204n78
Turhan Pasha, 6, 33–34, 68–69, 74–75
Tzitzifes, 51

Un coup d'oeil aux événements crétois (Girit Vekaiyine Atf-ı Nazar), 193n5
unmixing of populations, 4, 16–17, 84–85, 204n79
Uyar, Mesut, 186n18
Ümid (newspaper), 132–33
Üngör, Uğur Ümit, 171–72
Üsküdar, 120
Üsküp (Skopje), 136

Vamos, 41, 202n40
Vassos, Timoleon, 13
Venice, 69
Venizelos, Eleftherios, 72, 83, 86, 101–2, 208n63
Vienna, 56
violence: contemporary sectarian interpretations of, 6–7; grip of, 169–81; historiography on, 7–8, 12, 49, 194n13, 196n52; limits of hatred as an explanation of, 12, 149, 179–80, 188n33; representation of, 57, 116, 151, 155–60, 219n52
Voreadis, Antonios, 92

Walter, Barbara, 12
Whittall, 145, 217n24
Wilhelm II (emperor of Germany), 185n6
Wittenberg, Jason, 57
World War I, 3–5, 16, 25, 106, 135, 140, 149, 165, 169, 186n18, 196n56, 204n79, 214n76, 216n7
World War II, x, 26, 57, 67
Wratislaw, Albert C., 6, 214n79

Yanitsarakis (mayor), 60
Yeni Asır (newspaper), 154
Yeni Edirne (newspaper), 19–20, 127, 209n7, 214n84

Yeni Gazete (newspaper), 212n46
Yosmaoğlu, İpek, 8
Young Turks in exile, 15, 110, 116, 120–21, 172, 223n29
Yusuf Akçura, 116, 172
Yusuf Razi, 113, 156

Zahariadis, Mathaios, 55
Zeitun, 202n40
Zeynep Mehmet Hamitbeyzade, 94
Zionism, 16–17, 109, 219n51
Ziya Bey, 167

STANFORD **OTTOMAN WORLD** SERIES
Critical Studies in Empire, Nature, and Knowledge

Nükhet Varlık and Ali Yaycioğlu, editors

EDITORIAL BOARD
Julia Phillips Cohen, Nahyan Fancy, John-Paul Ghobrial,
Mayte Green-Mercado, Tijana Krstić, Harun Küçük,
Dana Sajdi, Fatih Yeşil

The Stanford Ottoman World Series showcases cutting-edge interdisciplinary scholarship in Ottoman history from the thirteenth to the twentieth centuries. Books in the series are concerned with three major themes—empire, nature, and knowledge—and the connections among them. The books in this series foster ambitious and innovative scholarship and open new paths in Ottoman studies and beyond.

———

ELIZABETH R. WILLIAMS, *States of Cultivation: Imperial Transition and Scientific Agriculture in the Eastern Mediterranean*   **2023**

The authorized representative in the EU for product safety and compliance is:
Mare Nostrum Group
B.V Doelen 72
4831 GR Breda
The Netherlands

www.ingramcontent.com/pod-product-compliance
Lightning Source LLC
Chambersburg PA
CBHW031805220426
43662CB00007B/530